岸本斉史

Naruto's already at volume 24!
In volume 24 of *Dragon Ball**,
Goku was about to fight Ginyu.
It was so awesome, I was way
too hyper reading it... I gotta
make *Naruto* more exciting!!

—*Masashi Kishimoto*, 2004

(* Vol. 24 of *Dragon Ball* was released as
Vol. 8 of *Dragon Ball Z* in the U.S. – Ed.)

Author/artist Masashi Kishimoto was born in 1974 in rural
Okayama Prefecture, Japan. After spending time in art college,
he won the Hop Step Award for new manga artists with his
manga **Karakuri** (Mechanism). Kishimoto decided to base his
next story on traditional Japanese culture. His first version of
Naruto, drawn in 1997, was a one-shot story about fox spirits;
his final version, which debuted in **Weekly Shonen Jump** in
1999, quickly became the most popular ninja manga in Japan.

NARUTO VOL. 24
The SHONEN JUMP Manga Edition

STORY AND ART BY MASASHI KISHIMOTO

Translation/Joe Yamazaki
English Adaptation/Naomi Kokubo & Eric-Jon Rössel Waugh
Letterer/Inori Fukuda Trant
Consultant/Mari Morimoto
Design/Yvonne Cai
Editor/Joel Enos

Editor in Chief, Books/Alvin Lu
Editor in Chief, Magazines/Marc Weidenbaum
VP of Publishing Licensing/Rika Inouye
VP of Sales/Gonzalo Ferreyra
Sr. VP of Marketing/Liza Coppola
Publisher/Hyoe Narita

NARUTO © 1999 by Masashi Kishimoto. All rights reserved.
First published in Japan in 1999 by SHUEISHA Inc., Tokyo. English
translation rights in the United States of America and Canada
arranged by SHUEISHA Inc. The stories, characters and
incidents mentioned in this publication are entirely fictional.

Printed in Canada

Published by VIZ Media, LLC
P.O. Box 77010
San Francisco, CA 94107

SHONEN JUMP Manga Edition
10 9 8 7 6 5 4 3 2 1
First printing, November 2007

THE WORLD'S
MOST POPULAR MANGA

www.viz.com

www.shonenjump.com

SHONEN JUMP MANGA EDITION

NARUTO™

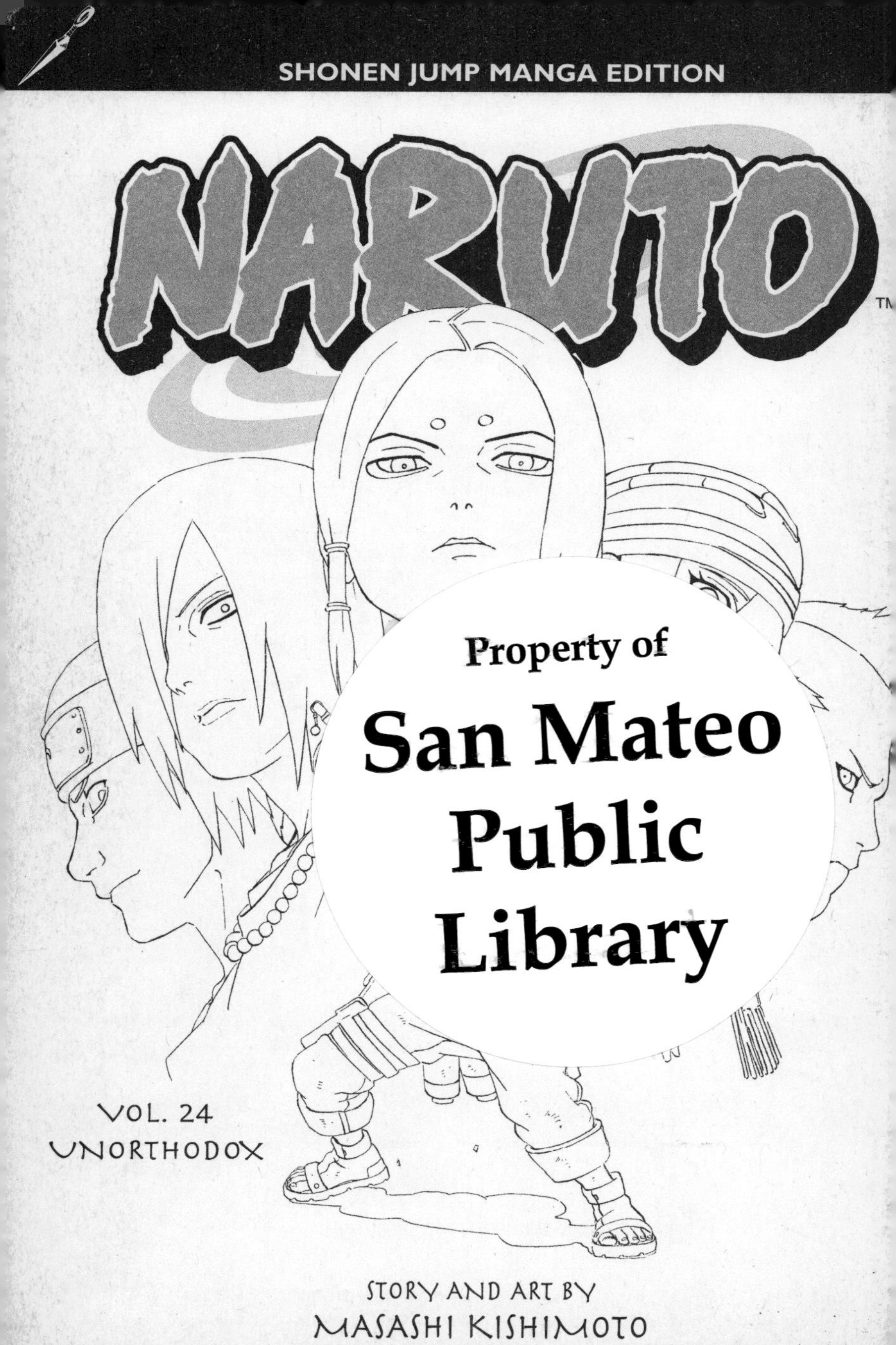

VOL. 24
UNORTHODOX

STORY AND ART BY
MASASHI KISHIMOTO

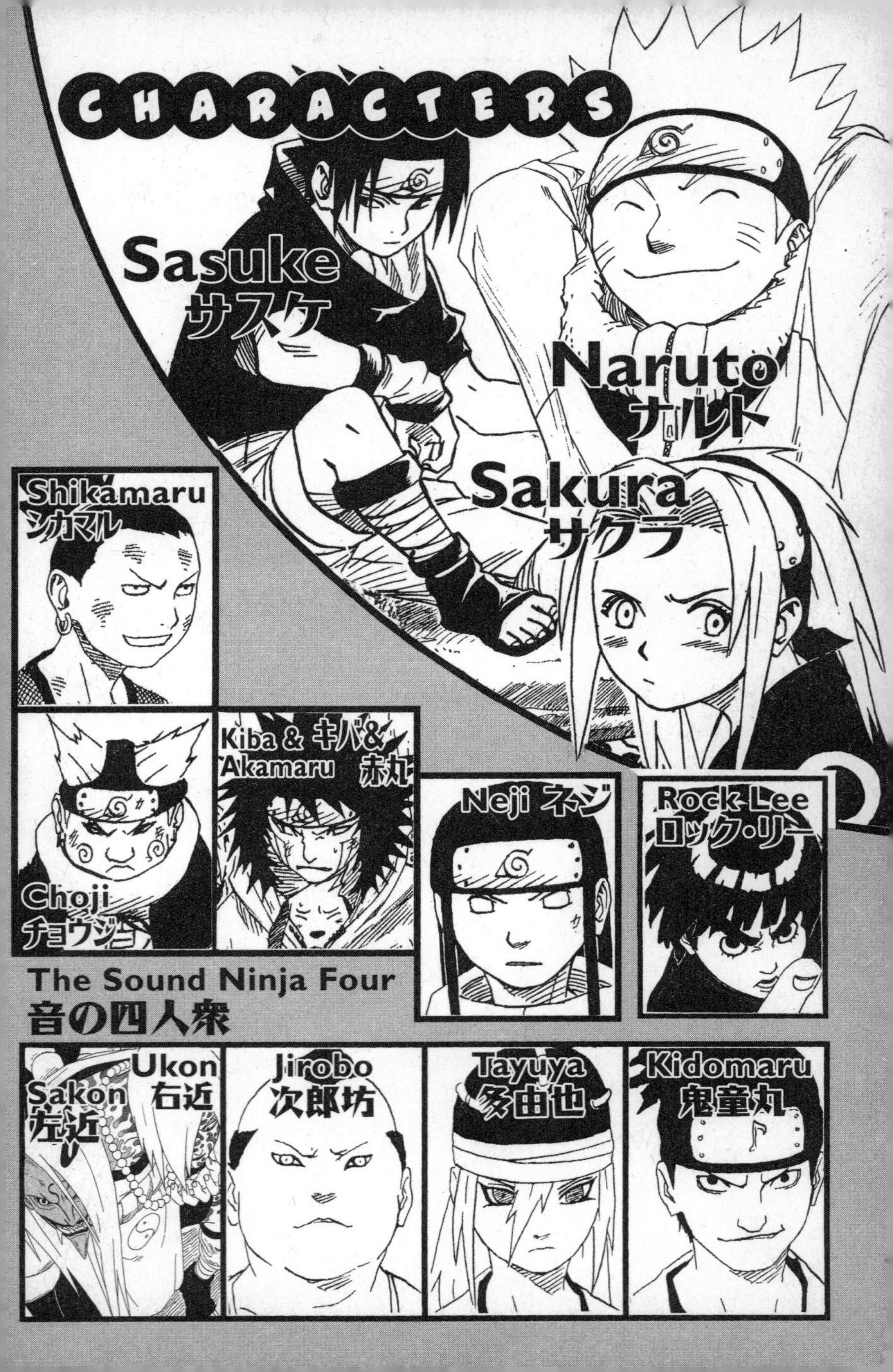
CHARACTERS
Naruto
ナルト
Sasuke
サスケ
Sakura
サクラ
Shikamaru
シカマル
Rock Lee
ロック・リー
Neji ネジ
Kiba & キバ&
Akamaru 赤丸
Choji
チョウジ
The Sound Ninja Four
音の四人衆
Kidomaru
鬼童丸
Tayuya
多由也
Jirobo
次郎坊
Ukon
右近
Sakon
左近

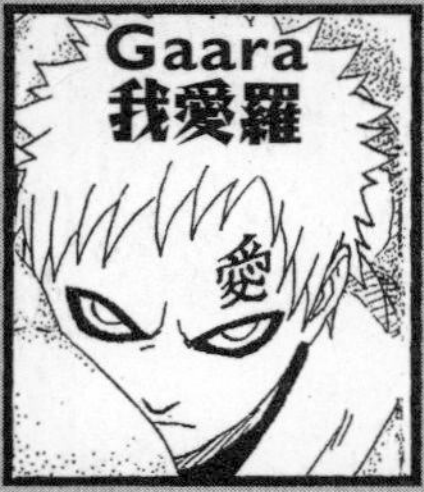
Gaara
我愛羅

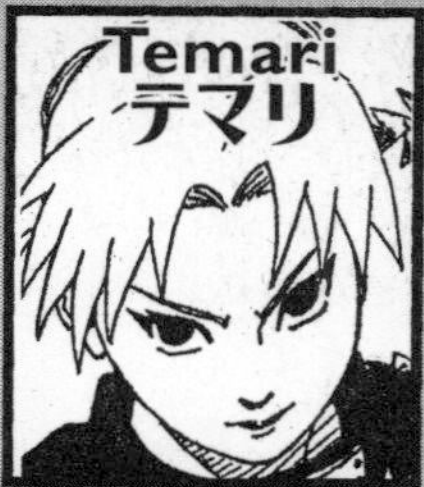
Temari
テマリ

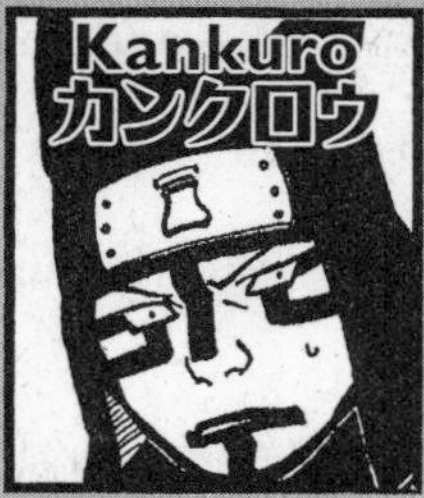
Kankuro
カンクロウ

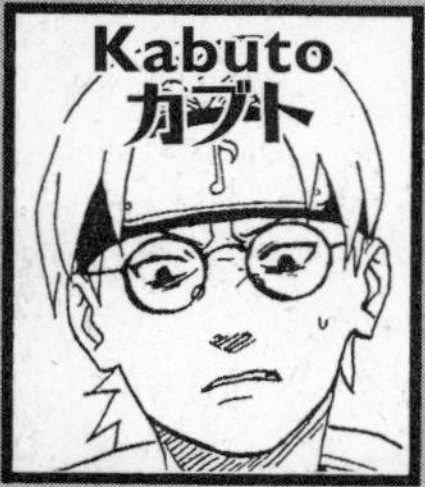
Kabuto
カブト

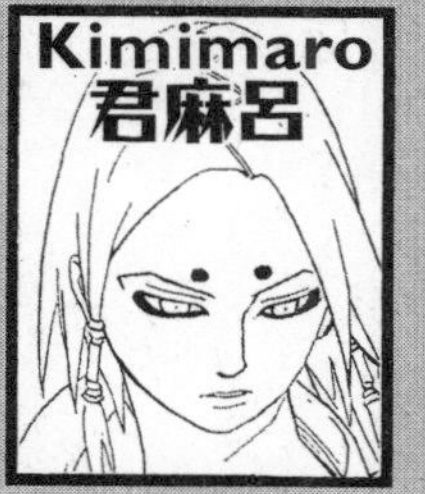
Kimimaro
君麻呂

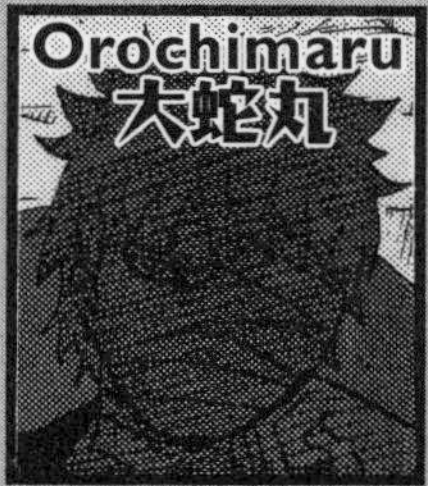
Orochimaru
大蛇丸

The Story So Far…

Naruto was once the bane of the Konohagakure Ninja Academy. Despite the rough start, he and his friends Sasuke and Sakura successfully join the ranks of the ninja. But during the final tournament of the Third Chunin Exam, the nefarious Orochimaru launches *Operation Destroy Konoha*, during which the Third Hokage sacrifices his own life.

In the aftermath, Tsunade steps up to become the Fifth Hokage. Charmed by the power of Orochimaru, Sasuke joins up with the Sound Ninja Four. During a battle with the Sound Four, Choji and Neji both fall, but Naruto, Shikamaru and Kiba are still standing…

NARUTO

VOL. 24
UNORTHODOX

CONTENTS

Number 209: Help Arrives!!

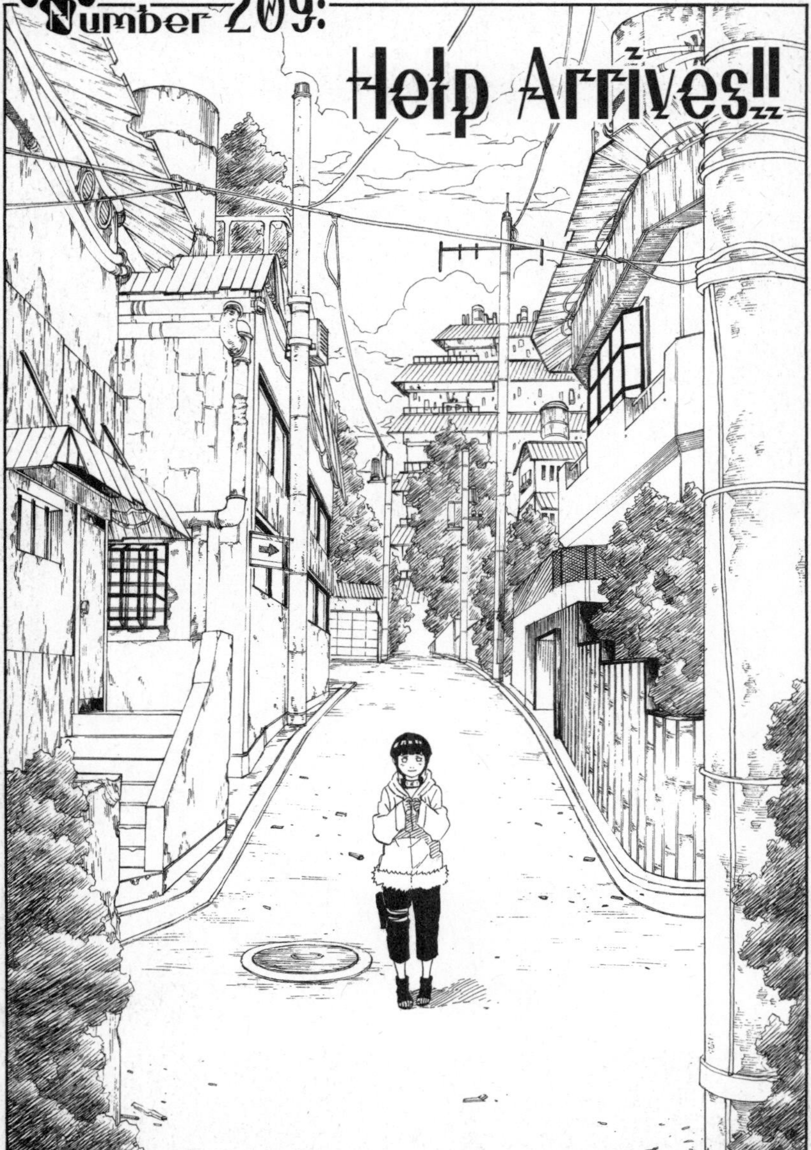

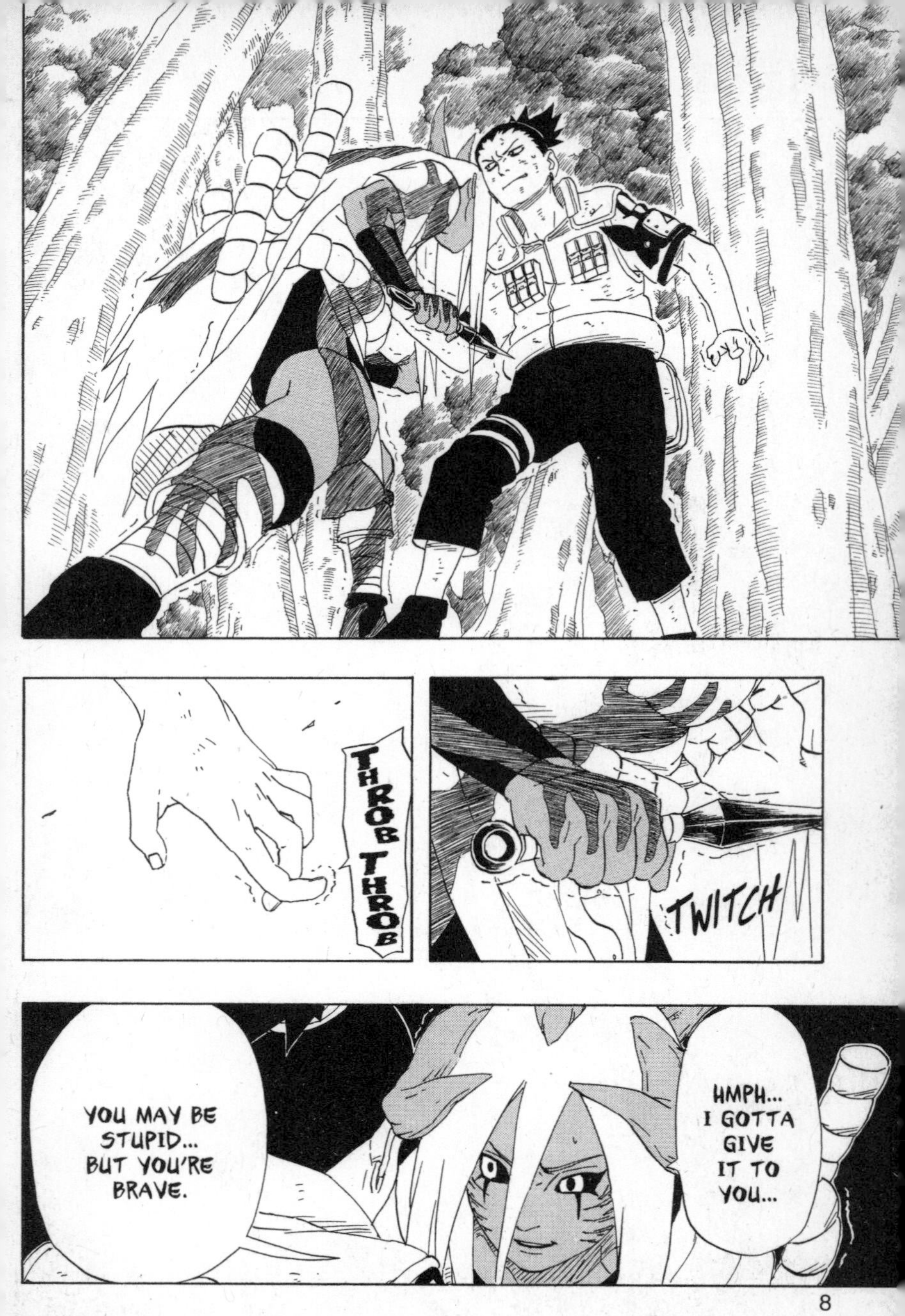
TWITCH
THROB THROB
HMPH... I GOTTA GIVE IT TO YOU...
YOU MAY BE STUPID... BUT YOU'RE BRAVE.

READ THIS WAY

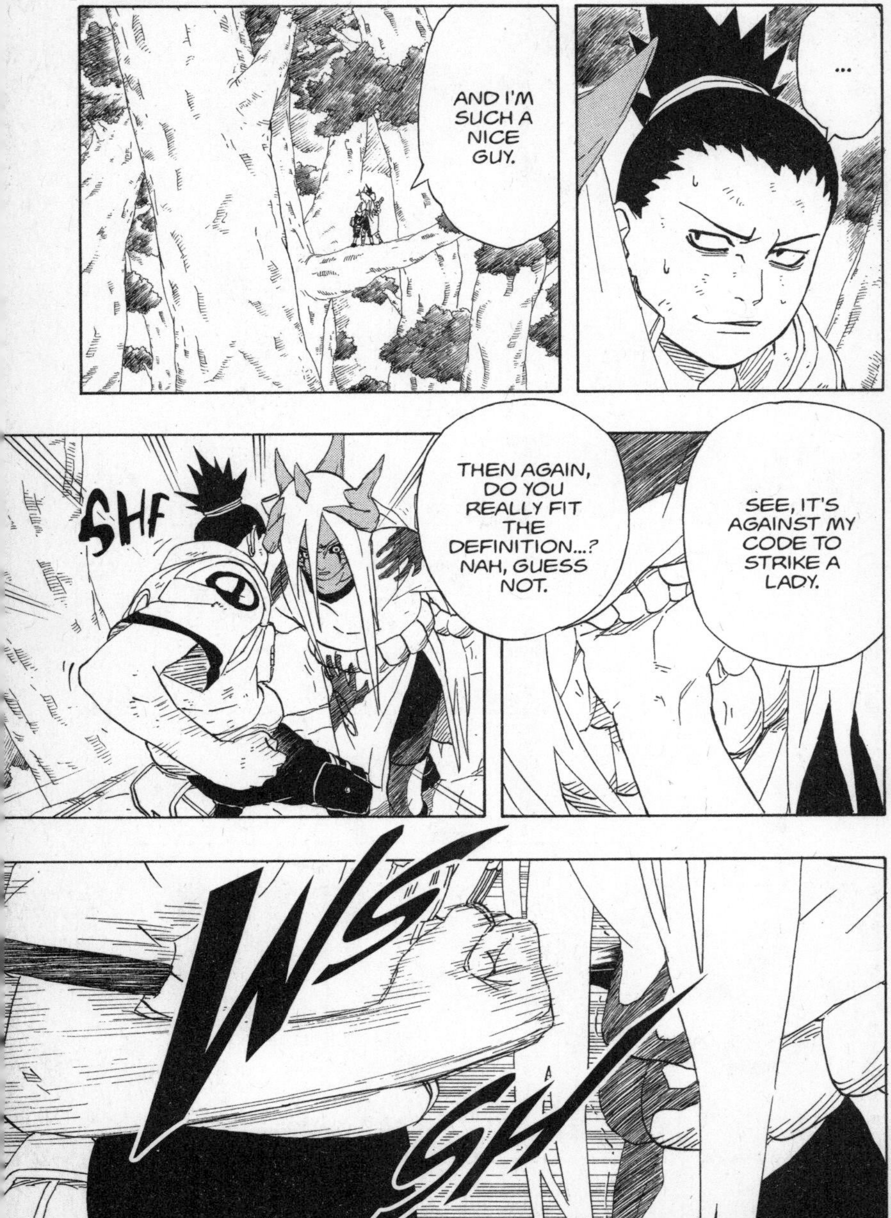

...
AND I'M SUCH A NICE GUY.
SEE, IT'S AGAINST MY CODE TO STRIKE A LADY.
THEN AGAIN, DO YOU REALLY FIT THE DEFINITION...? NAH, GUESS NOT.
SHF
WSSH

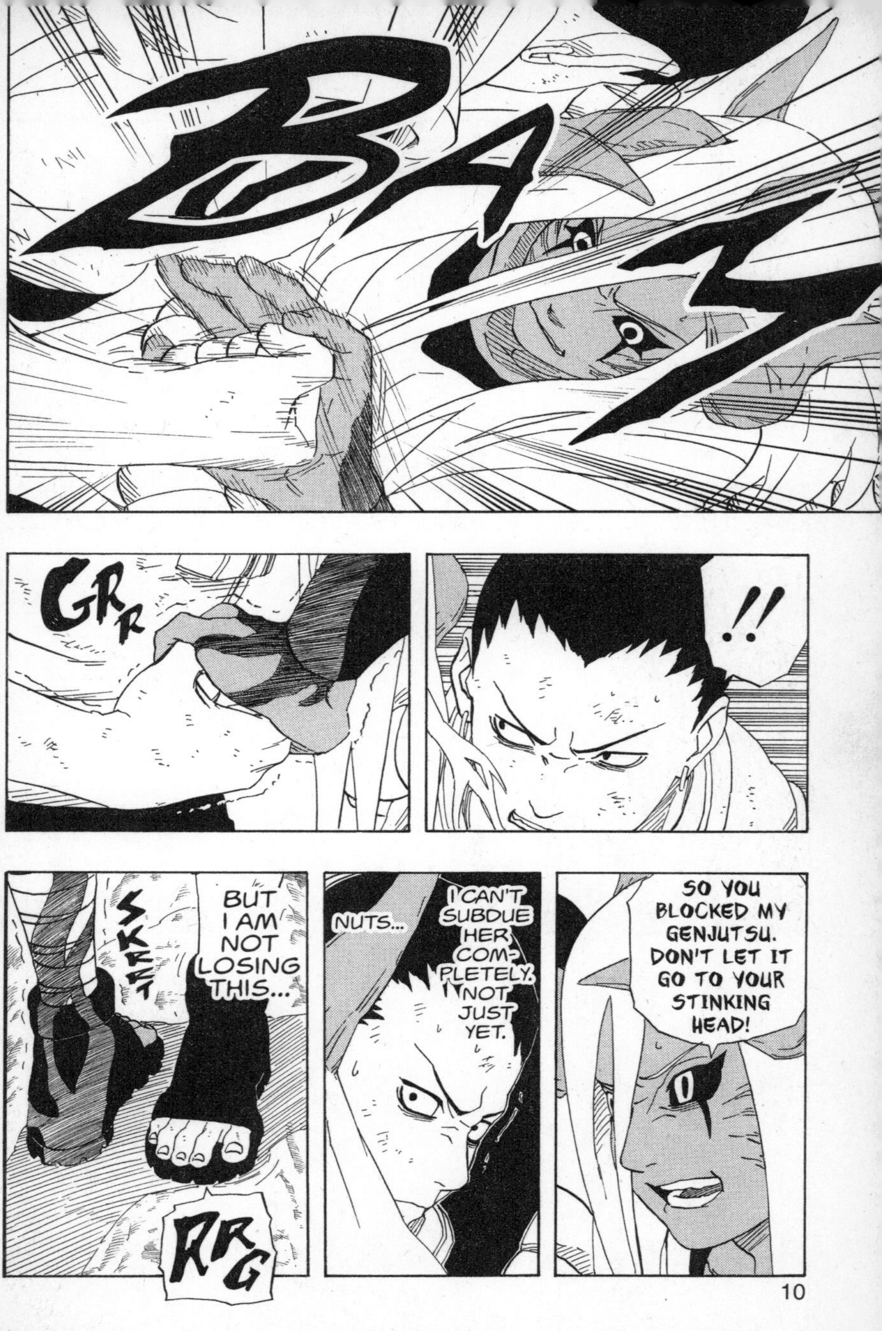
BAM
!!
GRR
SO YOU BLOCKED MY GENJUTSU. DON'T LET IT GO TO YOUR STINKING HEAD!
I CAN'T SUBDUE HER COMPLETELY. NOT JUST YET.
NUTS...
BUT I AM NOT LOSING THIS...
SKRET
RRG

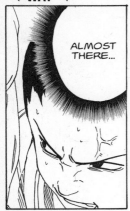

ALMOST THERE...

UGH
...

...!

GRR

SKUNNG

GWUR

GWUR

GWUR

ZWURR

ZWURR

?!

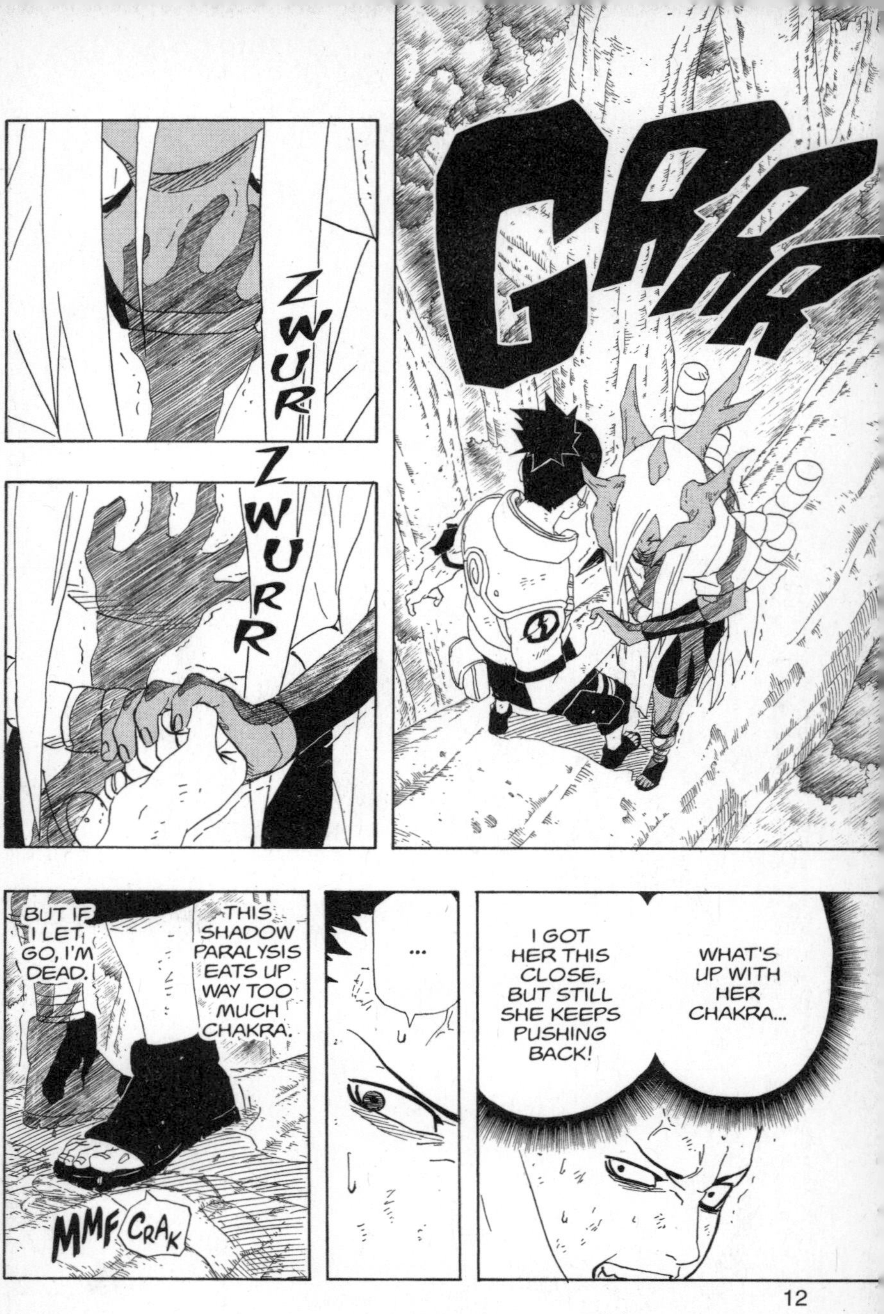
GAA
ZWUR
ZWURR
WHAT'S UP WITH HER CHAKRA...
I GOT HER THIS CLOSE, BUT STILL SHE KEEPS PUSHING BACK!
...
THIS SHADOW PARALYSIS EATS UP WAY TOO MUCH CHAKRA.
BUT IF I LET GO, I'M DEAD.
MMF
CRAK

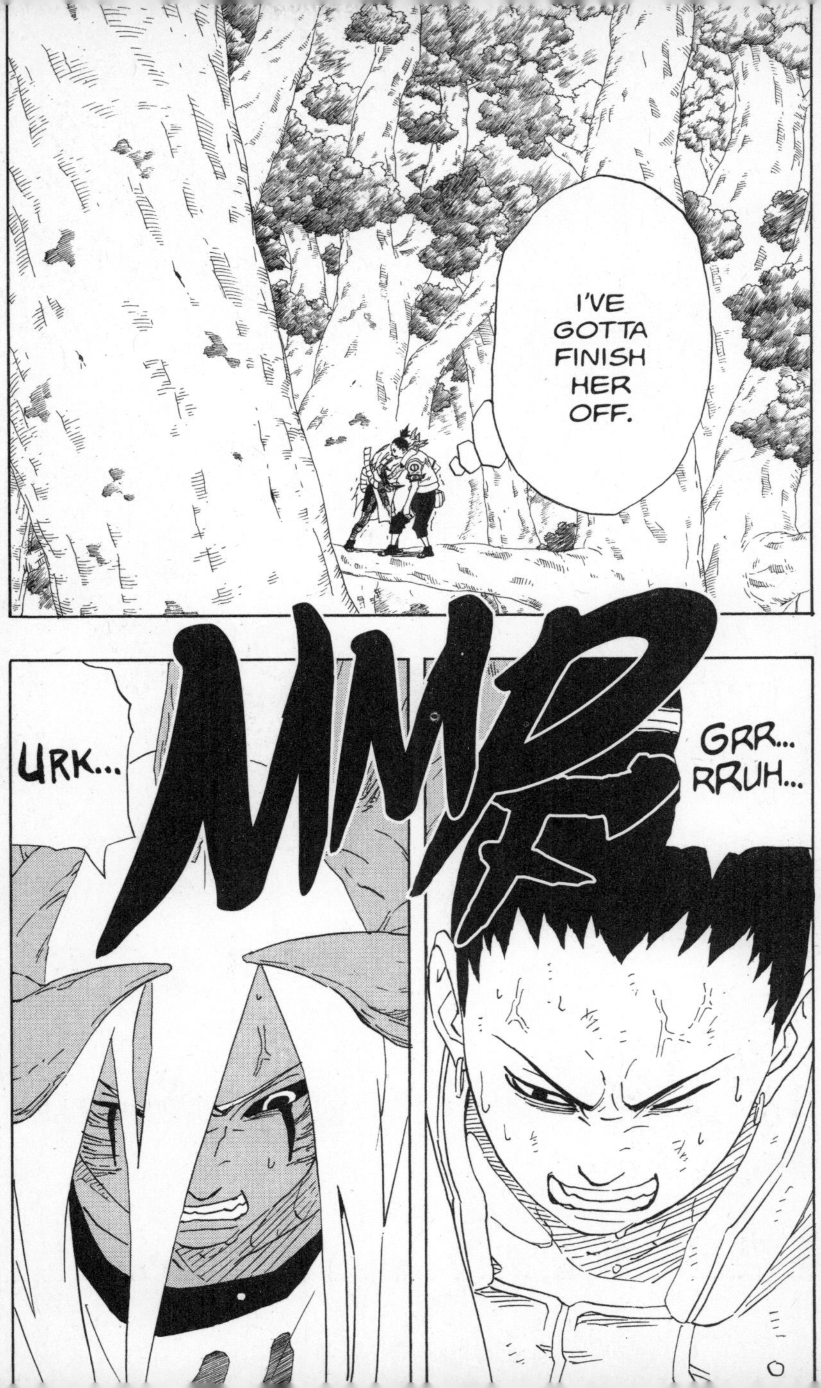
I'VE GOTTA FINISH HER OFF.
GRR... RRUH...
MMPF
URK...

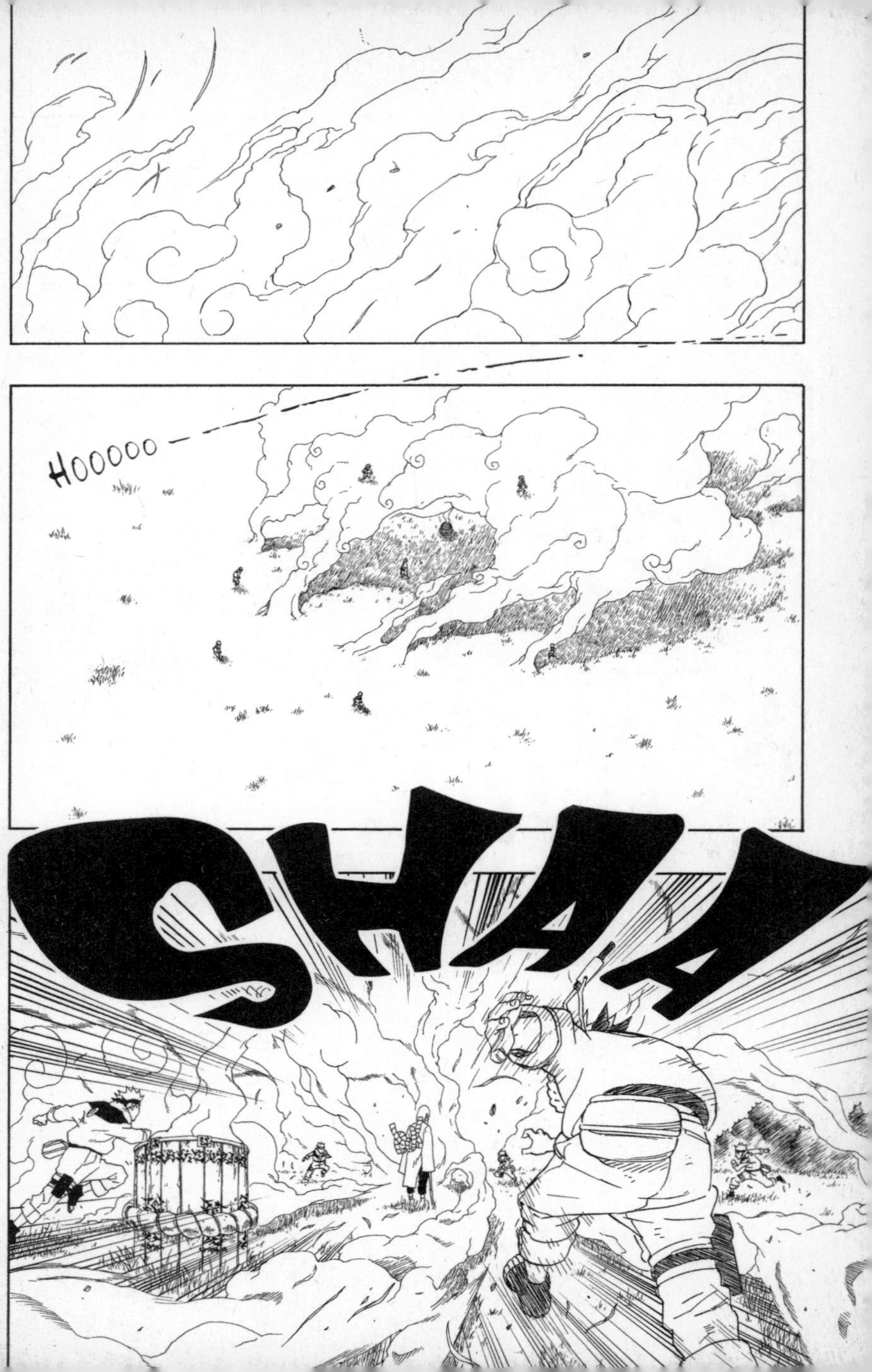
HOOOOO
SHAA

READ THIS WAY

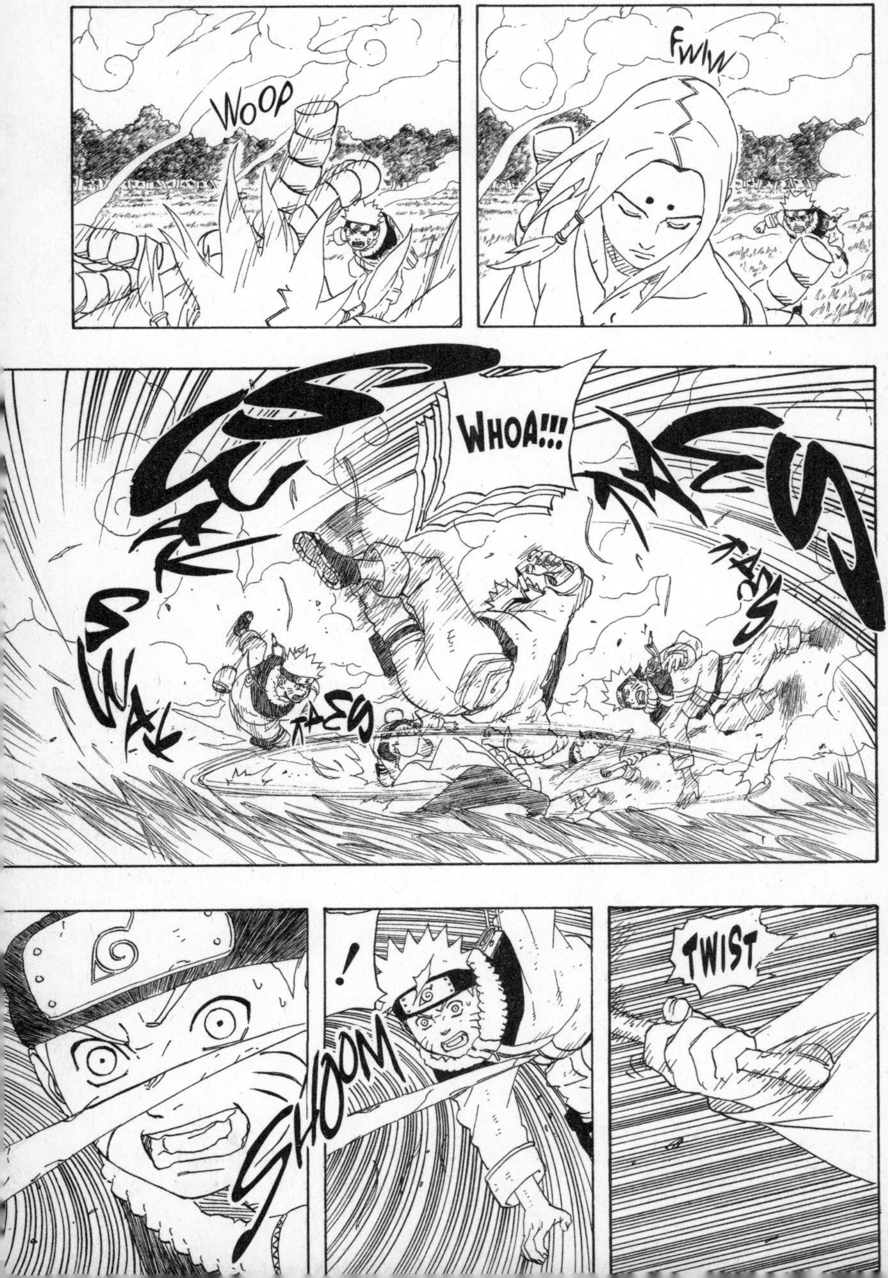
FWIW
WOOP
WHOA!!!
TWIST
!
SHOOM

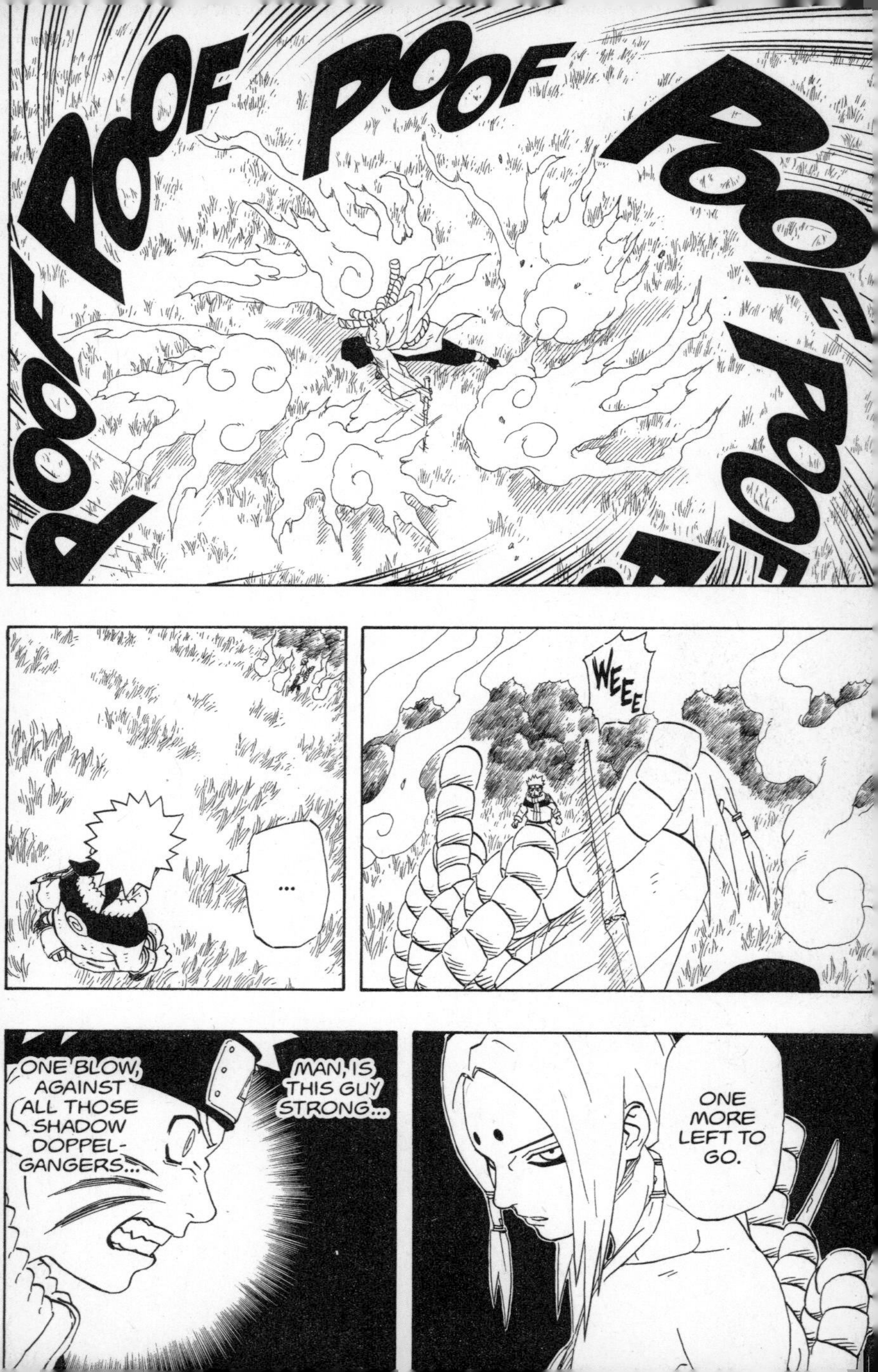
POOF POOF POOF
POOF
POOF POOF POOF
WEEE
...
ONE MORE LEFT TO GO.
MAN, IS THIS GUY STRONG...
ONE BLOW, AGAINST ALL THOSE SHADOW DOPPEL-GANGERS...

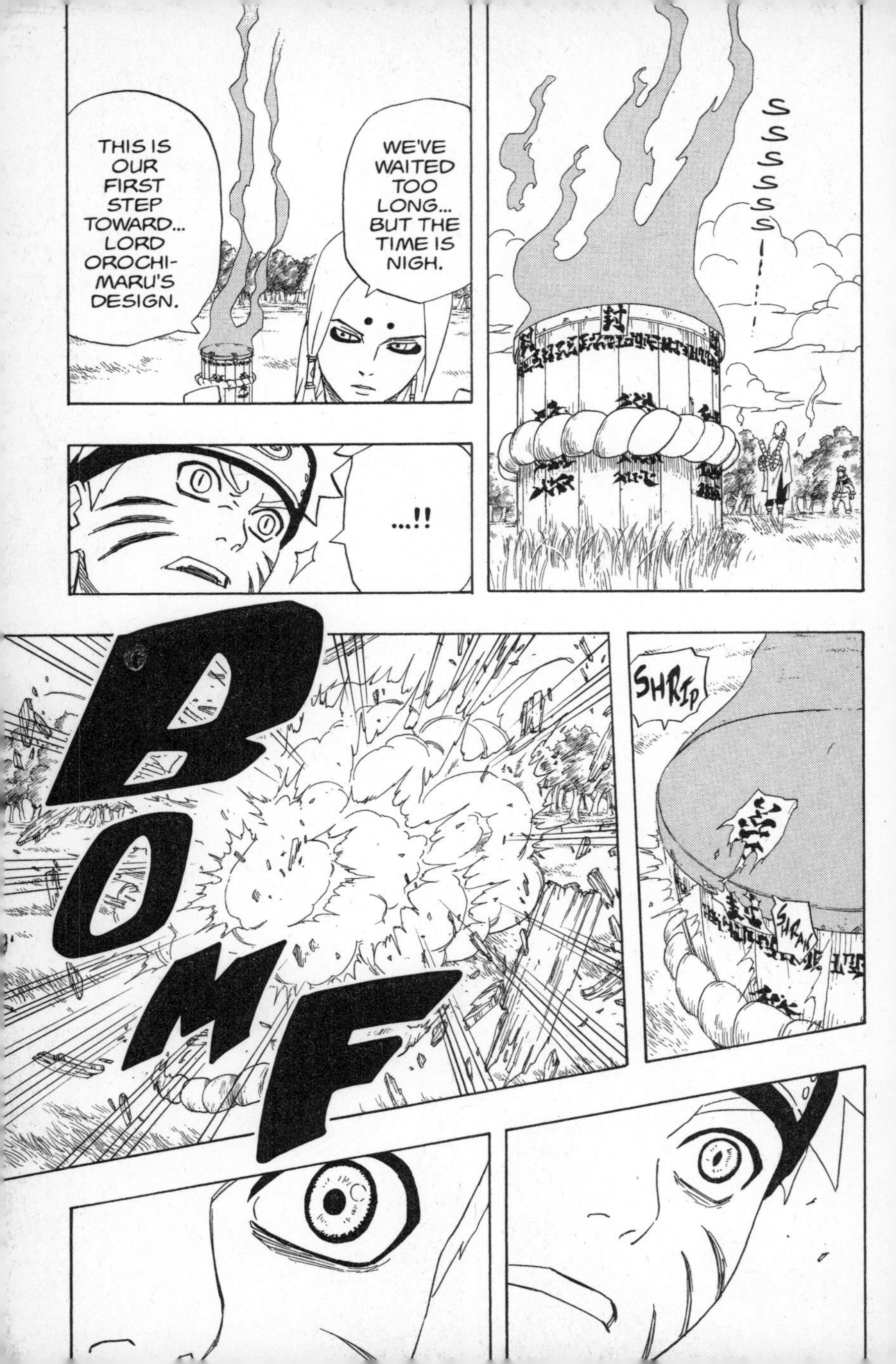
SSSSSS
WE'VE WAITED TOO LONG... BUT THE TIME IS NIGH.
THIS IS OUR FIRST STEP TOWARD... LORD OROCHIMARU'S DESIGN.
...!!
SHRIP
SHRAK
BOMF

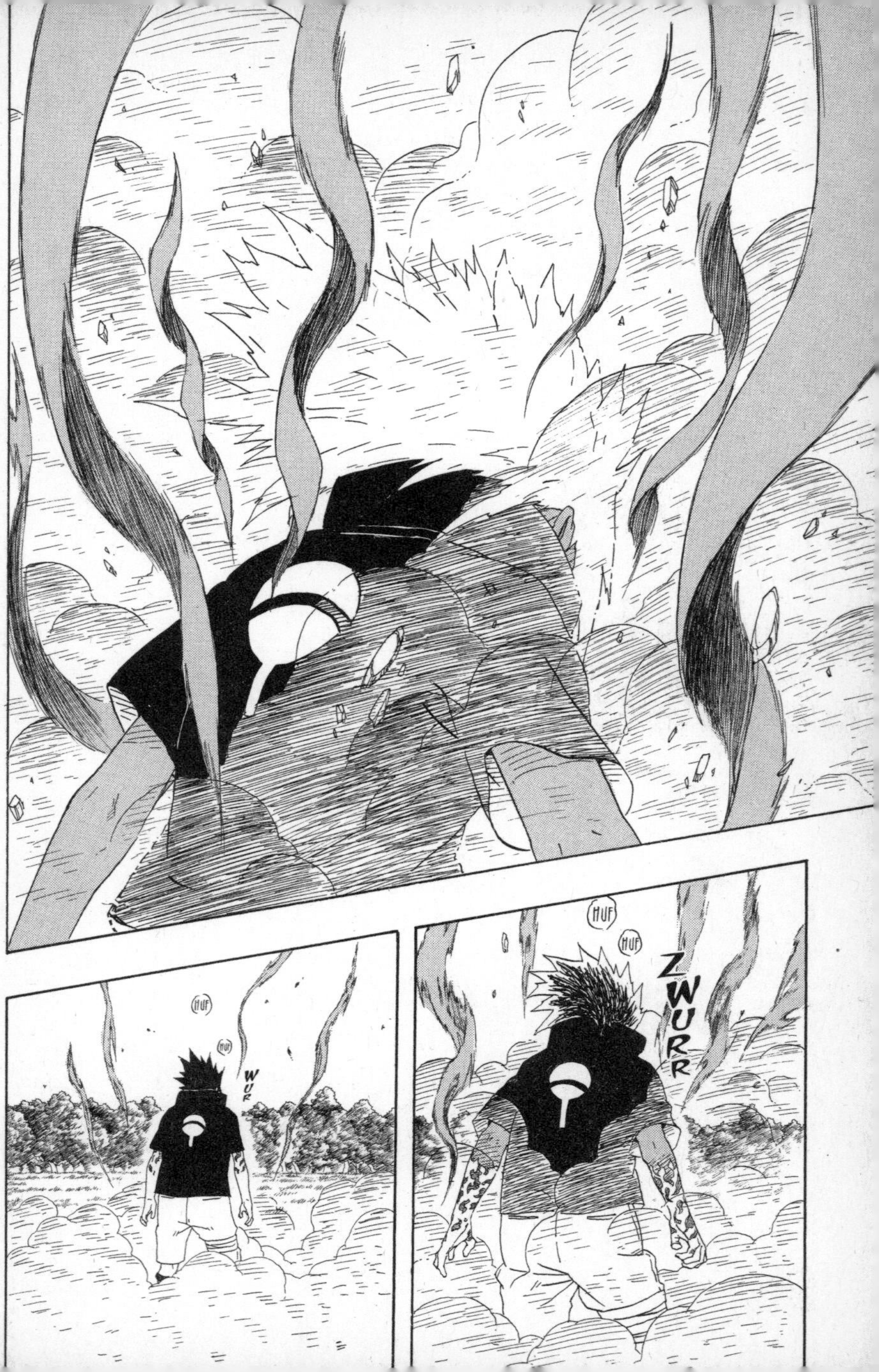
HUF
HUF
ZWURR
HUF
HUF
WUR

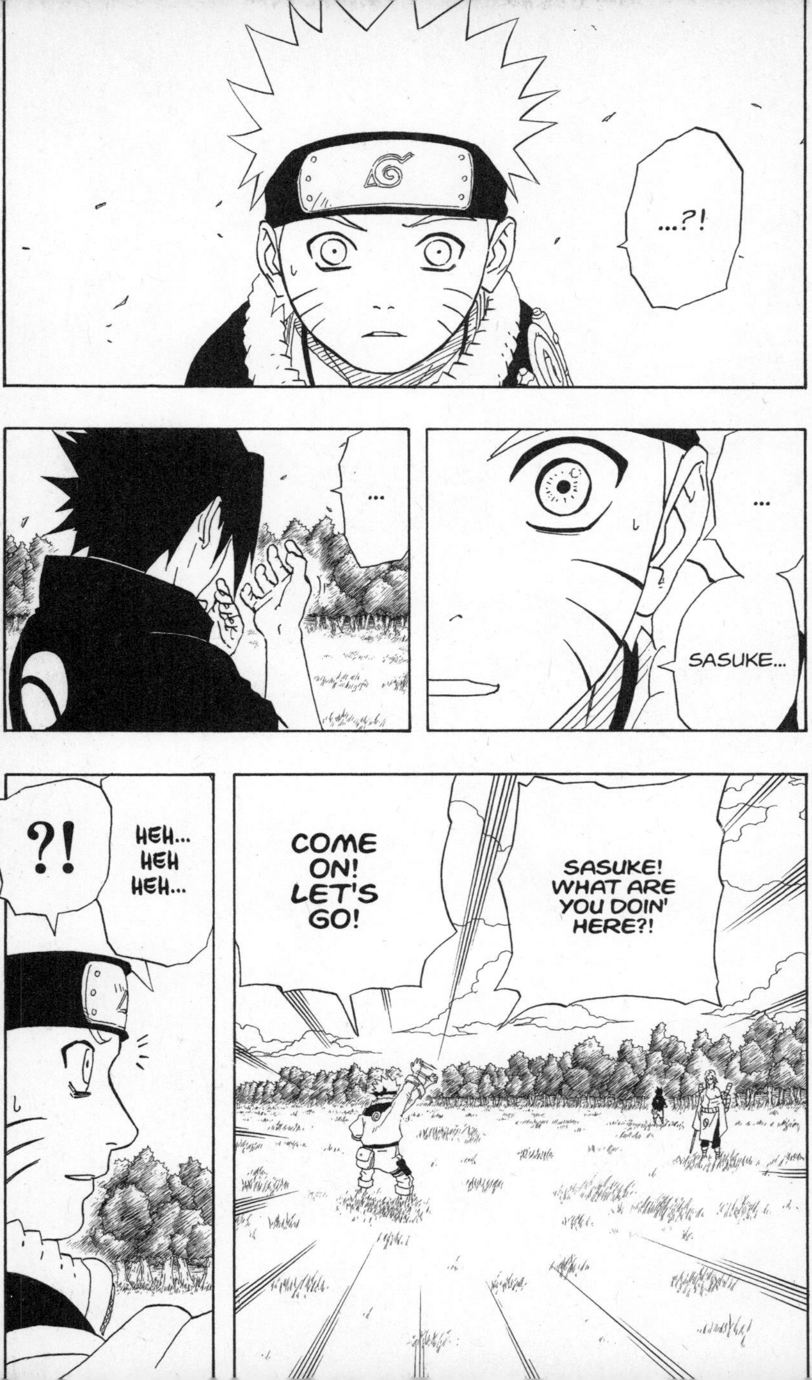
...?!
...
SASUKE...
...
SASUKE! WHAT ARE YOU DOIN' HERE?!
COME ON! LET'S GO!
HEH... HEH HEH...
?!

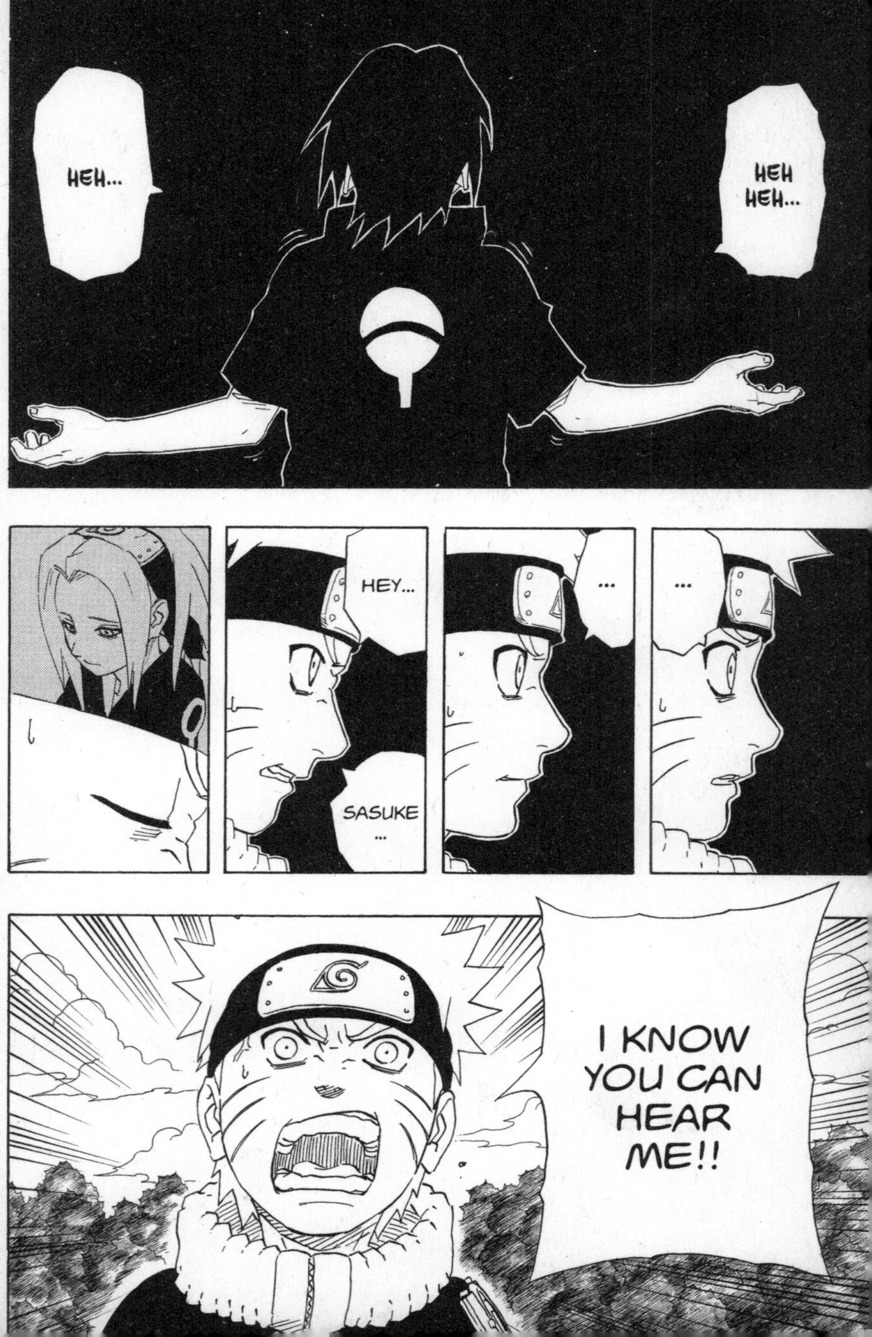
HEH HEH...
HEH...
...
...
HEY...
SASUKE ...
I KNOW YOU CAN HEAR ME!!

READ THIS WAY

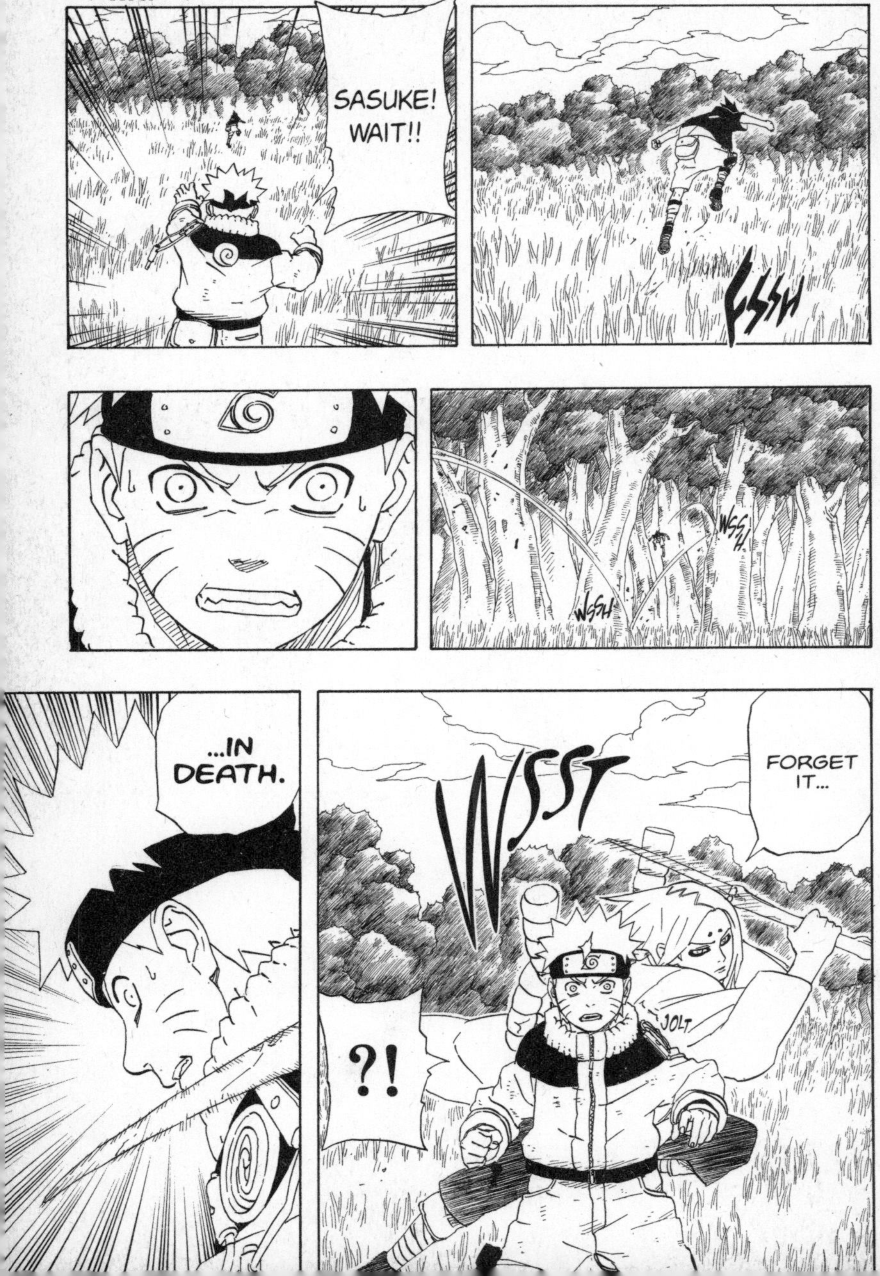
SSSH
SASUKE! WAIT!!
WSSH
WSSH
FORGET IT...
WSST
JOLT
?!
...IN DEATH.

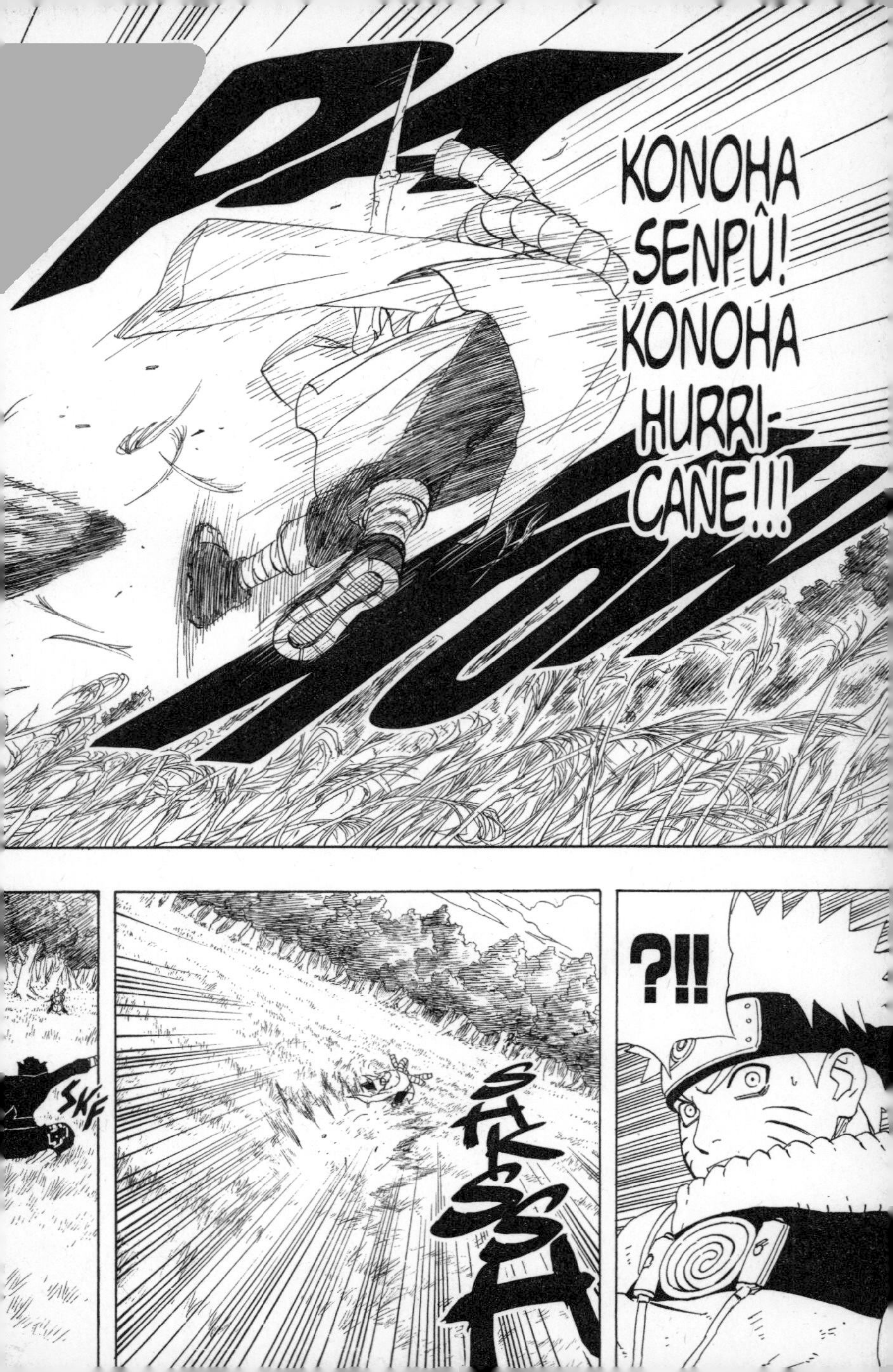
KONOHA SENPÛ!
KONOHA HURRI-CANE!!!
?!!
SKF

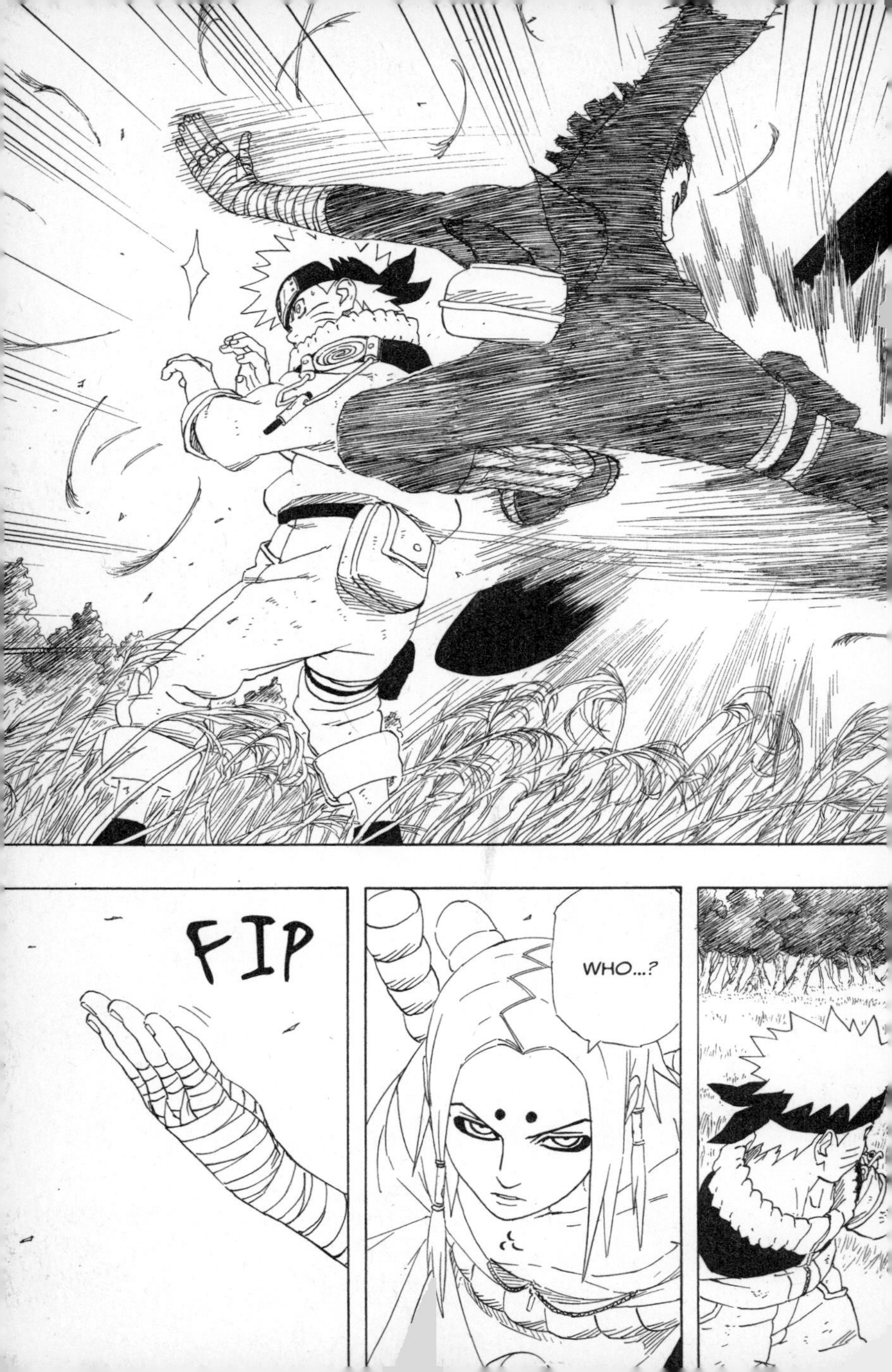
WHO...?
FIP

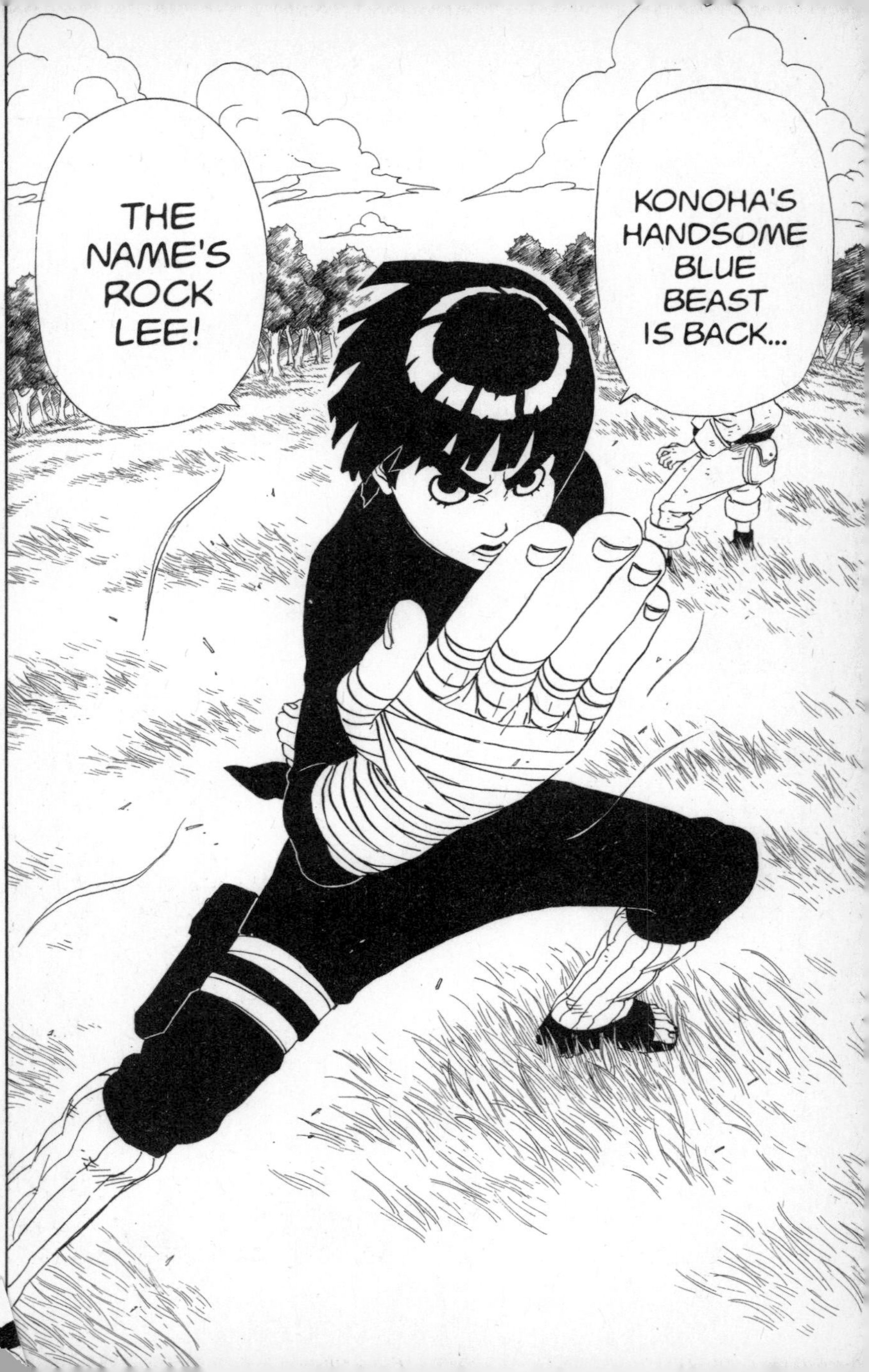
KONOHA'S HANDSOME BLUE BEAST IS BACK...
THE NAME'S ROCK LEE!

READ THIS WAY

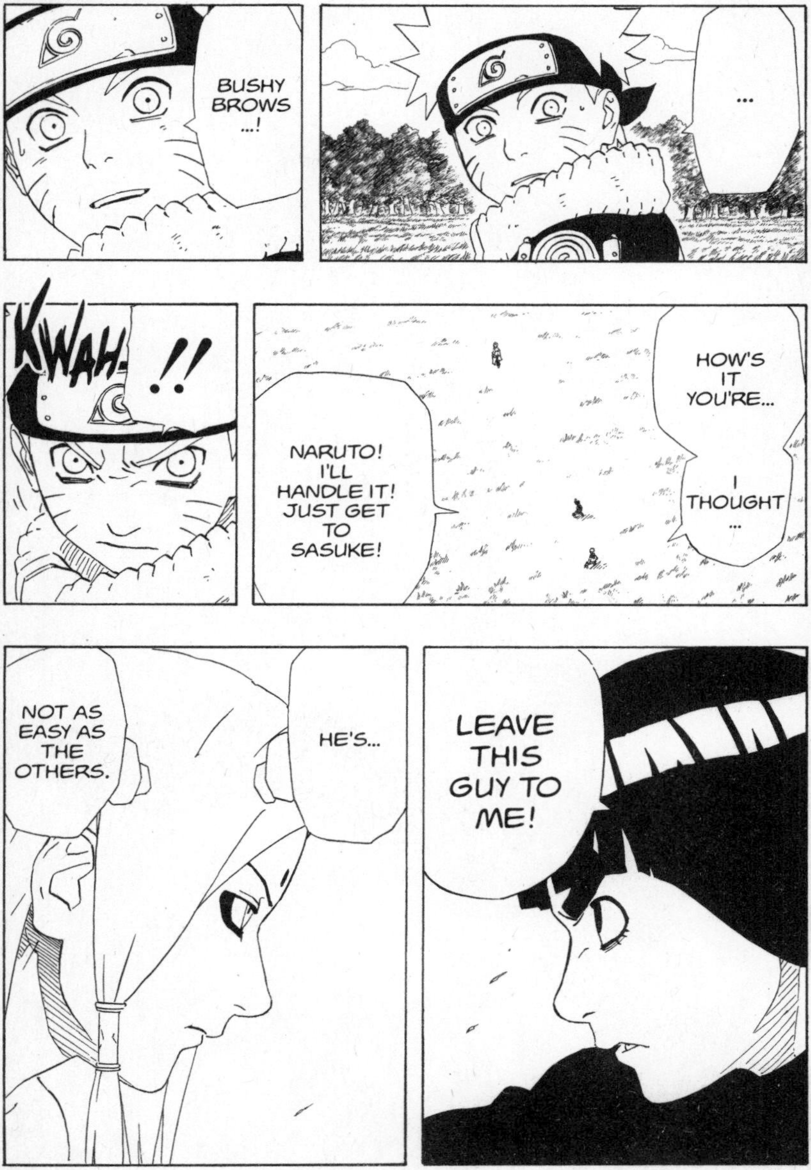

...
BUSHY BROWS ...!
HOW'S IT YOU'RE...
I THOUGHT ...
NARUTO! I'LL HANDLE IT! JUST GET TO SASUKE!
KWAH-!!
LEAVE THIS GUY TO ME!
HE'S...
NOT AS EASY AS THE OTHERS.

NARUTO™

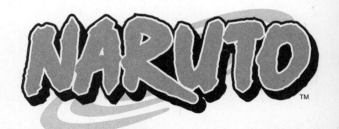

Number 210: Lee's Secret!!

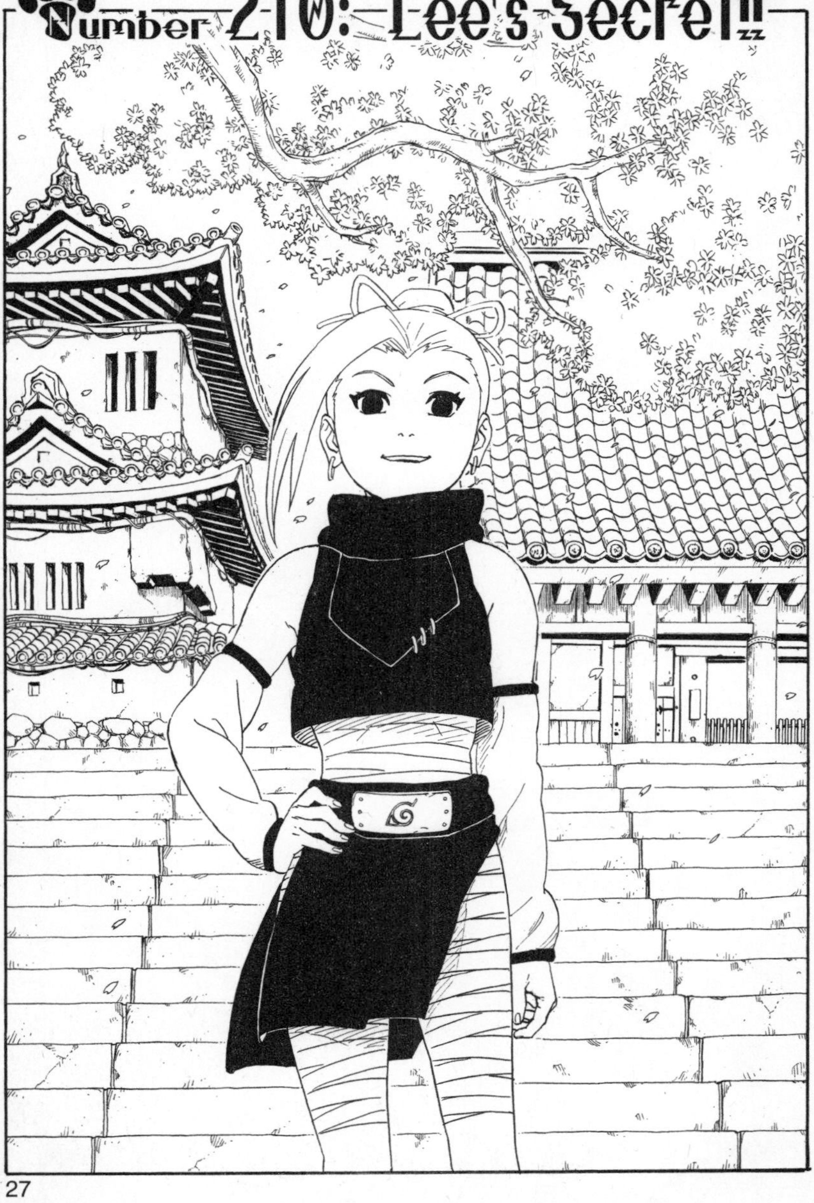

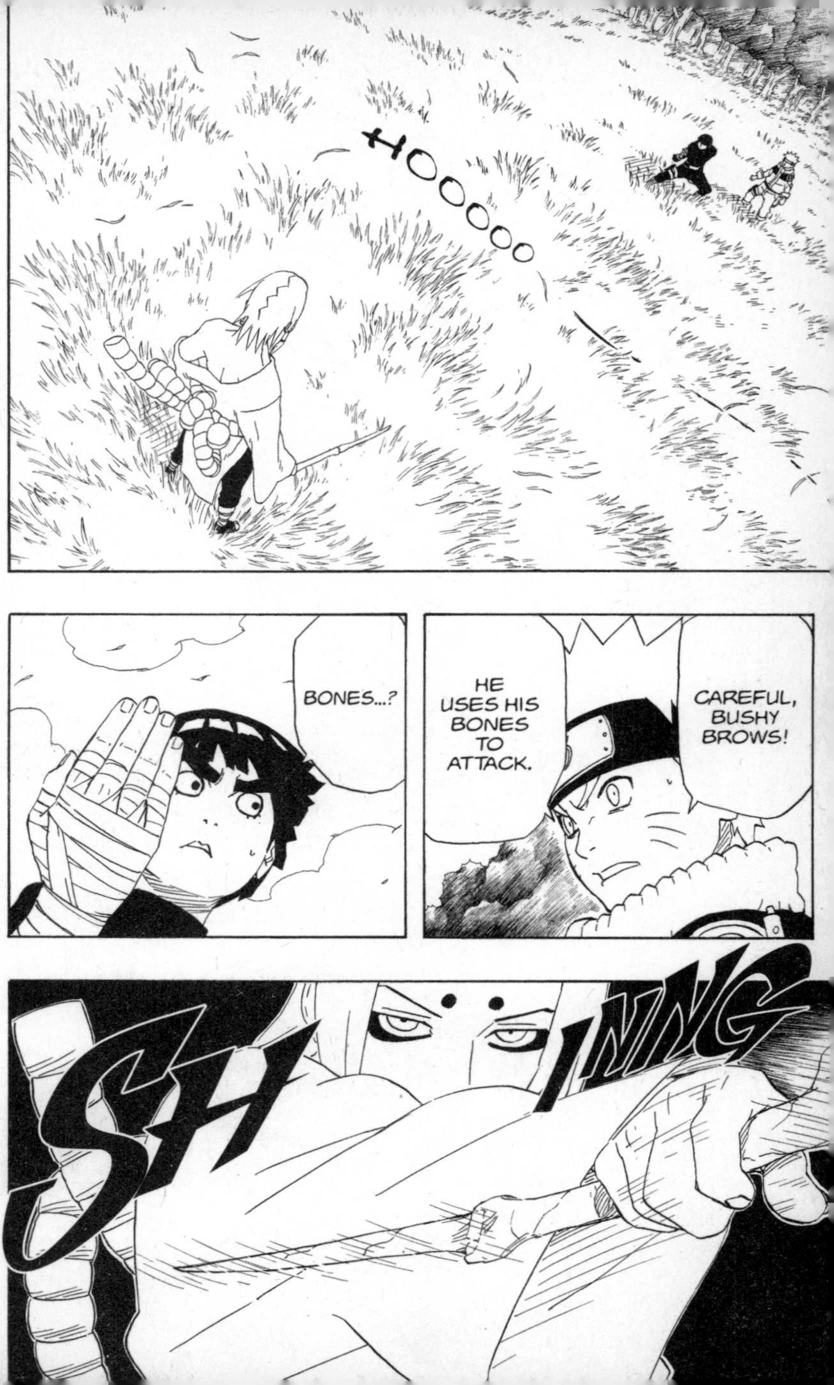
HOOOOO
CAREFUL, BUSHY BROWS!
HE USES HIS BONES TO ATTACK.
BONES...?
SHINNG

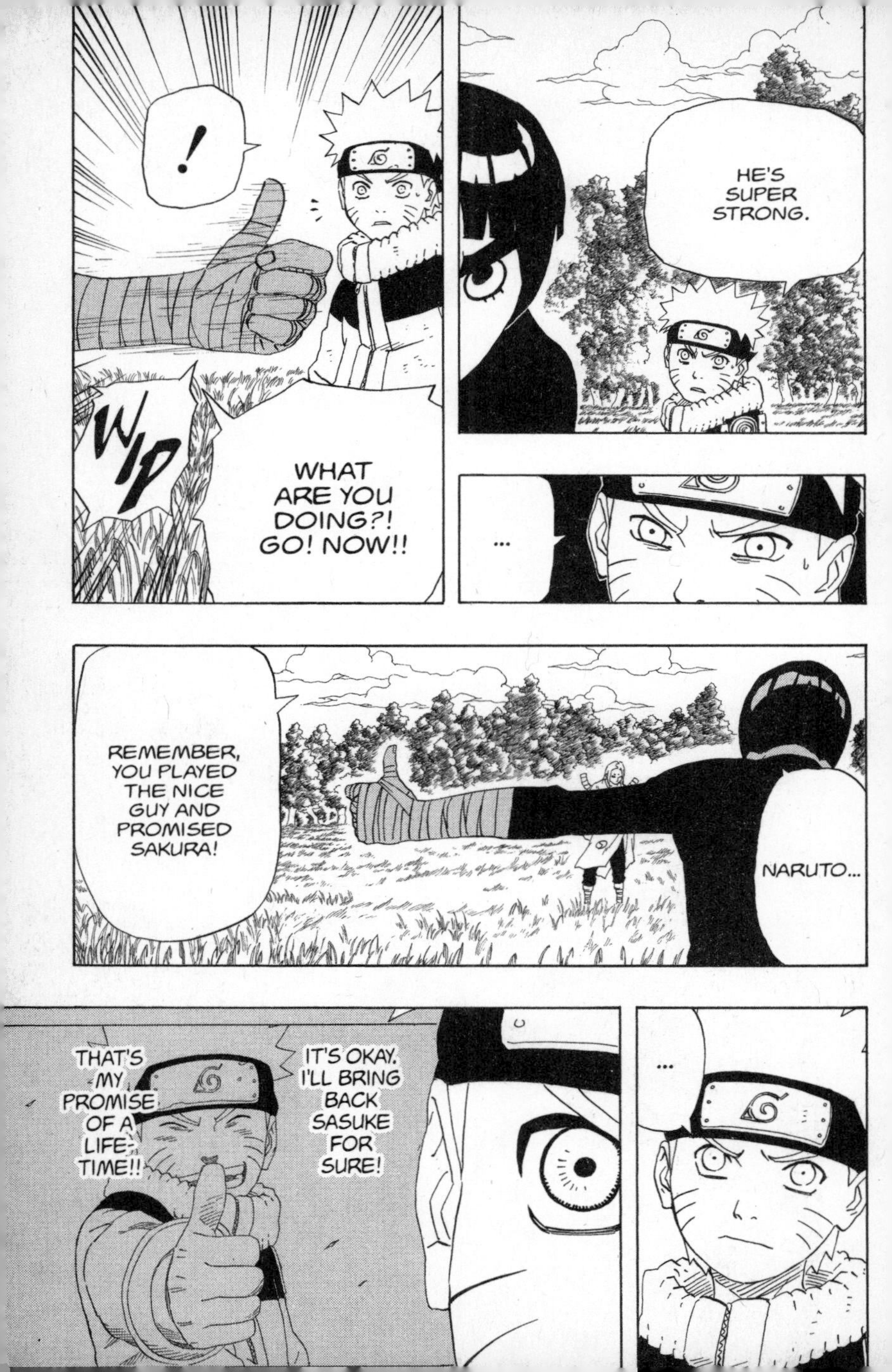
HE'S SUPER STRONG.
...
!
WIP
WHAT ARE YOU DOING?! GO! NOW!!
NARUTO...
REMEMBER, YOU PLAYED THE NICE GUY AND PROMISED SAKURA!
...
IT'S OKAY. I'LL BRING BACK SASUKE FOR SURE!
THAT'S MY PROMISE OF A LIFE-TIME!!

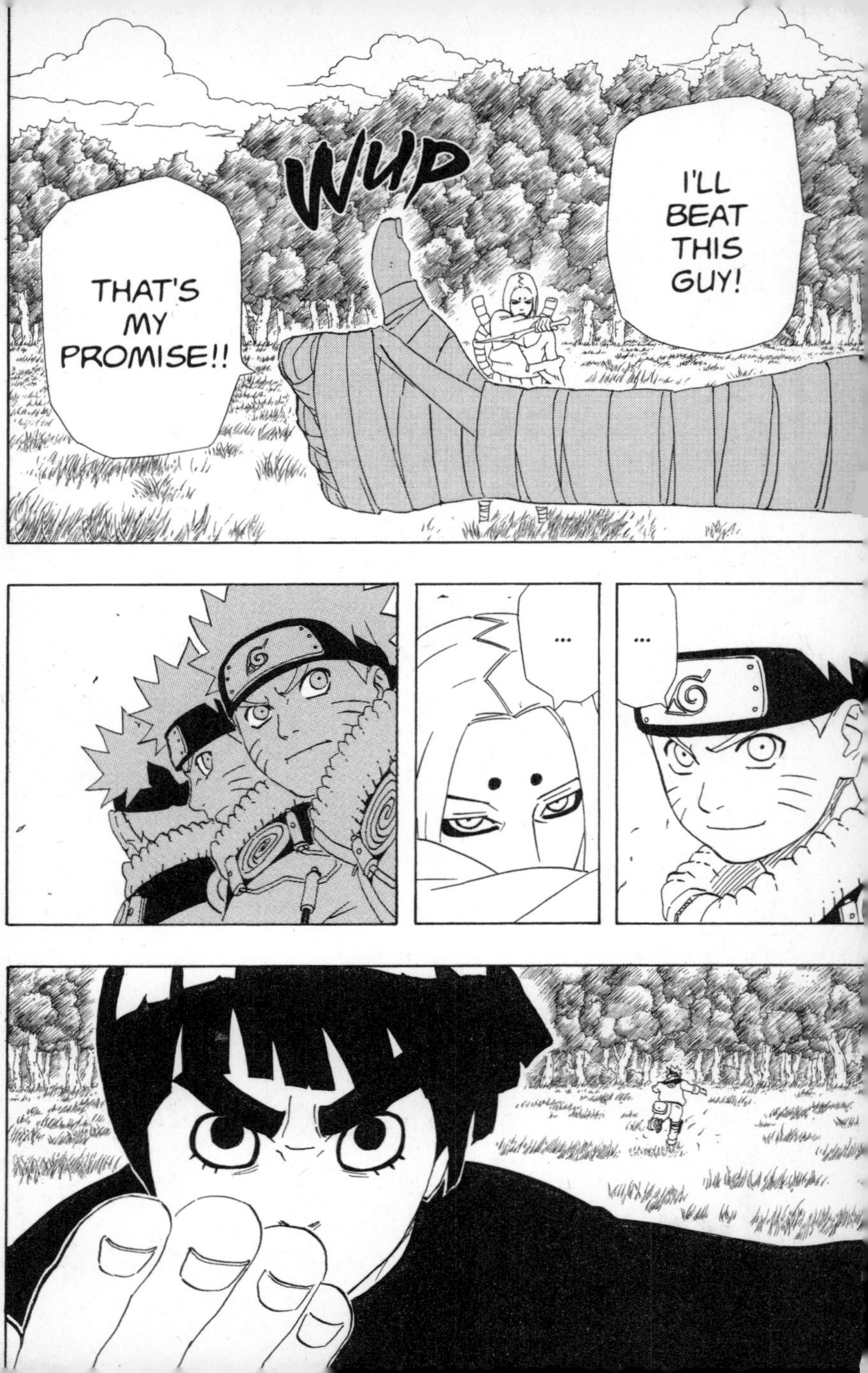
I'LL BEAT THIS GUY!
WUP
THAT'S MY PROMISE!!
...
...

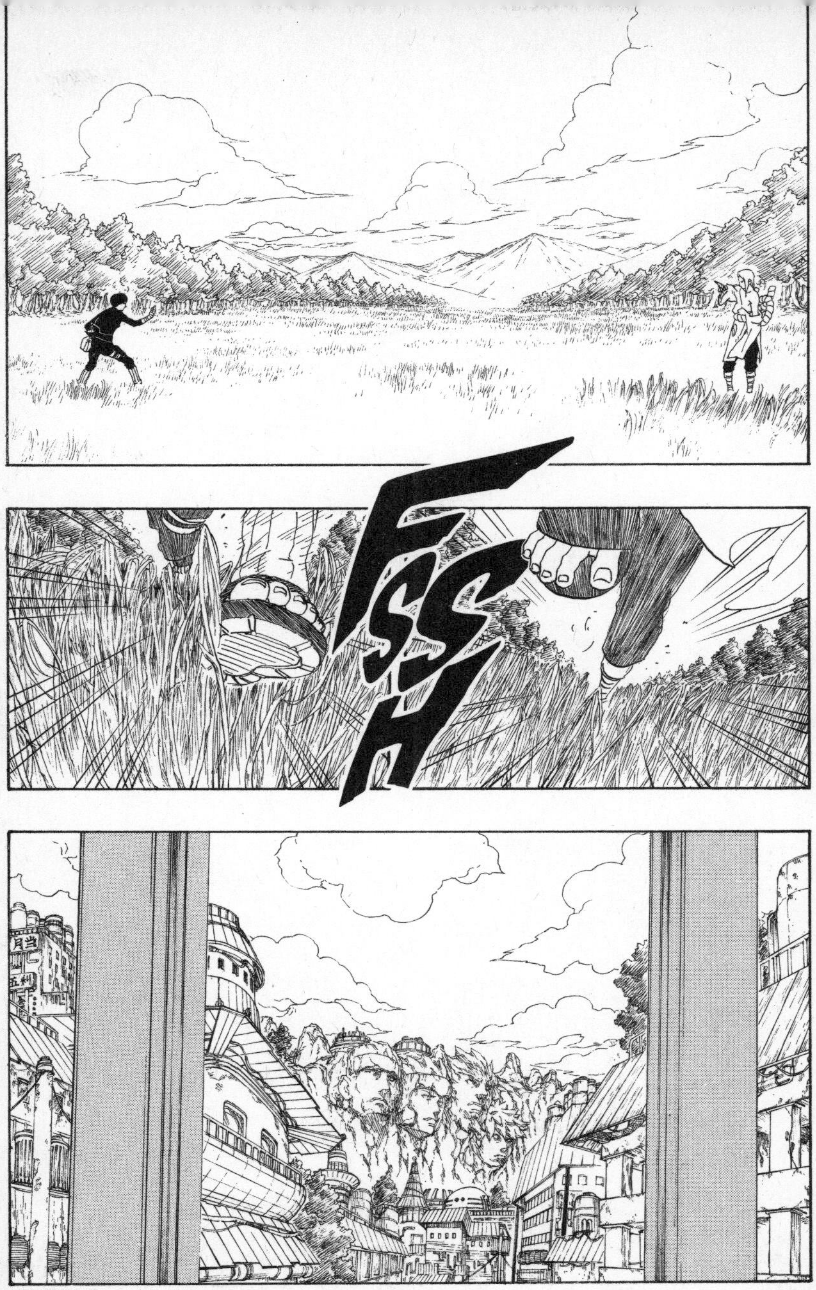
FSSH

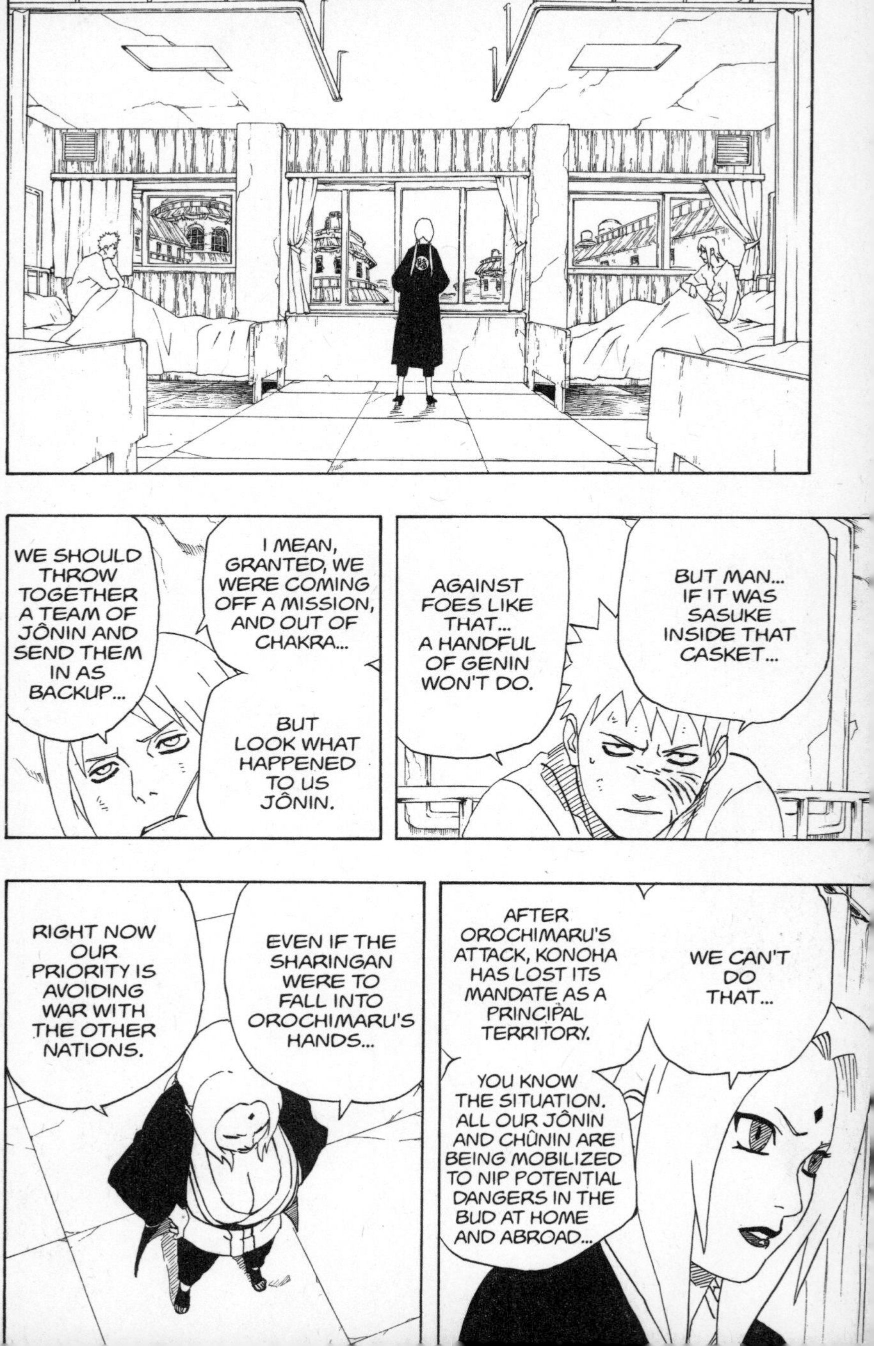
BUT MAN... IF IT WAS SASUKE INSIDE THAT CASKET...
AGAINST FOES LIKE THAT... A HANDFUL OF GENIN WON'T DO.
I MEAN, GRANTED, WE WERE COMING OFF A MISSION, AND OUT OF CHAKRA...
WE SHOULD THROW TOGETHER A TEAM OF JÔNIN AND SEND THEM IN AS BACKUP...
BUT LOOK WHAT HAPPENED TO US JÔNIN.
WE CAN'T DO THAT...
AFTER OROCHIMARU'S ATTACK, KONOHA HAS LOST ITS MANDATE AS A PRINCIPAL TERRITORY.
YOU KNOW THE SITUATION. ALL OUR JÔNIN AND CHÛNIN ARE BEING MOBILIZED TO NIP POTENTIAL DANGERS IN THE BUD AT HOME AND ABROAD...
EVEN IF THE SHARINGAN WERE TO FALL INTO OROCHIMARU'S HANDS...
RIGHT NOW OUR PRIORITY IS AVOIDING WAR WITH THE OTHER NATIONS.

READ THIS WAY

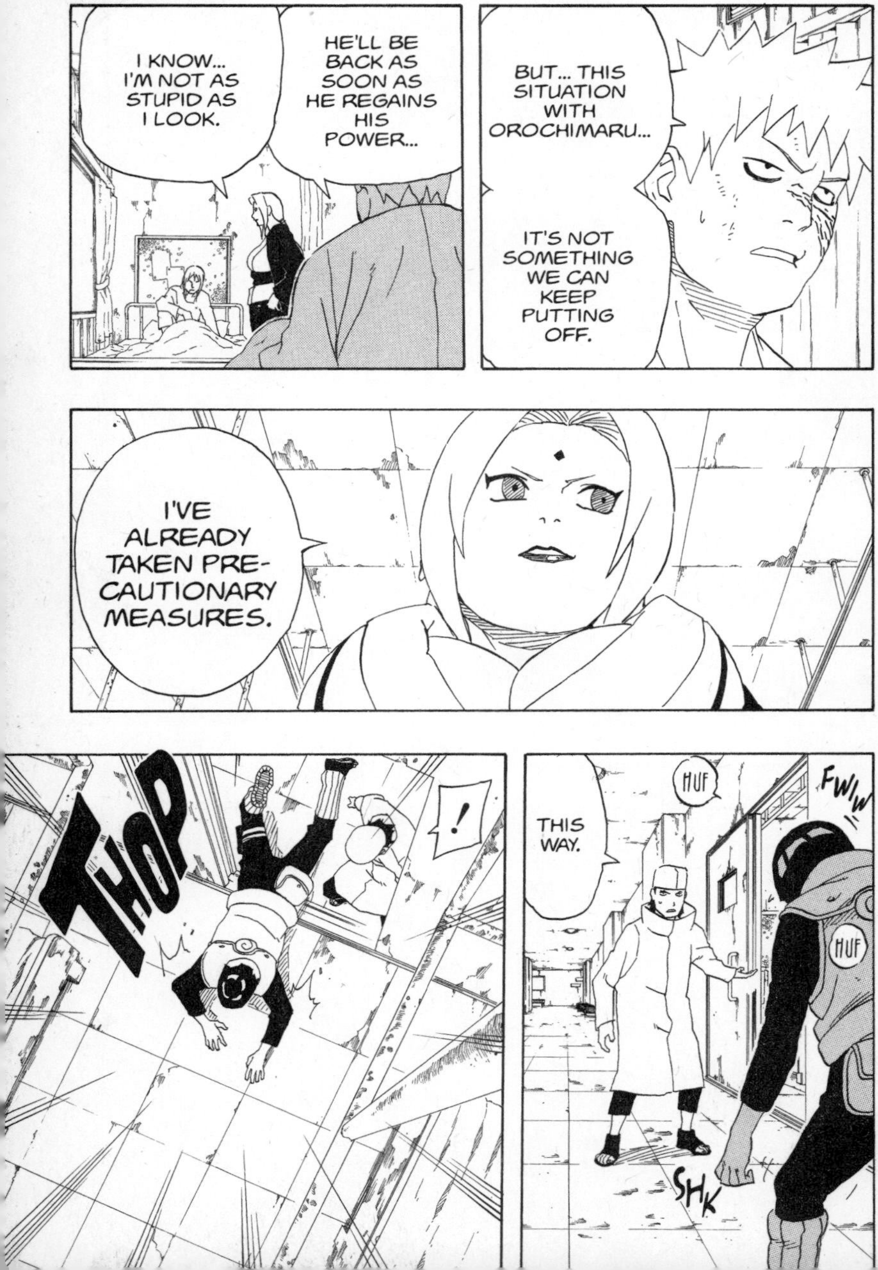
BUT... THIS SITUATION WITH OROCHIMARU...
IT'S NOT SOMETHING WE CAN KEEP PUTTING OFF.
HE'LL BE BACK AS SOON AS HE REGAINS HIS POWER...
I KNOW... I'M NOT AS STUPID AS I LOOK.
I'VE ALREADY TAKEN PRE-CAUTIONARY MEASURES.
FWIW
HUF
THIS WAY.
HUF
SHK
!
THOP

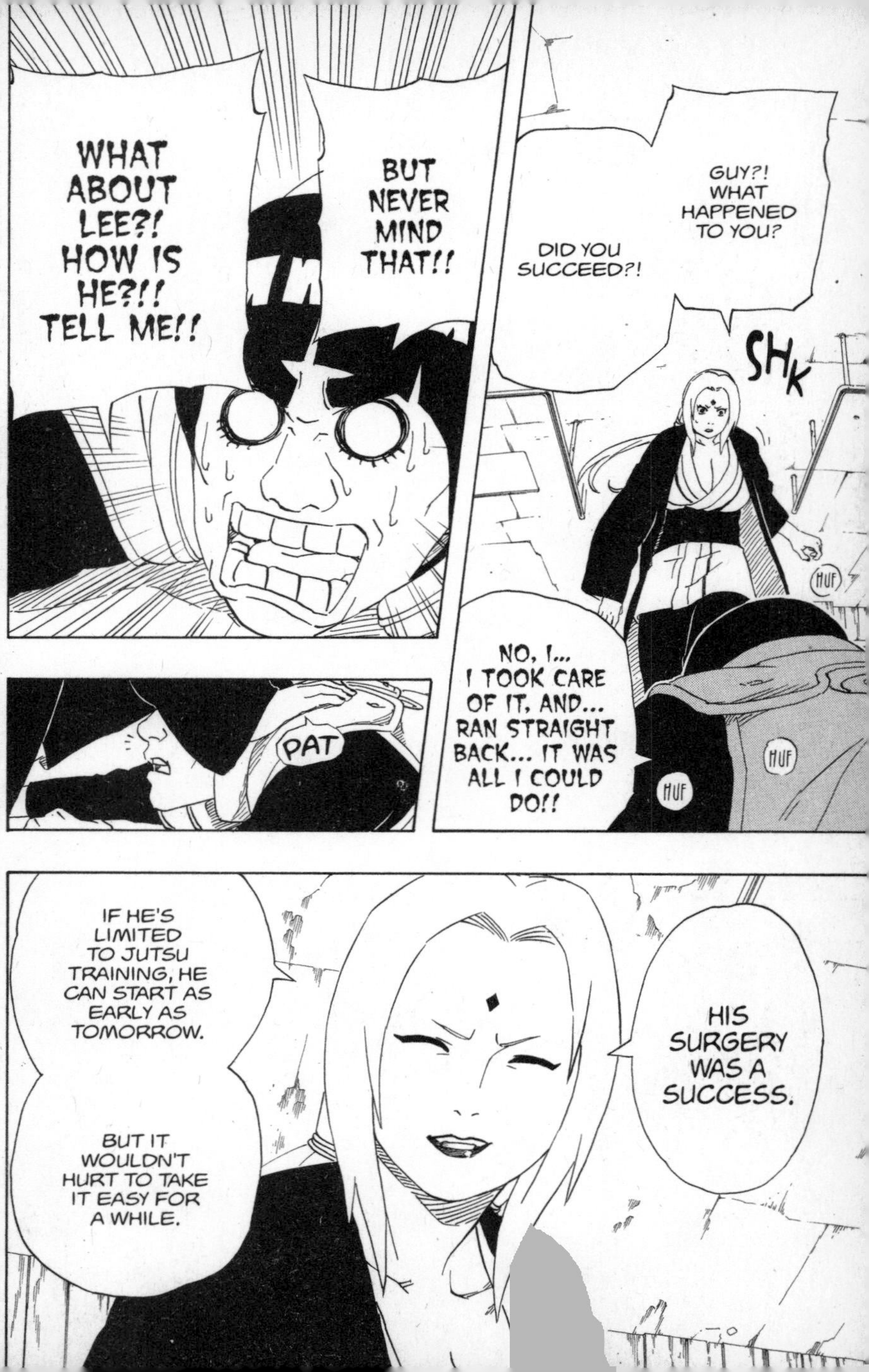
GUY?! WHAT HAPPENED TO YOU?
DID YOU SUCCEED?!
SHK
NO, I... I TOOK CARE OF IT, AND... RAN STRAIGHT BACK... IT WAS ALL I COULD DO!!
HUF
HUF
HUF
BUT NEVER MIND THAT!!
WHAT ABOUT LEE?! HOW IS HE?!! TELL ME!!
PAT
HIS SURGERY WAS A SUCCESS.
IF HE'S LIMITED TO JUTSU TRAINING, HE CAN START AS EARLY AS TOMORROW.
BUT IT WOULDN'T HURT TO TAKE IT EASY FOR A WHILE.

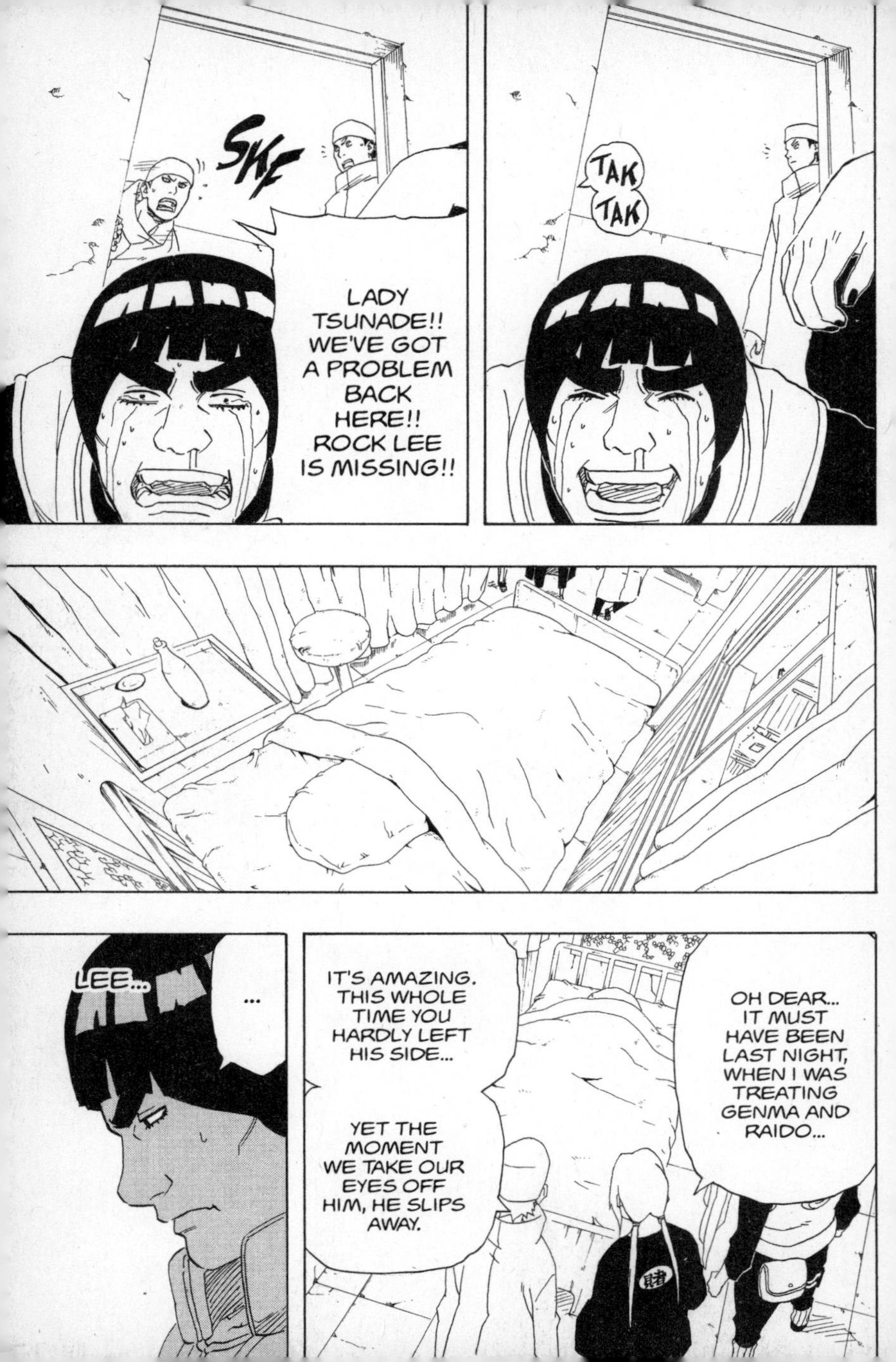
TAK TAK
SKF
LADY TSUNADE!! WE'VE GOT A PROBLEM BACK HERE!! ROCK LEE IS MISSING!!
OH DEAR... IT MUST HAVE BEEN LAST NIGHT, WHEN I WAS TREATING GENMA AND RAIDO...
IT'S AMAZING. THIS WHOLE TIME YOU HARDLY LEFT HIS SIDE...
YET THE MOMENT WE TAKE OUR EYES OFF HIM, HE SLIPS AWAY.
...
LEE...

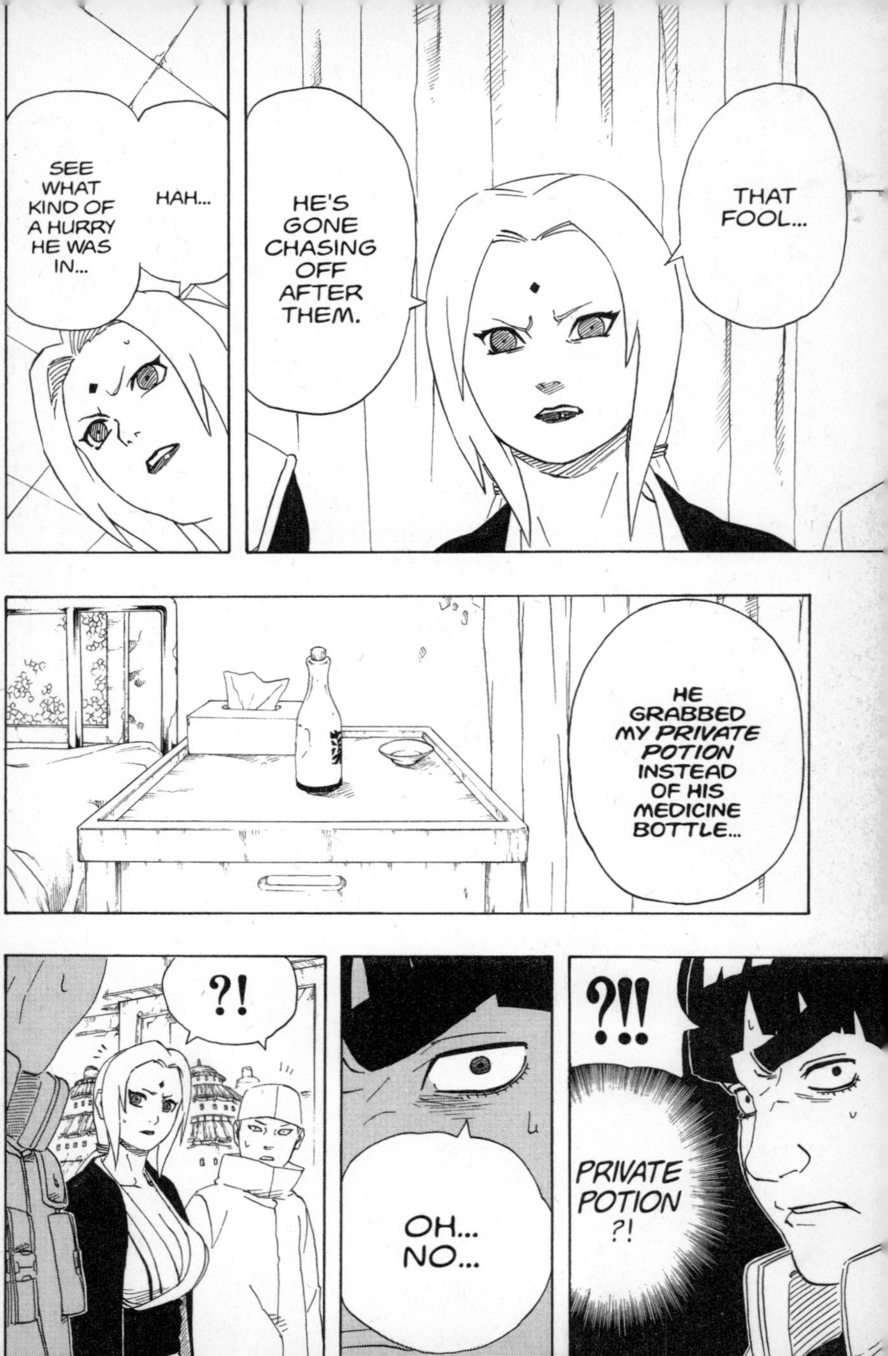
THAT FOOL...
HE'S GONE CHASING OFF AFTER THEM.
HAH...
SEE WHAT KIND OF A HURRY HE WAS IN...
HE GRABBED MY *PRIVATE POTION* INSTEAD OF HIS MEDICINE BOTTLE...
?!!
PRIVATE POTION ?!
OH... NO...
?!

...?!

NOW WHAT'S WRONG?

GUY?!

...

TWITCH

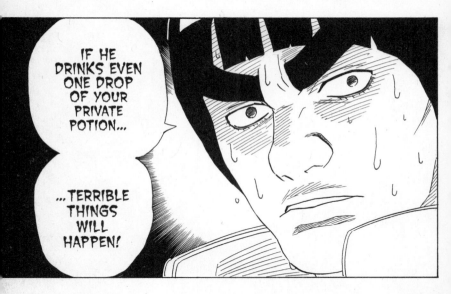

IF HE DRINKS EVEN ONE DROP OF YOUR PRIVATE POTION...

...TERRIBLE THINGS WILL HAPPEN!

TERRIBLE... THINGS?

...?!

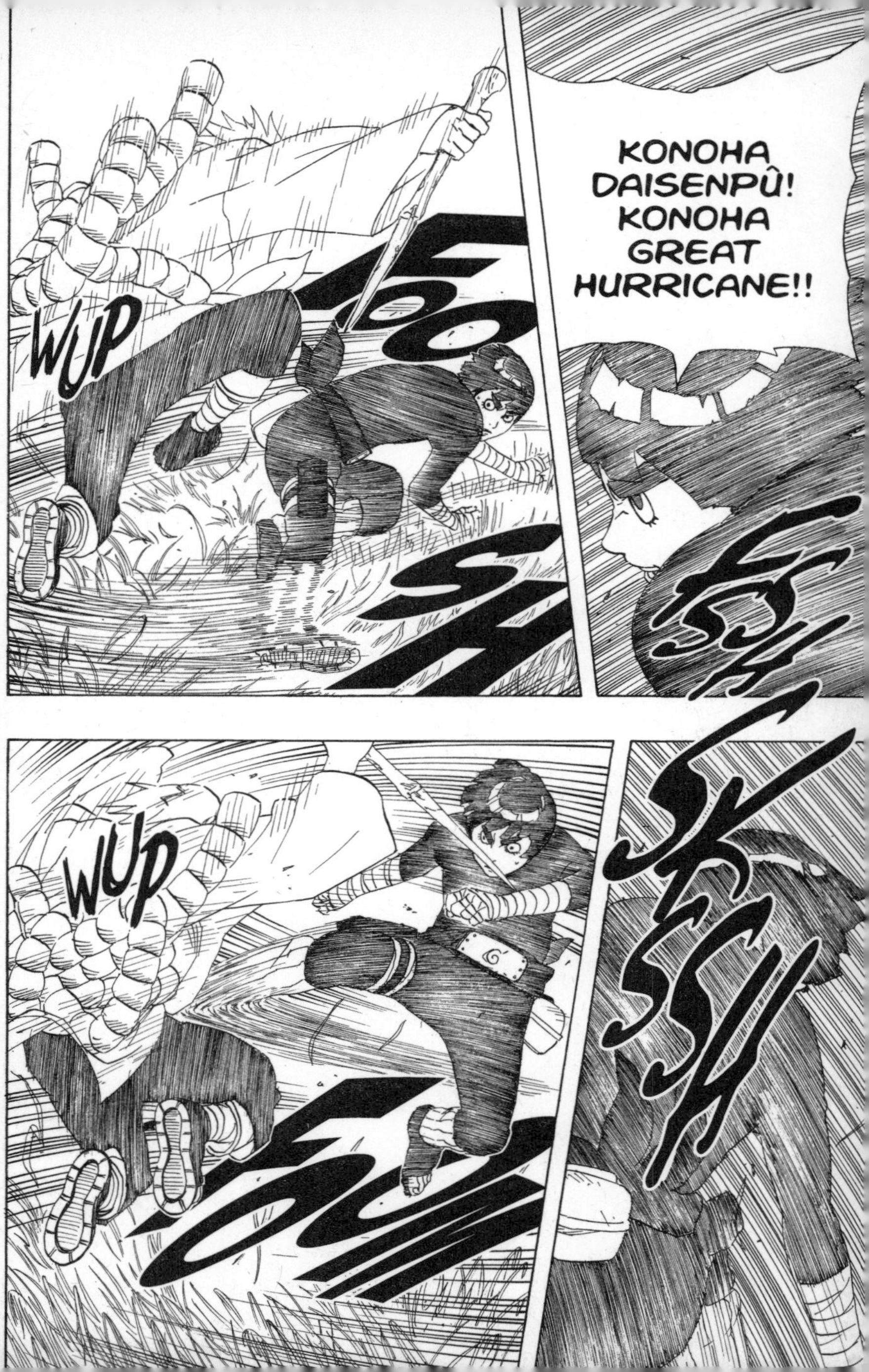
KONOHA DAISENPÛ! KONOHA GREAT HURRICANE!!
FSSH
FOOSH
WUP
WUP

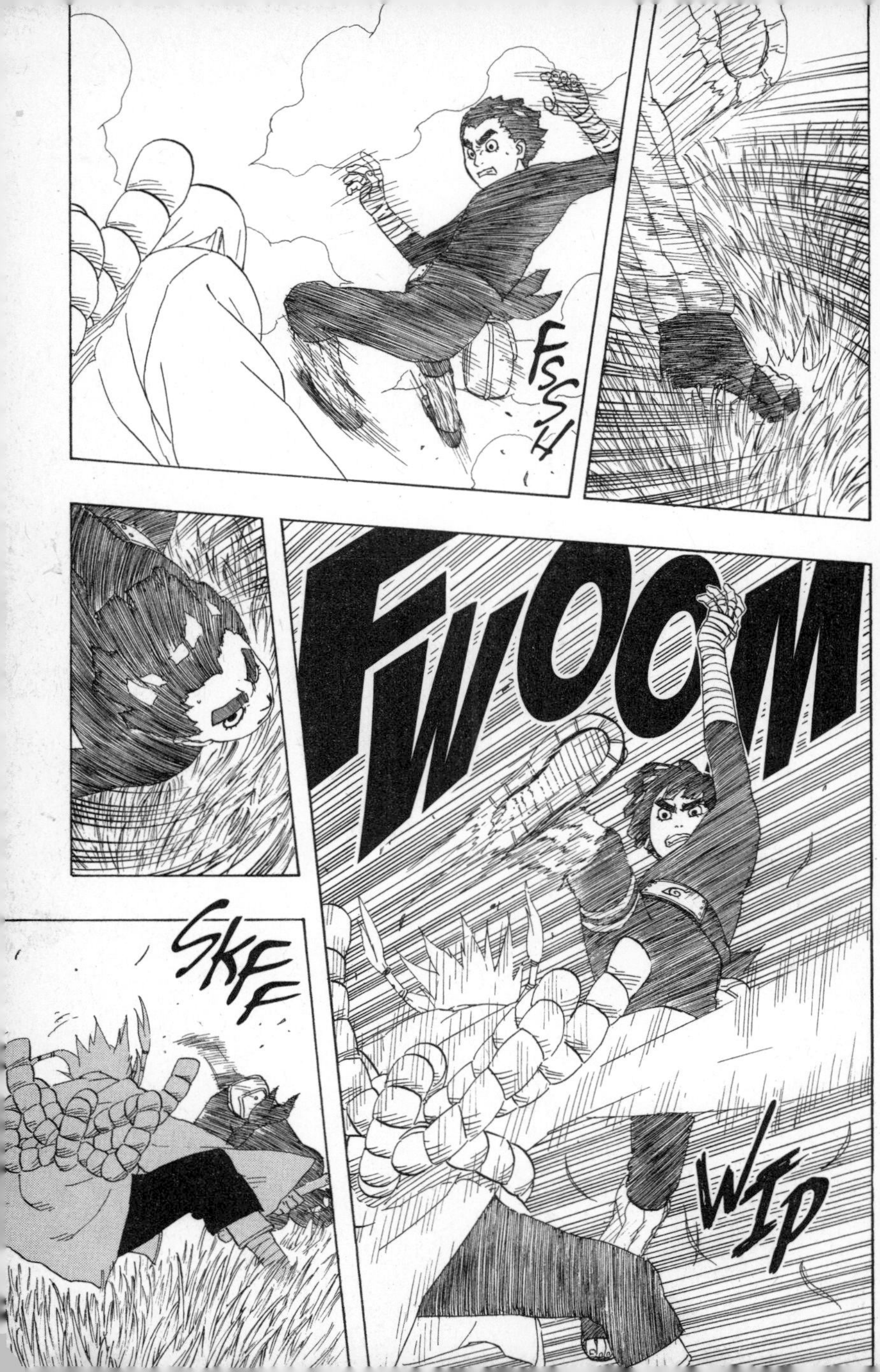
FSSH
FWOOM
WIP
SKFF

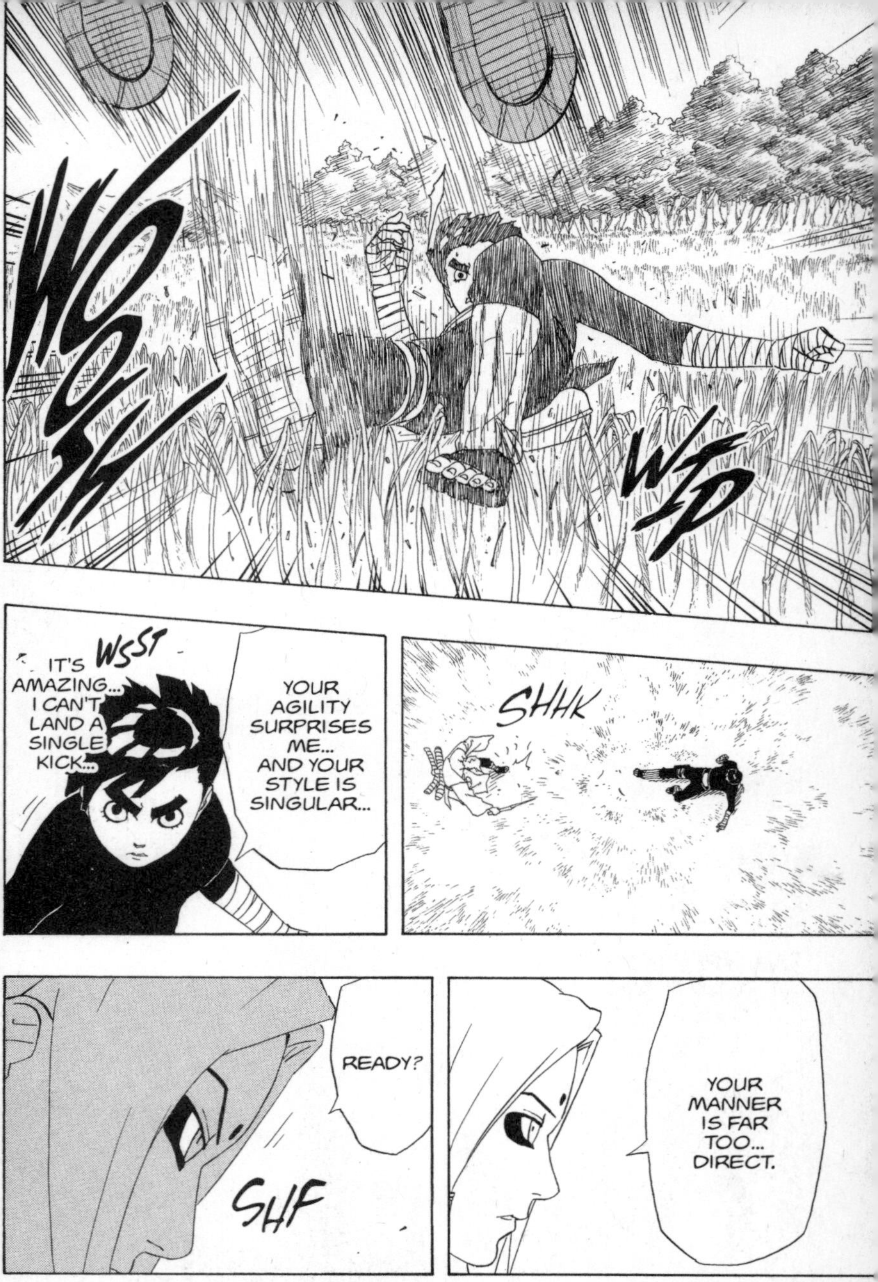
WIP
WOOSH
SHHK
YOUR AGILITY SURPRISES ME... AND YOUR STYLE IS SINGULAR...
WSST
IT'S AMAZING... I CAN'T LAND A SINGLE KICK...
YOUR MANNER IS FAR TOO... DIRECT.
READY?
SHF

READ THIS WAY

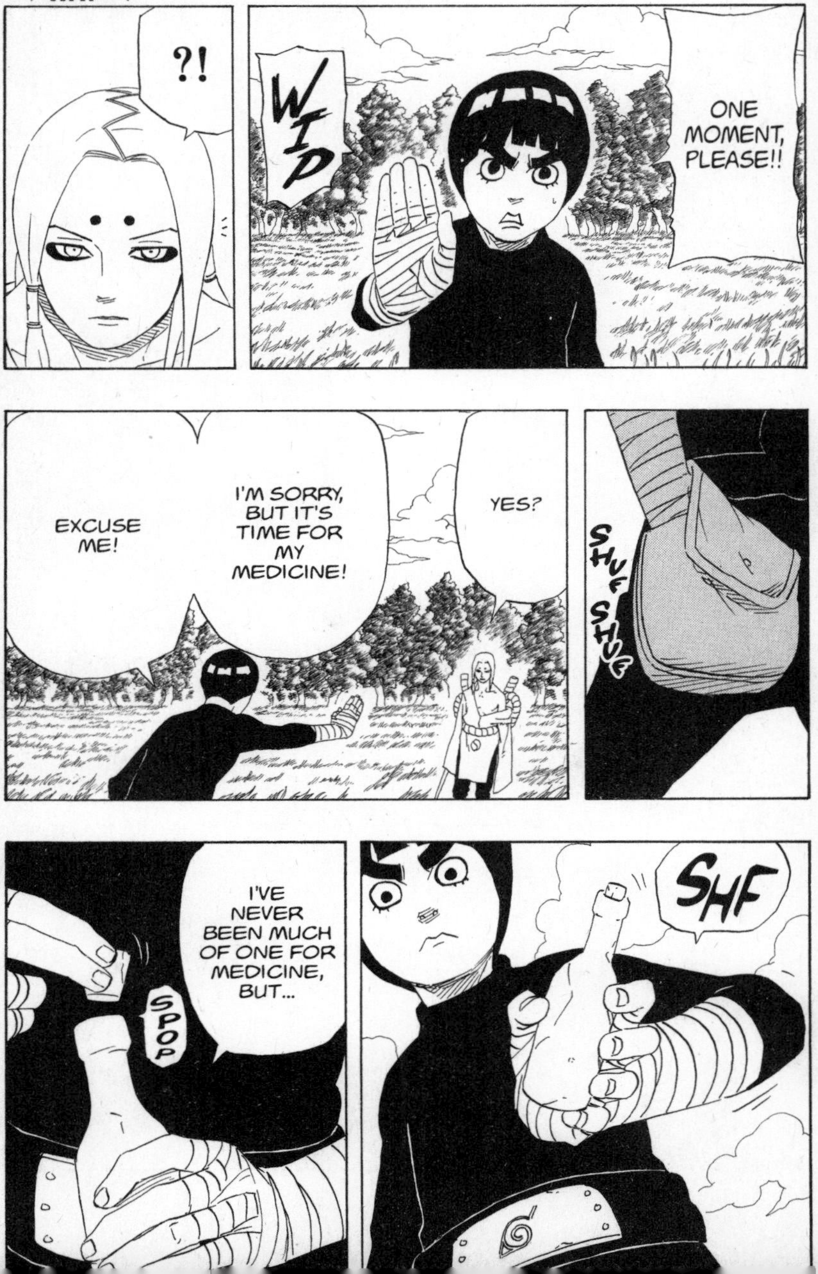
ONE MOMENT, PLEASE!!
WIP
?!
SHUF SHUF
YES?
EXCUSE ME!
I'M SORRY, BUT IT'S TIME FOR MY MEDICINE!
SHF
I'VE NEVER BEEN MUCH OF ONE FOR MEDICINE, BUT...
SPOP

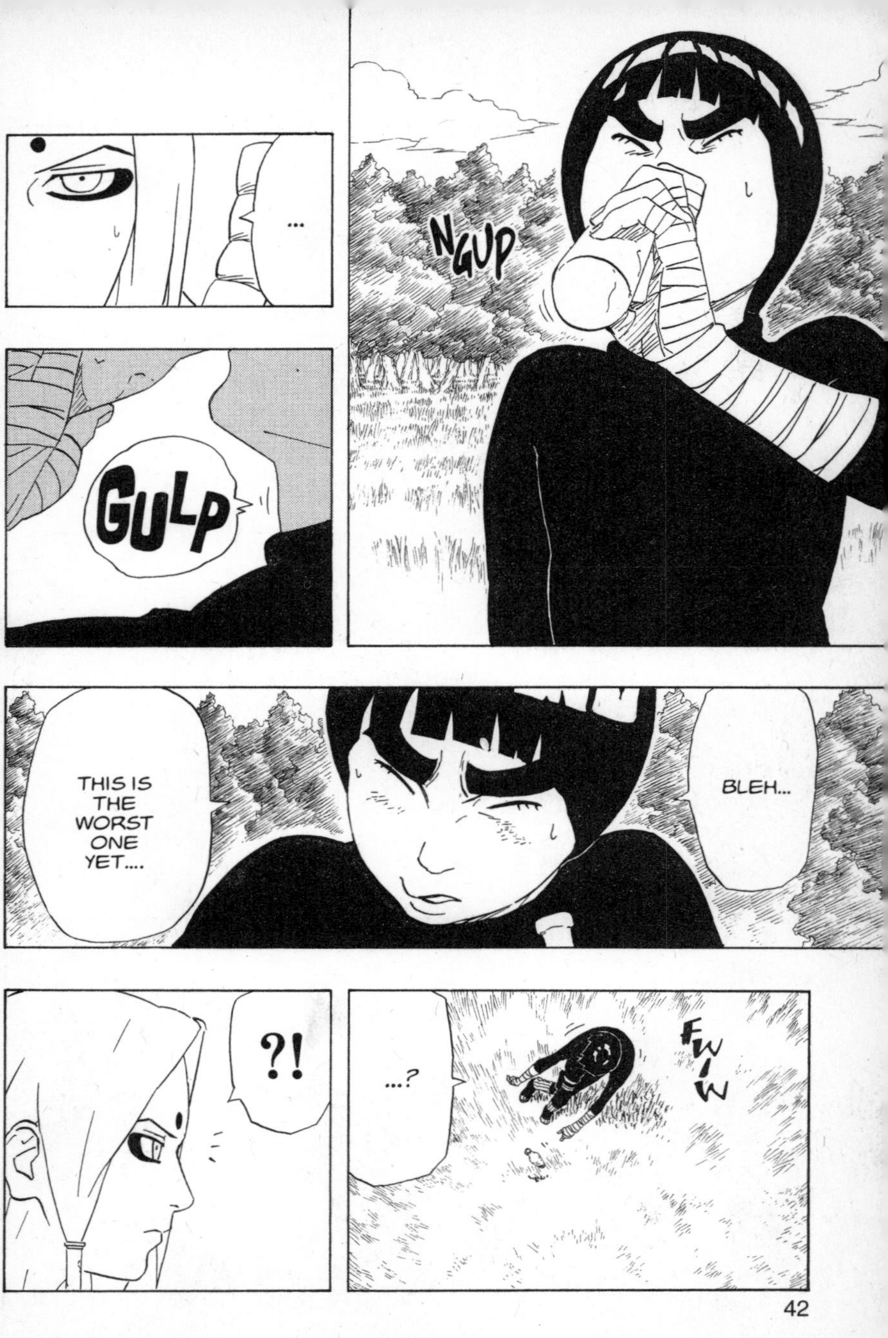
NGUP
...
GULP
BLEH...
THIS IS THE WORST ONE YET....
...?
FWIW
?!

READ THIS WAY

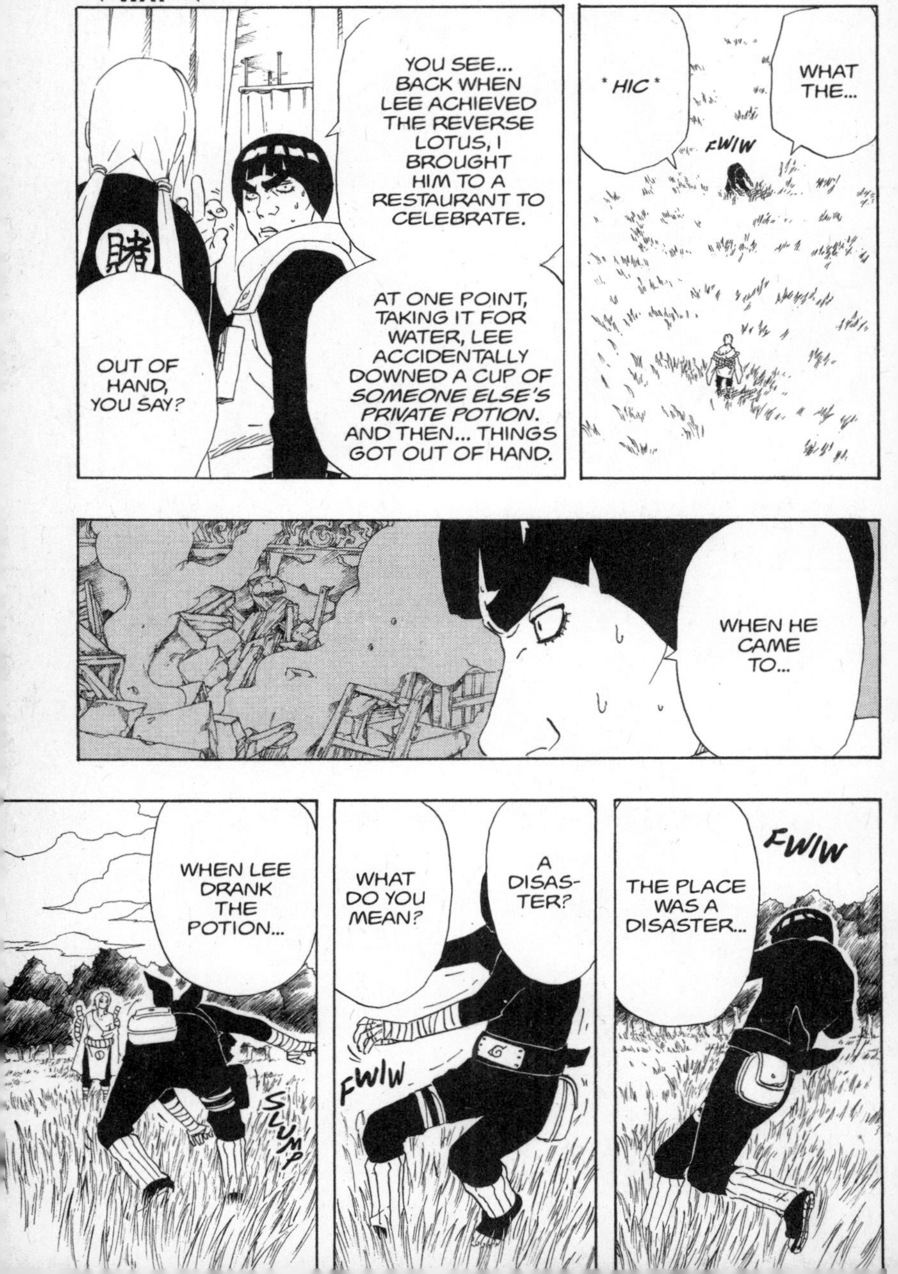
WHAT THE...
HIC
FWIW
YOU SEE... BACK WHEN LEE ACHIEVED THE REVERSE LOTUS, I BROUGHT HIM TO A RESTAURANT TO CELEBRATE.
AT ONE POINT, TAKING IT FOR WATER, LEE ACCIDENTALLY DOWNED A CUP OF *SOMEONE ELSE'S PRIVATE POTION.* AND THEN... THINGS GOT OUT OF HAND.
OUT OF HAND, YOU SAY?
WHEN HE CAME TO...
FWIW
THE PLACE WAS A DISASTER...
A DISASTER?
WHAT DO YOU MEAN?
FWIW
WHEN LEE DRANK THE POTION...
SLUMP

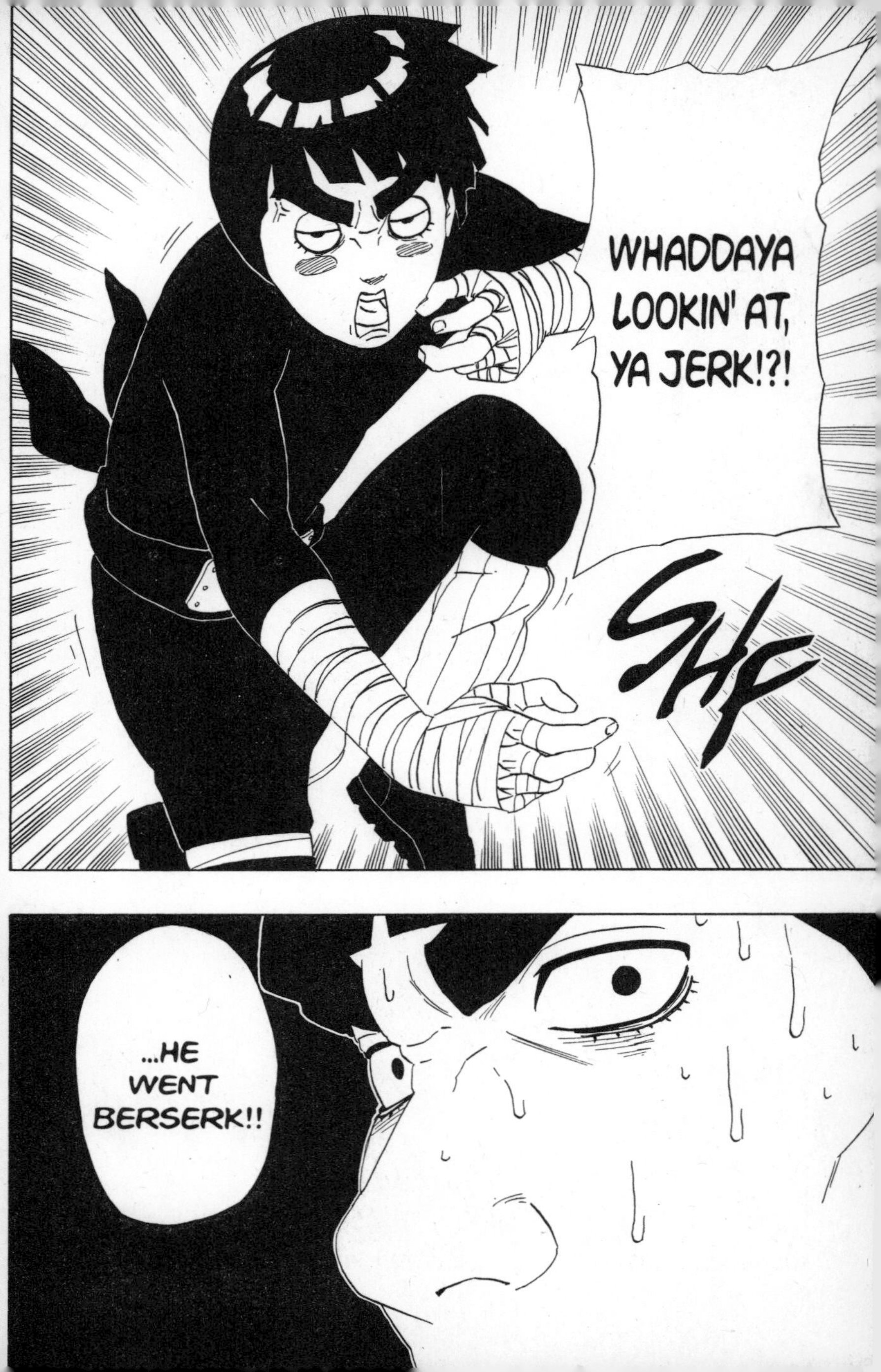
WHADDAYA LOOKIN' AT, YA JERK!?!
SHF
...HE WENT BERSERK!!

READ THIS WAY

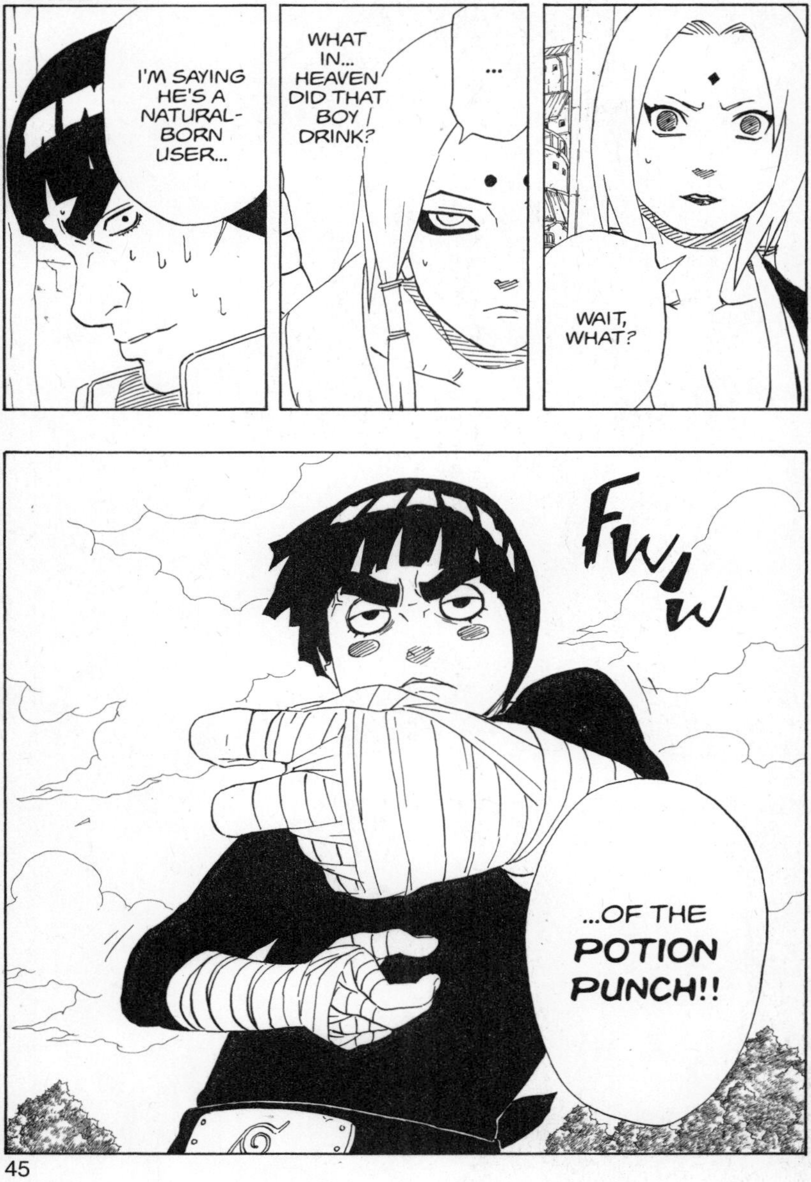
WAIT, WHAT?
...
WHAT IN... HEAVEN DID THAT BOY DRINK?
I'M SAYING HE'S A NATURAL-BORN USER...
FWIW
...OF THE POTION PUNCH!!

NARUTO™

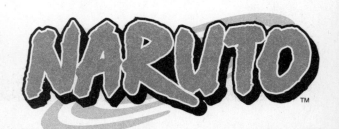

Number 211: Unorthodox...!!

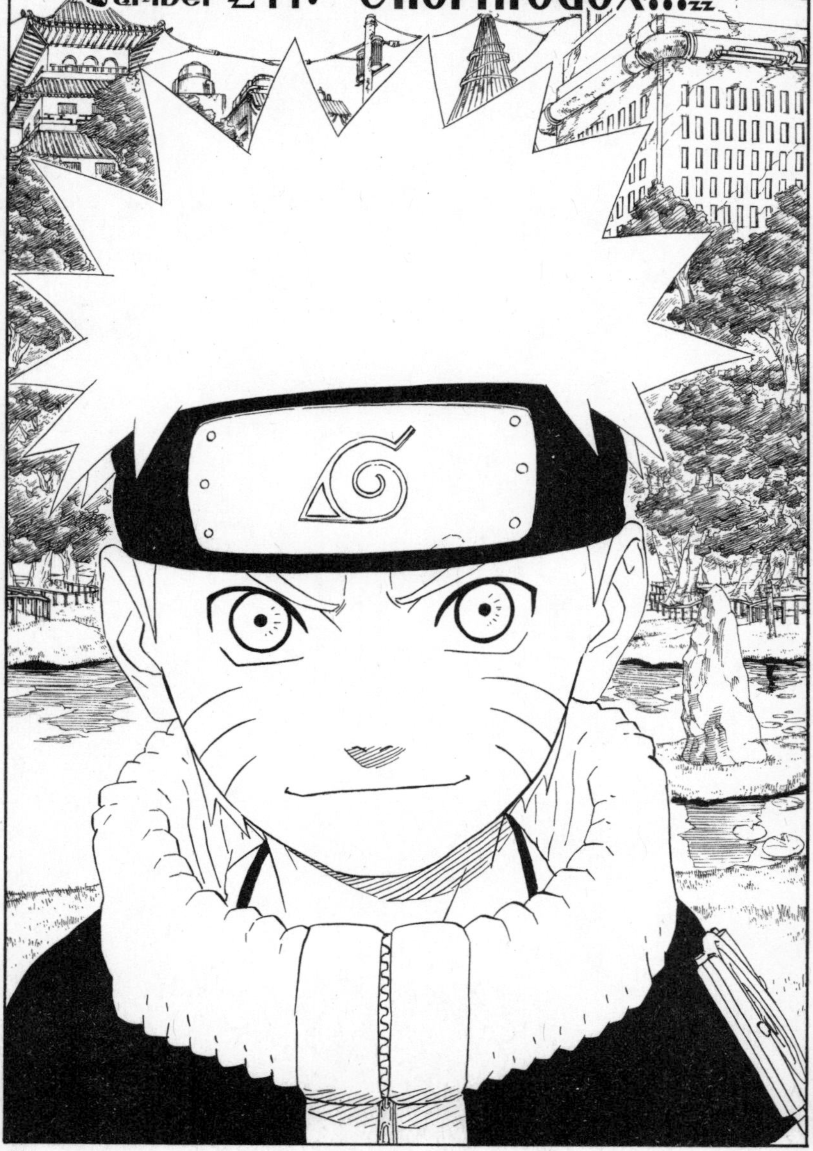

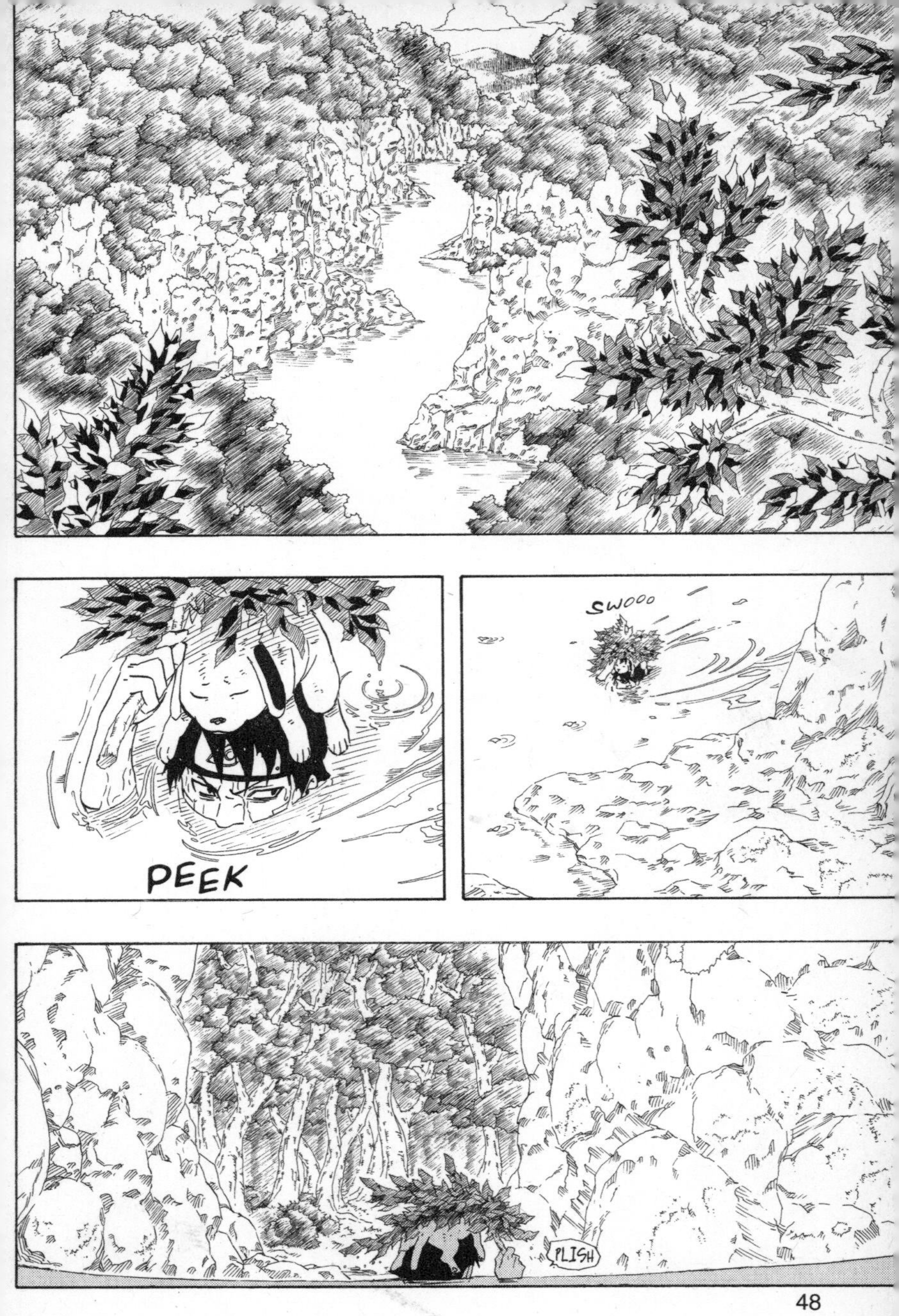
SWOOO
PEEK
PLISH

READ THIS WAY

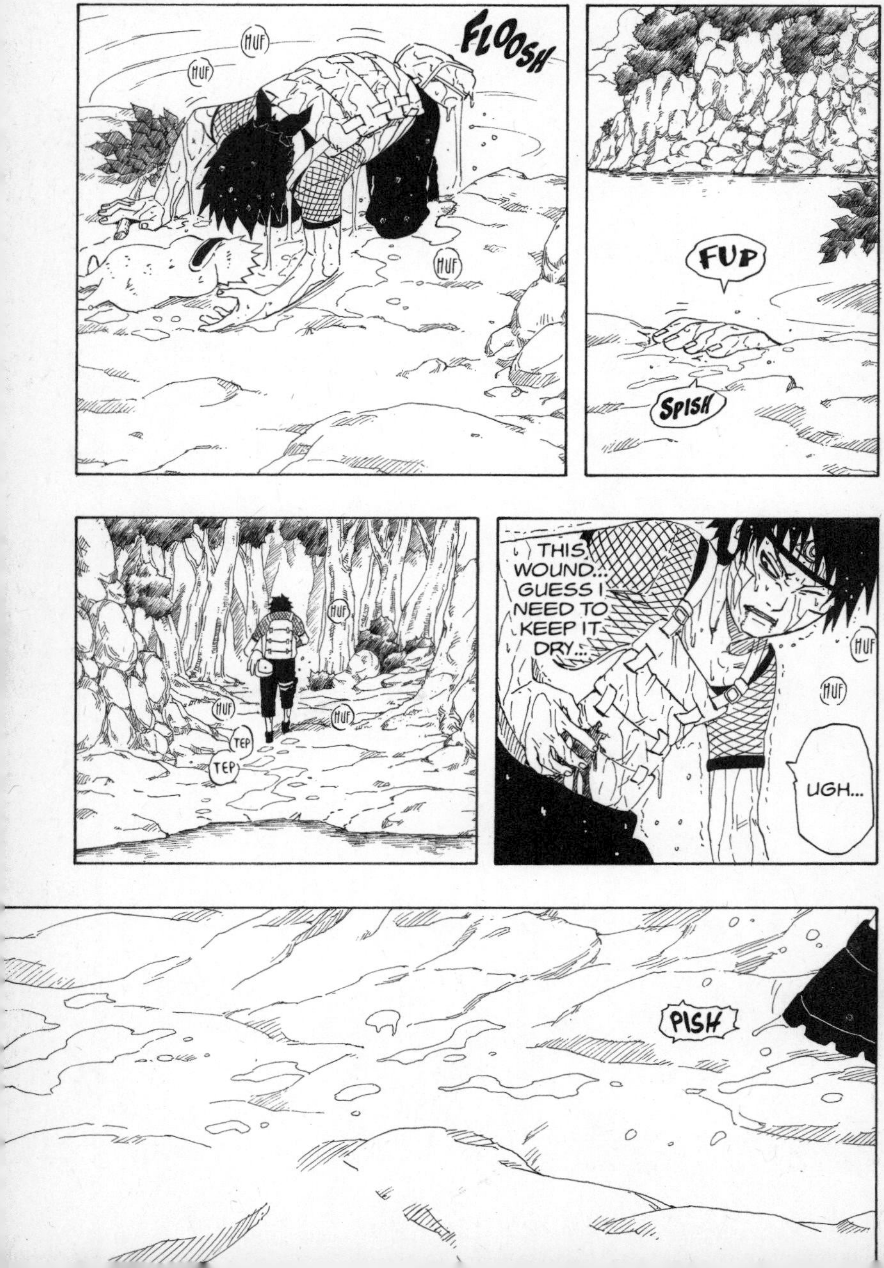
FUP
SPISH
FLOOSH
HUF
HUF
HUF
THIS WOUND... GUESS I NEED TO KEEP IT DRY...
HUF
HUF
UGH...
HUF
HUF
HUF
TEP
TEP
PISH

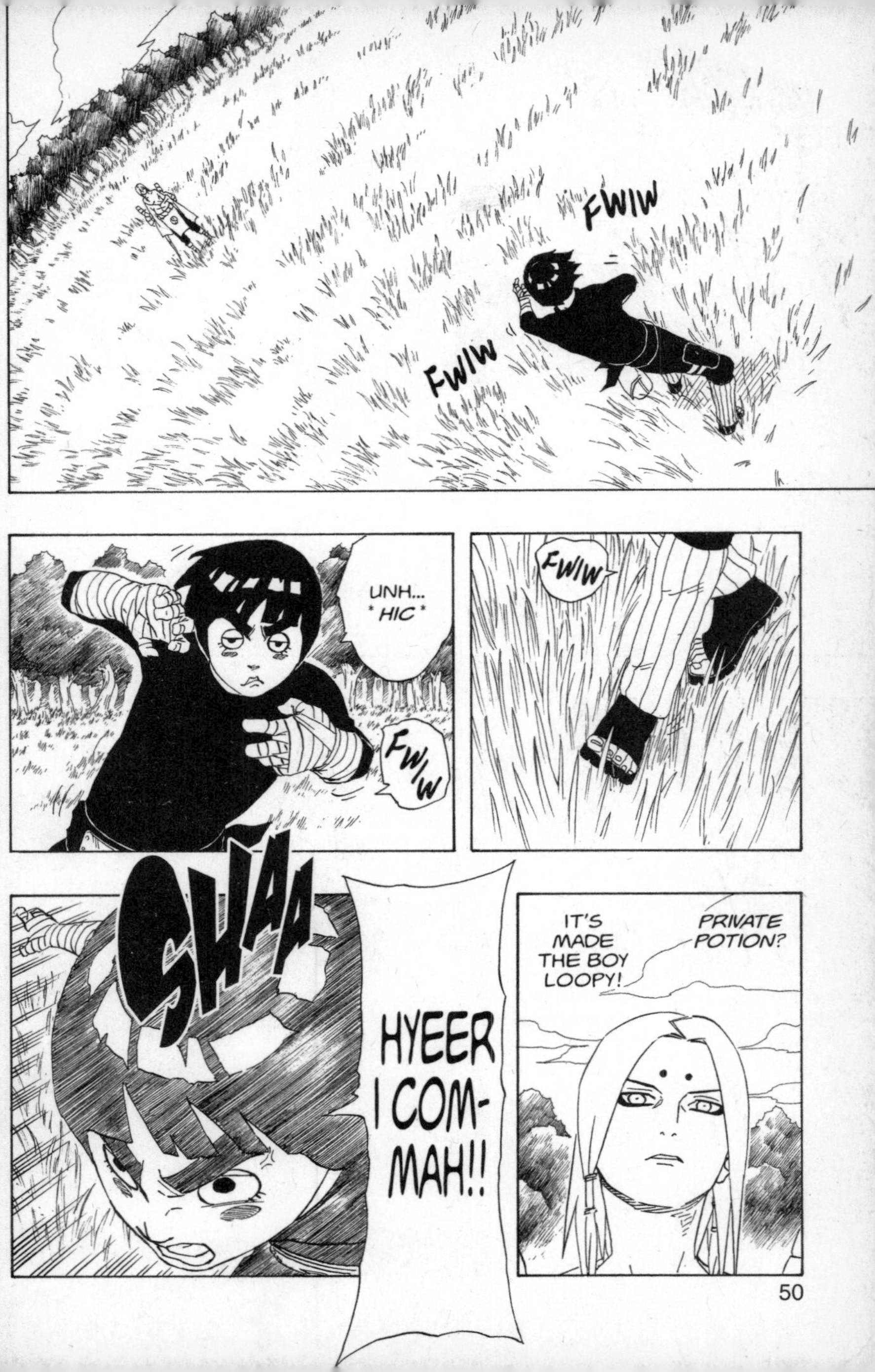

FWIW
FWIW
FWIW
UNH... *HIC*
FWIW
PRIVATE POTION?
IT'S MADE THE BOY LOOPY!
SHAA
HYEER I COMMAH!!

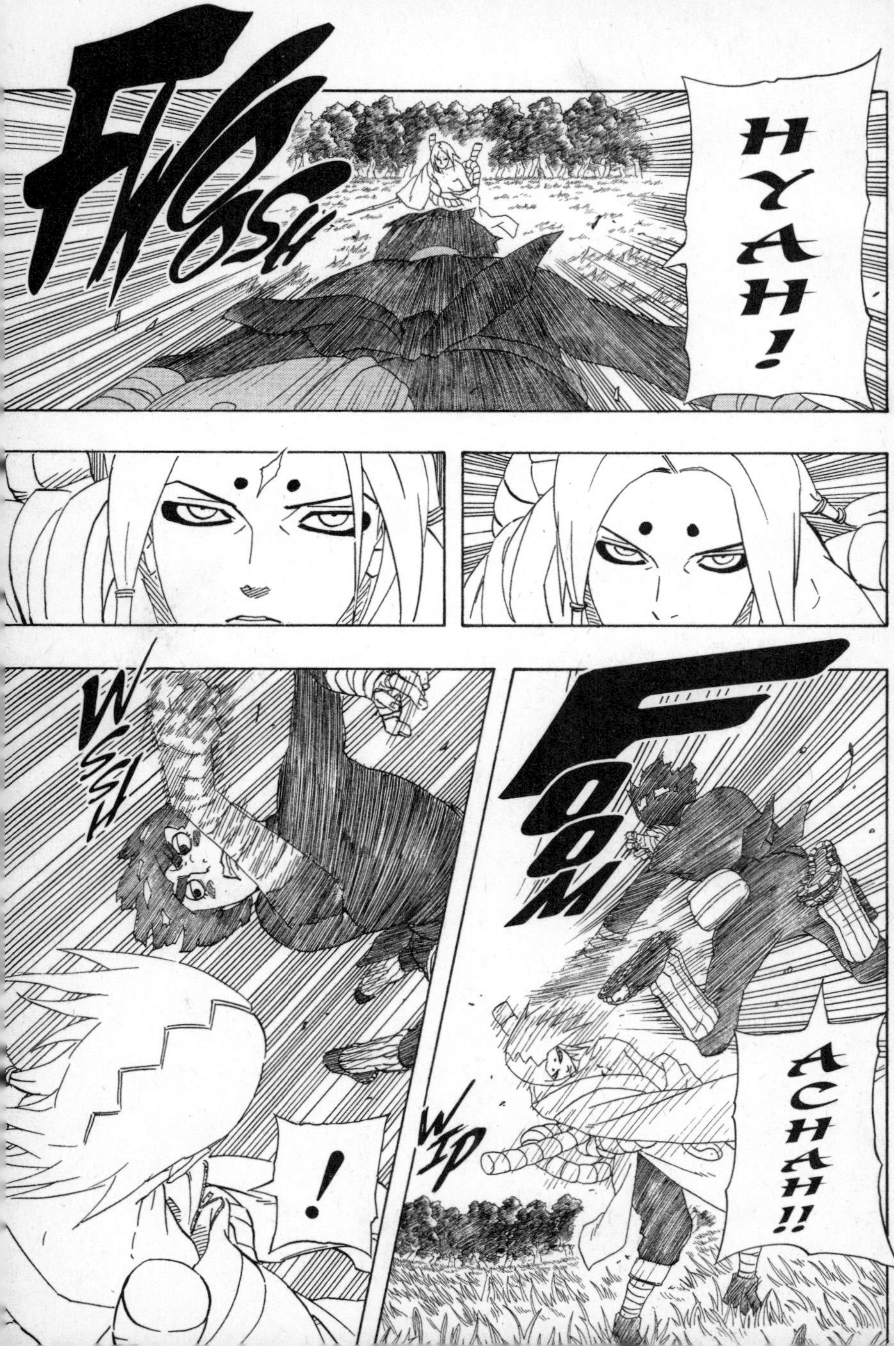

HYAH!
FWOOSH
FOOM
ACHAH!!
WSSH
WIP
!

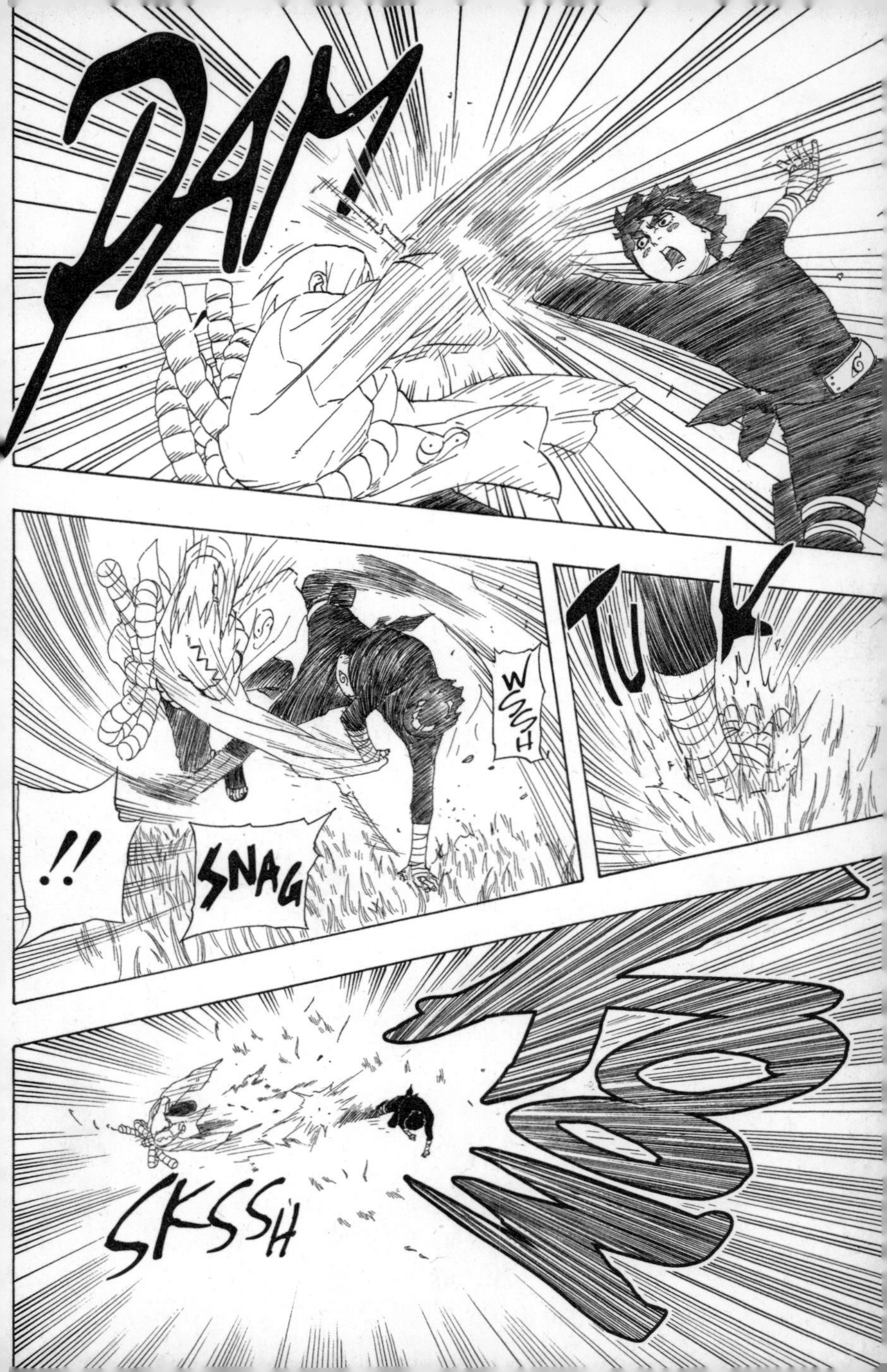
DAM
TUK
WSSH
SNAG
!!
SKSSH

READ THIS WAY

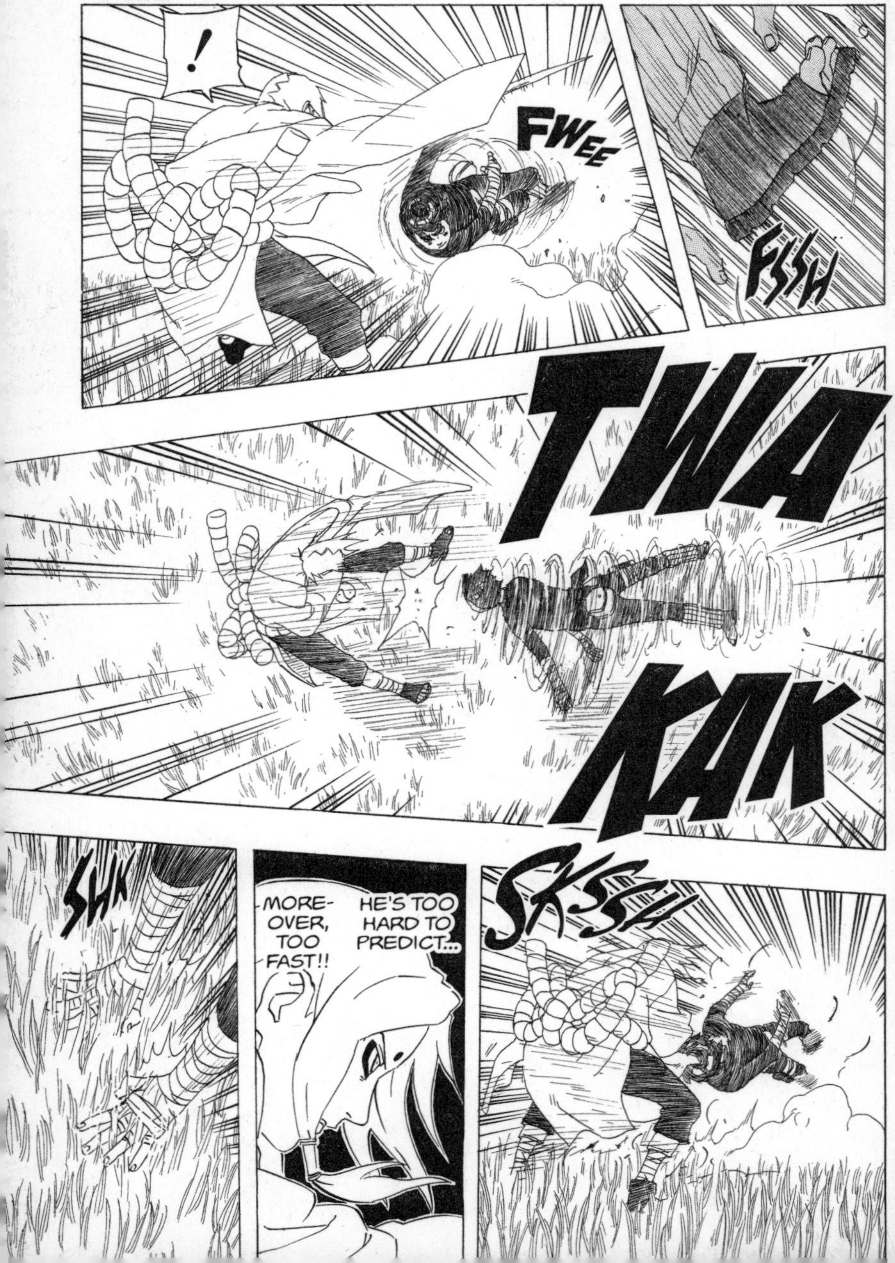
FSSH
FWEE
!
TWA KAK
SKSSH
HE'S TOO HARD TO PREDICT...
MORE-OVER, TOO FAST!!
SHK

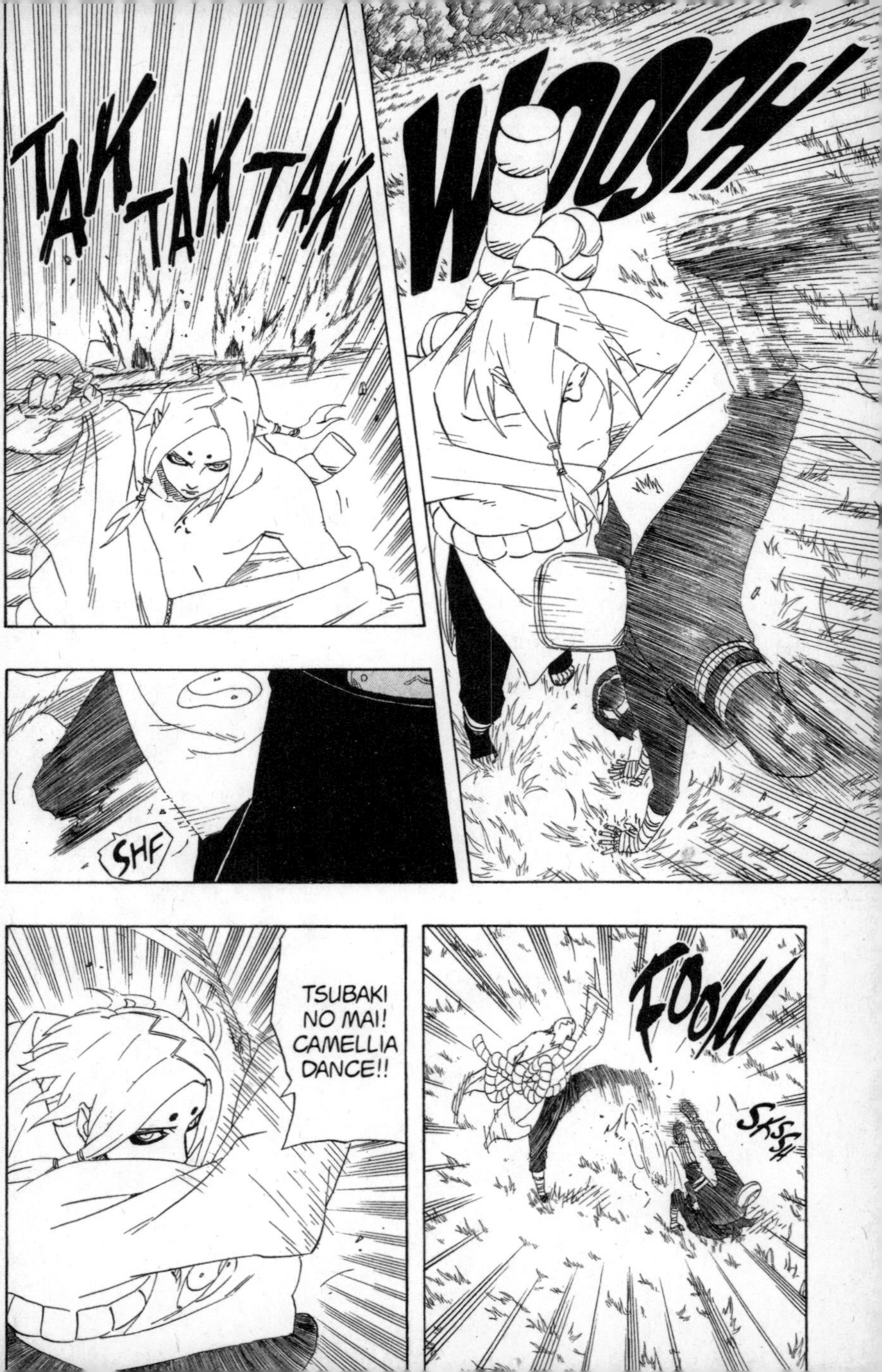
WHOOSH
TAK TAK TAK
SHF
FOOM
SKSSH
TSUBAKI NO MAI! CAMELLIA DANCE!!

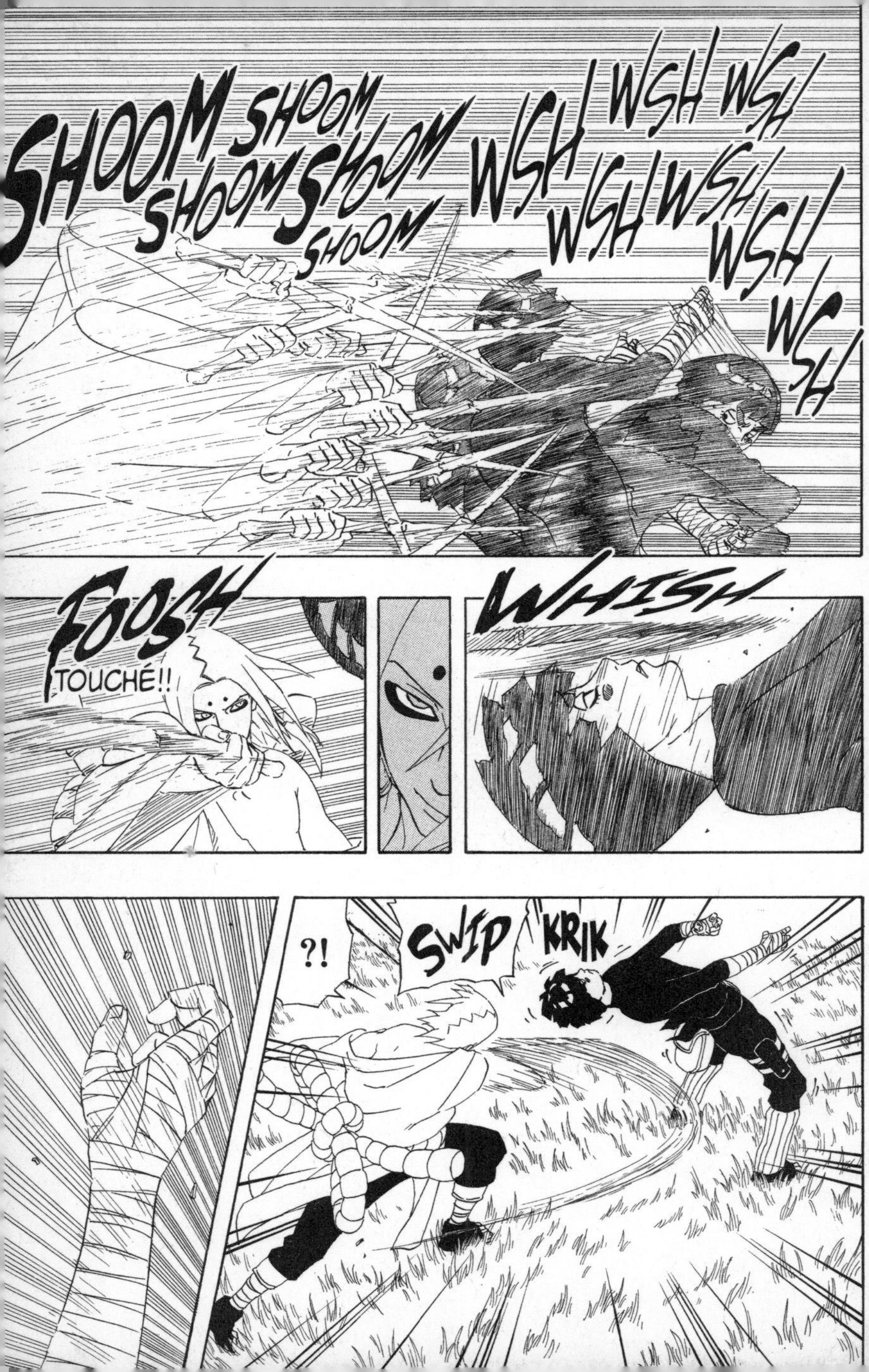
WSH WSH WSH
WSH WSH WSH
WSH
WSH
WSH
SHOOM SHOOM
SHOOM SHOOM
SHOOM
WHISH
FOOSH
TOUCHÉ!!
KRIK
SWIP
?!

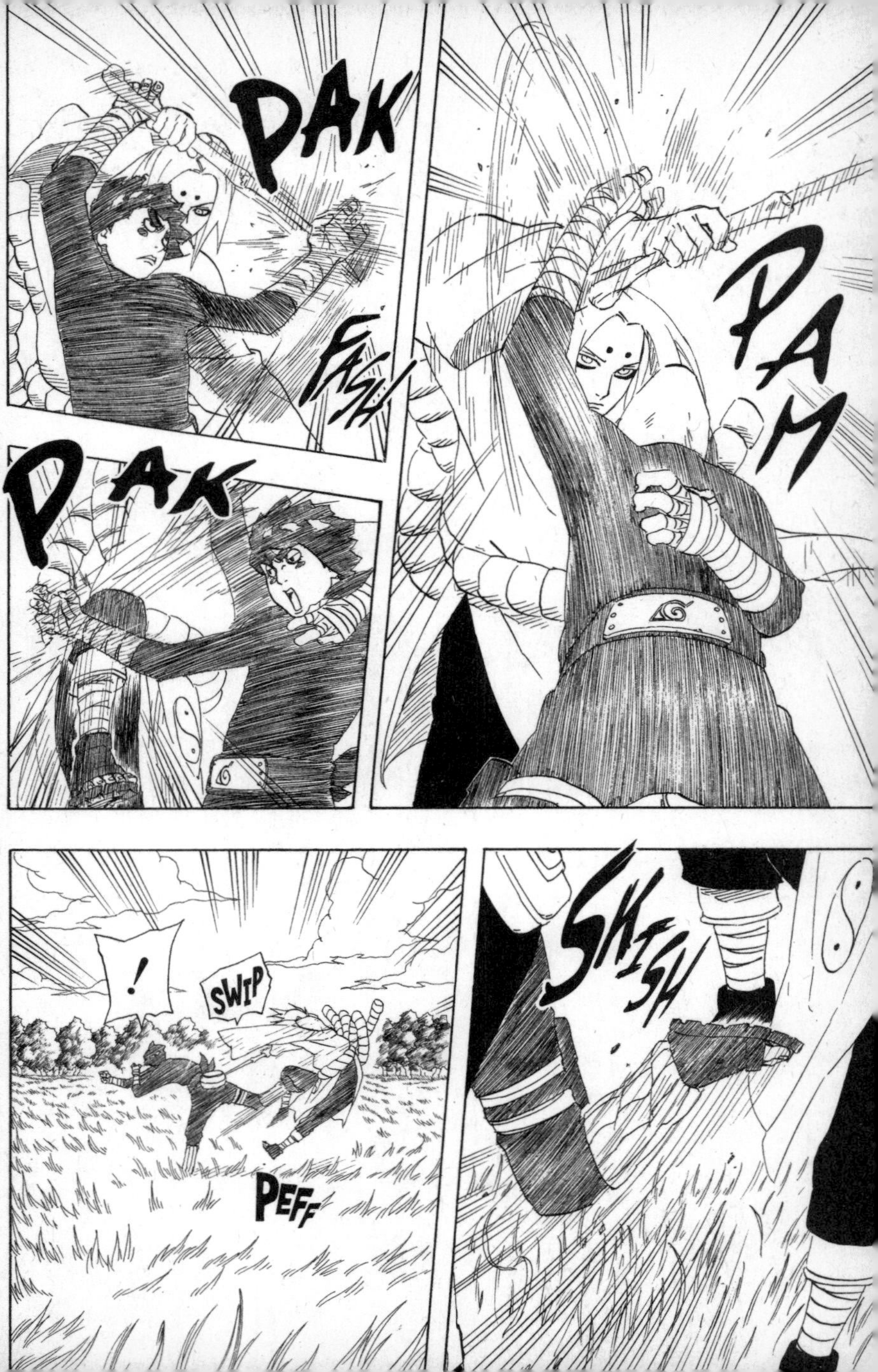
PAM
DAK
FASH
DAK
SKISH
!
SWIP
PEFF

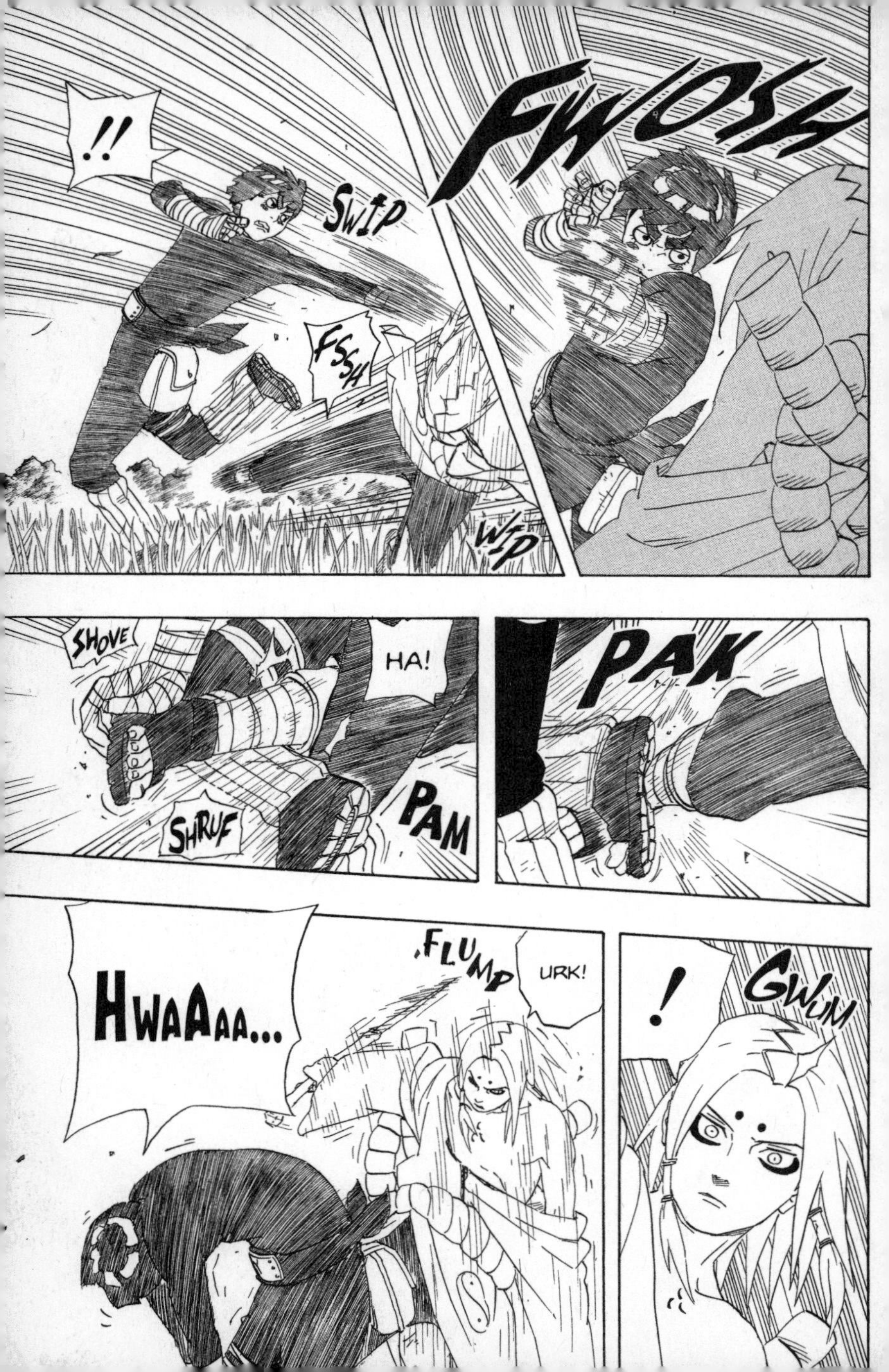
FWOSH
!!
SWIP
FSSH
WIP
PAK
HA!
SHOVE
PAM
SHRUF
!
GWUM
URK!
FLUMP
HWAAAA...

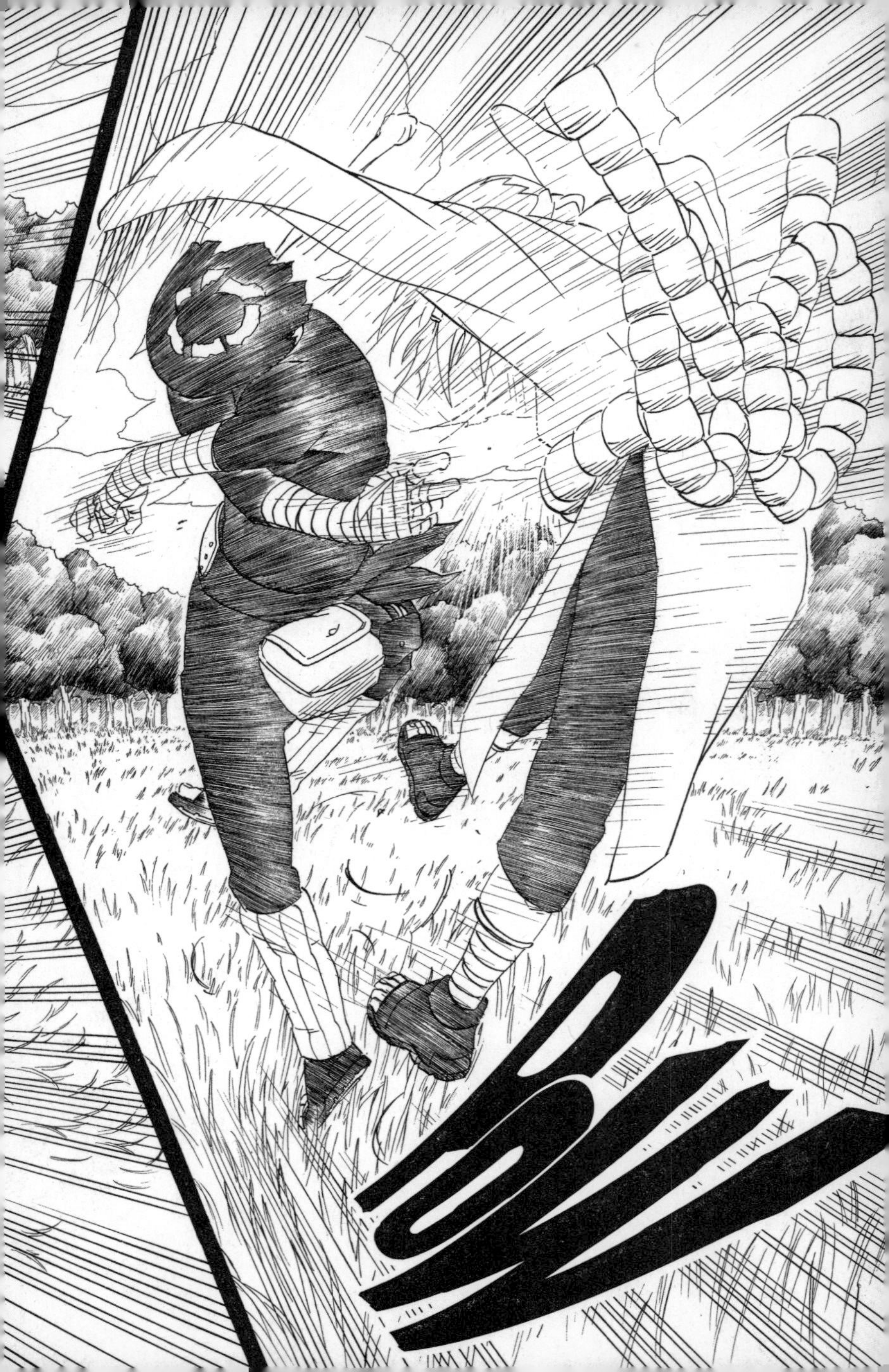

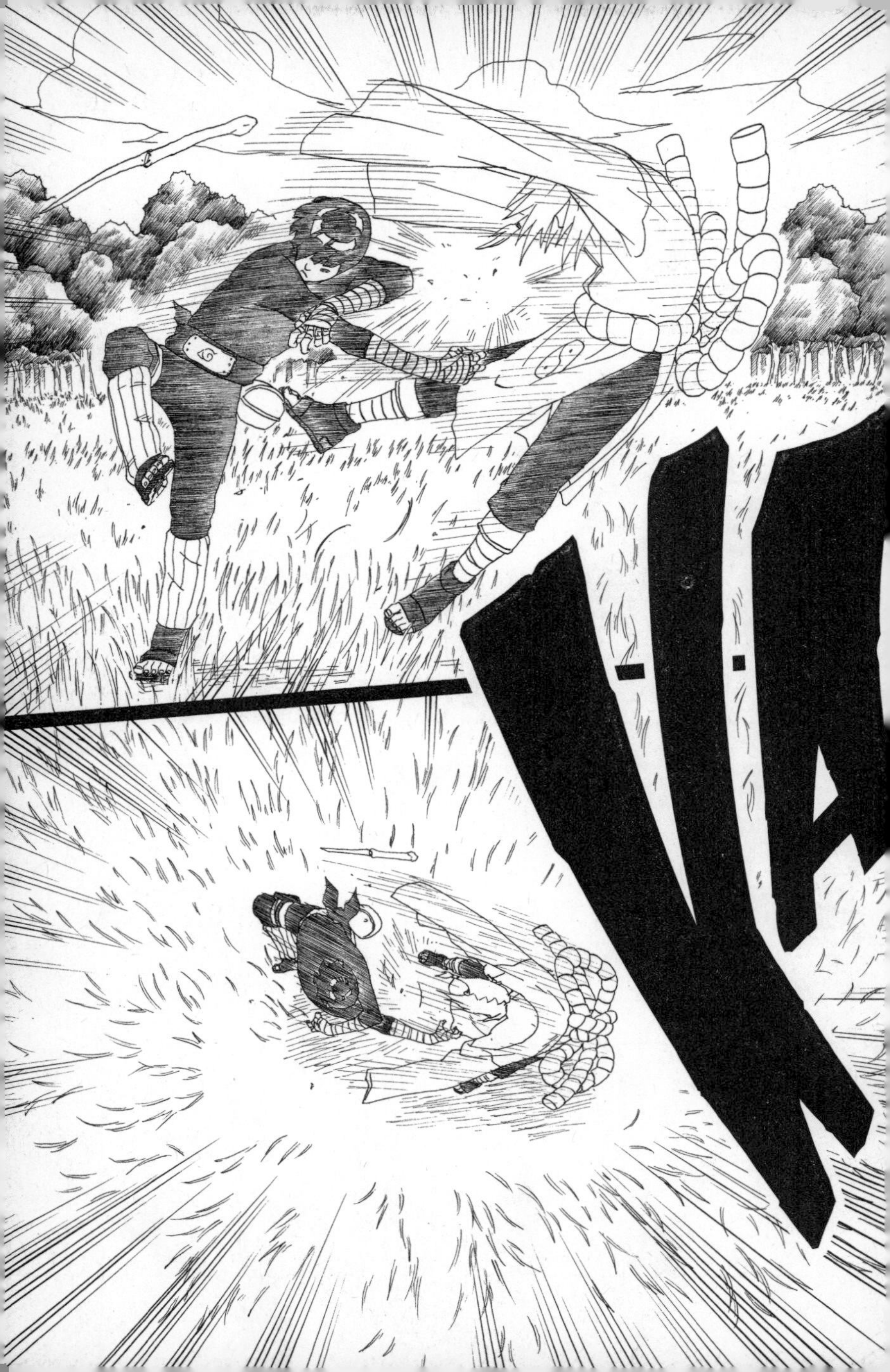

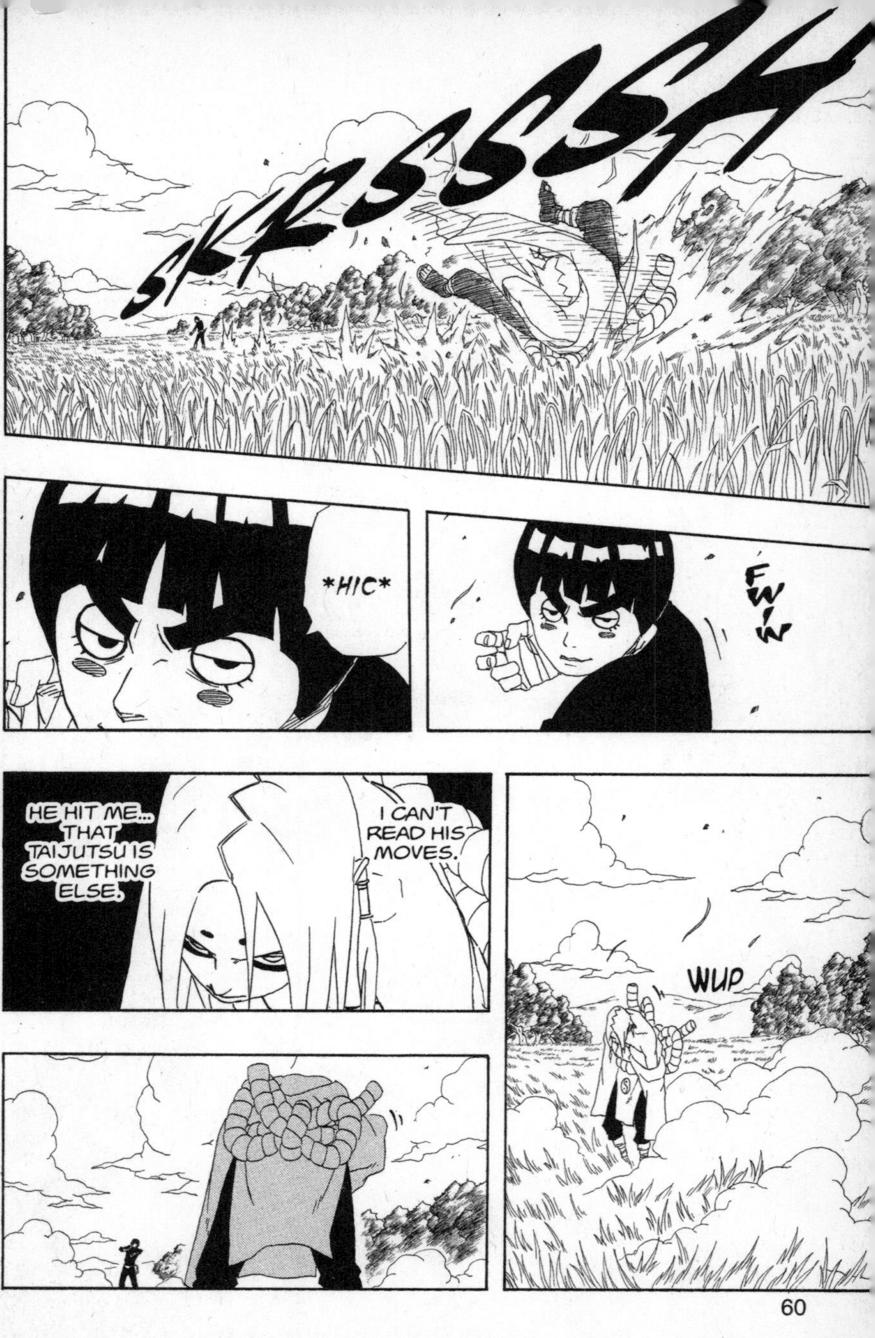
SKRSSSSH
FWIW
HIC
WUP
I CAN'T READ HIS MOVES.
HE HIT ME... THAT TAIJUTSU IS SOMETHING ELSE.

READ THIS WAY

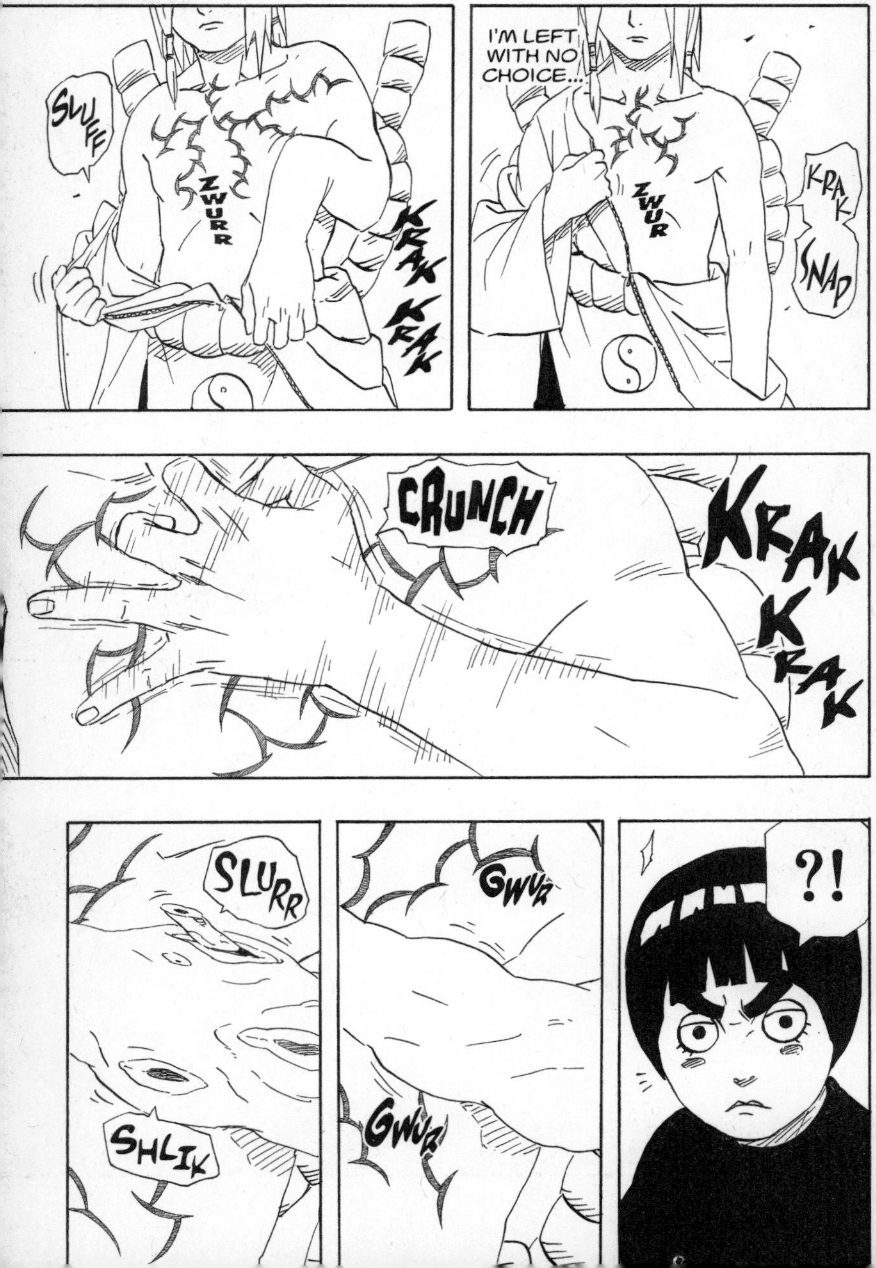
I'M LEFT WITH NO CHOICE...
ZWUR
KRAK
SNAP
SLUFF
ZWURR
KRAK KRAK
KRAK KRAK KRAK
CRUNCH
?!
GWUR
GWUR
SLURR
SHLIK

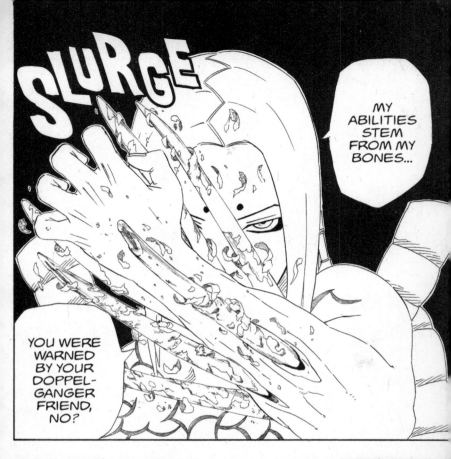

SLURGE

MY ABILITIES STEM FROM MY BONES...

YOU WERE WARNED BY YOUR DOPPEL-GANGER FRIEND, NO?

SHAAA

...!

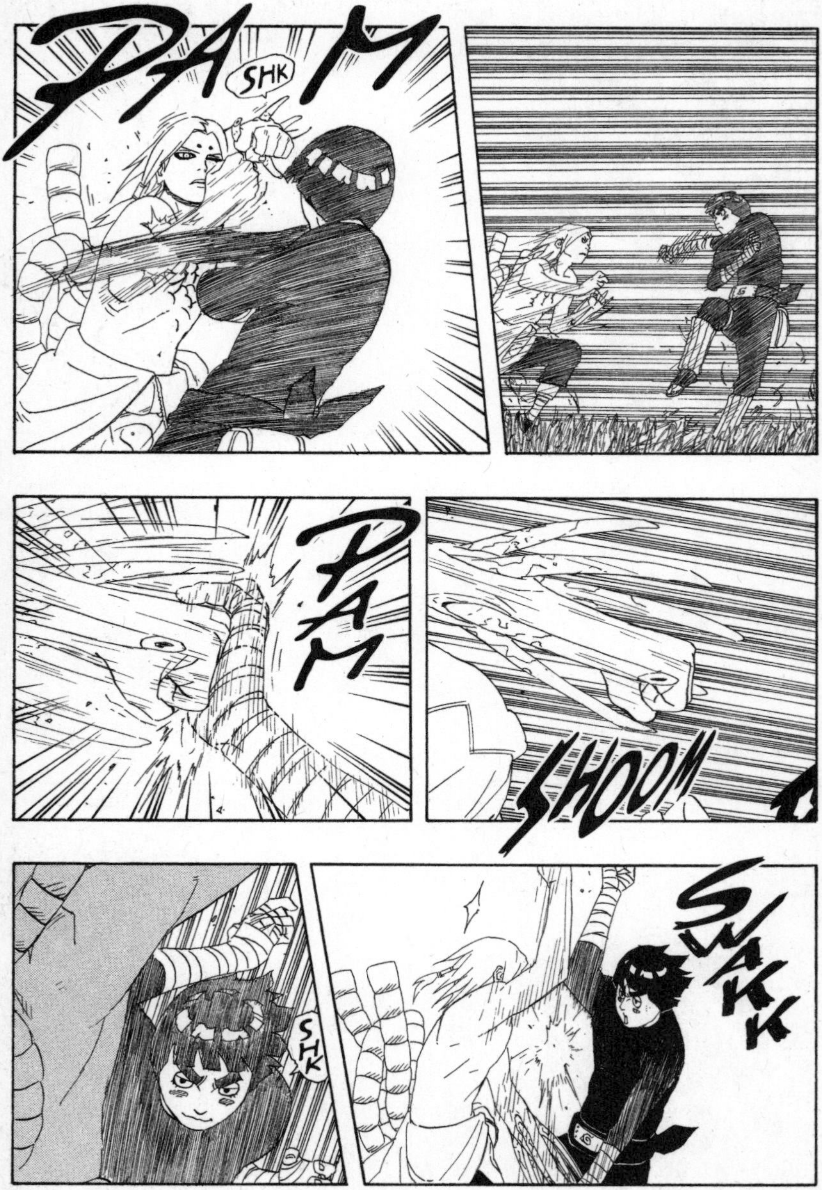
DAM
SHK
SHOOM
DAM
SWAKK
SHK

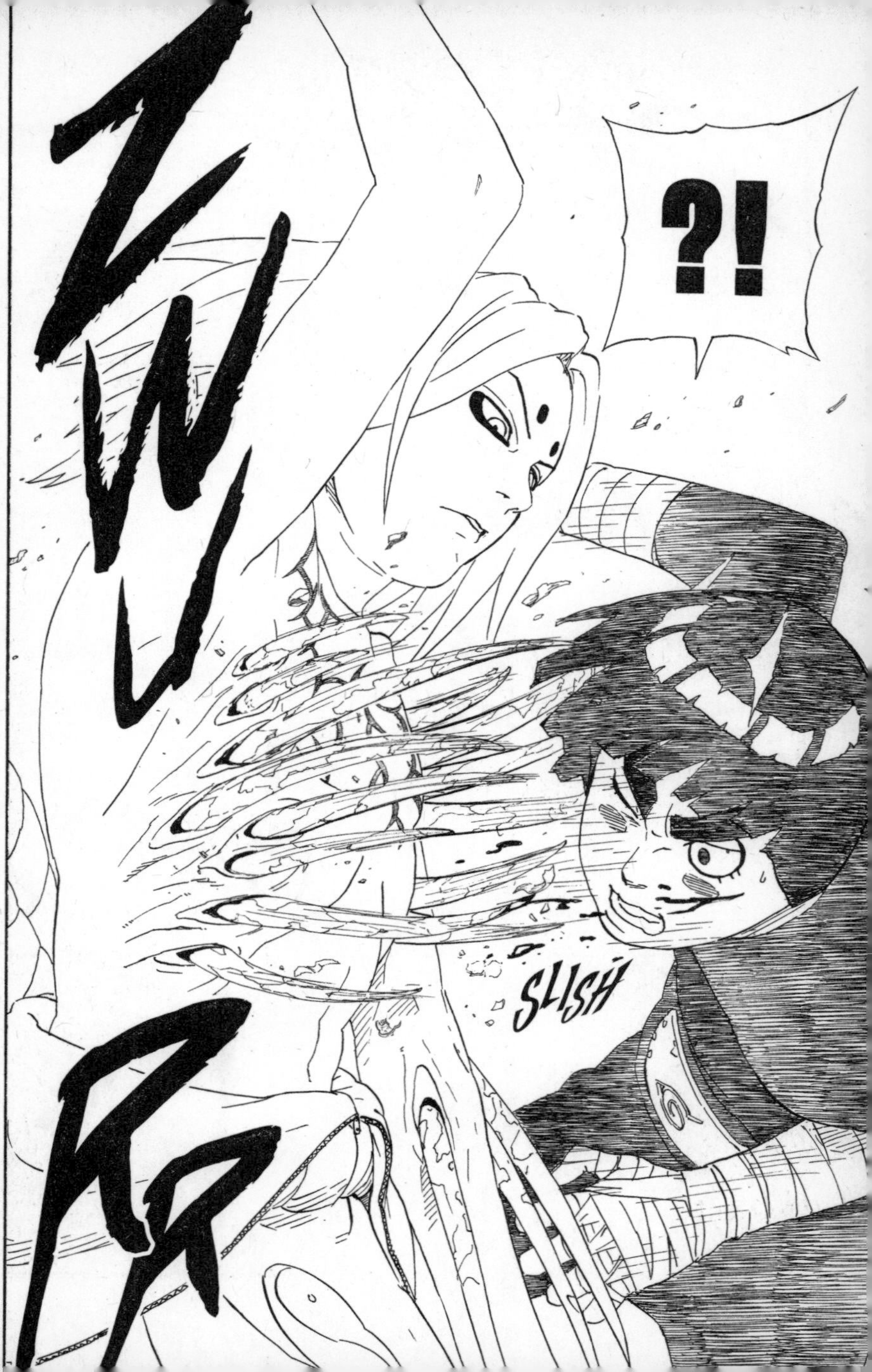
?!
SLISH

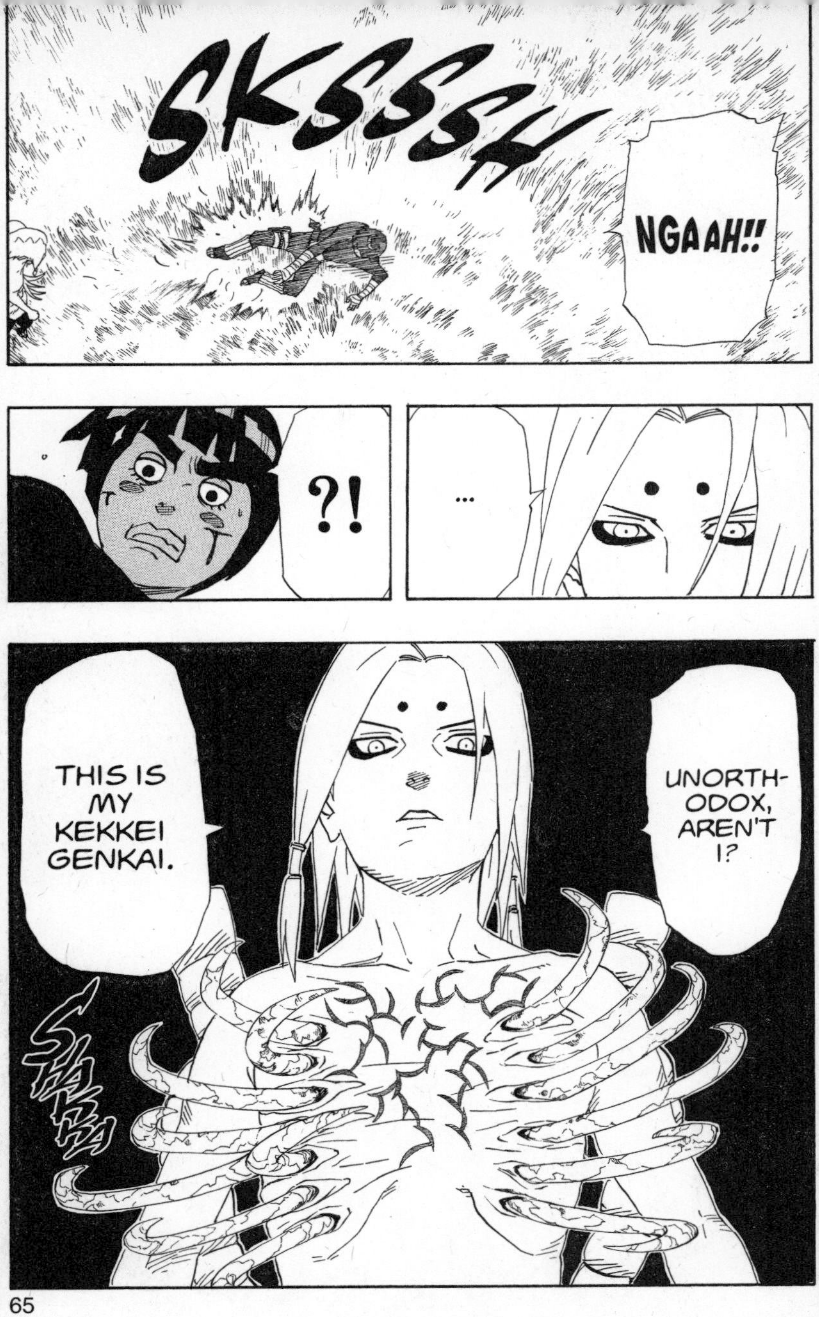
SKSSSH
NGAAH!!
...
?!
UNORTH-ODOX, AREN'T I?
THIS IS MY KEKKEI GENKAI.
SHAKA

NARUTO™

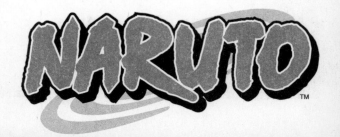

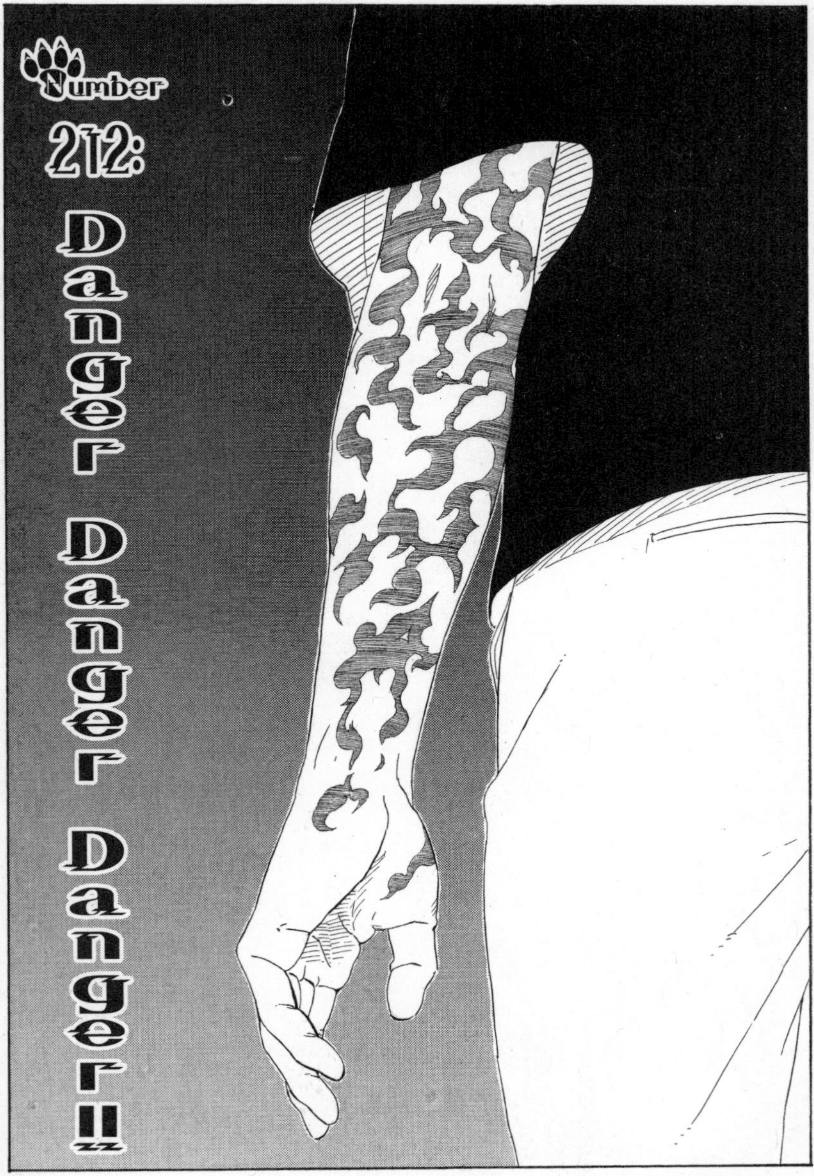
Number
212:
Danger Danger Danger!!

...!

LOOKS LIKE YOU'VE PULLED YOURSELF TOGETHER.

SHF

KEKKEI GENKAI?!

...?

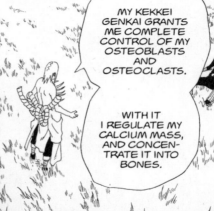

MY KEKKEI GENKAI GRANTS ME COMPLETE CONTROL OF MY OSTEOBLASTS AND OSTEOCLASTS.

WITH IT I REGULATE MY CALCIUM MASS, AND CONCENTRATE IT INTO BONES.

READ THIS WAY

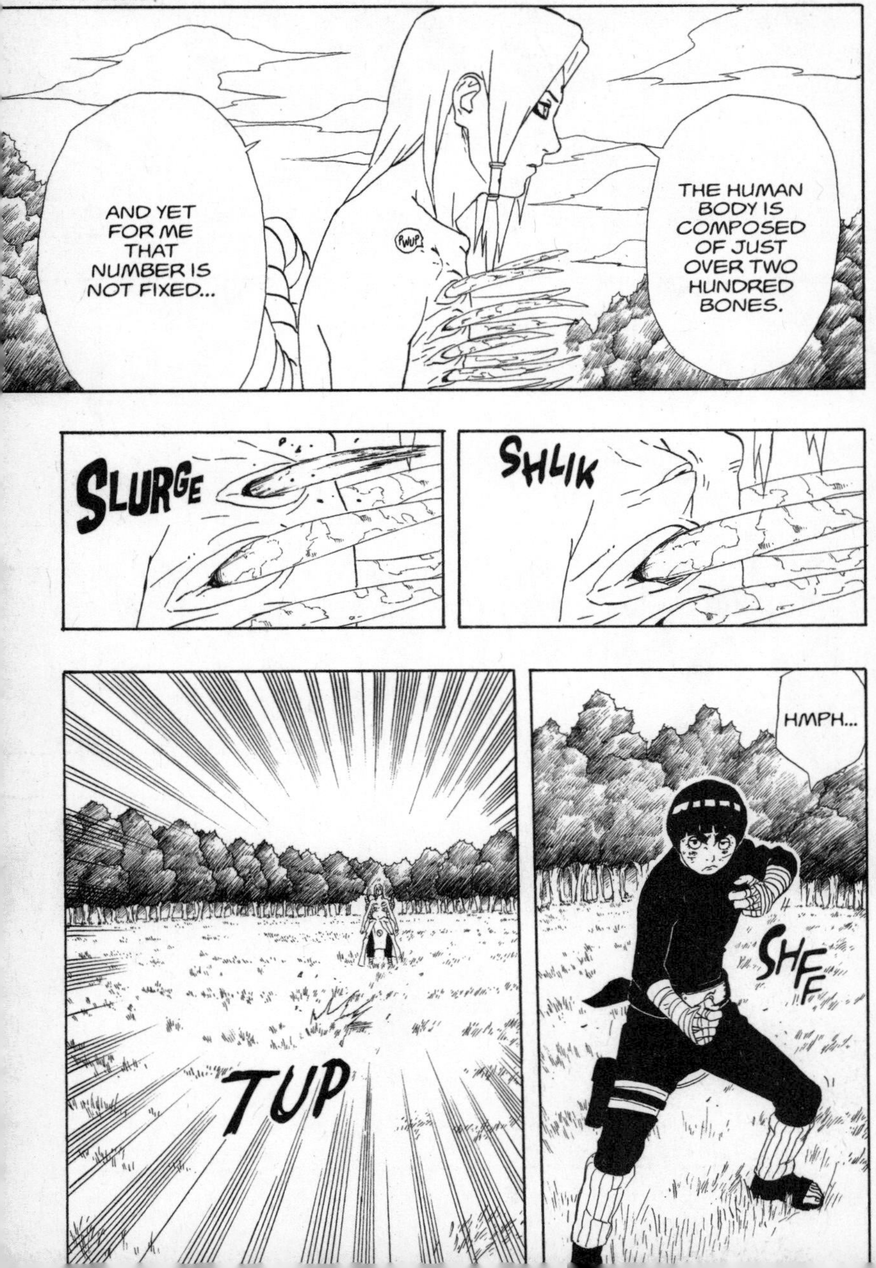
THE HUMAN BODY IS COMPOSED OF JUST OVER TWO HUNDRED BONES.
PWUP
AND YET FOR ME THAT NUMBER IS NOT FIXED...
SHLIK
SLURGE
HMPH...
SHFF
TUP

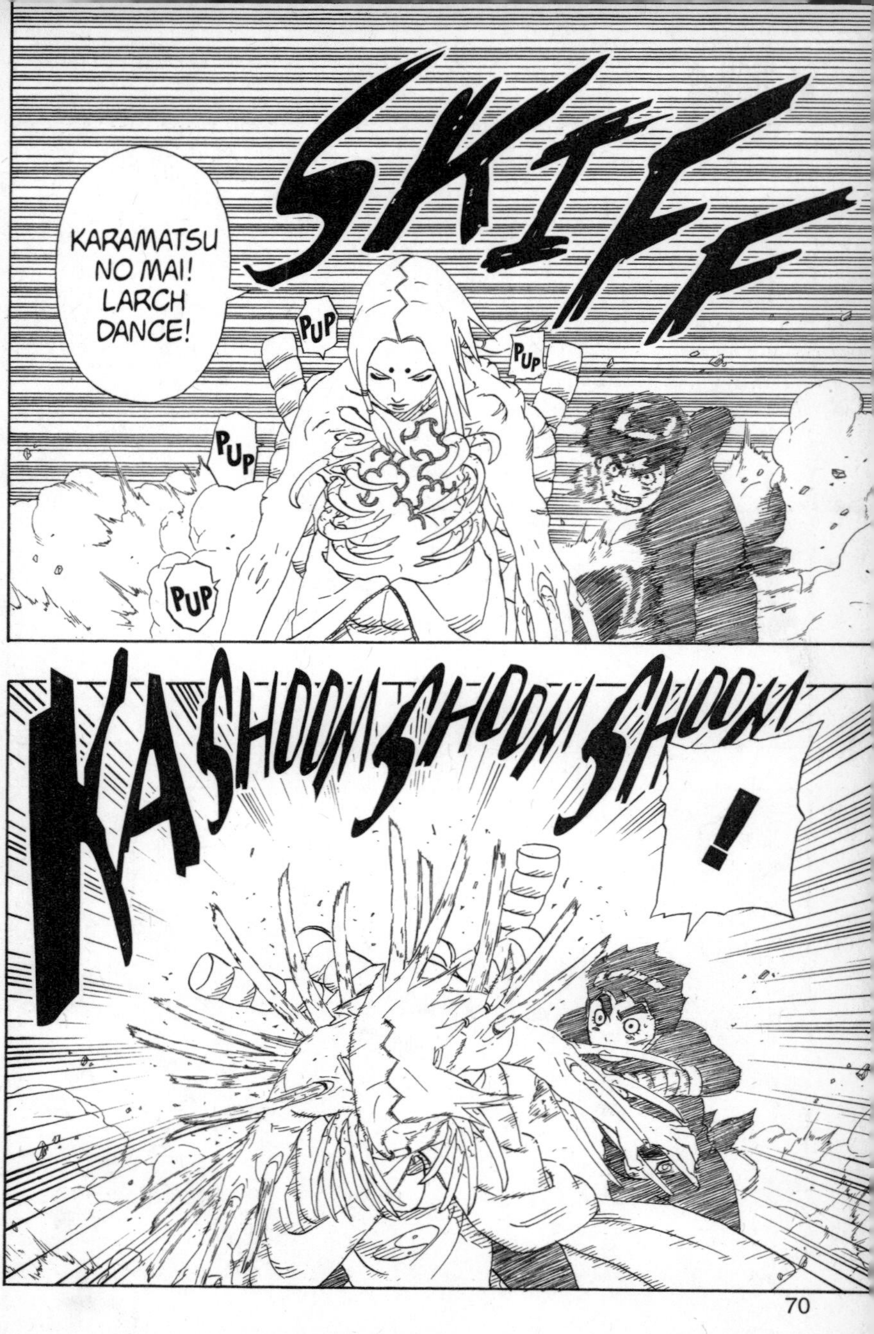
SKIFF
KARAMATSU NO MAI! LARCH DANCE!
PUP
PUP
PUP
PUP
KASHOOM SHOOM SH SHOOM
!

READ THIS WAY

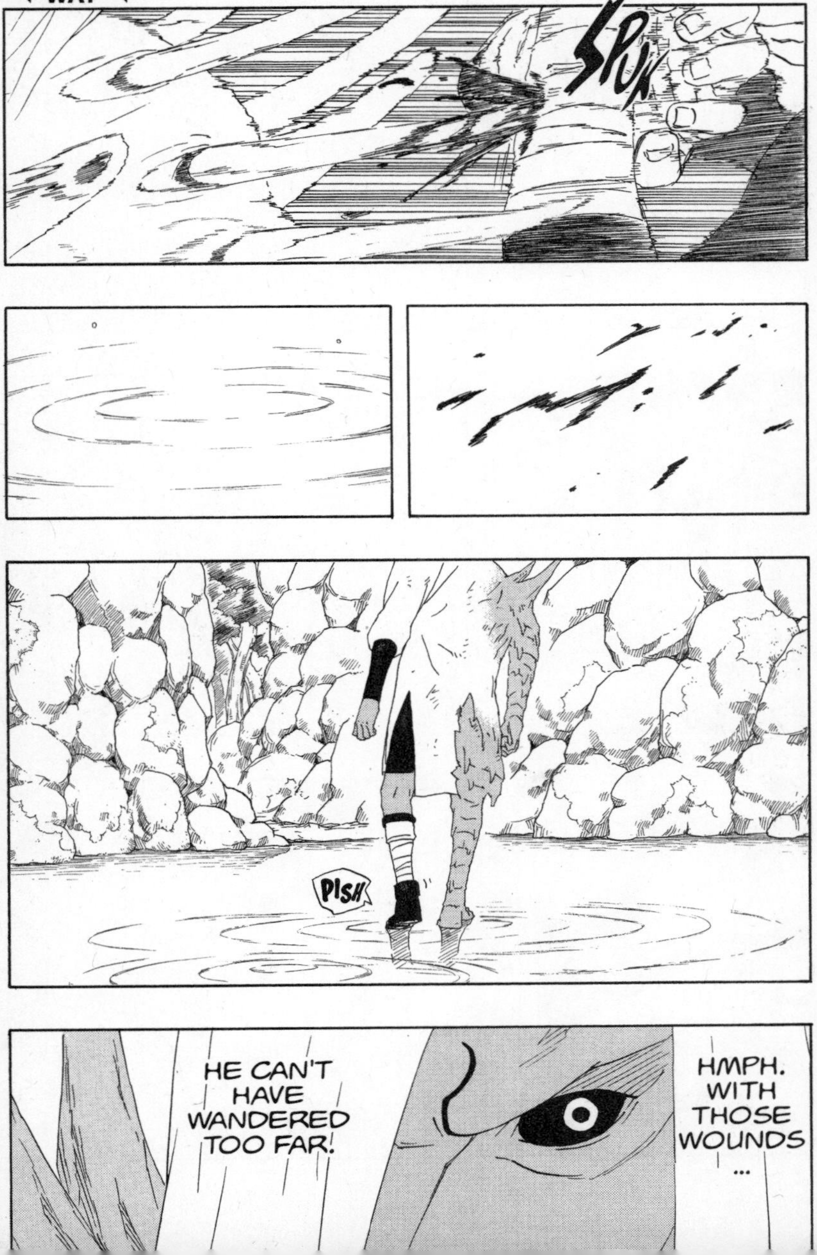
SPLUK
PISH
HMPH. WITH THOSE WOUNDS ...
HE CAN'T HAVE WANDERED TOO FAR.

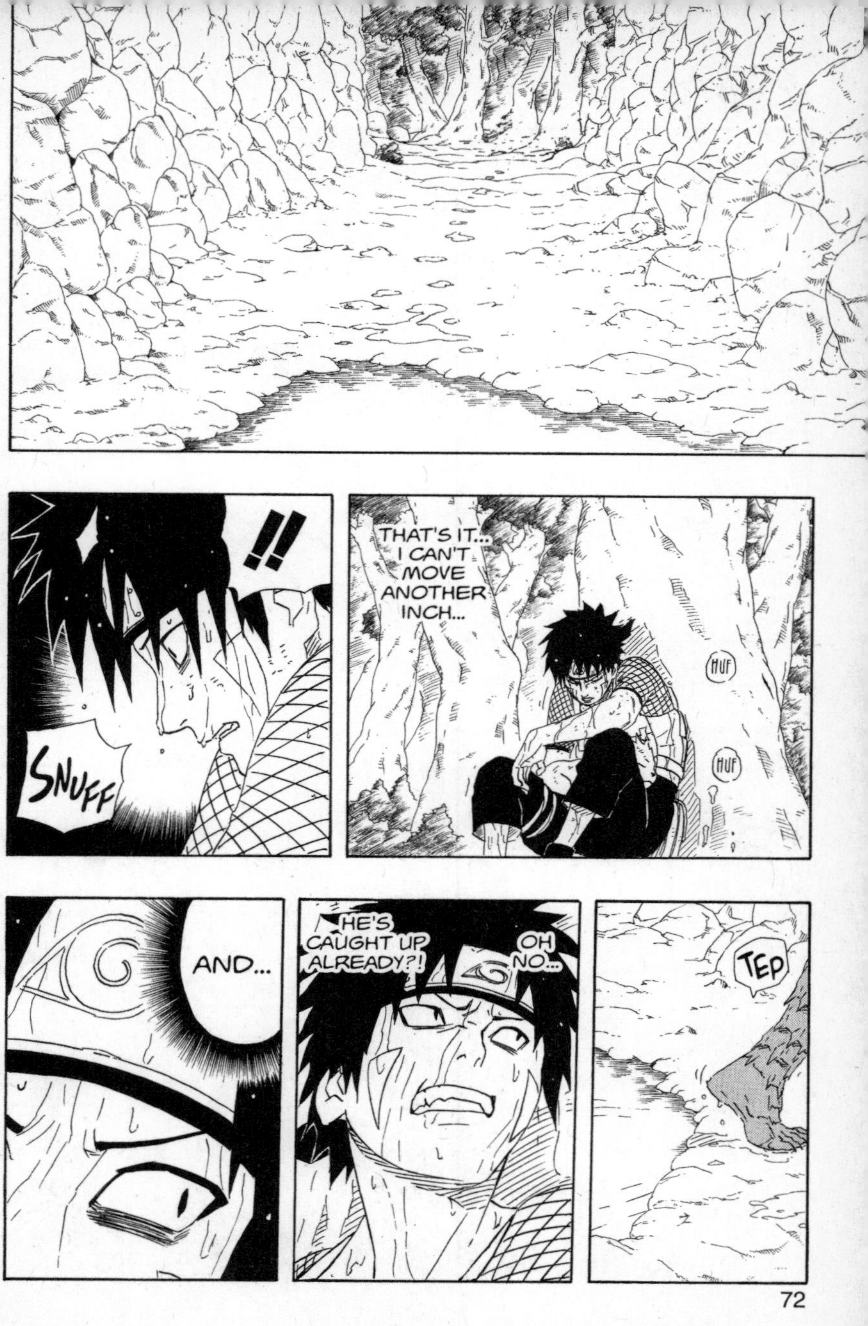
THAT'S IT... I CAN'T MOVE ANOTHER INCH...
HUF
HUF
!!
SNUFF
TEP
OH NO...
HE'S CAUGHT UP ALREADY?!
AND...

READ THIS WAY

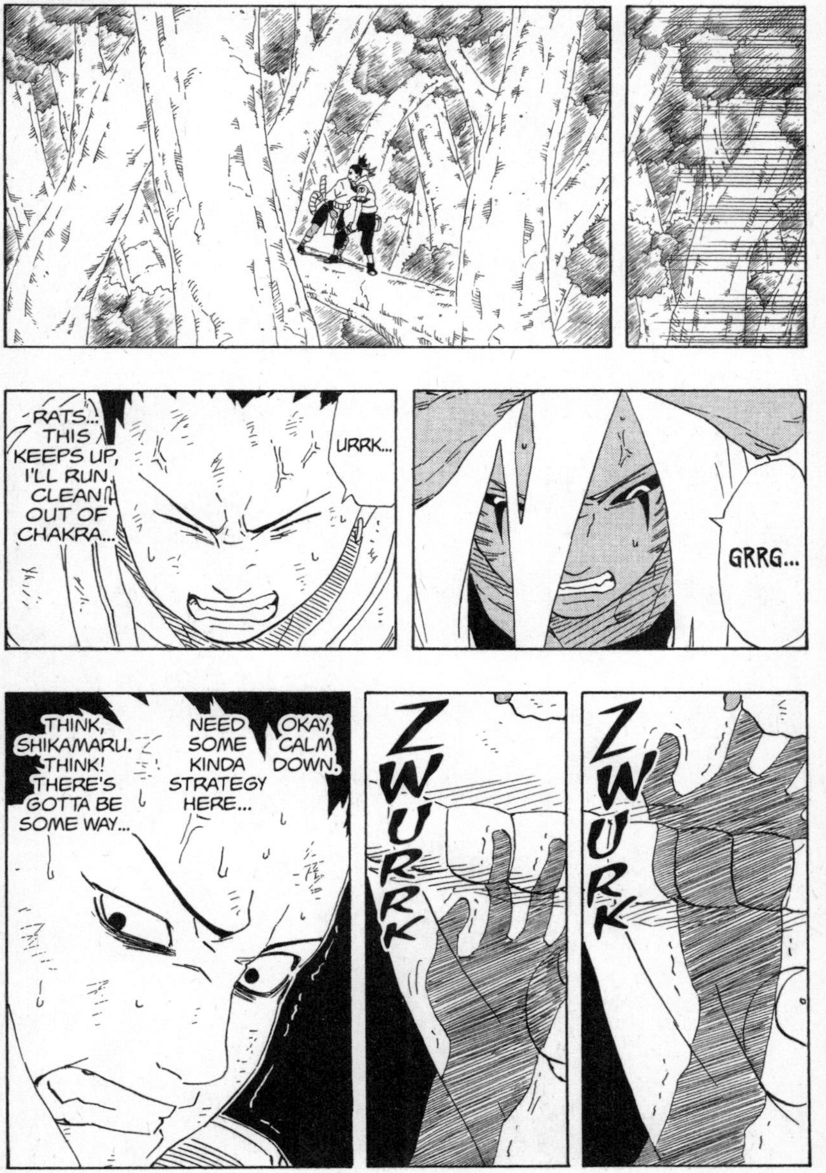
GRRG...
URRK...
RATS... THIS KEEPS UP, I'LL RUN CLEAN OUT OF CHAKRA...
ZWURK
ZWURRK
OKAY, CALM DOWN.
NEED SOME KINDA STRATEGY HERE...
THINK, SHIKAMARU. THINK! THERE'S GOTTA BE SOME WAY...

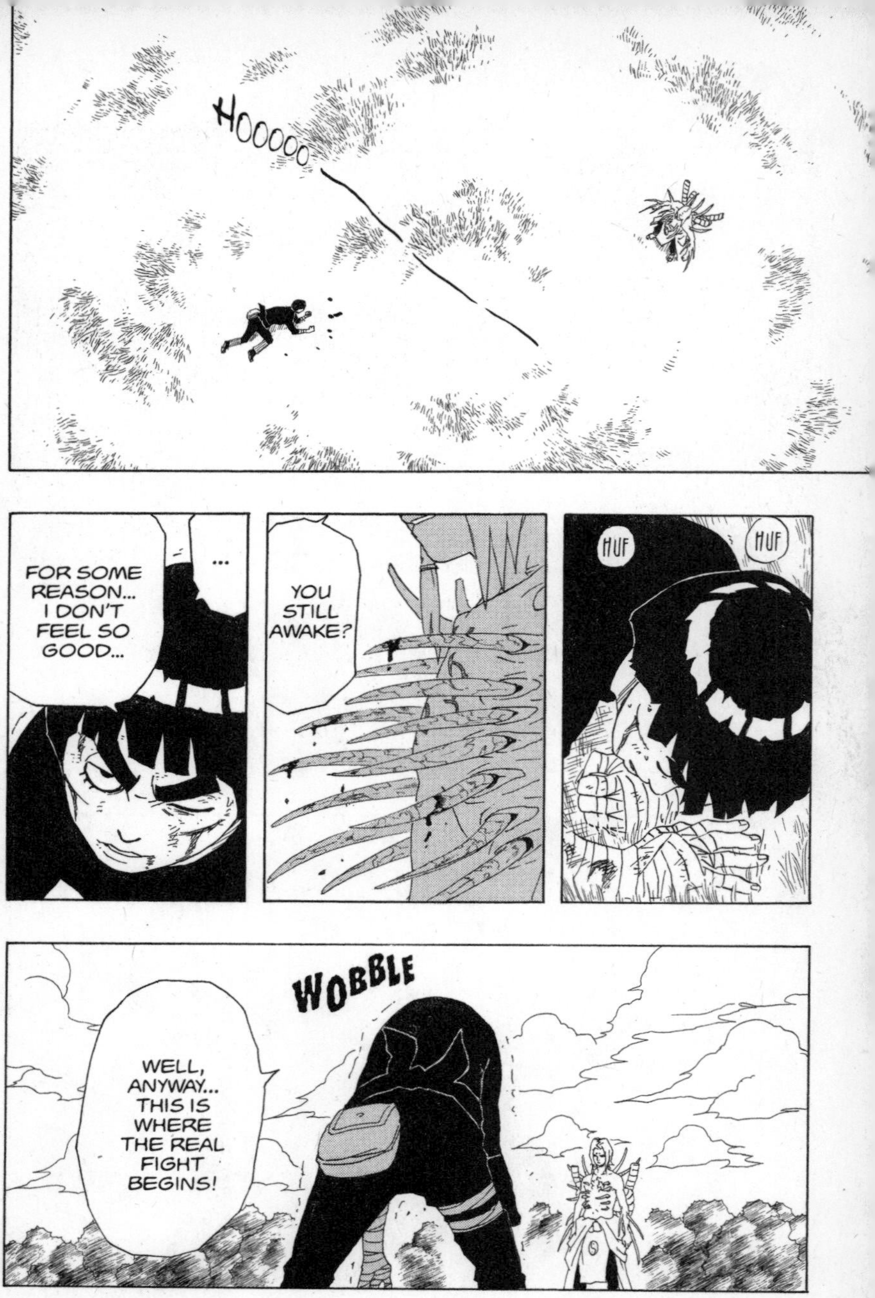
HOOOOO
HUF
HUF
YOU STILL AWAKE?
...
FOR SOME REASON... I DON'T FEEL SO GOOD...
WOBBLE
WELL, ANYWAY... THIS IS WHERE THE REAL FIGHT BEGINS!

READ THIS WAY

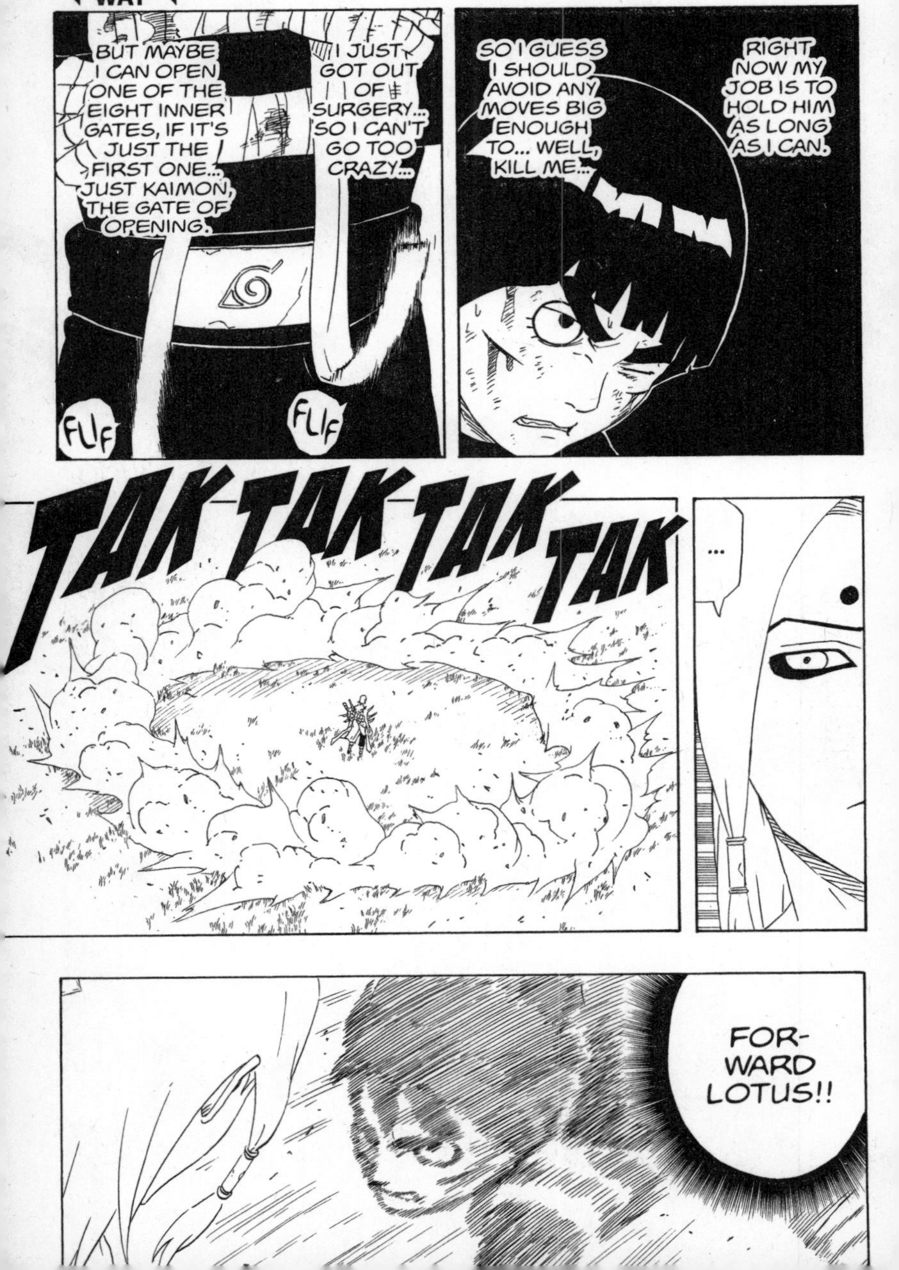
RIGHT NOW MY JOB IS TO HOLD HIM AS LONG AS I CAN.
SO I GUESS I SHOULD AVOID ANY MOVES BIG ENOUGH TO... WELL, KILL ME...
I JUST GOT OUT OF SURGERY... SO I CAN'T GO TOO CRAZY...
BUT MAYBE I CAN OPEN ONE OF THE EIGHT INNER GATES, IF IT'S JUST THE FIRST ONE... JUST KAIMON, THE GATE OF OPENING.
FLIF
FLIF
...
TAK TAK TAK TAK
FOR-WARD LOTUS!!

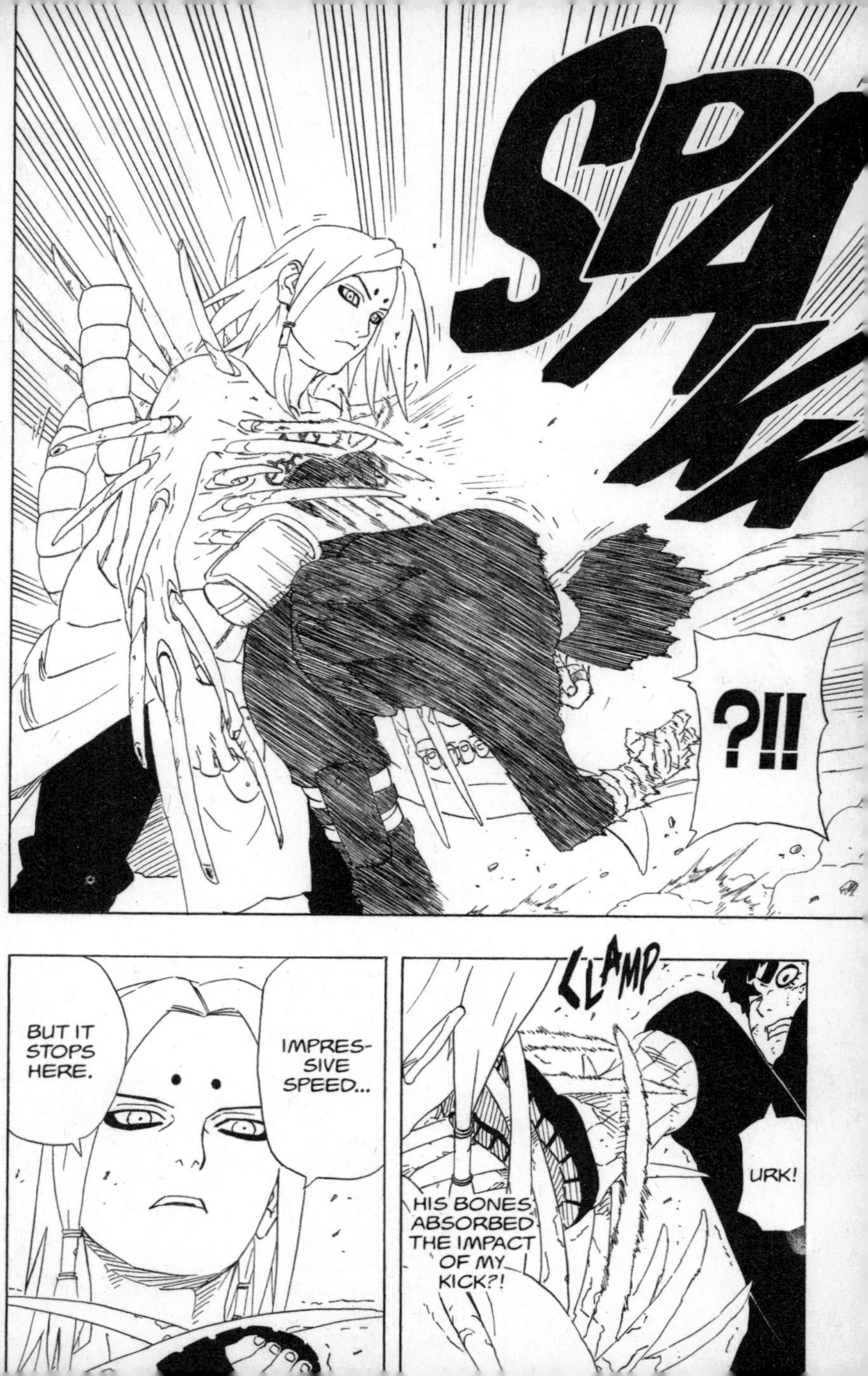
SPAM
?!!
CLAMP
URK!
HIS BONES ABSORBED THE IMPACT OF MY KICK?!
IMPRES-SIVE SPEED...
BUT IT STOPS HERE.

READ THIS WAY

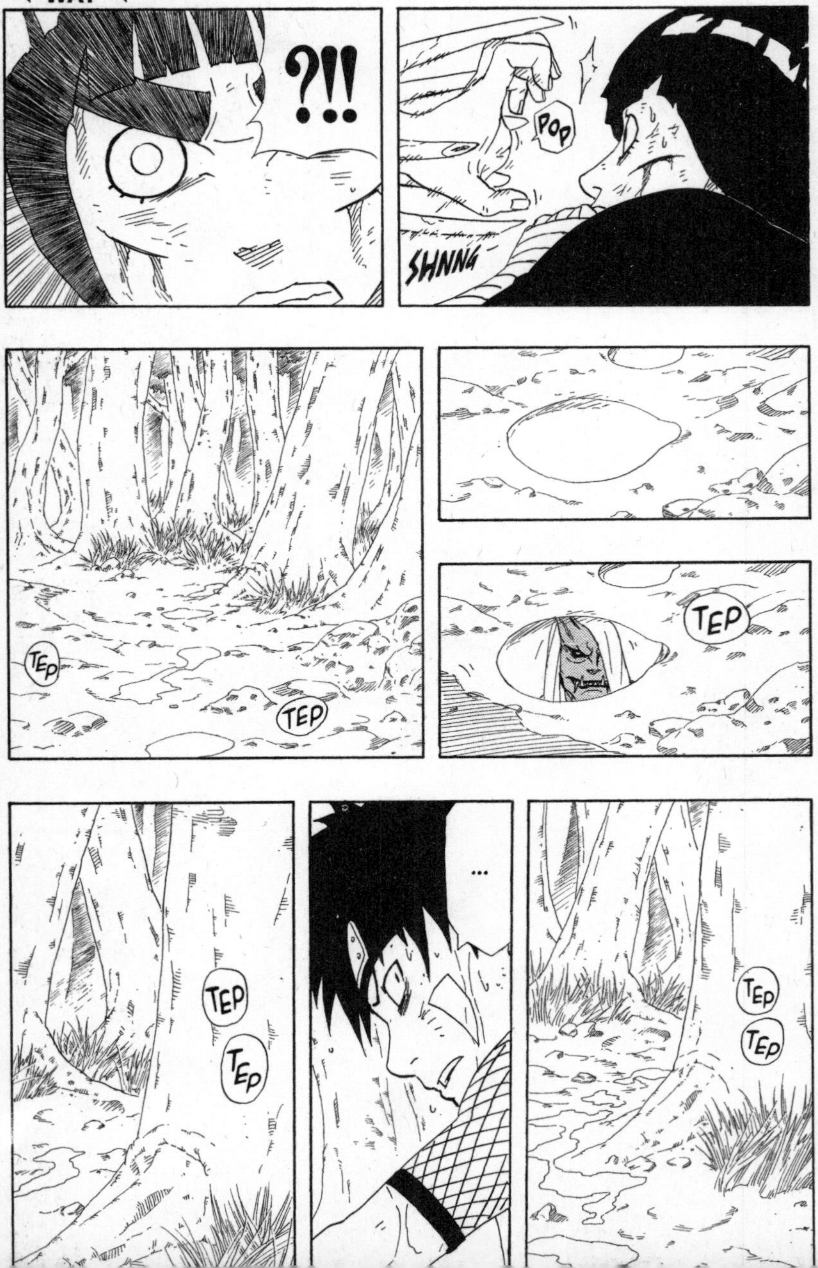
POP
SHNNG
?!!
TEP
TEP
TEP
TEP
TEP
...
TEP
TEP

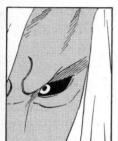

GRUNT!

TEP

UNGH...

GRR...

READ THIS WAY

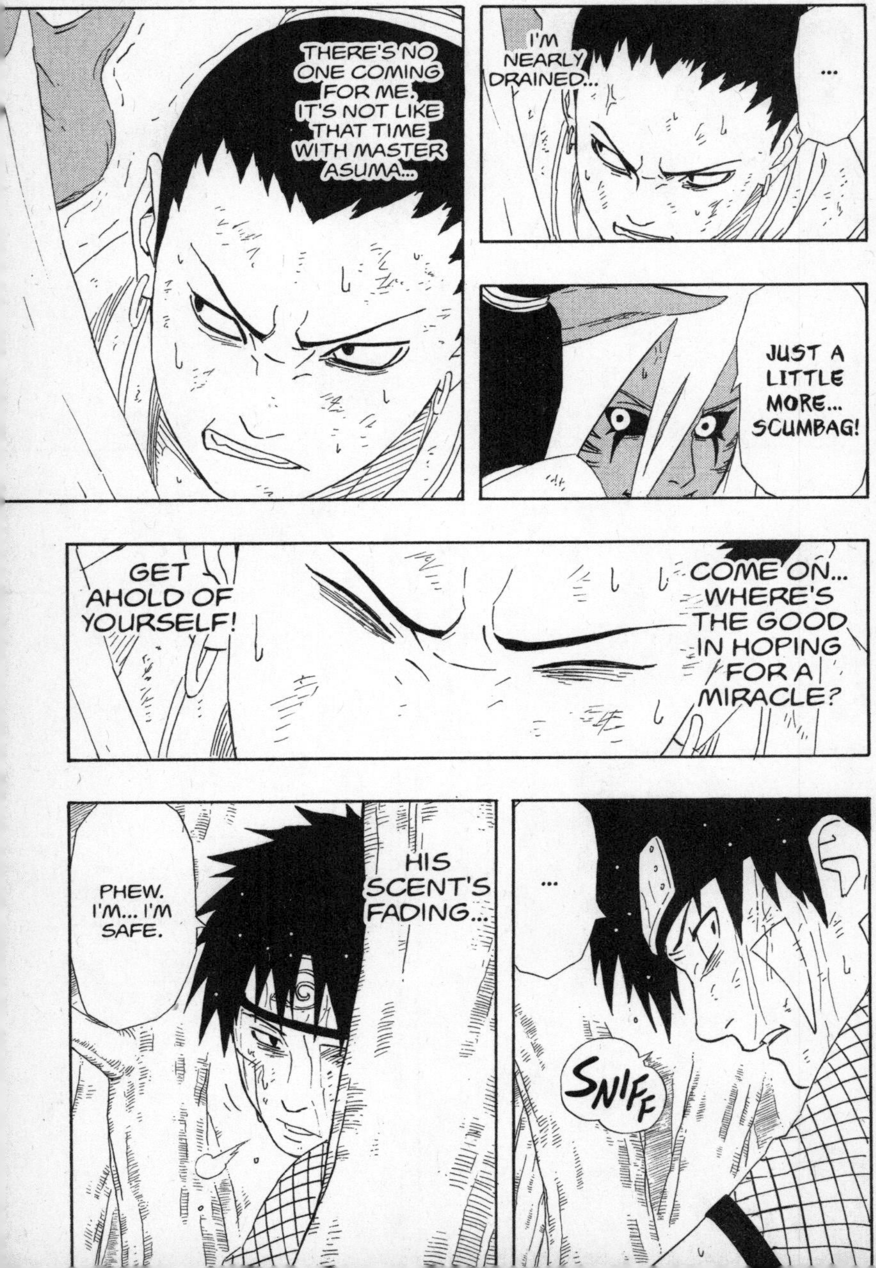
...
I'M NEARLY DRAINED...
JUST A LITTLE MORE... SCUMBAG!
THERE'S NO ONE COMING FOR ME. IT'S NOT LIKE THAT TIME WITH MASTER ASUMA...
COME ON... WHERE'S THE GOOD IN HOPING FOR A MIRACLE?
GET AHOLD OF YOURSELF!
...
SNIFF
HIS SCENT'S FADING...
PHEW. I'M... I'M SAFE.

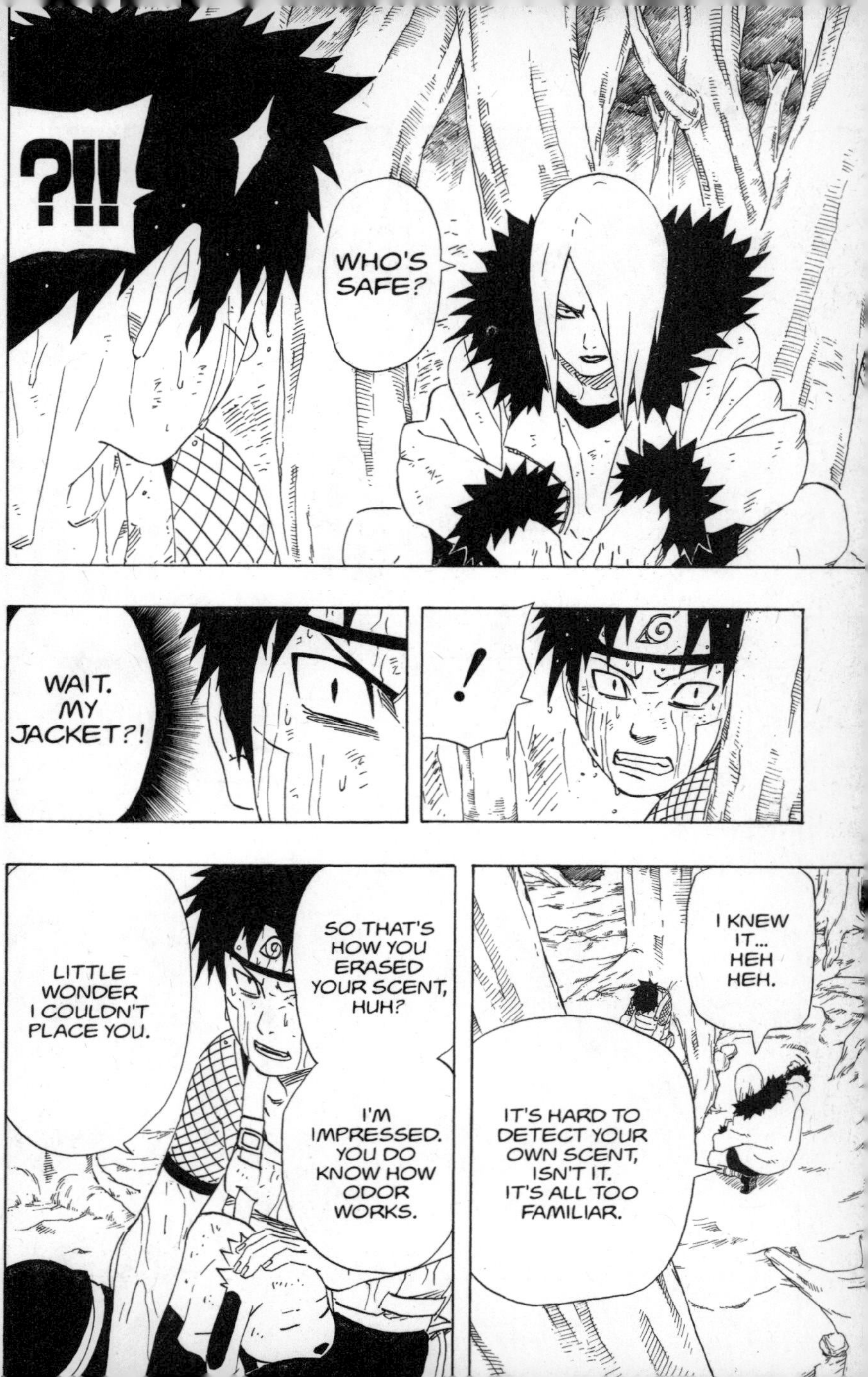
WHO'S SAFE?
?!!
!
WAIT. MY JACKET?!
I KNEW IT... HEH HEH.
IT'S HARD TO DETECT YOUR OWN SCENT, ISN'T IT. IT'S ALL TOO FAMILIAR.
SO THAT'S HOW YOU ERASED YOUR SCENT, HUH?
LITTLE WONDER I COULDN'T PLACE YOU.
I'M IMPRESSED. YOU DO KNOW HOW ODOR WORKS.

READ THIS WAY

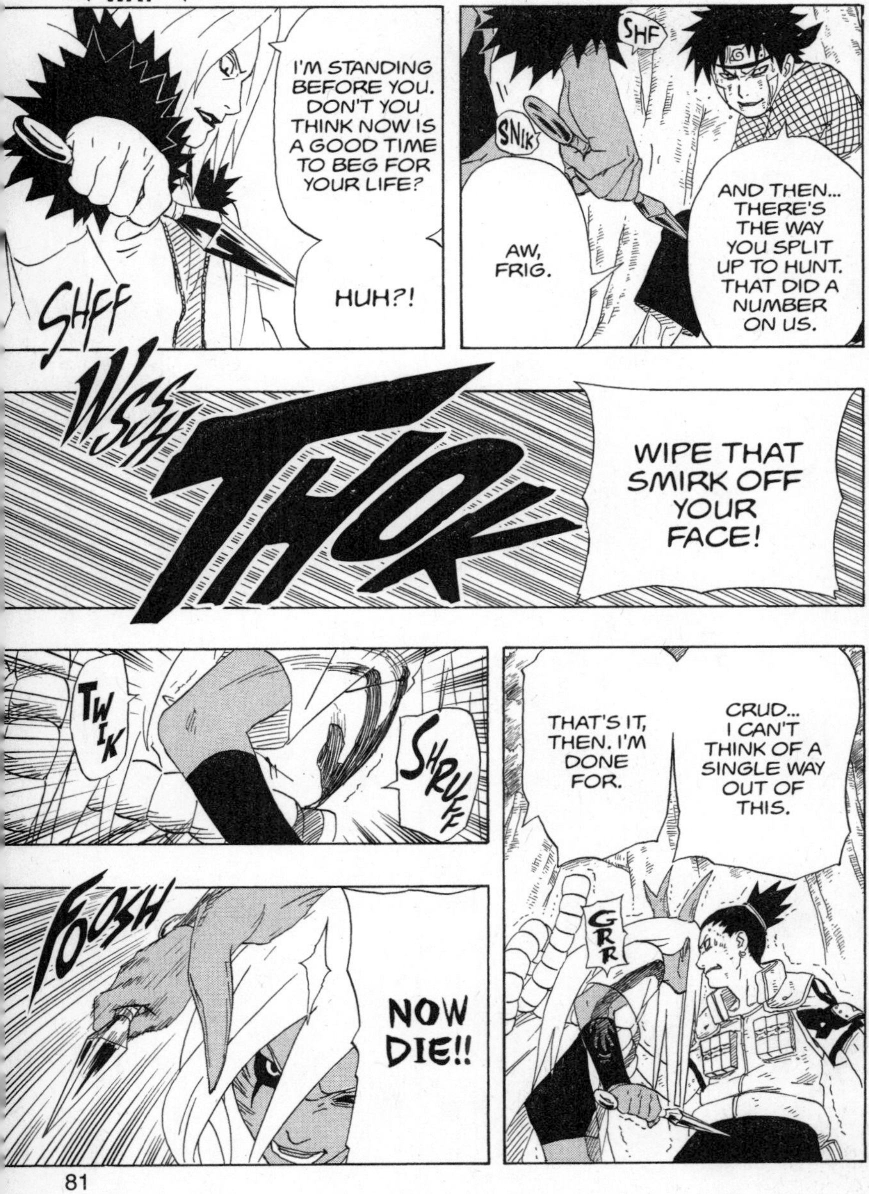
SHF
AND THEN... THERE'S THE WAY YOU SPLIT UP TO HUNT. THAT DID A NUMBER ON US.
SNIK
AW, FRIG.
I'M STANDING BEFORE YOU. DON'T YOU THINK NOW IS A GOOD TIME TO BEG FOR YOUR LIFE?
HUH?!
SHFF
WIPE THAT SMIRK OFF YOUR FACE!
THOK
WSSH
CRUD... I CAN'T THINK OF A SINGLE WAY OUT OF THIS.
THAT'S IT, THEN. I'M DONE FOR.
GRR
SHRUFF
TWIK
NOW DIE!!
FOOSH

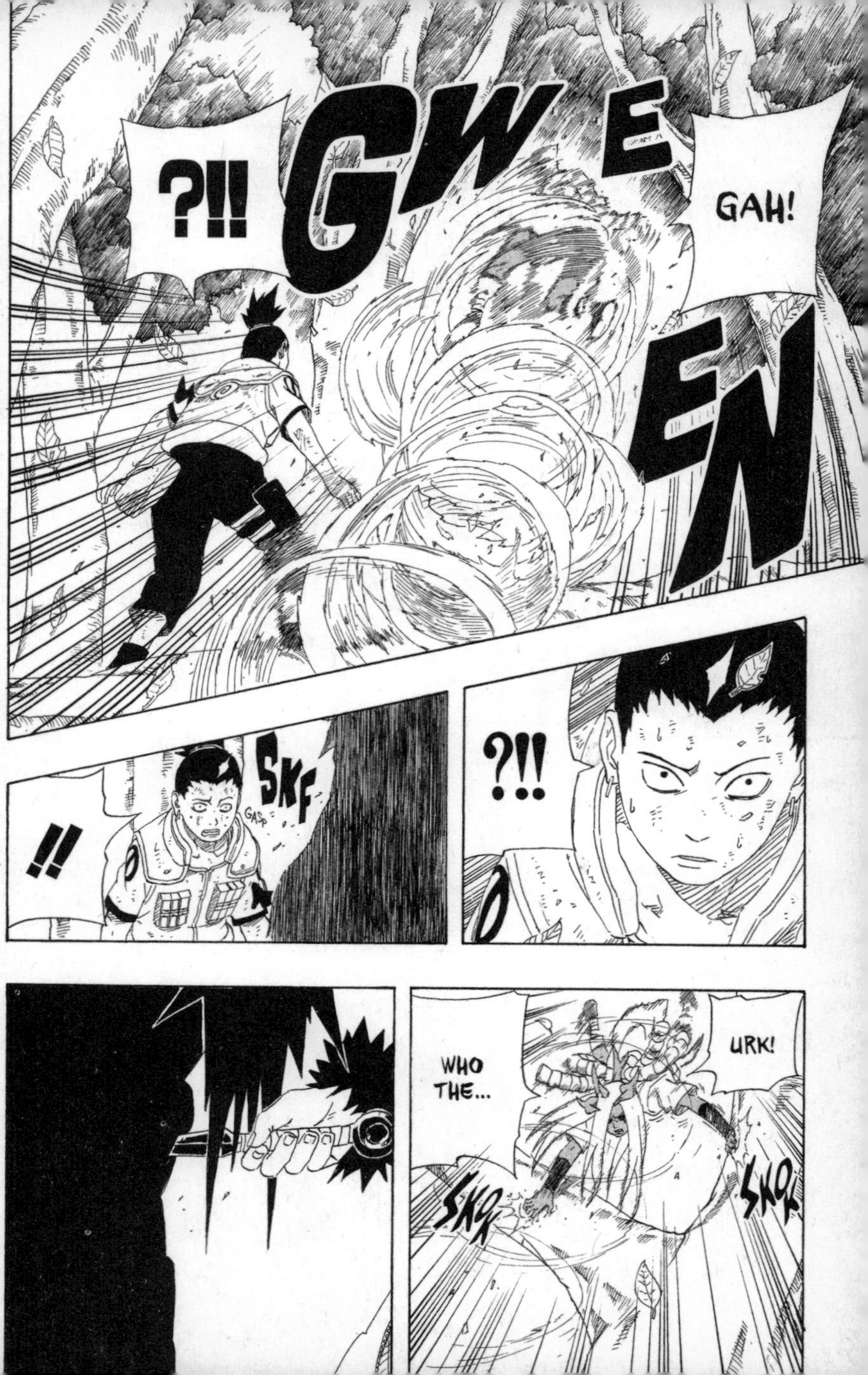
GAH!
GWEEN
?!!
?!!
SKF
GASP
!!
URK!
WHO THE...
SKOK
SKOK

READ THIS WAY

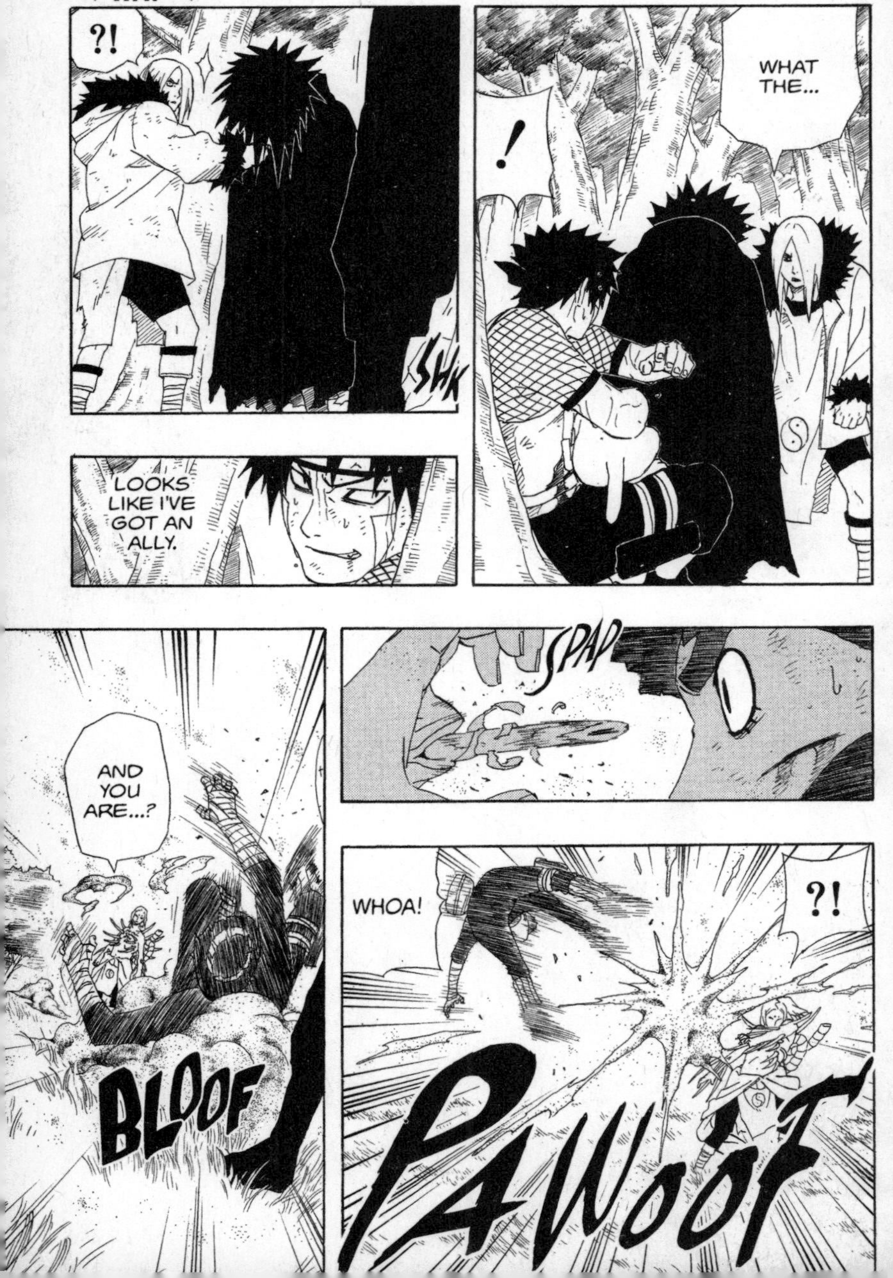
WHAT THE...
!
?!
SHK
LOOKS LIKE I'VE GOT AN ALLY.
SPAP
?!
WHOA!
PAWOOF
AND YOU ARE...?
BLOOF

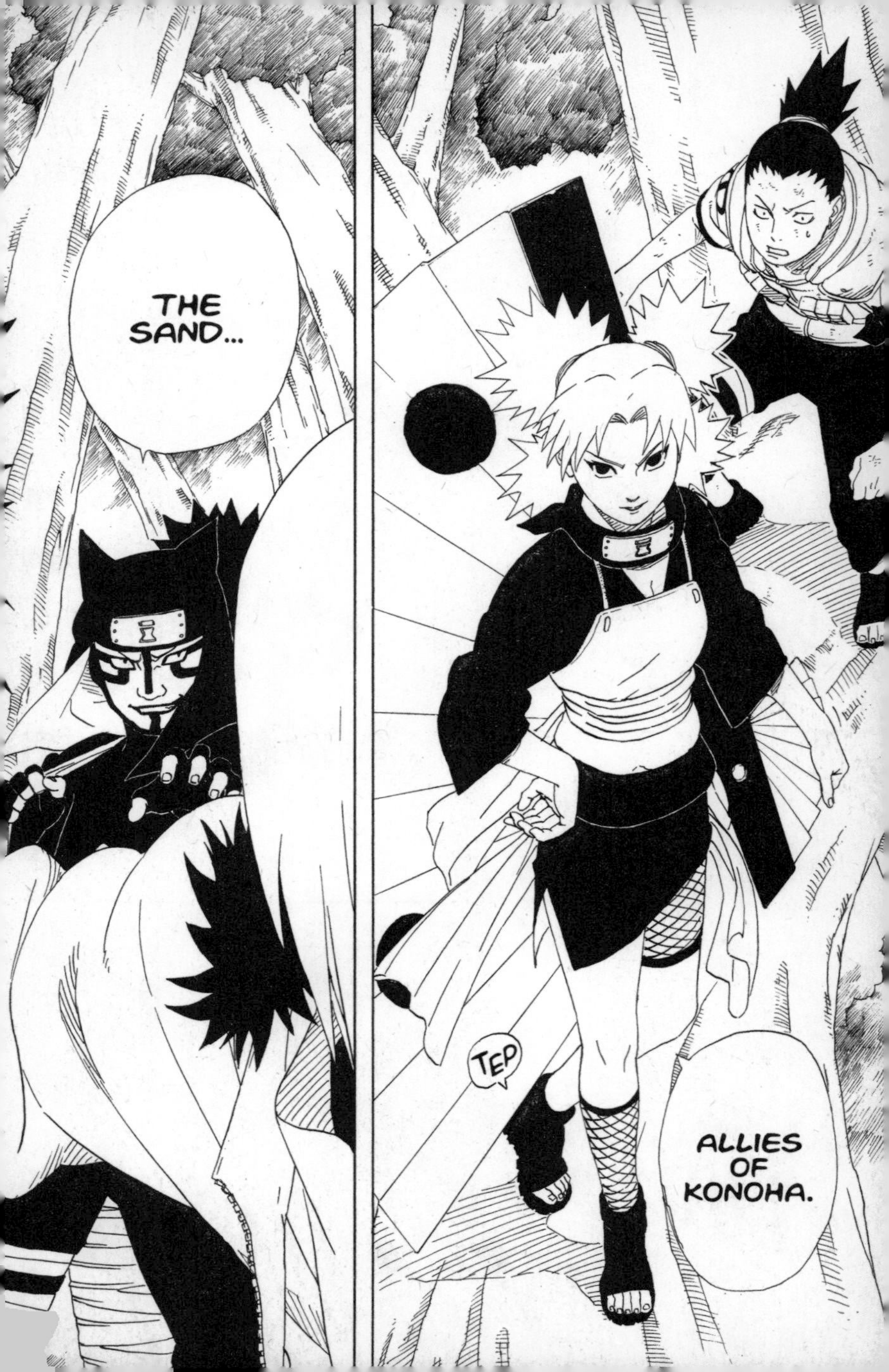
TEP
ALLIES OF KONOHA.
THE SAND...

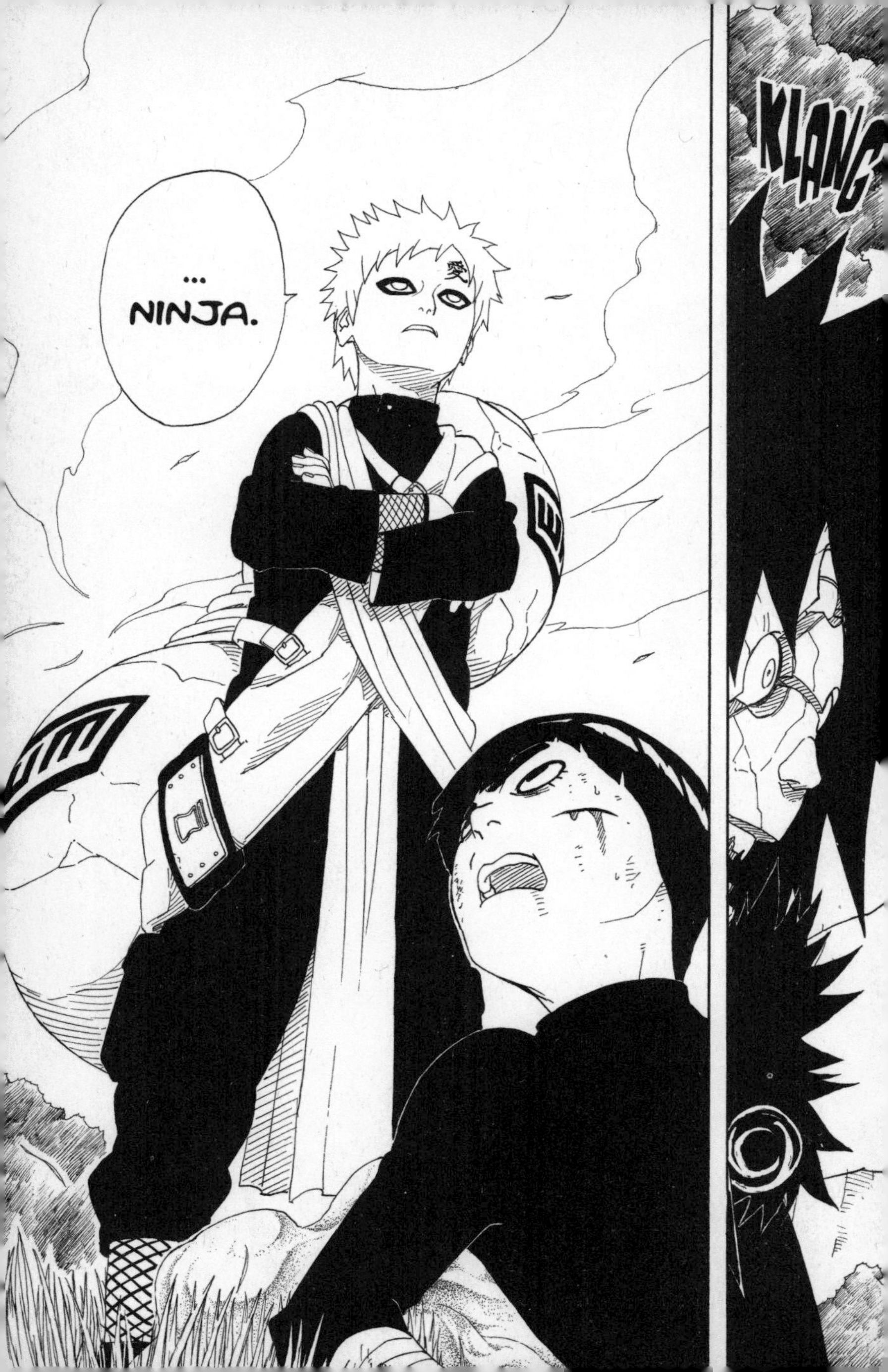
KLANG
... NINJA.

NARUTO™

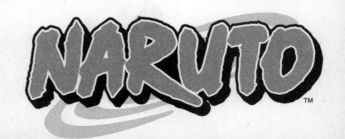

Number 213: Debt...!!

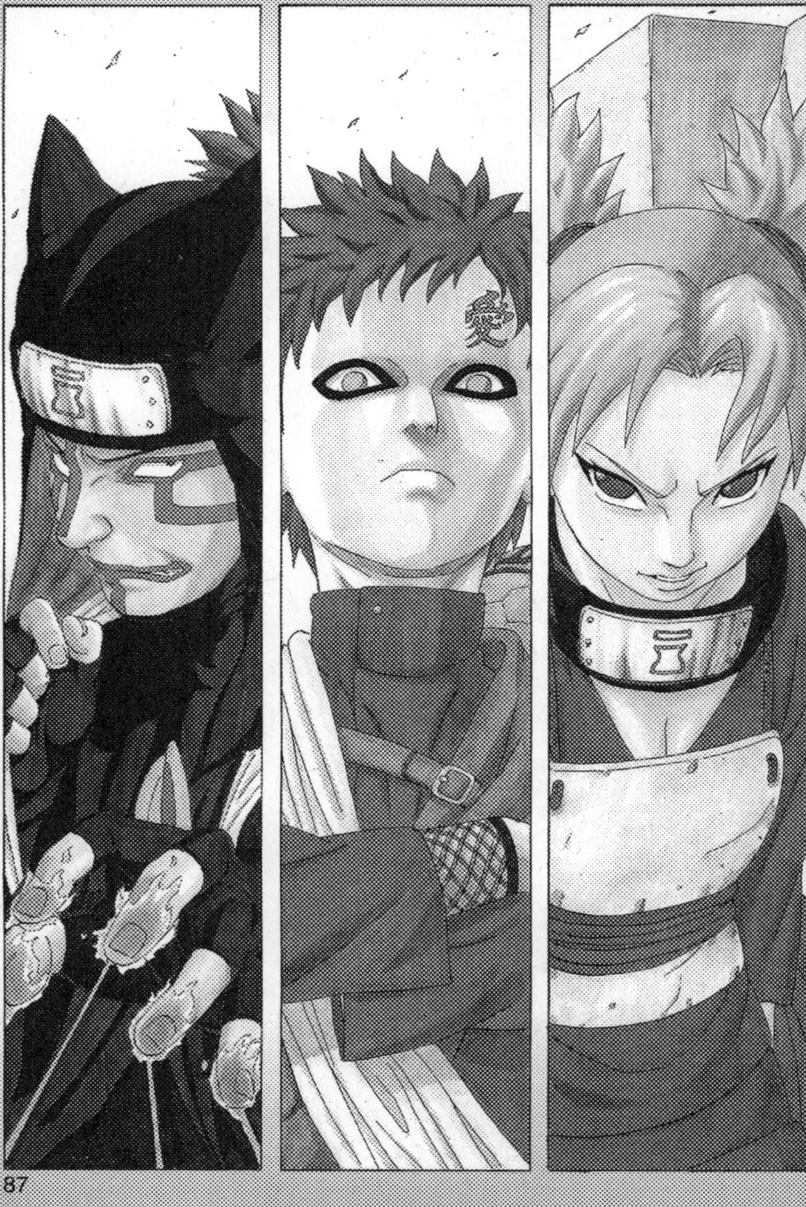

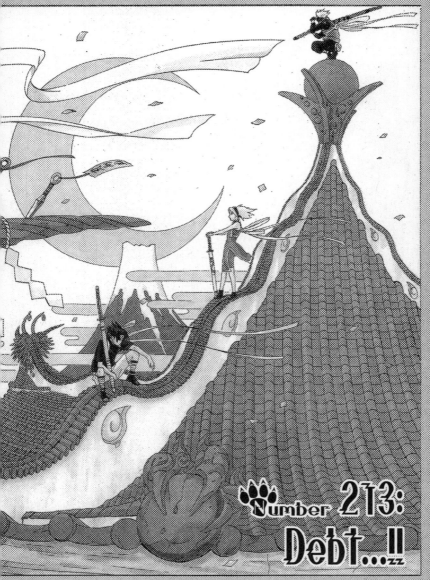

Number 213:
Debt...!!

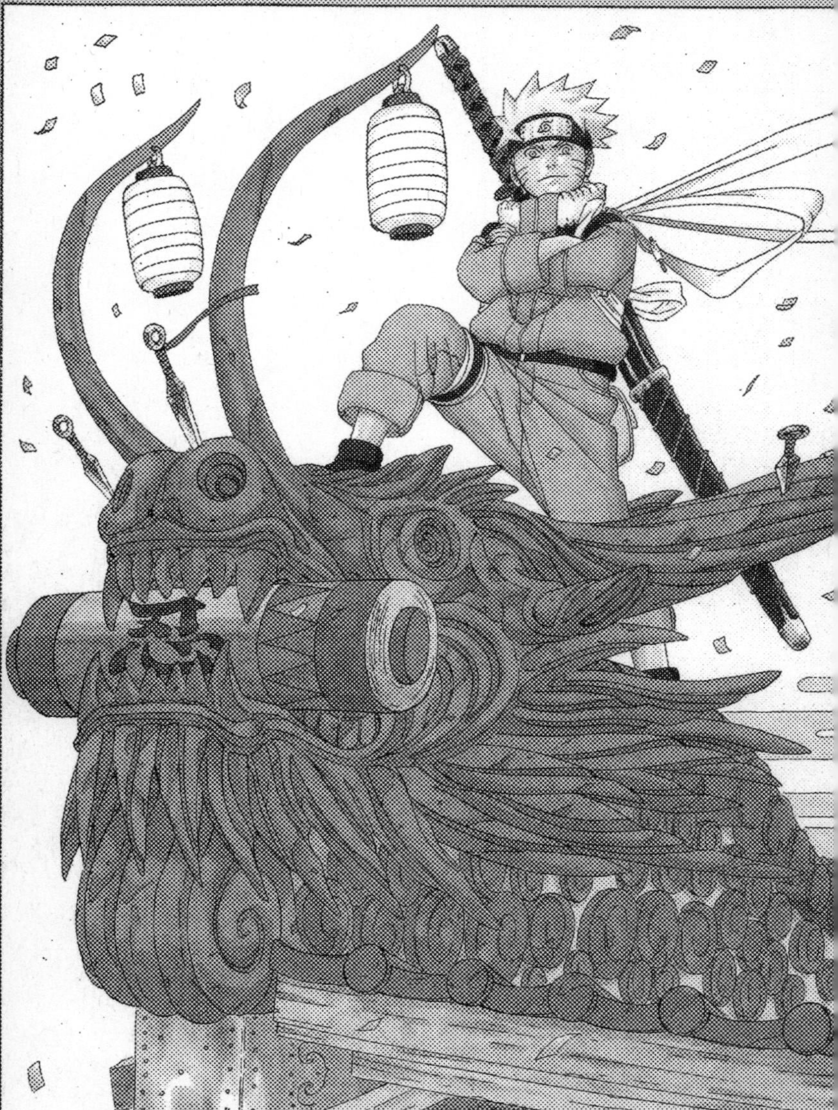

NARUTO -ナルト-

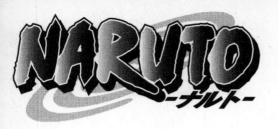

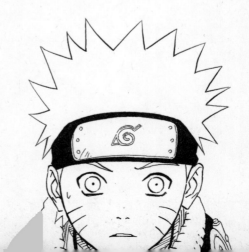

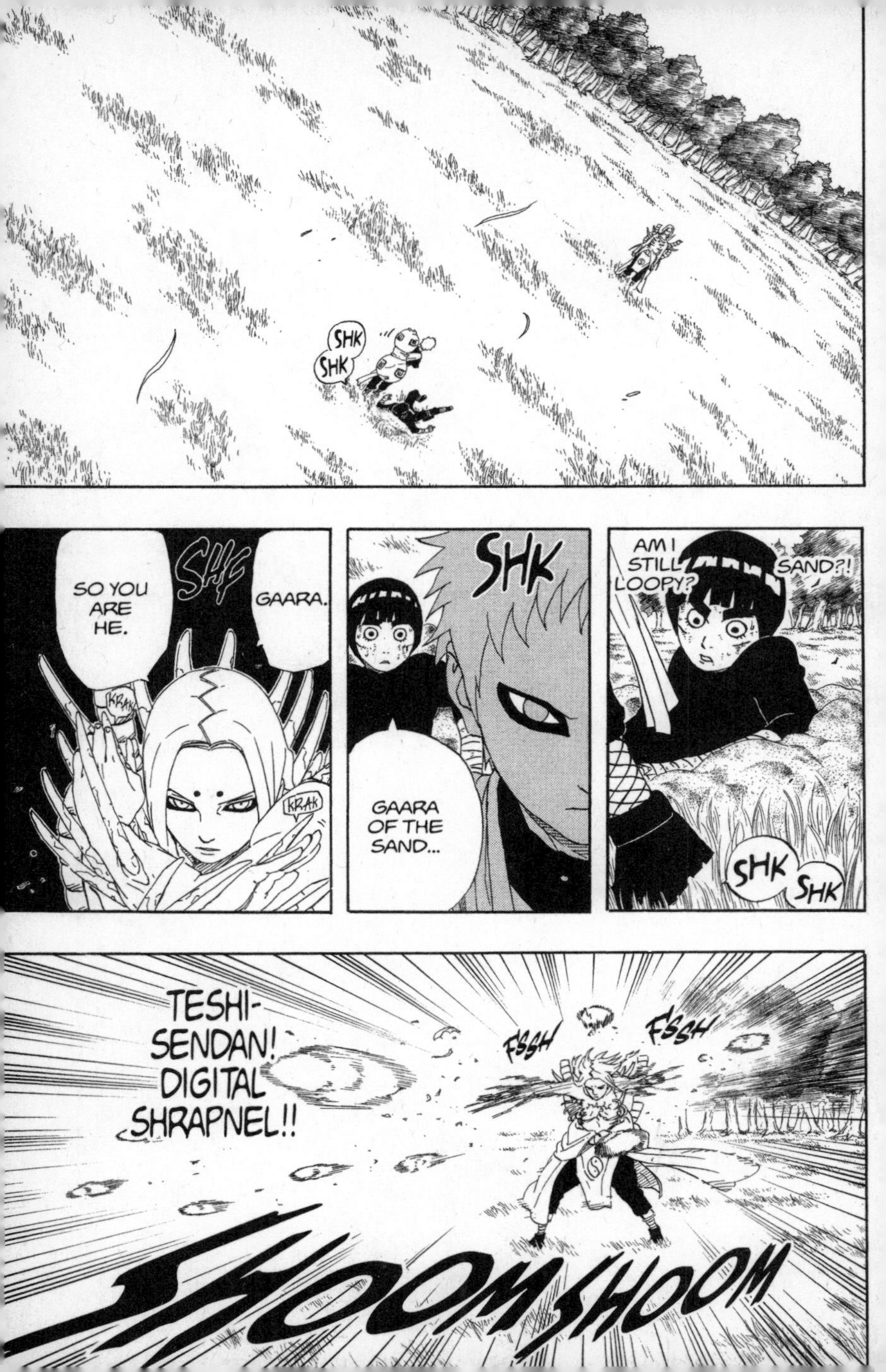
SHK
SHK
SAND?!
AM I STILL LOOPY?
SHK
SHK
SHK
GAARA OF THE SAND...
GAARA.
SHK
SO YOU ARE HE.
KRAK
KRAK
FSSH
FSSH
TESHI-SENDAN! DIGITAL SHRAPNEL!!
SHOOM SHOOM

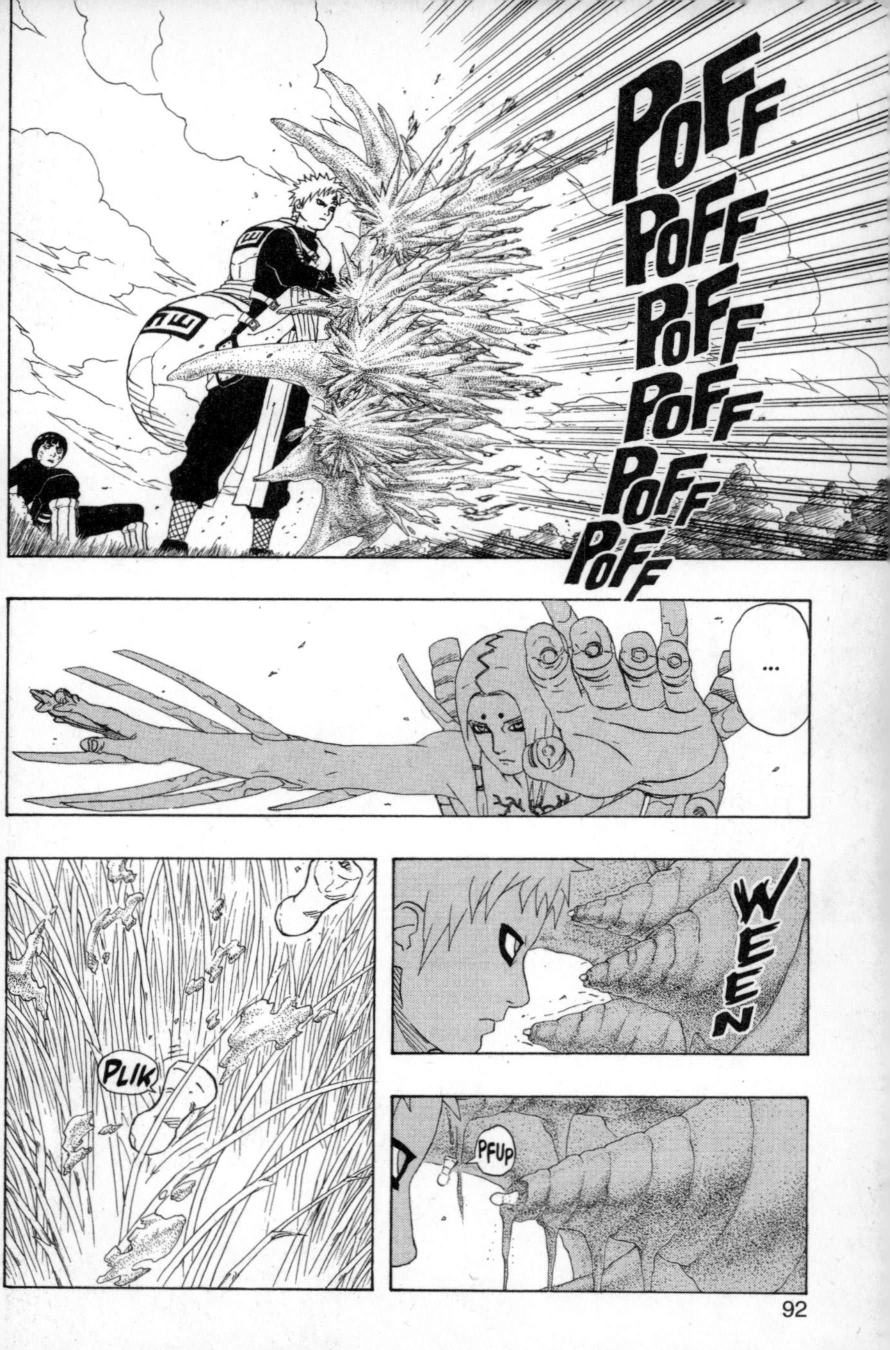
POFF POFF POFF POFF POFF POFF POFF
...
WEEN
PFUP
PLIK

READ THIS WAY

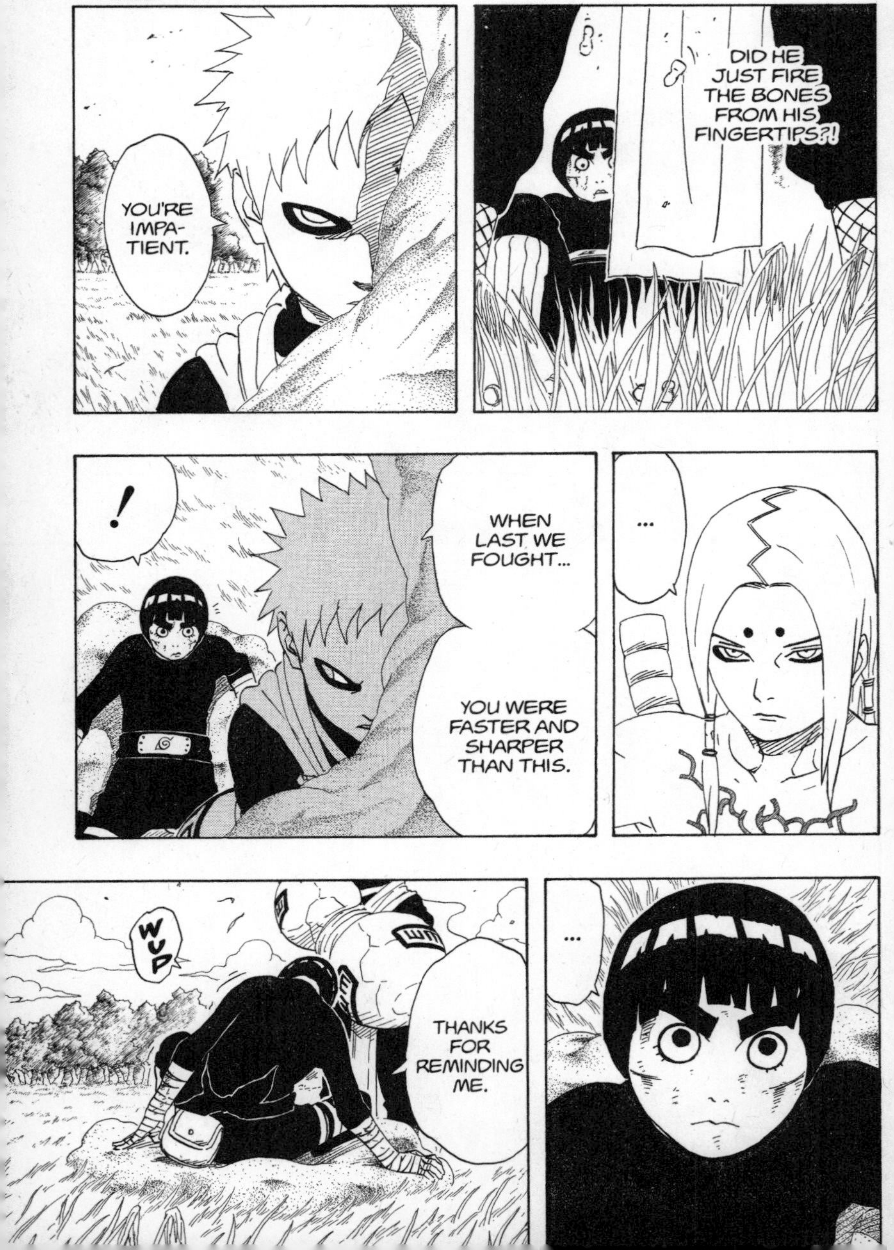
DID HE JUST FIRE THE BONES FROM HIS FINGERTIPS?!
YOU'RE IMPA-TIENT.
...
WHEN LAST WE FOUGHT...
!
YOU WERE FASTER AND SHARPER THAN THIS.
...
WUP
THANKS FOR REMINDING ME.

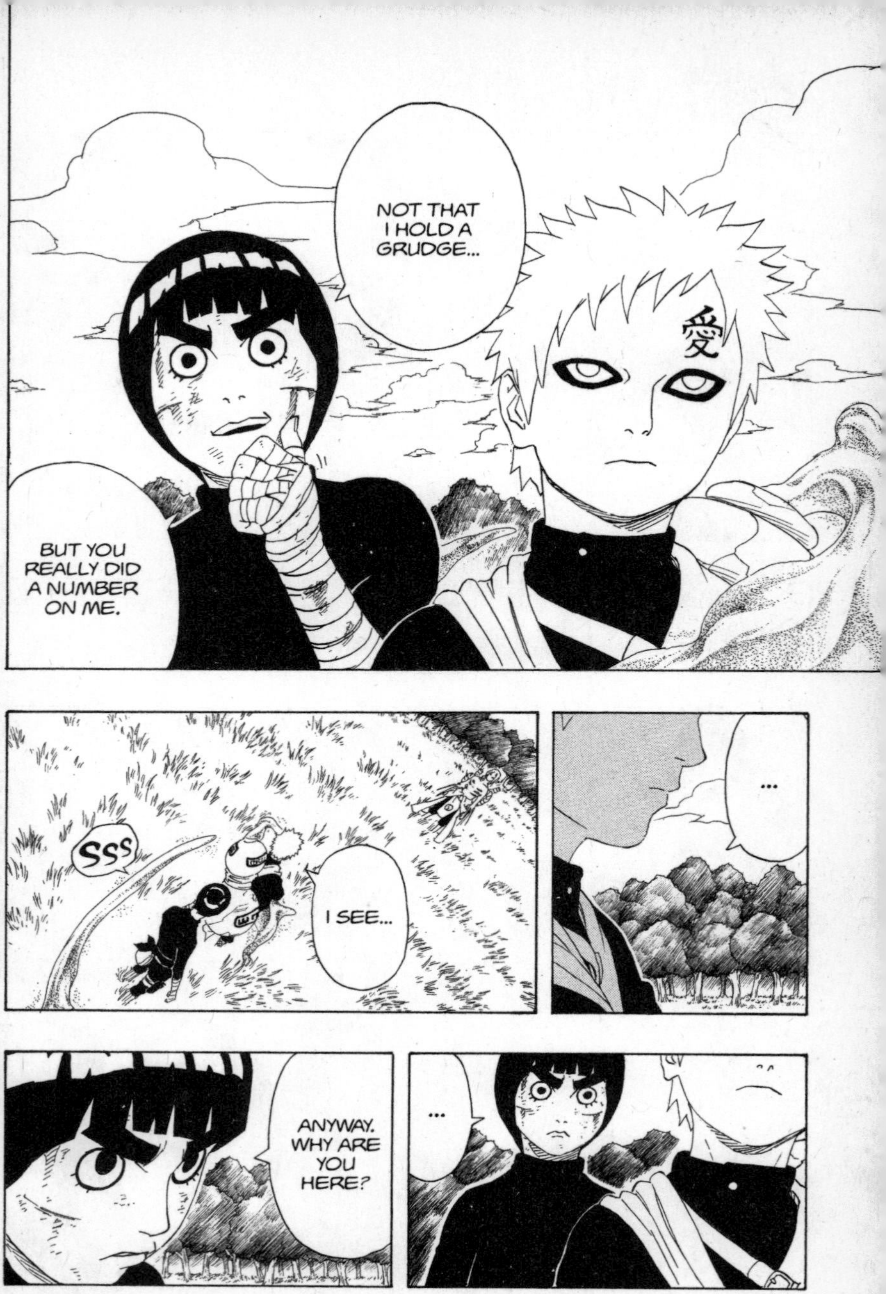
NOT THAT I HOLD A GRUDGE...
BUT YOU REALLY DID A NUMBER ON ME.
...
I SEE...
SSS
...
ANYWAY. WHY ARE YOU HERE?

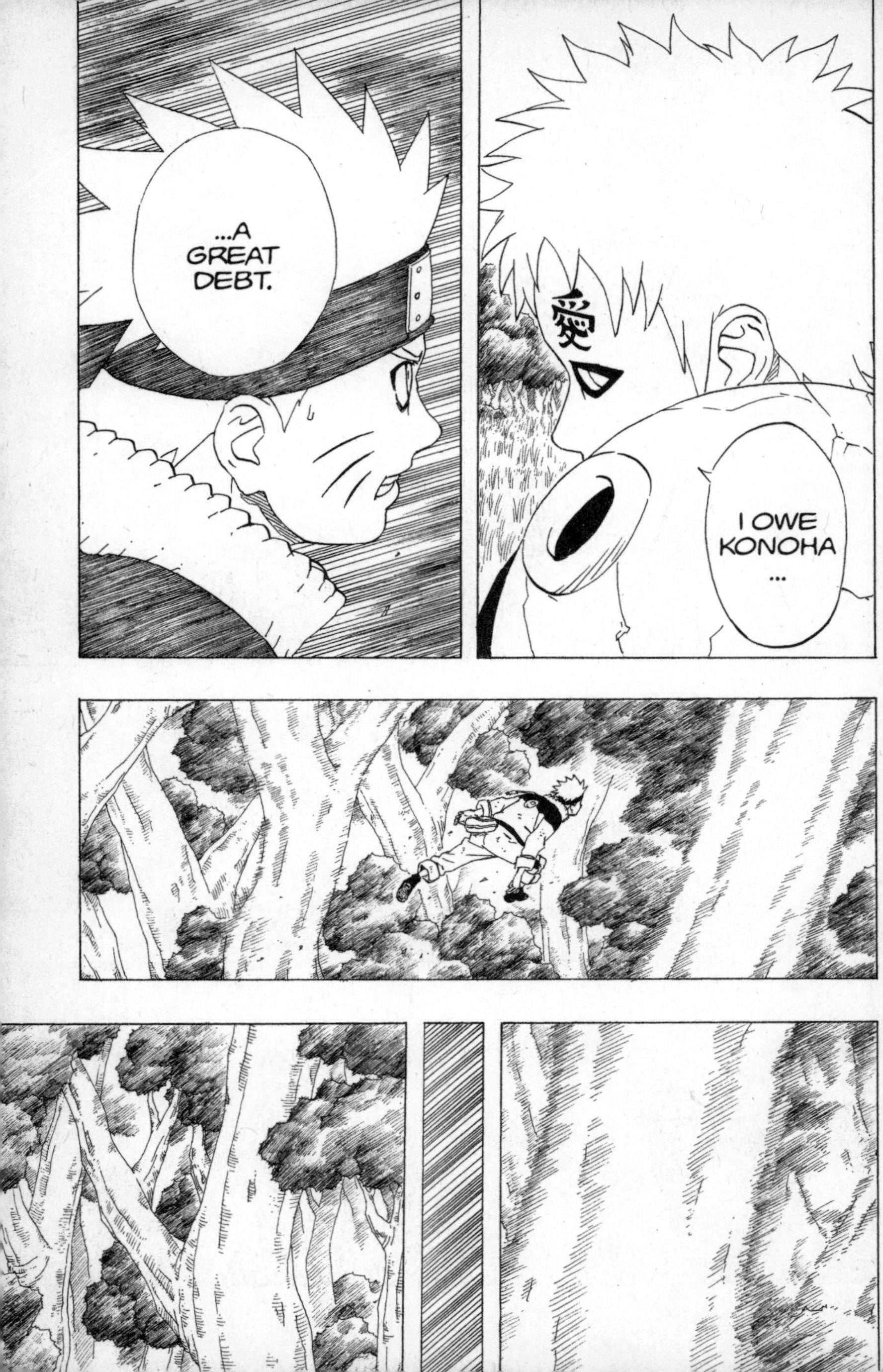
I OWE KONOHA ...
...A GREAT DEBT.

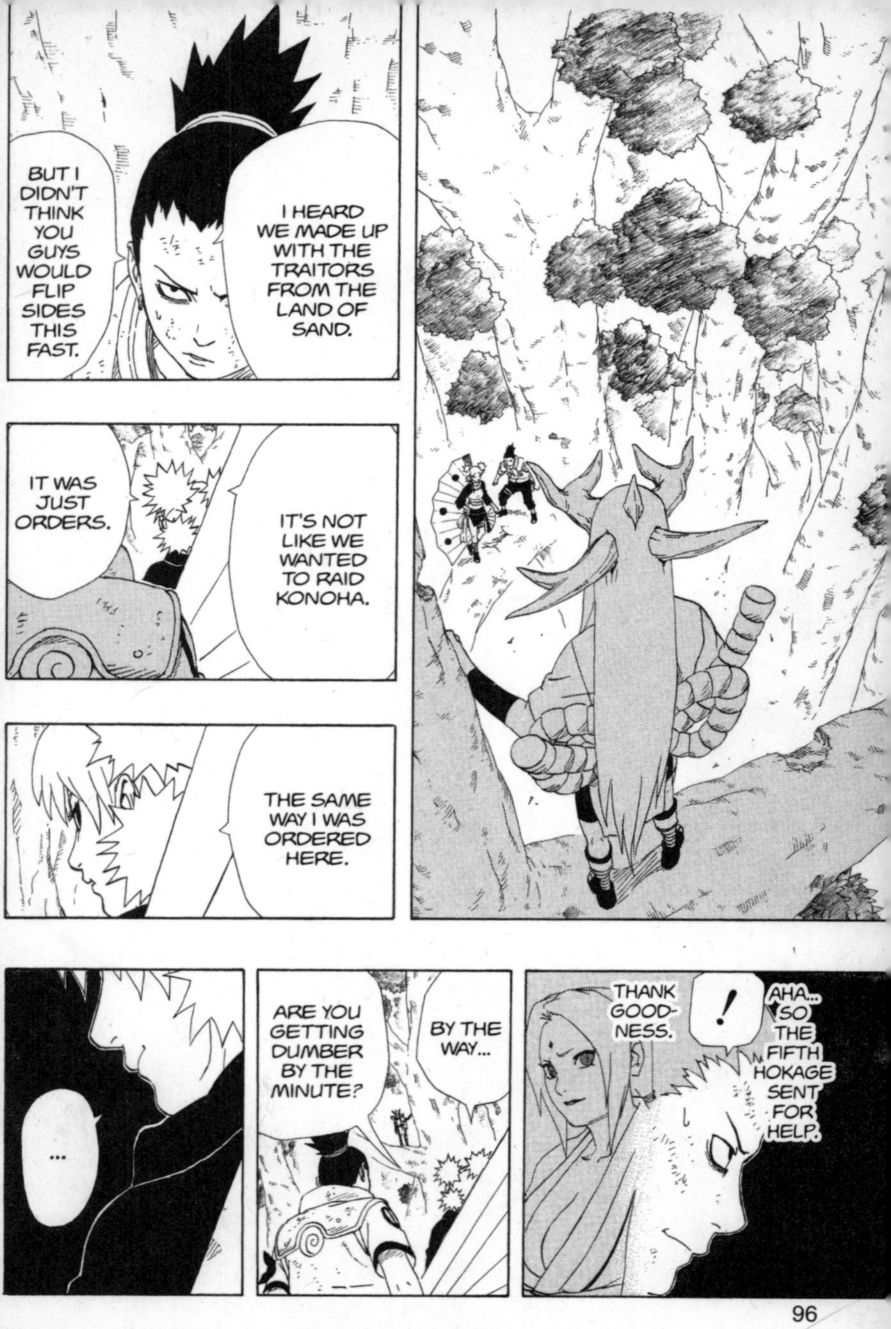
I HEARD WE MADE UP WITH THE TRAITORS FROM THE LAND OF SAND.
BUT I DIDN'T THINK YOU GUYS WOULD FLIP SIDES THIS FAST.
IT'S NOT LIKE WE WANTED TO RAID KONOHA.
IT WAS JUST ORDERS.
THE SAME WAY I WAS ORDERED HERE.
AHA... SO THE FIFTH HOKAGE SENT FOR HELP.
!
THANK GOOD-NESS.
BY THE WAY...
ARE YOU GETTING DUMBER BY THE MINUTE?
...

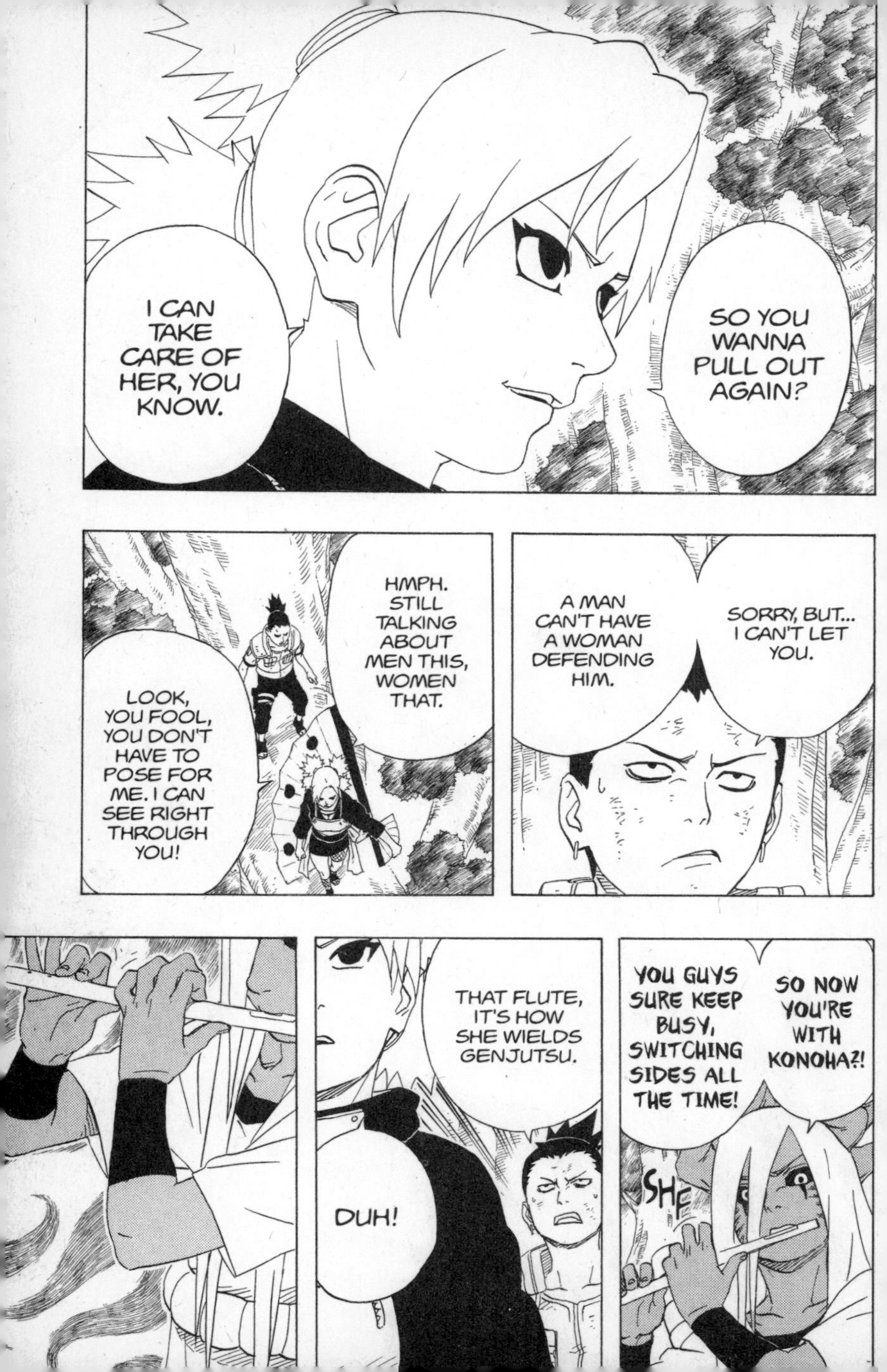
SO YOU WANNA PULL OUT AGAIN?
I CAN TAKE CARE OF HER, YOU KNOW.
SORRY, BUT... I CAN'T LET YOU.
A MAN CAN'T HAVE A WOMAN DEFENDING HIM.
HMPH. STILL TALKING ABOUT MEN THIS, WOMEN THAT.
LOOK, YOU FOOL, YOU DON'T HAVE TO POSE FOR ME. I CAN SEE RIGHT THROUGH YOU!
SO NOW YOU'RE WITH KONOHA?!
YOU GUYS SURE KEEP BUSY, SWITCHING SIDES ALL THE TIME!
SHF
THAT FLUTE, IT'S HOW SHE WIELDS GENJUTSU.
DUH!

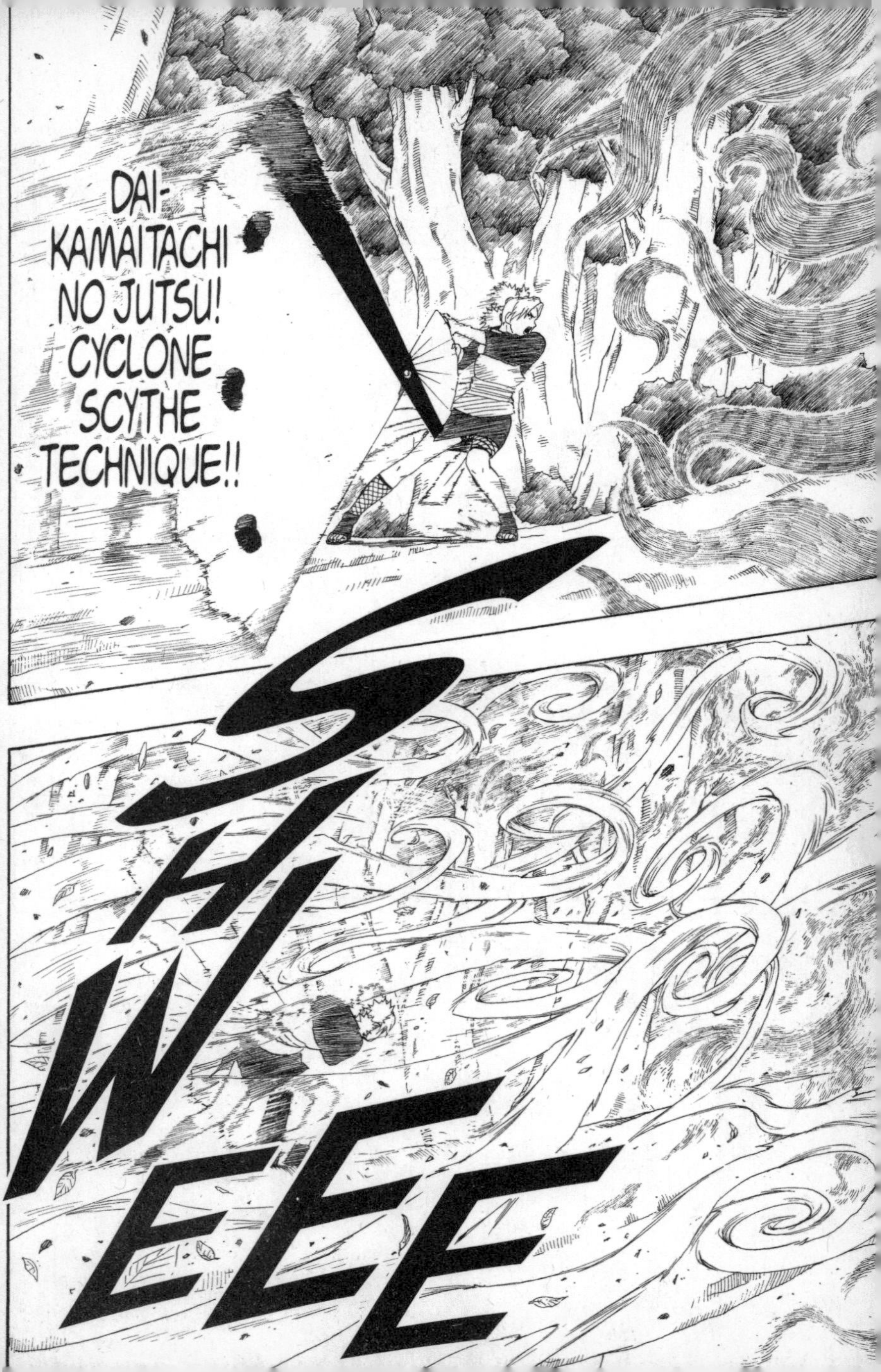
DAI-KAMAITACHI NO JUTSU! CYCLONE SCYTHE TECHNIQUE!!
SHWEEE

READ THIS WAY

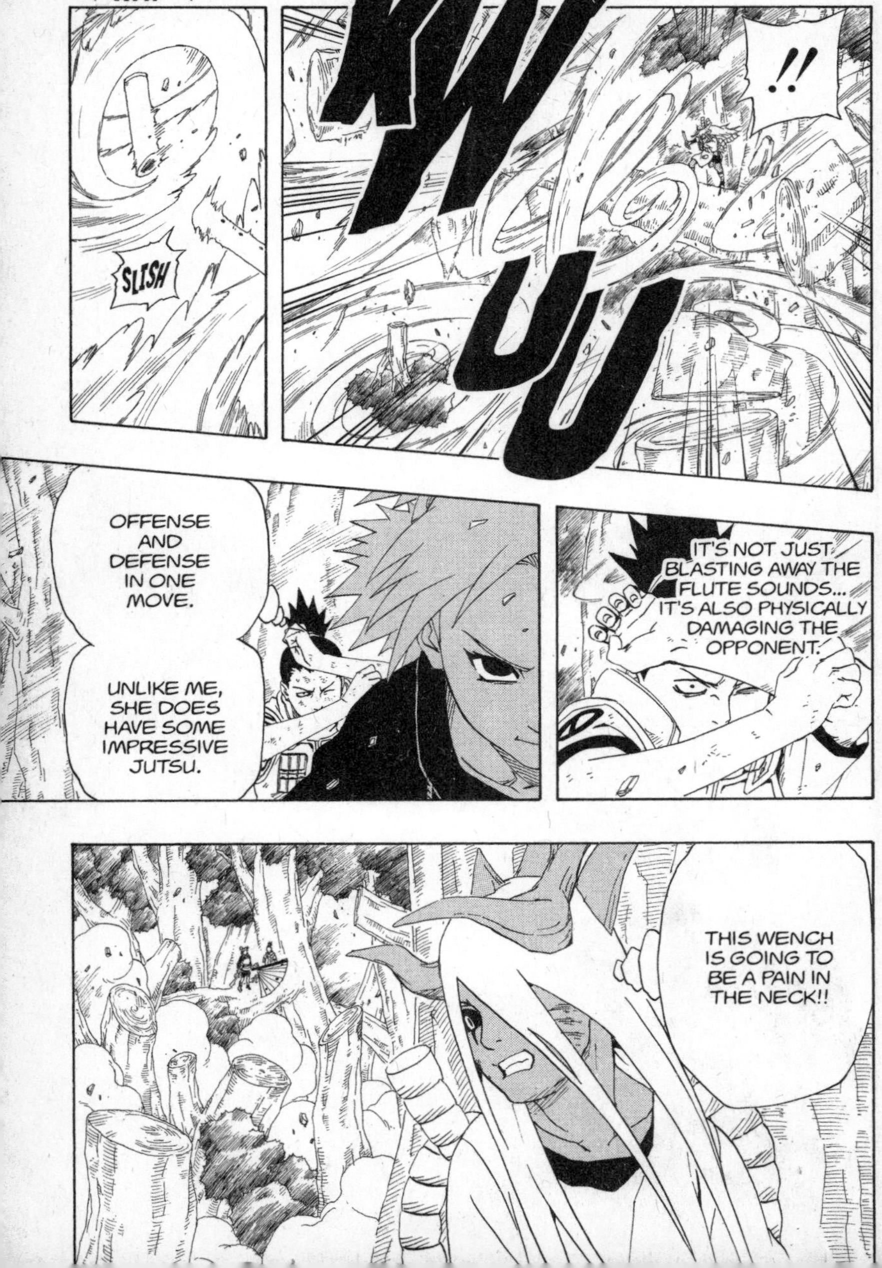
KWUUU
!!
SLISH
IT'S NOT JUST BLASTING AWAY THE FLUTE SOUNDS... IT'S ALSO PHYSICALLY DAMAGING THE OPPONENT.
OFFENSE AND DEFENSE IN ONE MOVE.
UNLIKE ME, SHE DOES HAVE SOME IMPRESSIVE JUTSU.
THIS WENCH IS GOING TO BE A PAIN IN THE NECK!!

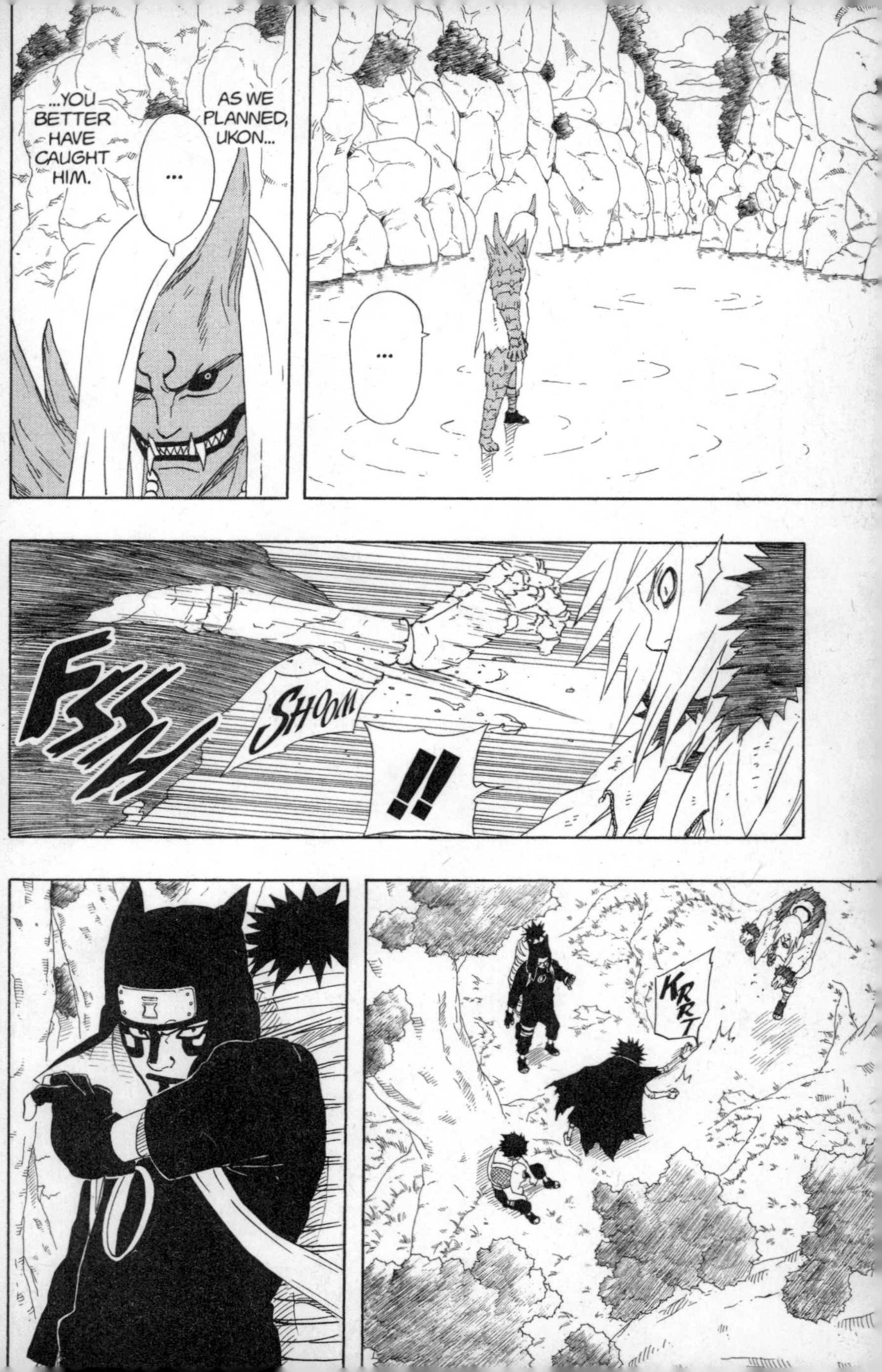
...
AS WE PLANNED, UKON...
...
...YOU BETTER HAVE CAUGHT HIM.
!!
SHOOM
FSSH
KRRT

READ THIS WAY

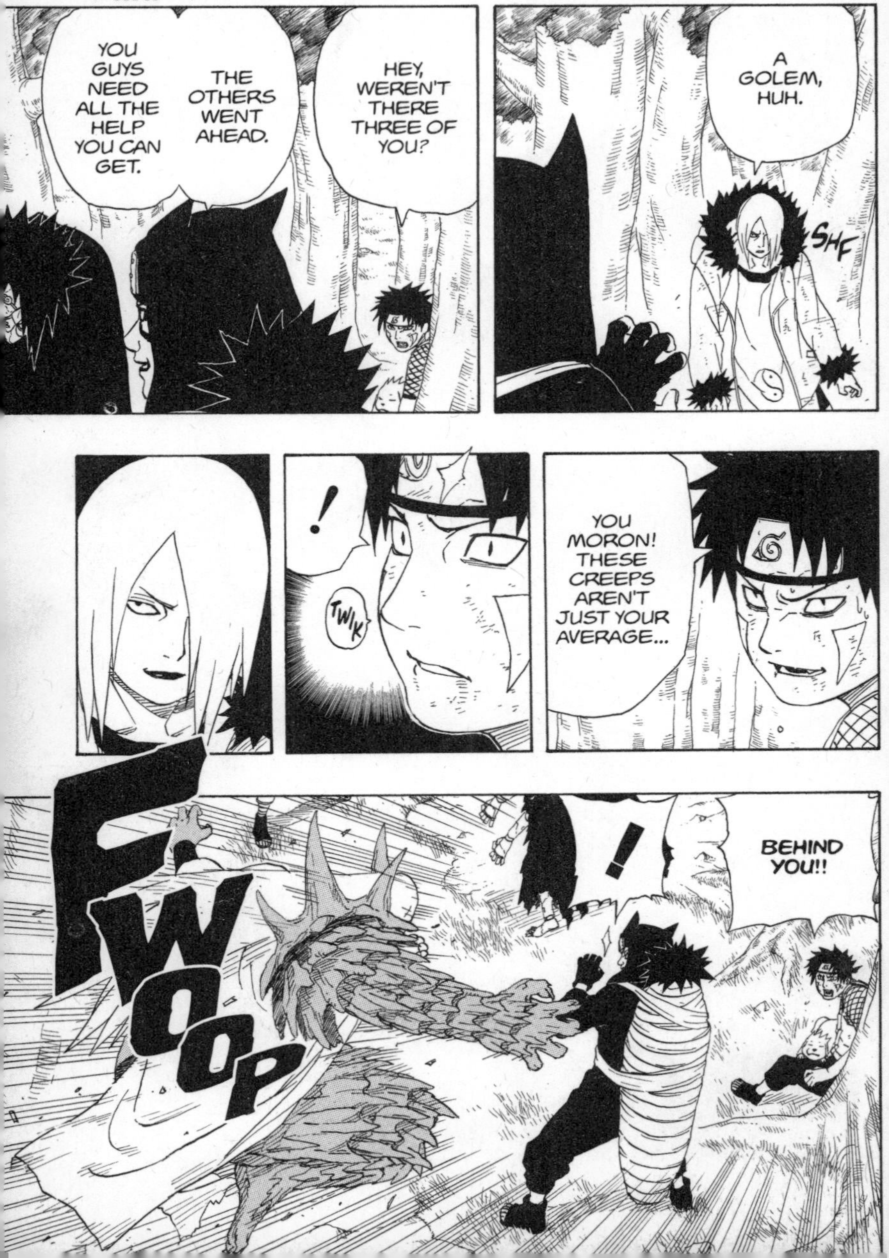

A GOLEM, HUH.
SHF
HEY, WEREN'T THERE THREE OF YOU?
THE OTHERS WENT AHEAD.
YOU GUYS NEED ALL THE HELP YOU CAN GET.
YOU MORON! THESE CREEPS AREN'T JUST YOUR AVERAGE...
!
TWIK
BEHIND YOU!!
!
FWOOP

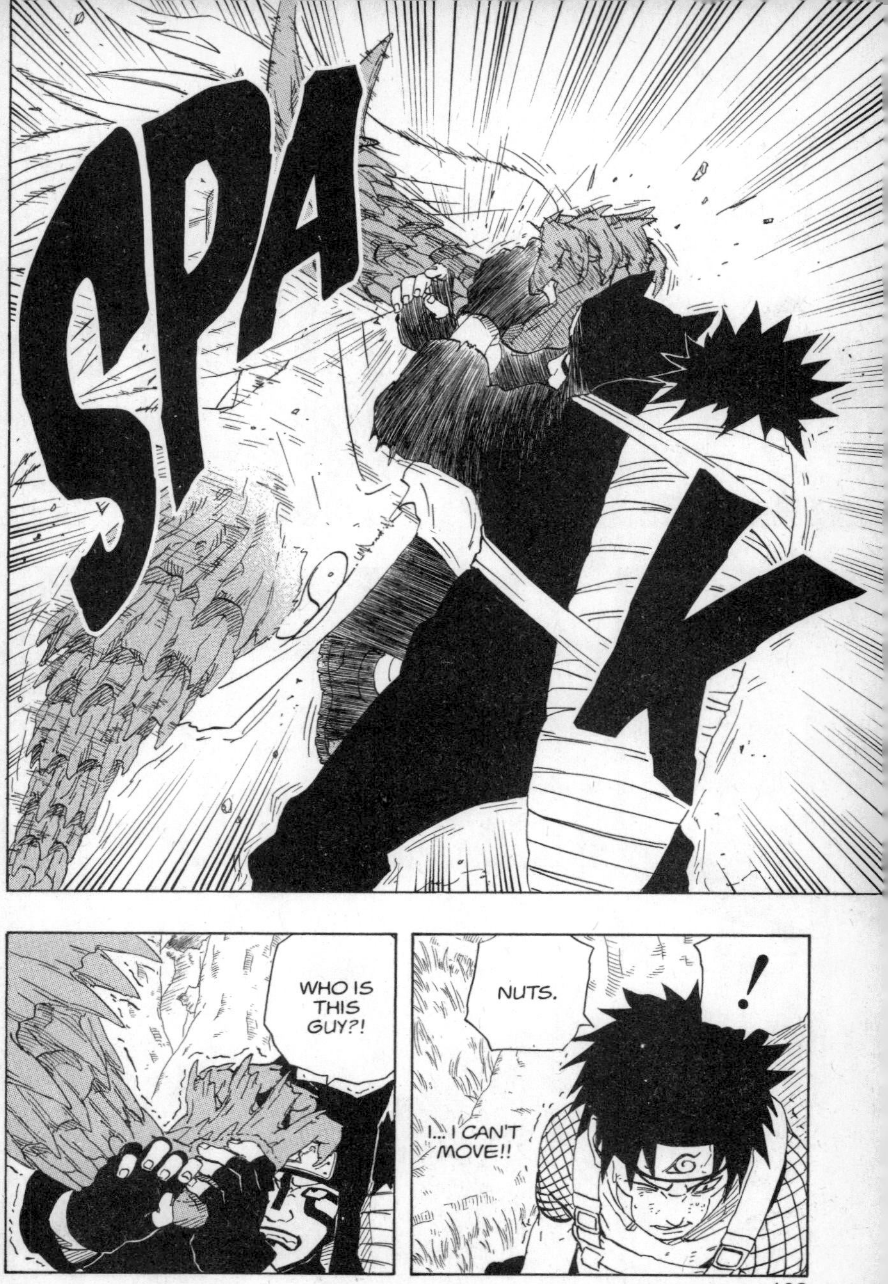
SPAK
NUTS.
!
I... I CAN'T MOVE!!
WHO IS THIS GUY?!

READ THIS WAY

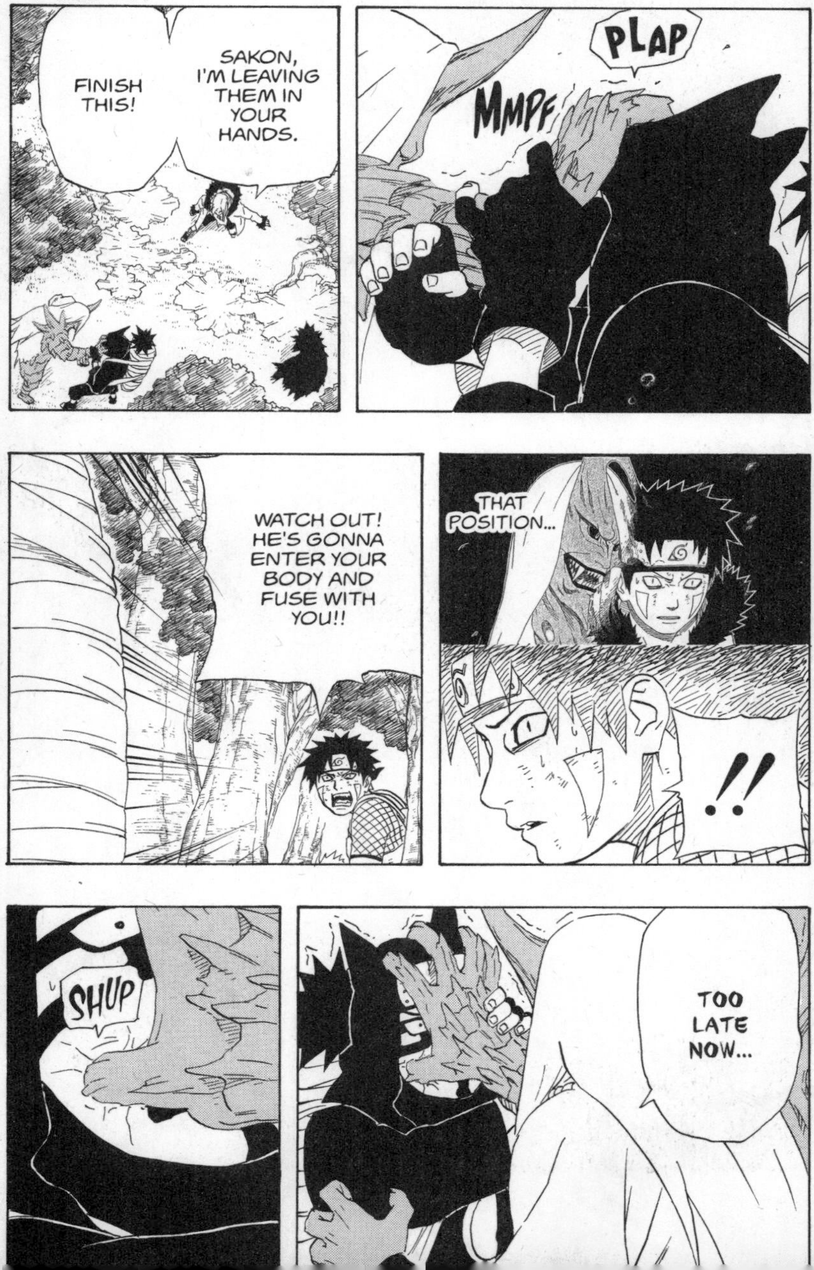
PLAP
MMPF
SAKON, I'M LEAVING THEM IN YOUR HANDS.
FINISH THIS!
THAT POSITION...
!!
WATCH OUT! HE'S GONNA ENTER YOUR BODY AND FUSE WITH YOU!!
TOO LATE NOW...
SHUP

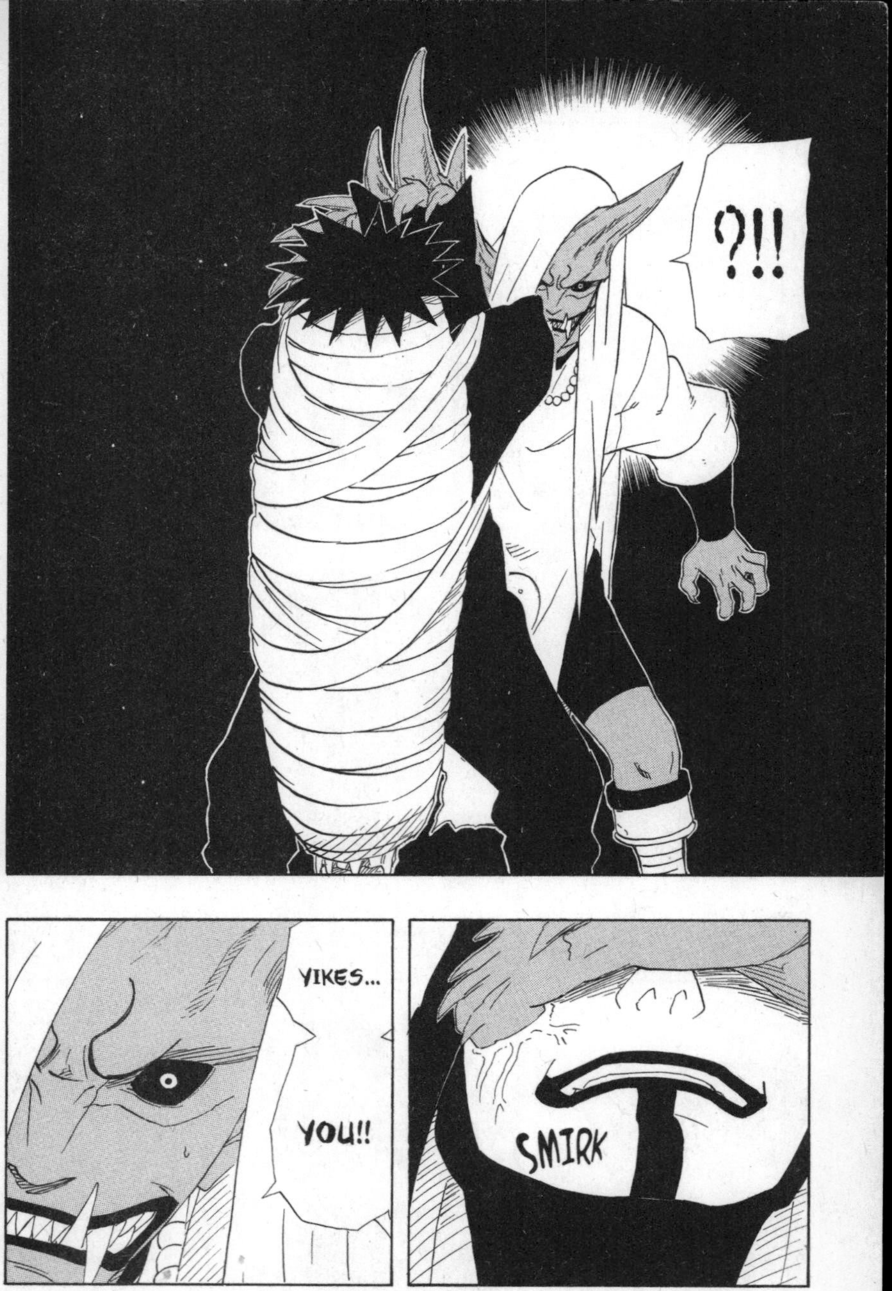
?!!
SMIRK
YIKES...
YOU!!

READ THIS WAY

?!
TAK
SAKON?! WHAT IS IT?!
PLIK
PLIK
SSSSS
SHUFF
SHUFF
SHUFF
?!
?!
?!!

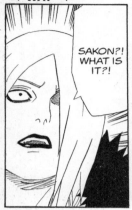

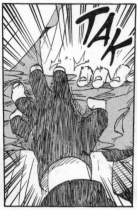

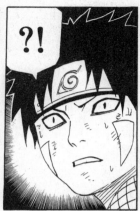

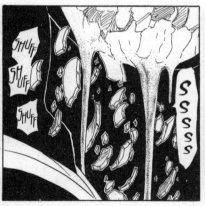

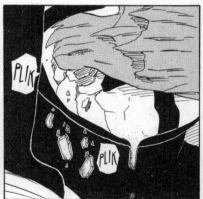

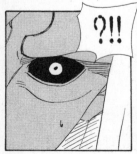

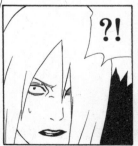

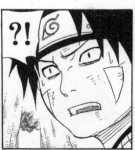

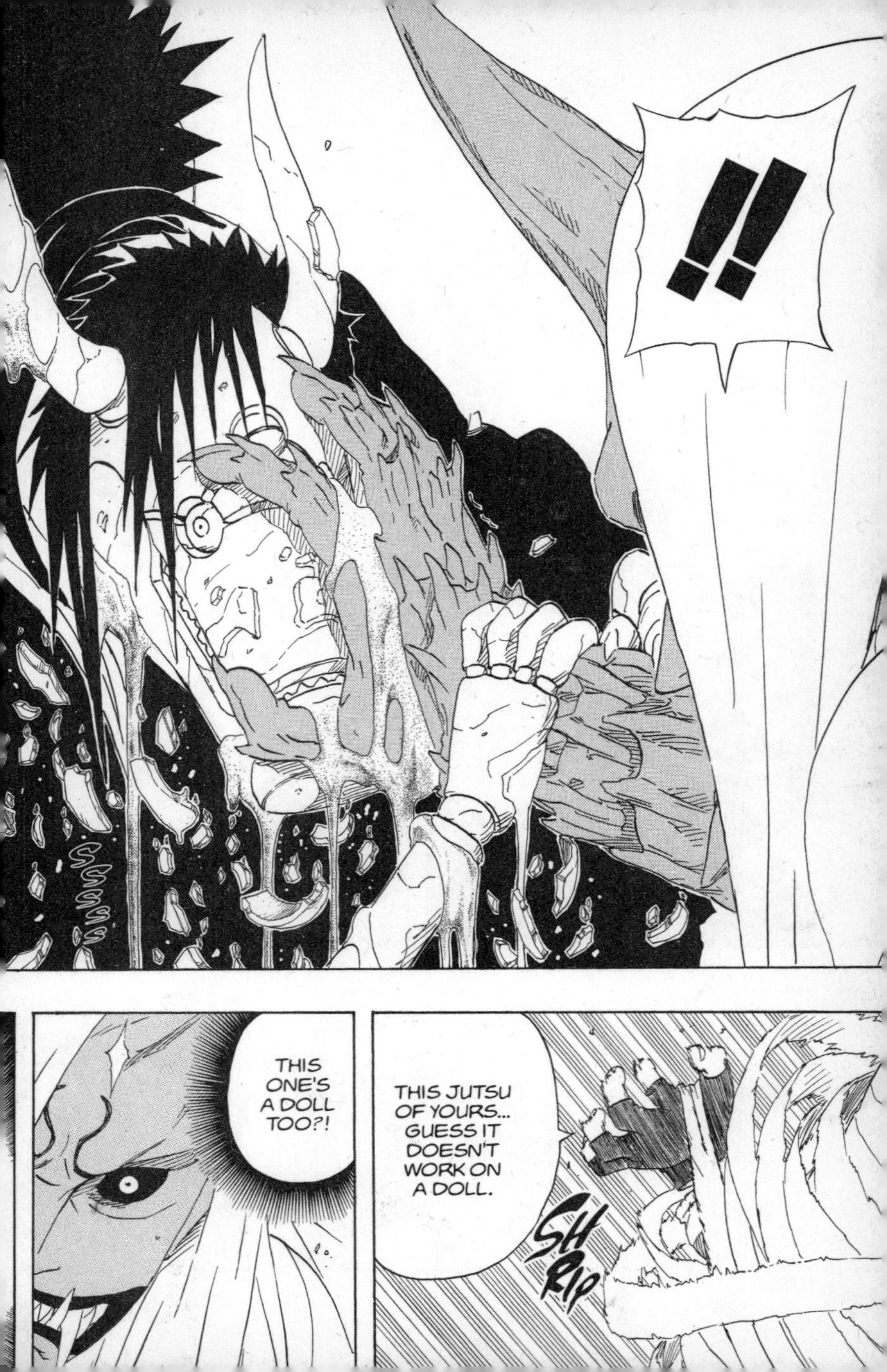
!!
THIS JUTSU OF YOURS... GUESS IT DOESN'T WORK ON A DOLL.
SHRIP
THIS ONE'S A DOLL TOO?!

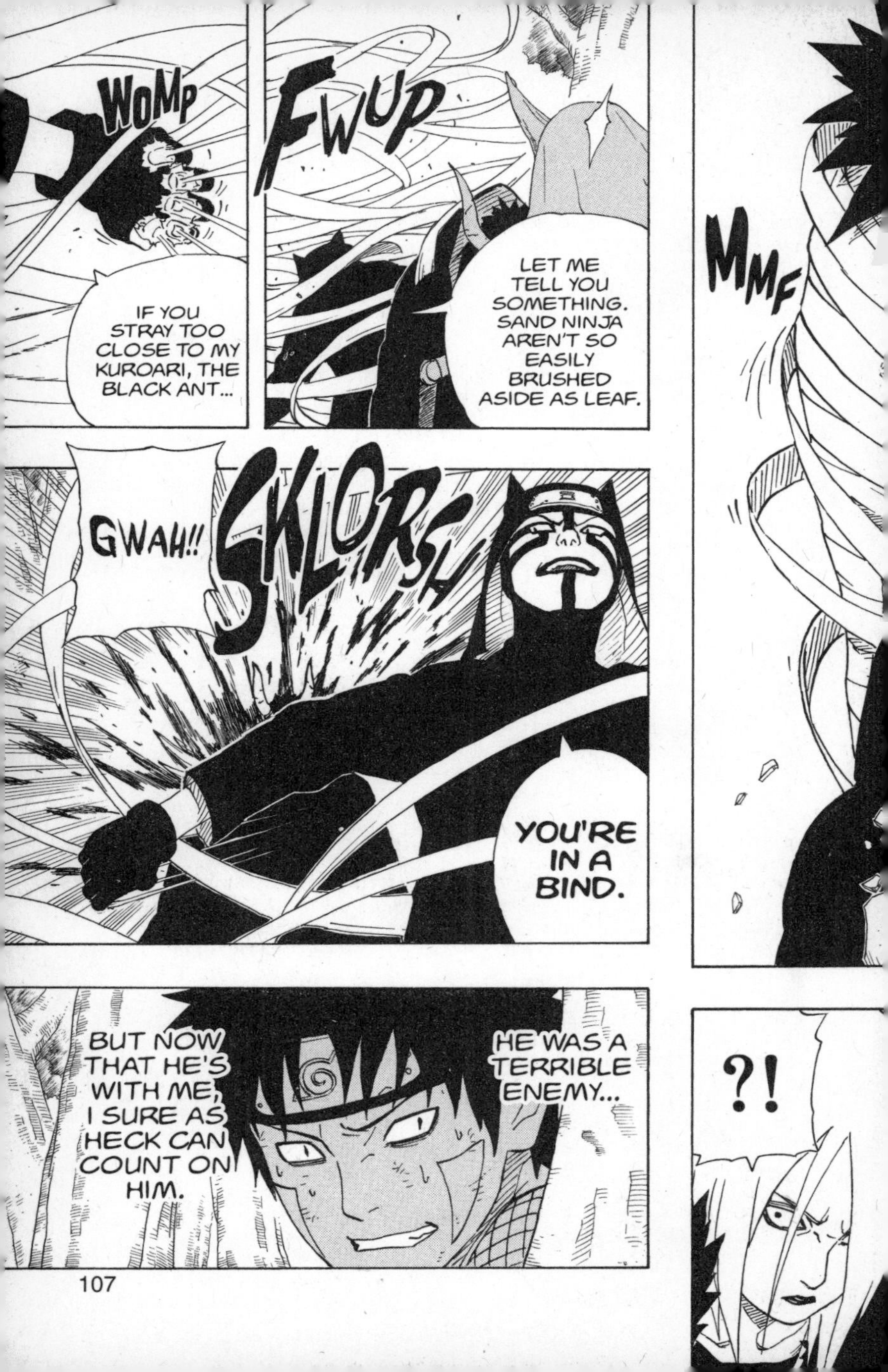
MMF
FWUP
LET ME TELL YOU SOMETHING. SAND NINJA AREN'T SO EASILY BRUSHED ASIDE AS LEAF.
WOMP
IF YOU STRAY TOO CLOSE TO MY KUROARI, THE BLACK ANT...
SKLORSH
GWAH!!
YOU'RE IN A BIND.
HE WAS A TERRIBLE ENEMY...
BUT NOW THAT HE'S WITH ME, I SURE AS HECK CAN COUNT ON HIM.
?!

THE WORLD OF KISHIMOTO MASASHI
PERSONAL HISTORY:
THE TOO-EMBARRASSING-TO-WRITE-ABOUT STORY, PART 3

THE MORE I ADD TO THIS PERSONAL HISTORY, THE MORE MISERY I RELIVE FROM MY EMBARRASSING PAST. I ASK MYSELF WHETHER I ONLY DREDGE UP ALL THESE STUPID MEMORIES OUT OF A COMPULSION TO FILL IN THE PAGES BETWEEN CHAPTERS. YET STILL I PERSIST. WELL, AT LEAST YOU CAN NEVER SAY I HELD BACK ON YOU AS AN ENTERTAINER.

THE THINGS I'M ABOUT TO DISCLOSE MAY GET A LITTLE INTENSE FOR SOME READERS. STILL, HERE WE GO.

THIS INCIDENT IS WEDGED IN MY BRAIN... IT WAS BACK IN KINDERGARTEN, THE DAY OF THE "POTATO DIGGING TOURNA-MENT." THAT AUTUMN, THAT DAY, IN THE MIDST OF HARVESTING SEASON, JUST FOR THAT EVENT, OUR SCHOOL INVITED OUR FAMILIES TO JOIN US. KIDS, PARENTS, TEACHERS, ALL OF US GOT TOGETHER TO HARVEST THE SWEET POTATOES WE'D PLANTED AT A NEARBY FARM. IN THE COUNTRYSIDE, YOU SEE, KINDERGARTENS HOLD THESE HEARTWARMING COMMUNITY FUNCTIONS, INTENDED TO BRING KIDS, PARENTS, AND TEACHERS CLOSER TOGETHER.

I WAS DIGGING AWAY IN HIGH SPIRITS, TELLING MYSELF "I'LL FIND THE BIGGEST POTATO OF ALL, AND SURPRISE EVERY-BODY!" AND THEN THERE IT WAS, A MONOLITH AMONGST POTATOES. IN MY DELIGHT, I STARTED DIGGING LIKE A STARVING MAN. MIND YOU, FOR ALL MY HASTE I WAS CAREFUL NOT TO BREAK THE ROOT. AND THEN THERE I WAS, CLUTCHING A GIANT POTATO.

IN UNISON, EVERYBODY SCREAMED: "WOW!!" AND "THAT'S HUGE!" AND SO ON. I WAS IN ANOTHER WORLD. SO THEN... I DON'T KNOW WHY I DID THIS, BUT I STARTED RUNNING AND ROLLING AROUND THE FIELD, GRASPING MY PRECIOUS POTATO. THEN THE THOUGHT HIT ME: "I GOTTA SHOW MOM THIS POTATO!" SO I GLANCED AROUND FOR HER AND REAL-IZED SHE WASN'T THERE. SHE WAS ACTUALLY DOWN AT MY TWIN BROTHER'S PLOT. SEE, THE FARM WAS TERRACED, AND HIS PLOT WAS IN A FIELD BELOW. SO I PELTED STRAIGHT TOWARD HER, SPRINTING FROM FIELD TO FIELD, HOPPING DOWN THE TERRACES AND EVERYTHING.

AND THAT'S WHEN IT HAPPENED. I WAS IN SUCH A HURRY I WASN'T LOOKING, BUT IN THE LOWER FIELD, IN THE FIVE SQUARE METER AREA WHERE I WAS DUE TO LAND, WAS A HEAPING PILE OF A TYPICAL RURAL ARTIFACT...

AS YOU MAY HAVE SURMISED, IT WAS, YES, A MOUNTAIN OF
COW MANURE!

-- TO BE CONTINUED --

Number 214: Retreat...!!

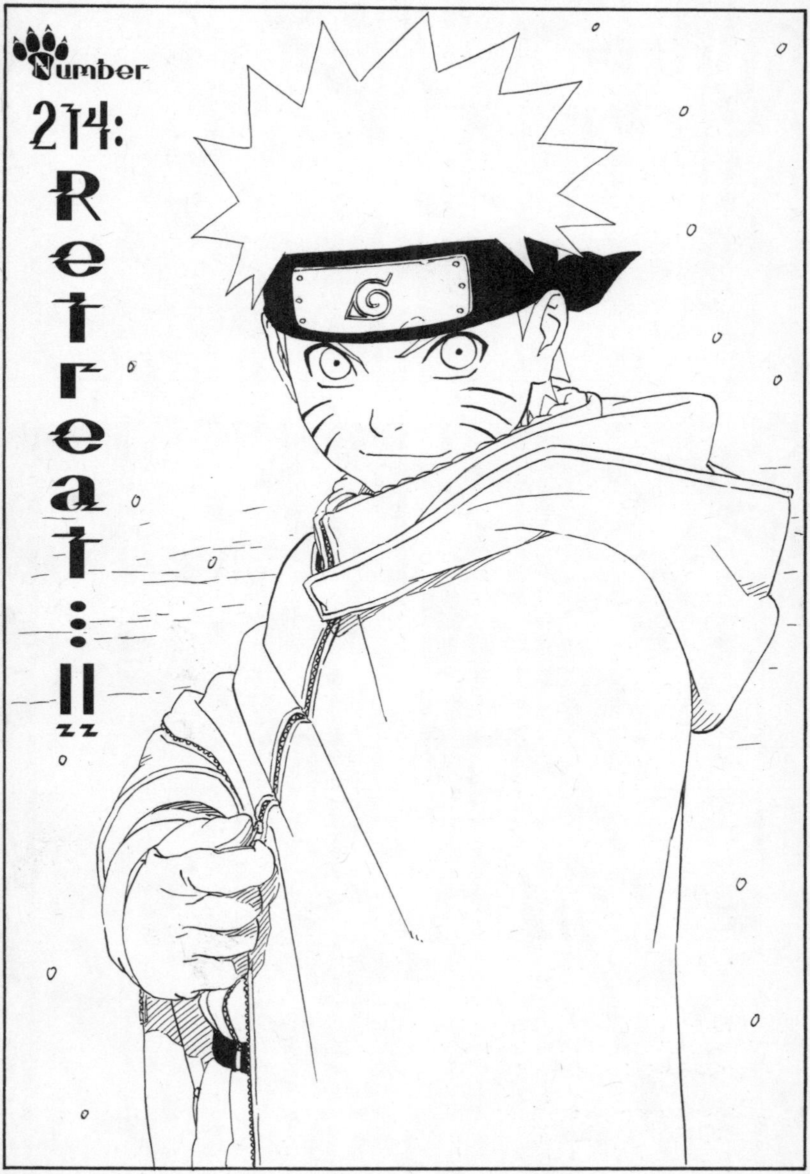

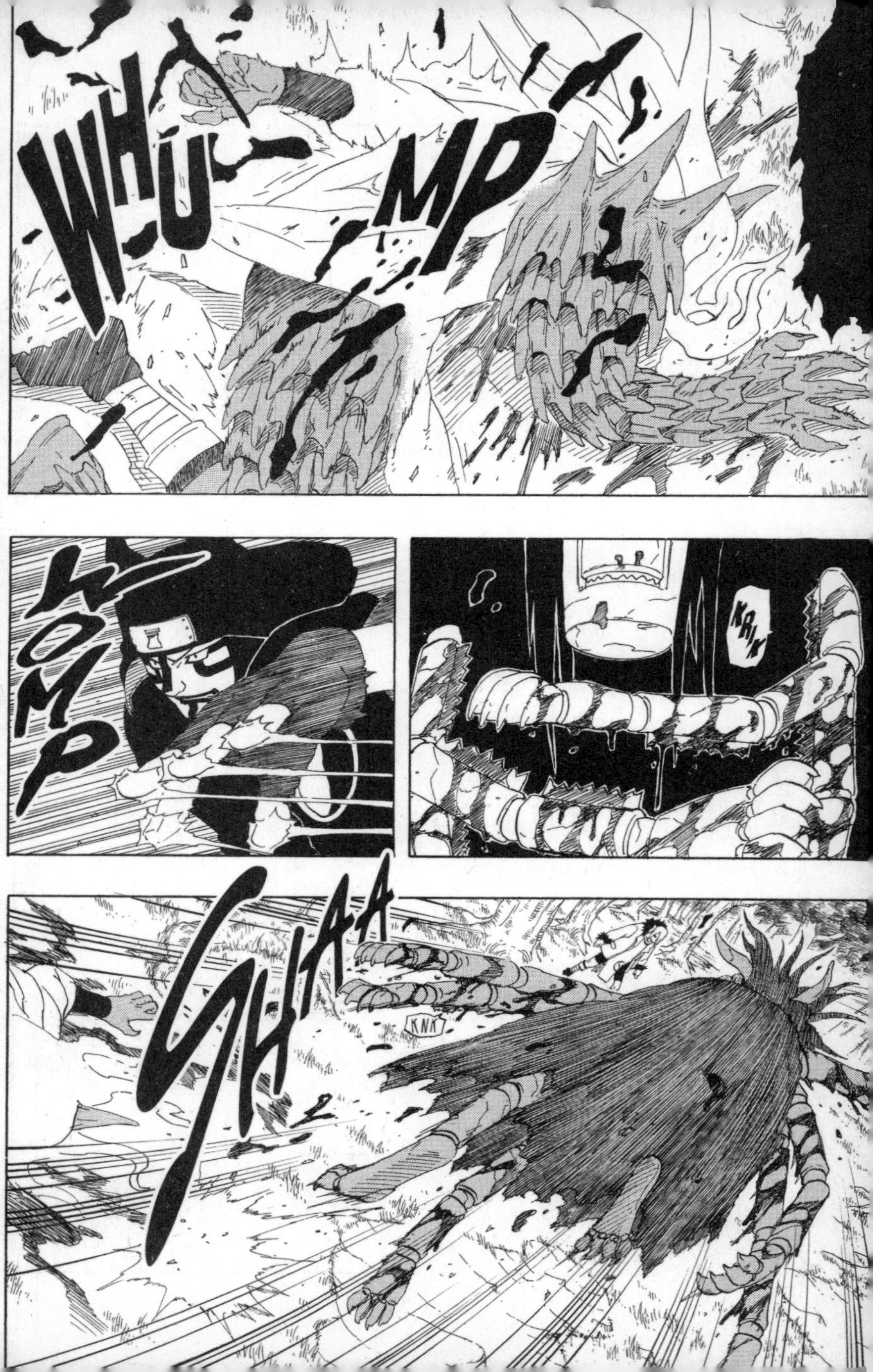
WHUMP
KRIK
WOMP
SHAA
KNK

READ THIS WAY

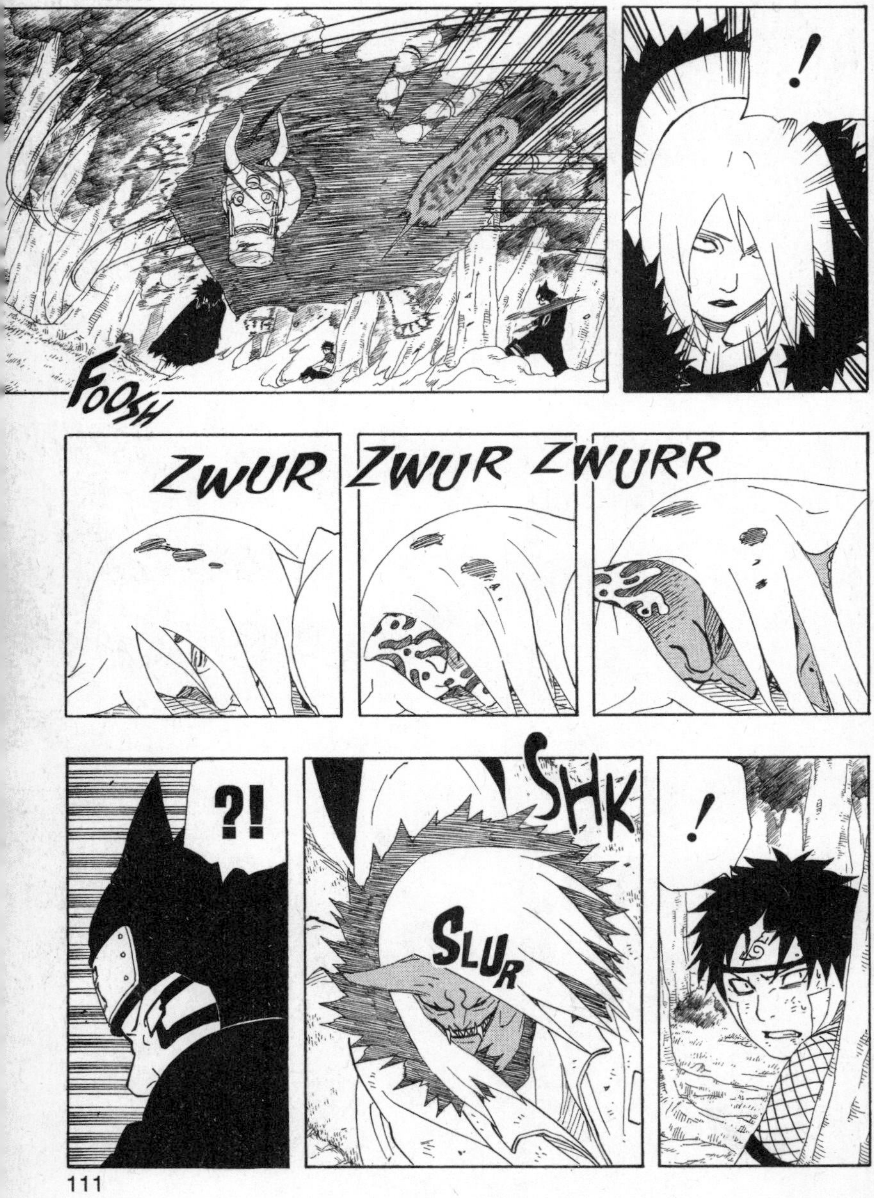

!
FOOSH
ZWURR
ZWUR
ZWUR
!
SHK
SLUR
?!

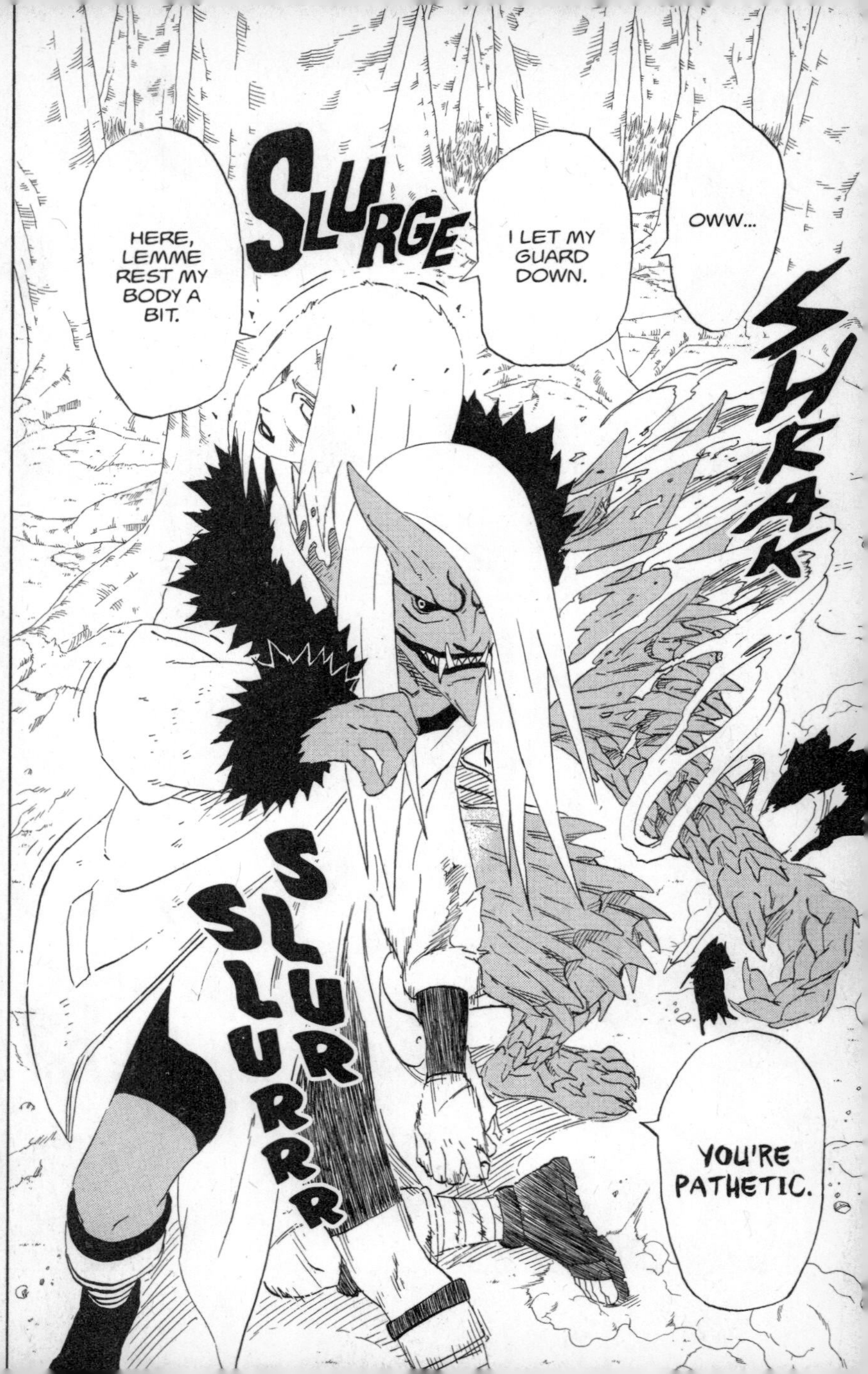
OWW...
I LET MY GUARD DOWN.
SLURGE
HERE, LEMME REST MY BODY A BIT.
SHRAK
SLURR
SLURRR
YOU'RE PATHETIC.

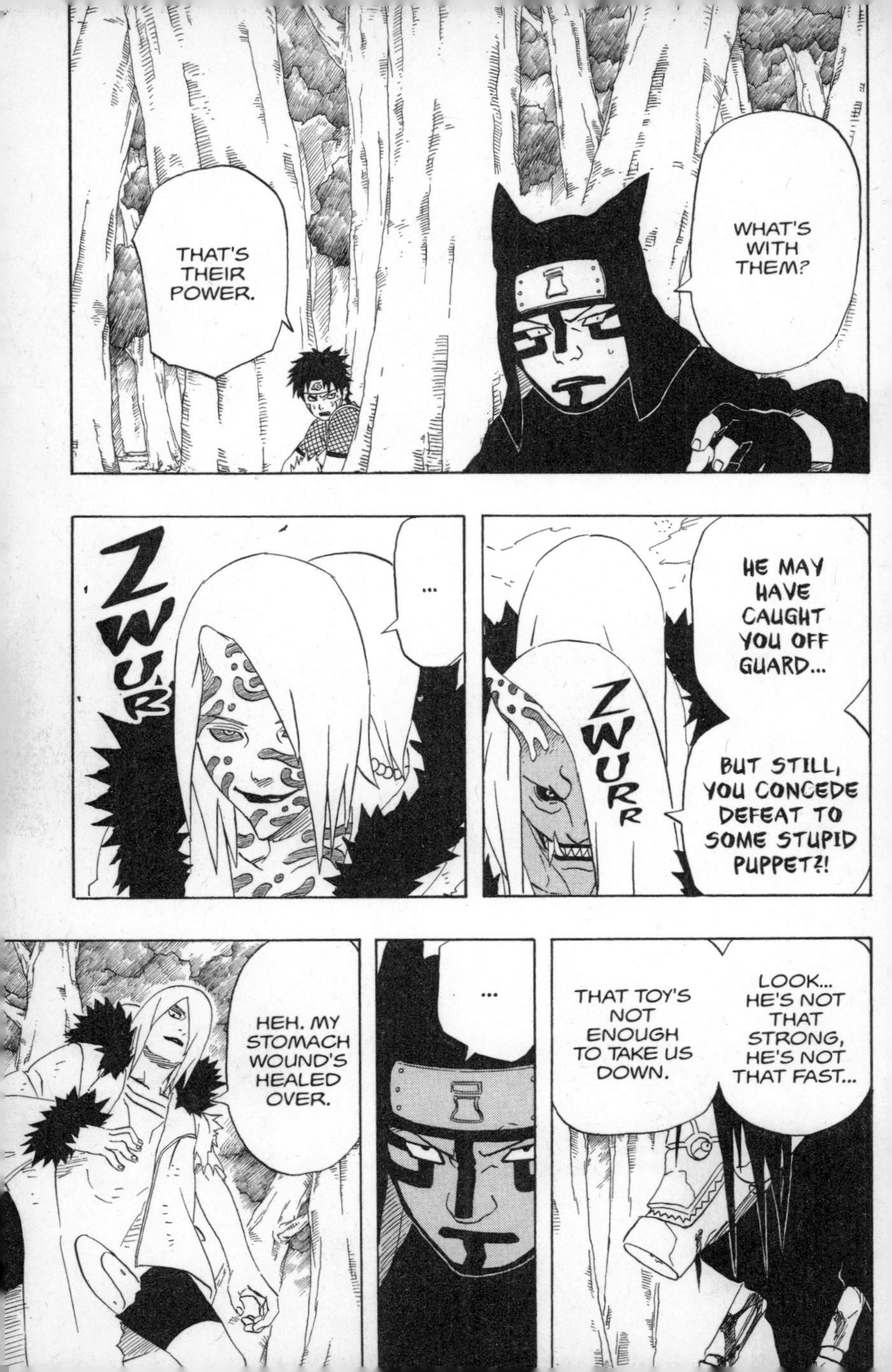
WHAT'S WITH THEM?
THAT'S THEIR POWER.
HE MAY HAVE CAUGHT YOU OFF GUARD...
BUT STILL, YOU CONCEDE DEFEAT TO SOME STUPID PUPPET?!
ZWURR
...
ZWURR
LOOK... HE'S NOT THAT STRONG, HE'S NOT THAT FAST...
THAT TOY'S NOT ENOUGH TO TAKE US DOWN.
...
HEH. MY STOMACH WOUND'S HEALED OVER.

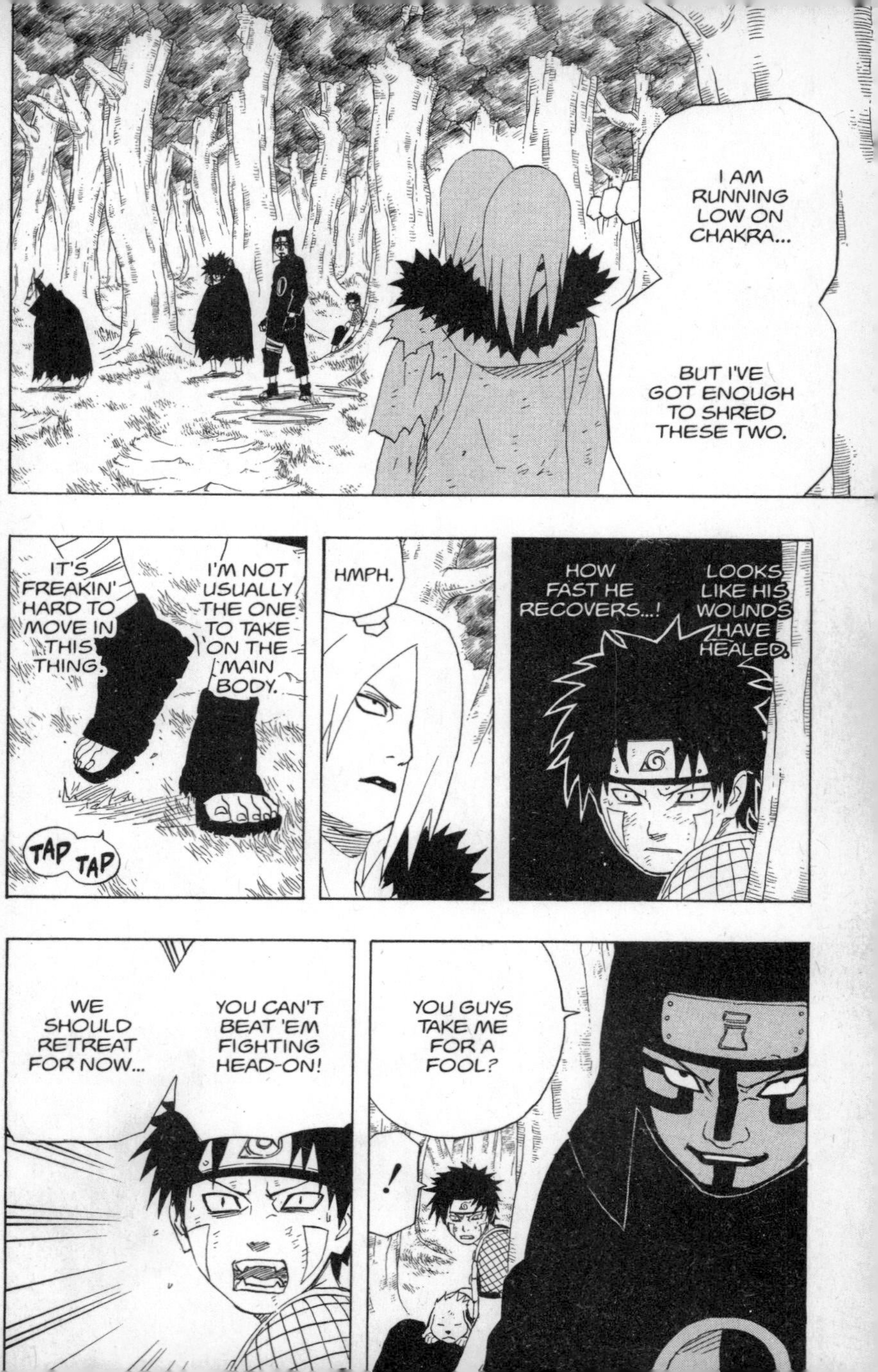
I AM RUNNING LOW ON CHAKRA...
BUT I'VE GOT ENOUGH TO SHRED THESE TWO.
LOOKS LIKE HIS WOUNDS HAVE HEALED.
HOW FAST HE RECOVERS...!
HMPH.
I'M NOT USUALLY THE ONE TO TAKE ON THE MAIN BODY.
IT'S FREAKIN' HARD TO MOVE IN THIS THING.
TAP TAP
YOU GUYS TAKE ME FOR A FOOL?
!
YOU CAN'T BEAT 'EM FIGHTING HEAD-ON!
WE SHOULD RETREAT FOR NOW...

« READ THIS WAY «

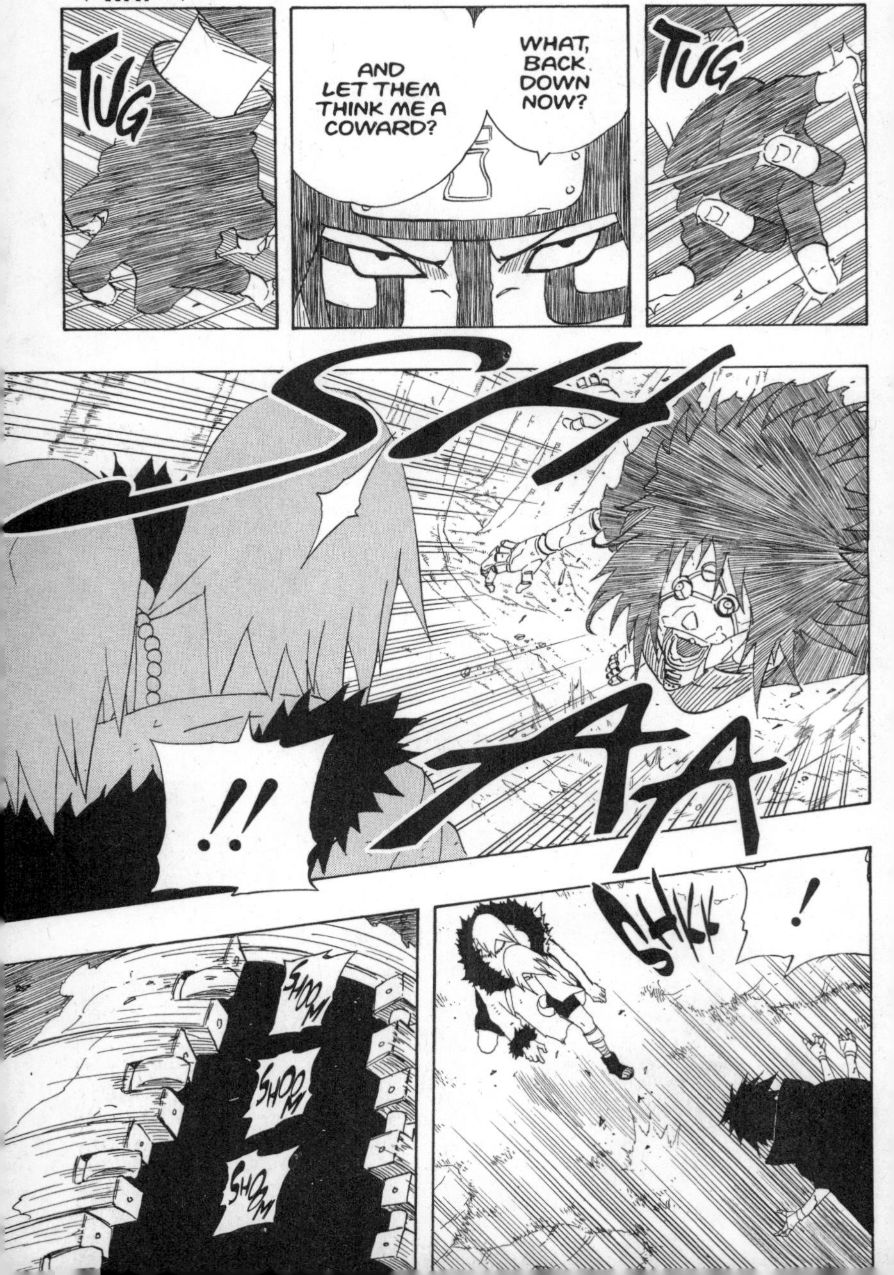
TUG
WHAT, BACK DOWN NOW?
AND LET THEM THINK ME A COWARD?
TUG
SHAA
!!
!
SHKK
SHOOM
SHOOM
SHOOM

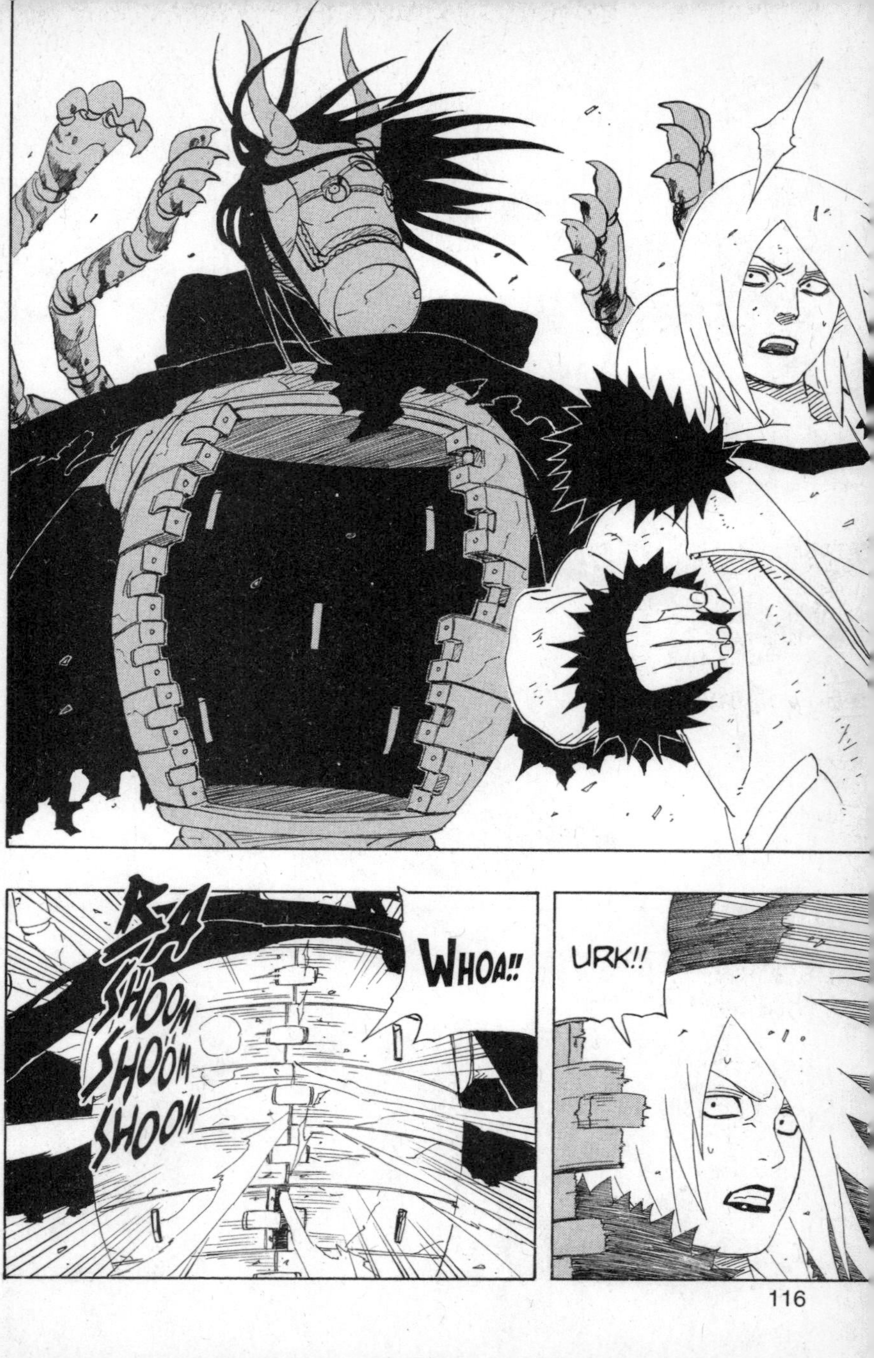
URK!!
WHOA!!
BA SHOOM SHOOM SHOOM

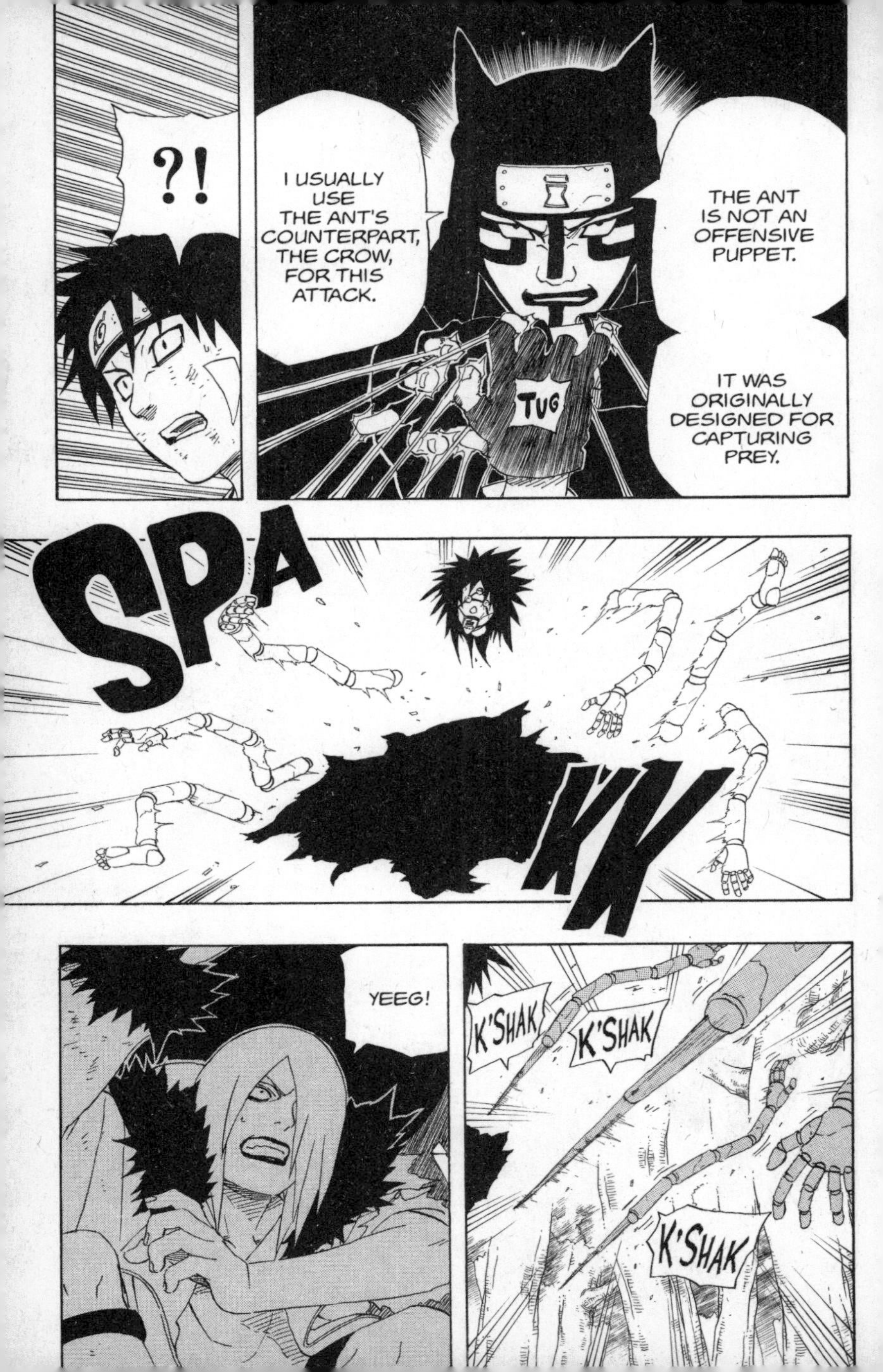
THE ANT IS NOT AN OFFENSIVE PUPPET.
IT WAS ORIGINALLY DESIGNED FOR CAPTURING PREY.
I USUALLY USE THE ANT'S COUNTERPART, THE CROW, FOR THIS ATTACK.
TUG
?!
SPAKK
K'SHAK
K'SHAK
K'SHAK
YEEG!

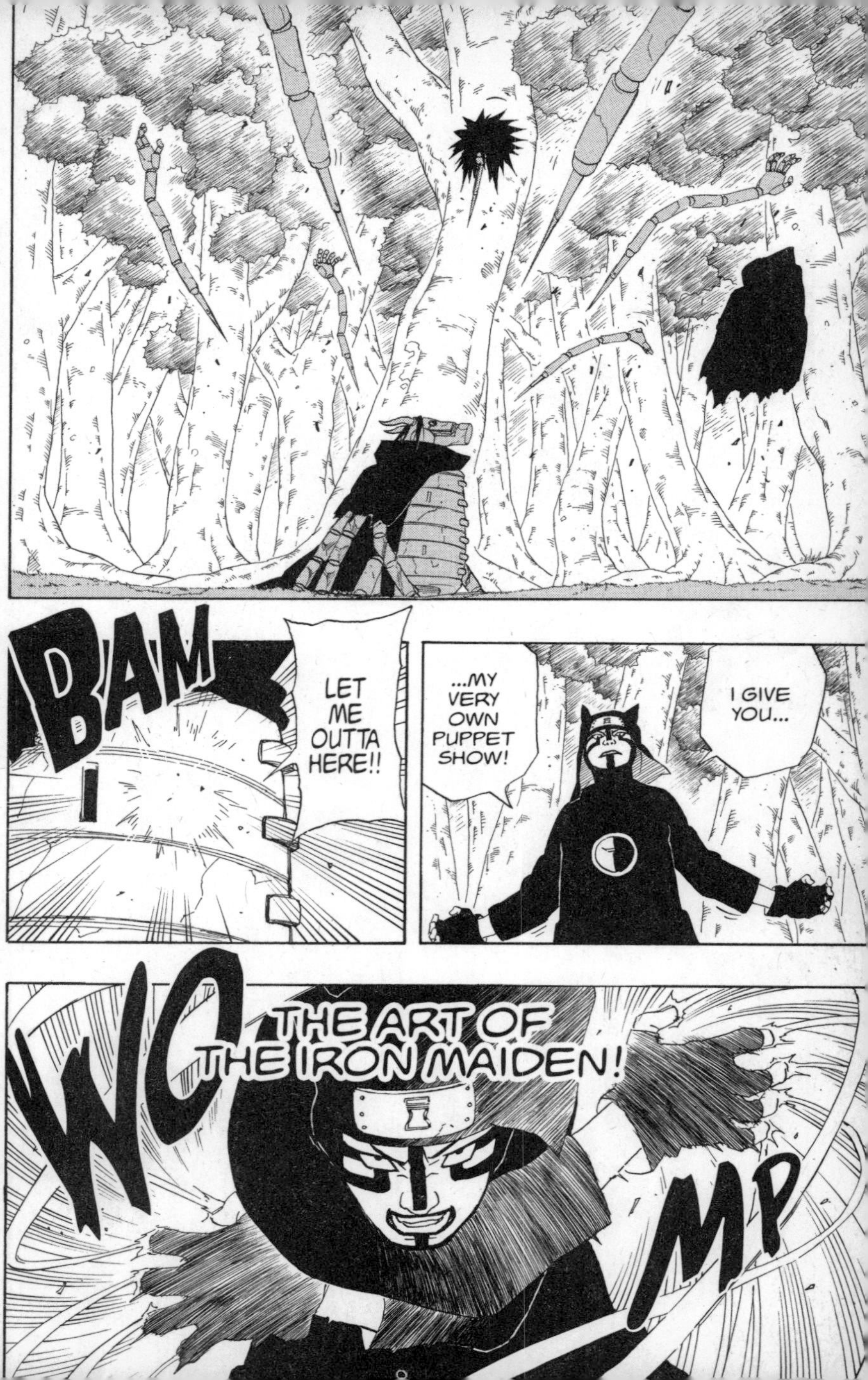
I GIVE YOU...
...MY VERY OWN PUPPET SHOW!
LET ME OUTTA HERE!!
BAM
THE ART OF THE IRON MAIDEN!
WHOMP

READ THIS WAY

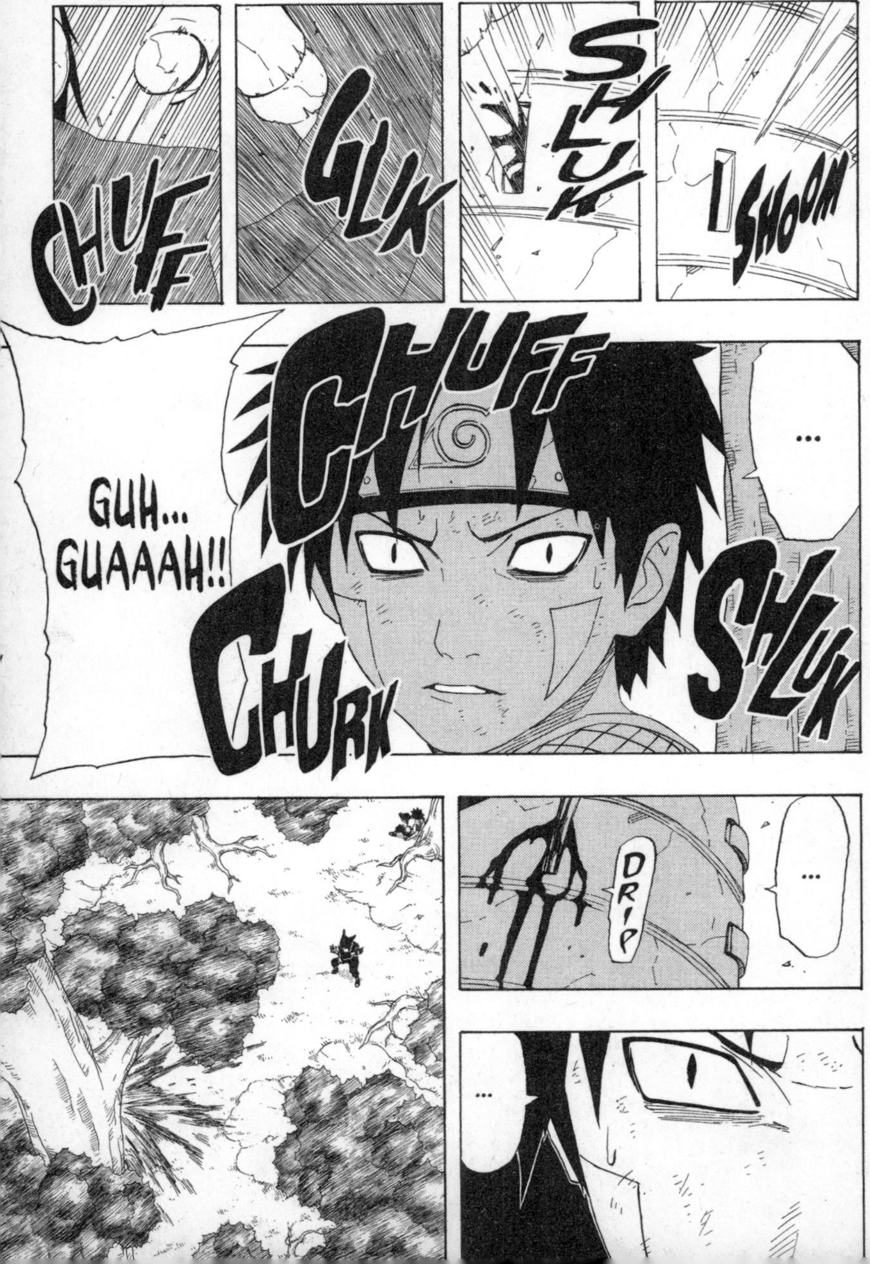
SHOOM
SHLUK
GLUK
CHUFF
...
CHUFF
SHLUK
CHURK
GUH... GUAAAH!!
...
DRIP
...

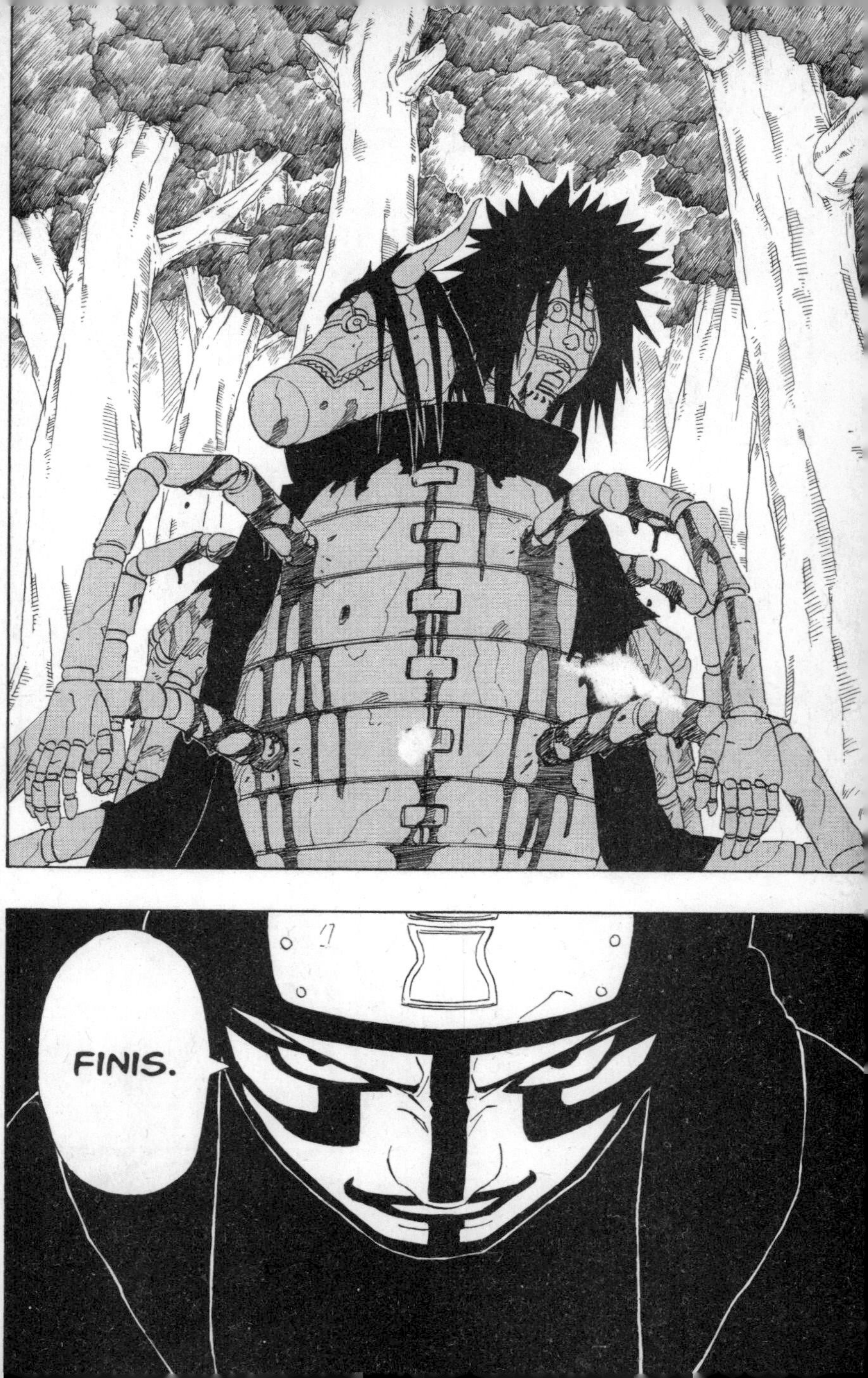
FINIS.

READ THIS WAY

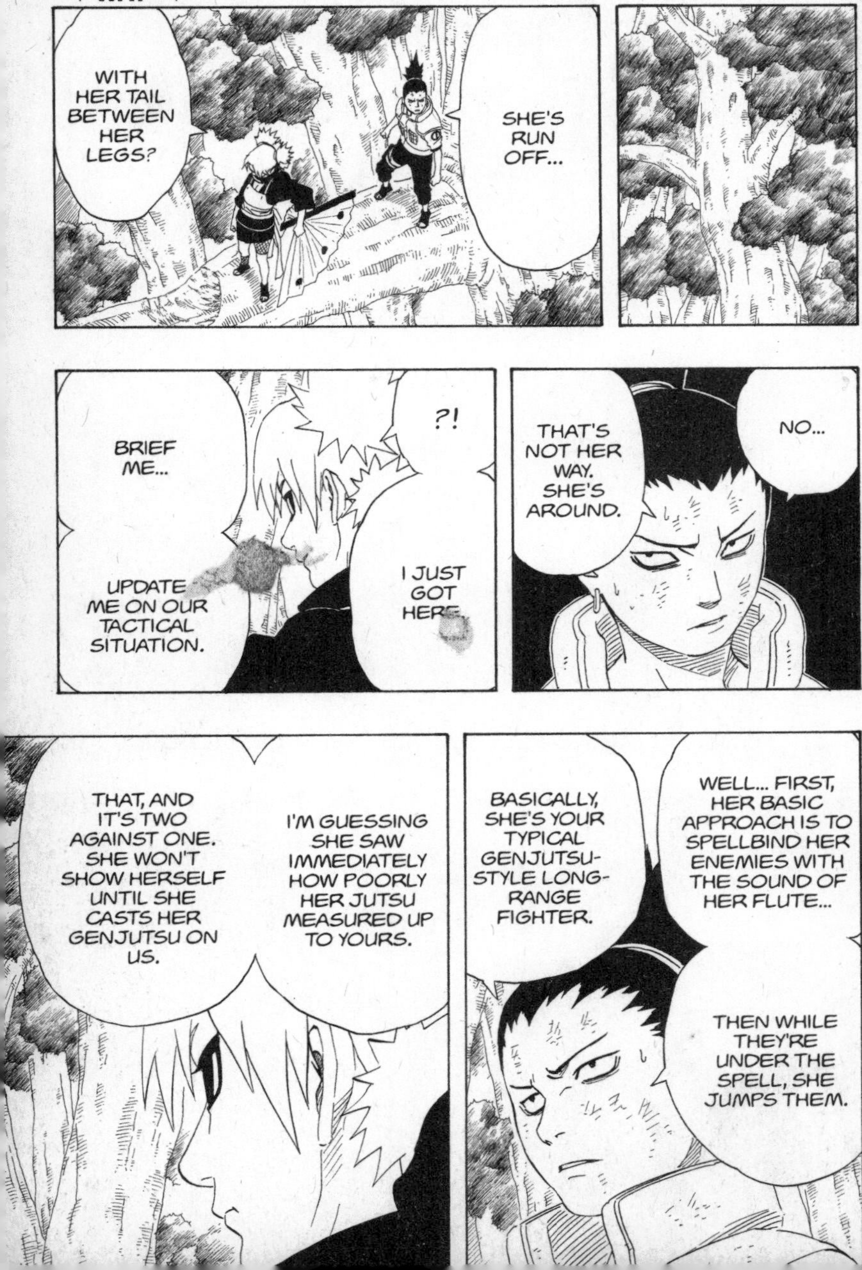
SHE'S RUN OFF...
WITH HER TAIL BETWEEN HER LEGS?
NO...
THAT'S NOT HER WAY. SHE'S AROUND.
?!
I JUST GOT HERE.
BRIEF ME...
UPDATE ME ON OUR TACTICAL SITUATION.
WELL... FIRST, HER BASIC APPROACH IS TO SPELLBIND HER ENEMIES WITH THE SOUND OF HER FLUTE...
THEN WHILE THEY'RE UNDER THE SPELL, SHE JUMPS THEM.
BASICALLY, SHE'S YOUR TYPICAL GENJUTSU-STYLE LONG-RANGE FIGHTER.
I'M GUESSING SHE SAW IMMEDIATELY HOW POORLY HER JUTSU MEASURED UP TO YOURS.
THAT, AND IT'S TWO AGAINST ONE. SHE WON'T SHOW HERSELF UNTIL SHE CASTS HER GENJUTSU ON US.

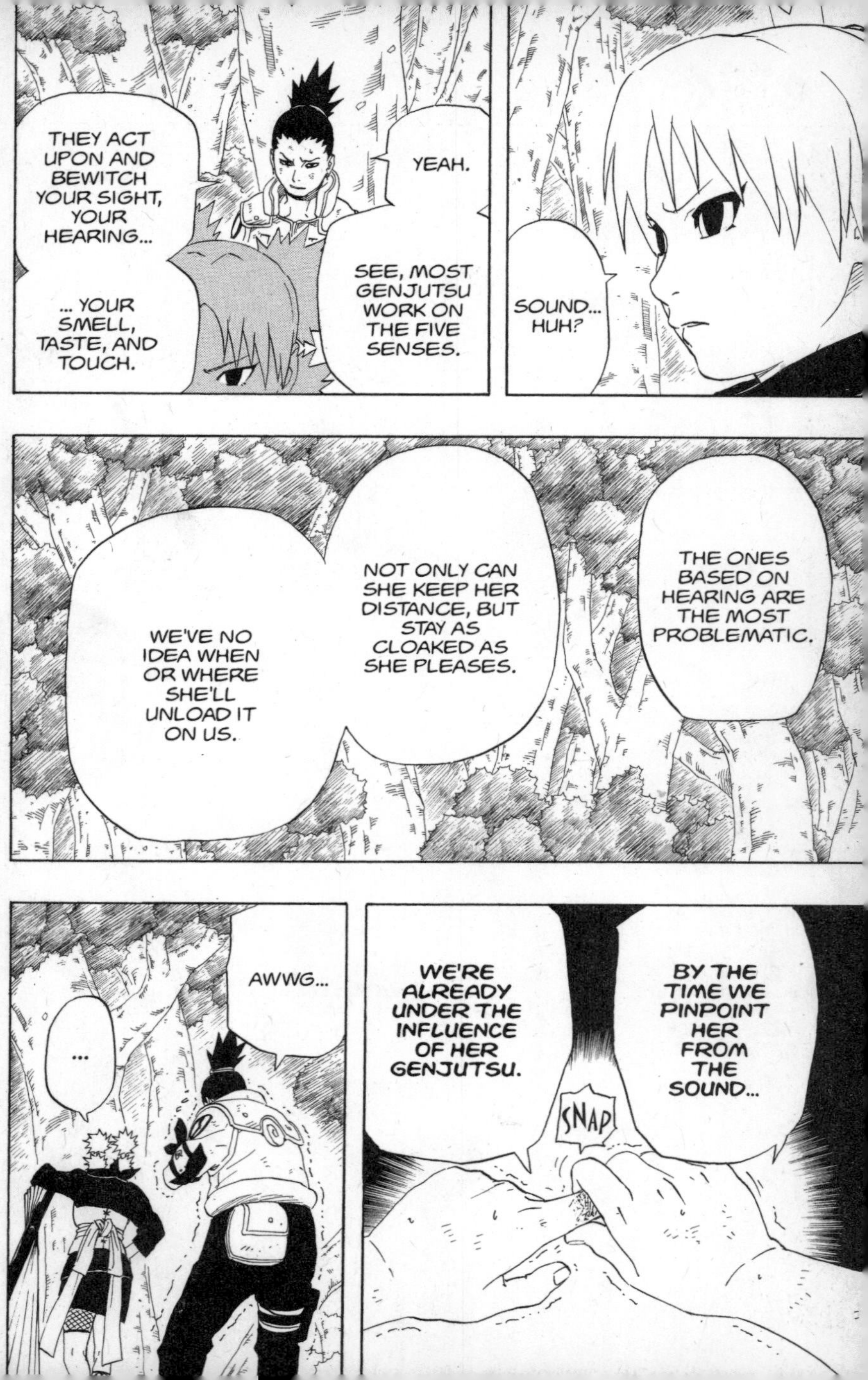
SOUND... HUH?
YEAH.
SEE, MOST GENJUTSU WORK ON THE FIVE SENSES.
THEY ACT UPON AND BEWITCH YOUR SIGHT, YOUR HEARING...
... YOUR SMELL, TASTE, AND TOUCH.
THE ONES BASED ON HEARING ARE THE MOST PROBLEMATIC.
NOT ONLY CAN SHE KEEP HER DISTANCE, BUT STAY AS CLOAKED AS SHE PLEASES.
WE'VE NO IDEA WHEN OR WHERE SHE'LL UNLOAD IT ON US.
BY THE TIME WE PINPOINT HER FROM THE SOUND...
WE'RE ALREADY UNDER THE INFLUENCE OF HER GENJUTSU.
SNAP
AWWG...
...

READ THIS WAY

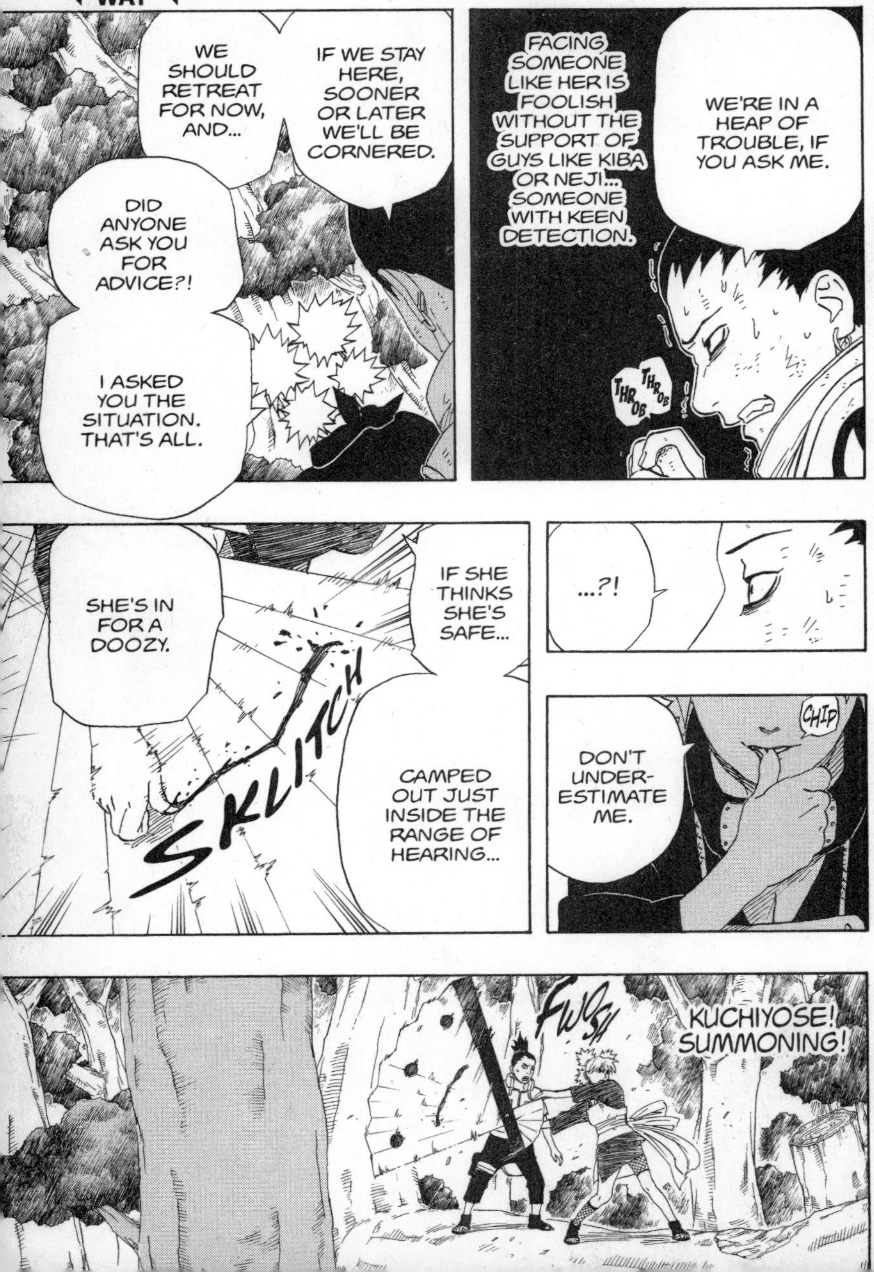
WE'RE IN A HEAP OF TROUBLE, IF YOU ASK ME.
FACING SOMEONE LIKE HER IS FOOLISH WITHOUT THE SUPPORT OF GUYS LIKE KIBA OR NEJI... SOMEONE WITH KEEN DETECTION.
THROB THROB
IF WE STAY HERE, SOONER OR LATER WE'LL BE CORNERED.
WE SHOULD RETREAT FOR NOW, AND...
DID ANYONE ASK YOU FOR ADVICE?!
I ASKED YOU THE SITUATION. THAT'S ALL.
...?!
CHIP
DON'T UNDER-ESTIMATE ME.
IF SHE THINKS SHE'S SAFE...
CAMPED OUT JUST INSIDE THE RANGE OF HEARING...
SHE'S IN FOR A DOOZY.
SKLITCH
KUCHIYOSE! SUMMONING!
FWOSH

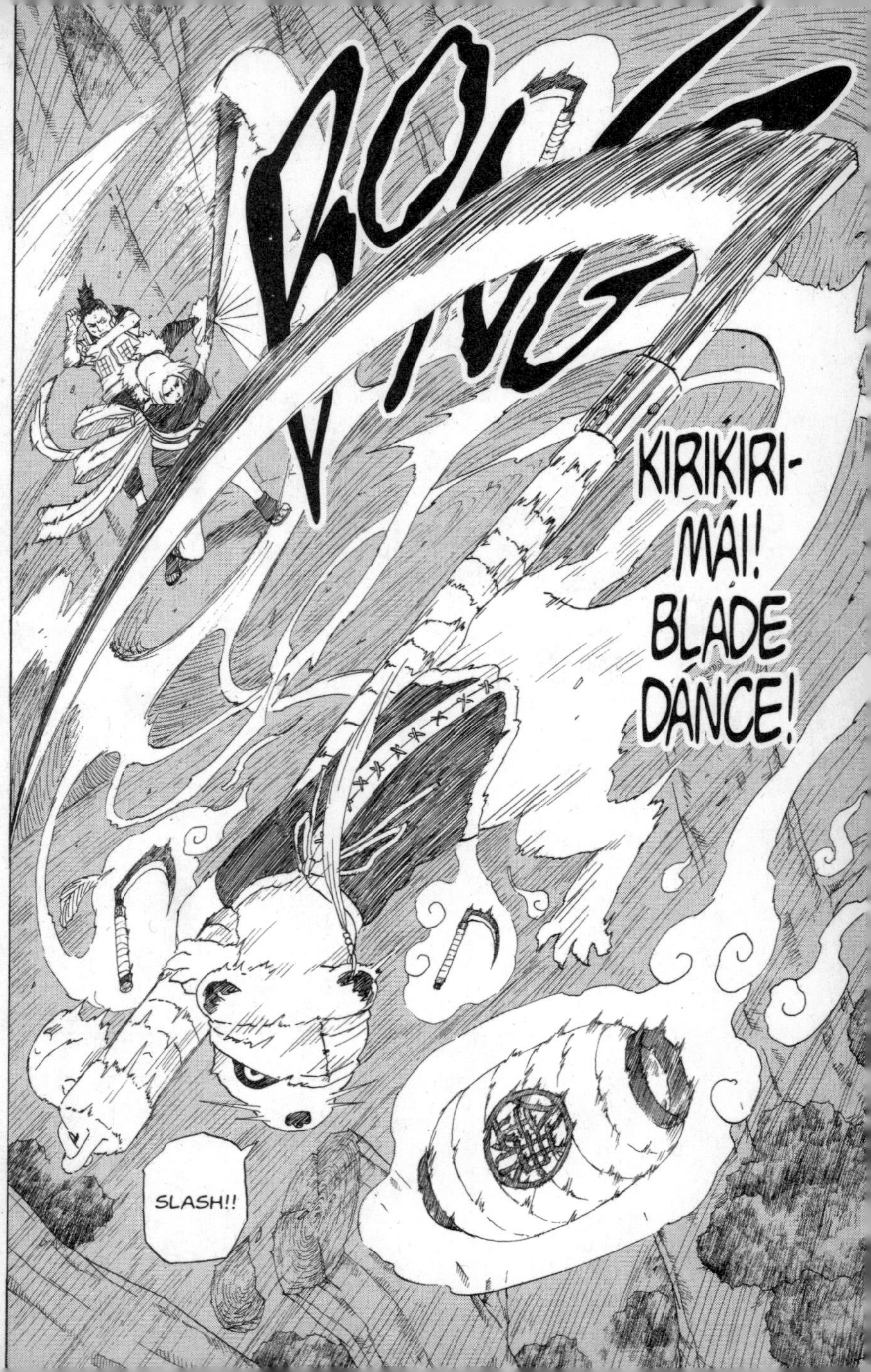
KIRIKIRI-MAI! BLADE DANCE!
SLASH!!

READ THIS WAY

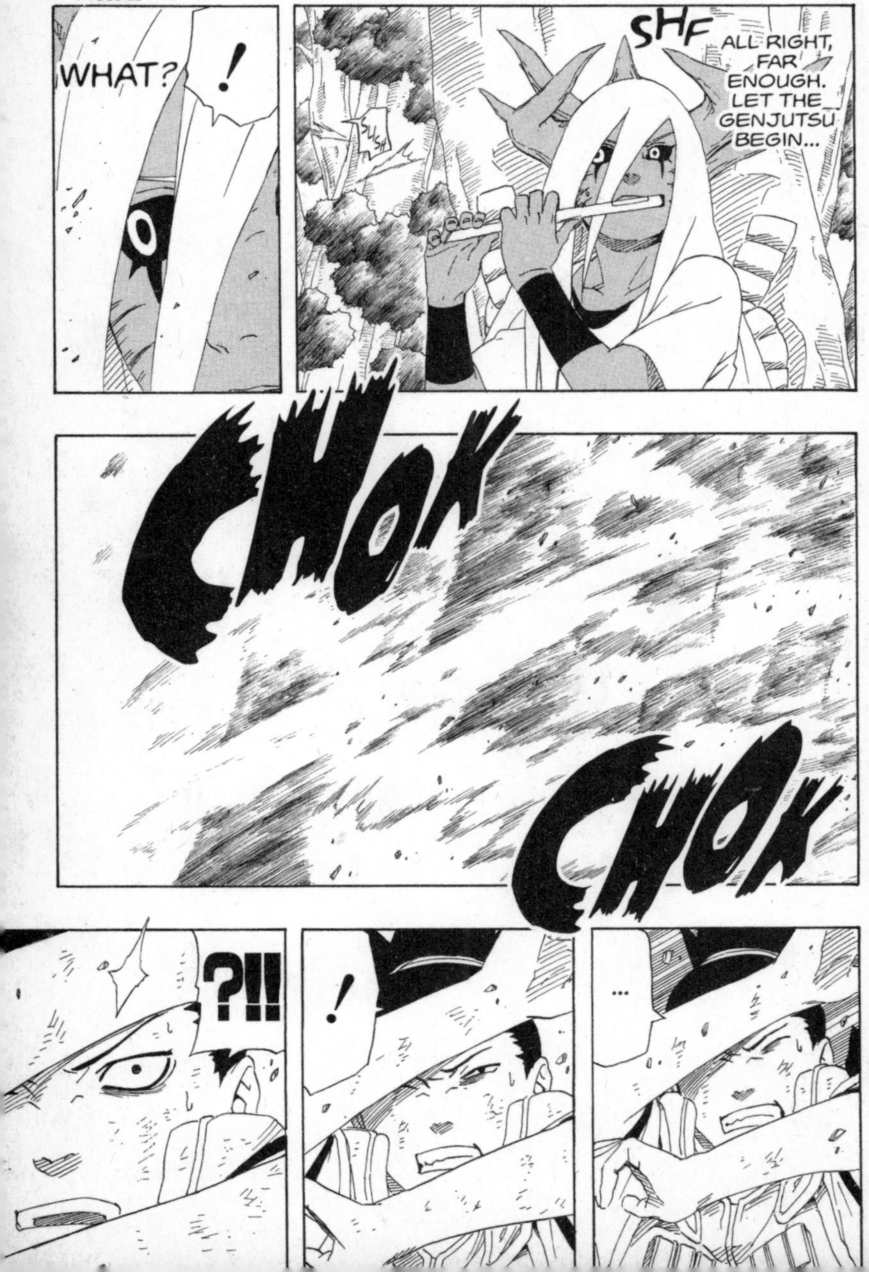
ALL RIGHT, FAR ENOUGH. LET THE GENJUTSU BEGIN...
SHF
SUSH
!
WHAT?
CHOK
CHOK
...
!
?!!

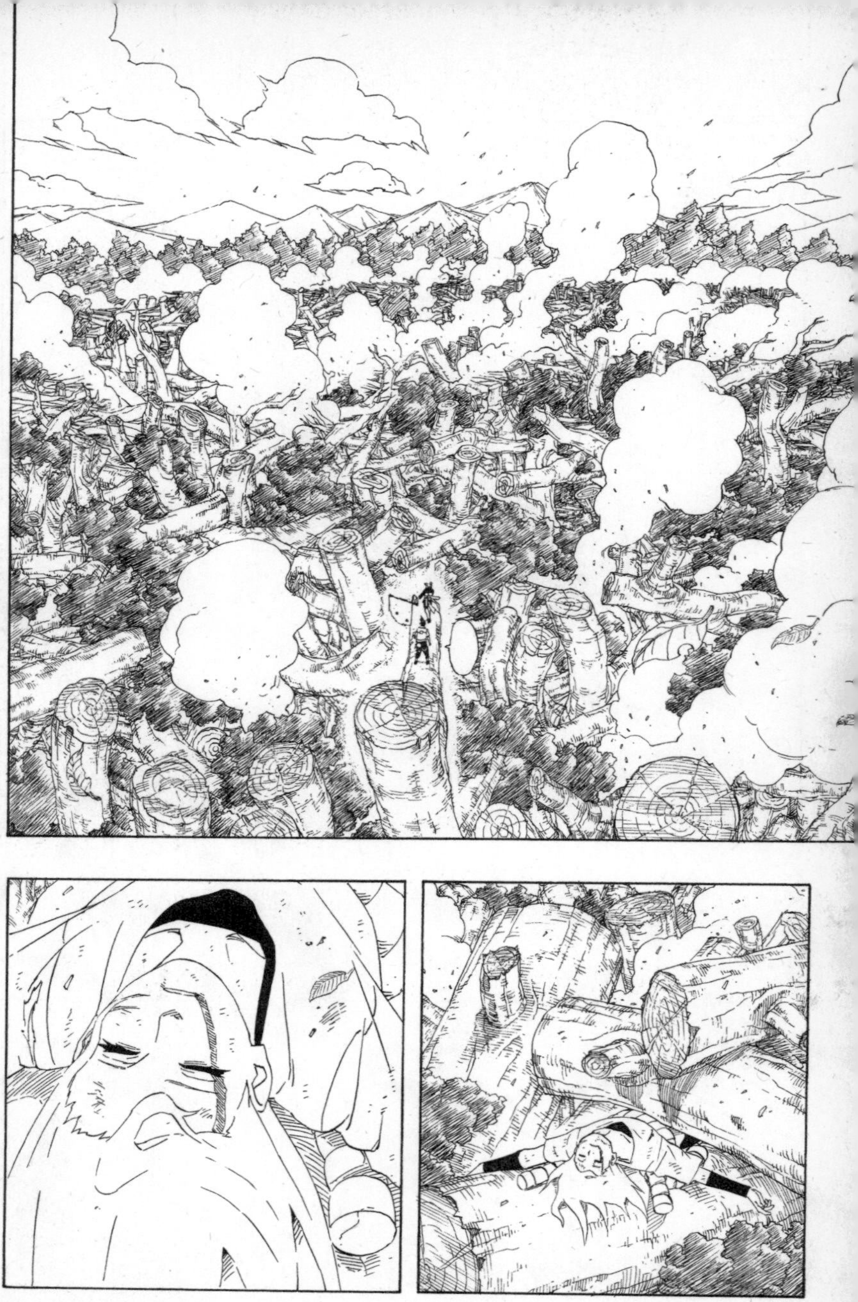

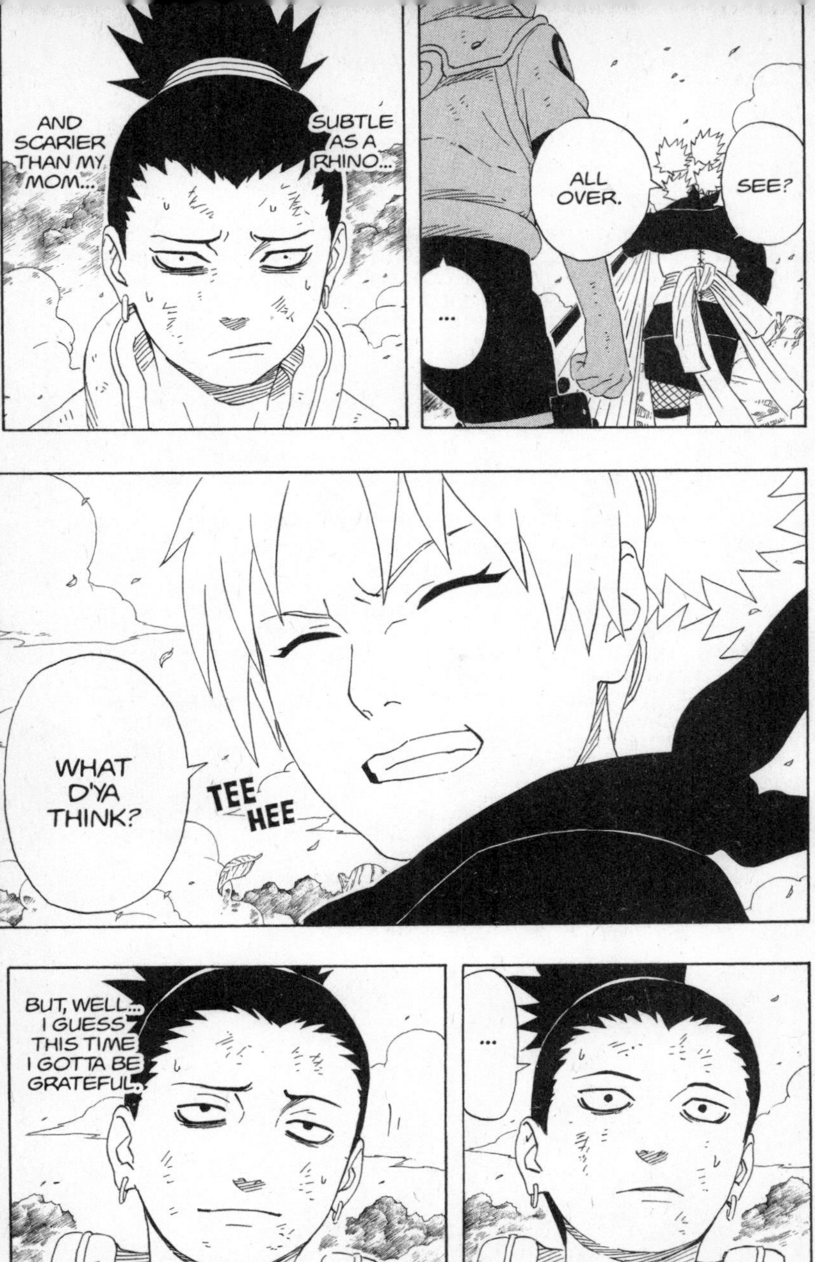
SEE?
ALL OVER.
...
SUBTLE AS A RHINO...
AND SCARIER THAN MY MOM...
TEE HEE
WHAT D'YA THINK?
...
BUT, WELL... I GUESS THIS TIME I GOTTA BE GRATEFUL.

THE WORLD OF KISHIMOTO MASASHI
PERSONAL HISTORY:
THE TOO-EMBARRASSING-TO-WRITE-ABOUT STORY, PART 4

THE IMAGE OF THAT SCENE IS ACID-ETCHED INTO MY MIND. I REMEMBER MY THOUGHTS, HOVERING THERE IN MIDAIR. WHAT WOULD HAPPEN IF I LOST MY BALANCE? OH NO. DON'T LET ME FALL DOWN. THAT'S IT, FORGET THE LEGS. IF I JUST LAND WITH MY UPPER BODY STRAIGHT, LIKE A GYMNAST...

ANYWAY, NEVER MIND THE POTATO. I TOSSED IT ASIDE. **SQUELCH**. IT HIT THE MOUND FIRST. HEARING THAT SOUND GAVE ME THE RESOLVE I NEEDED. **SQUISH SMUSSH!** BOTH MY LEGS, PLANTED IN THE DUNG! IT WAS DEEPER THAN I HAD ENVISIONED. BUT ACTUALLY, THAT WAS A GODSEND. CEMENTED KNEE-DEEP, I MANAGED TO MAINTAIN MY BALANCE.

INSTEAD OF SURPRISING EVERYBODY WITH MY PRIZE POTATO, I WOUND UP STIRRING THEM IN A DIFFERENT WAY.

AND THEN CAME THE MISERY. I CALLED TO A NEARBY CLASS-MATE FOR HELP. HE RAN TO THE NEAREST TEACHER, SCREAMING FULL BLAST: "MASASHI'S BURIED IN POO!" I'LL NEVER FORGET WHAT HAPPENED NEXT... THE TEACHER REFUSED TO HELP ME. I GUESS SHE WAS AVERSE TO RURAL ARTIFACTS. TO MY RELIEF AND HER CREDIT, MY MOTHER THEN CAME TO THE RESCUE, LIFTING ME OUT OF MY PREDICAMENT WITHOUT HESITATION. IN THAT MOMENT I LEARNED AWE FOR THE LOVE OF A MOTHER.

TO THIS DAY WHEN A YAM CROSSES MY PATH, IT BRINGS ME BACK TO THAT EVENT. AND NOW THE MORAL (IN TWO PARTS): NO GOOD EVER COMES FROM BEING CAUGHT UP WITH THINGS; AND WHEN IT COMES TO IT, MOTHERS ARE BRAVE!

Number 215: Gaara of the Sand

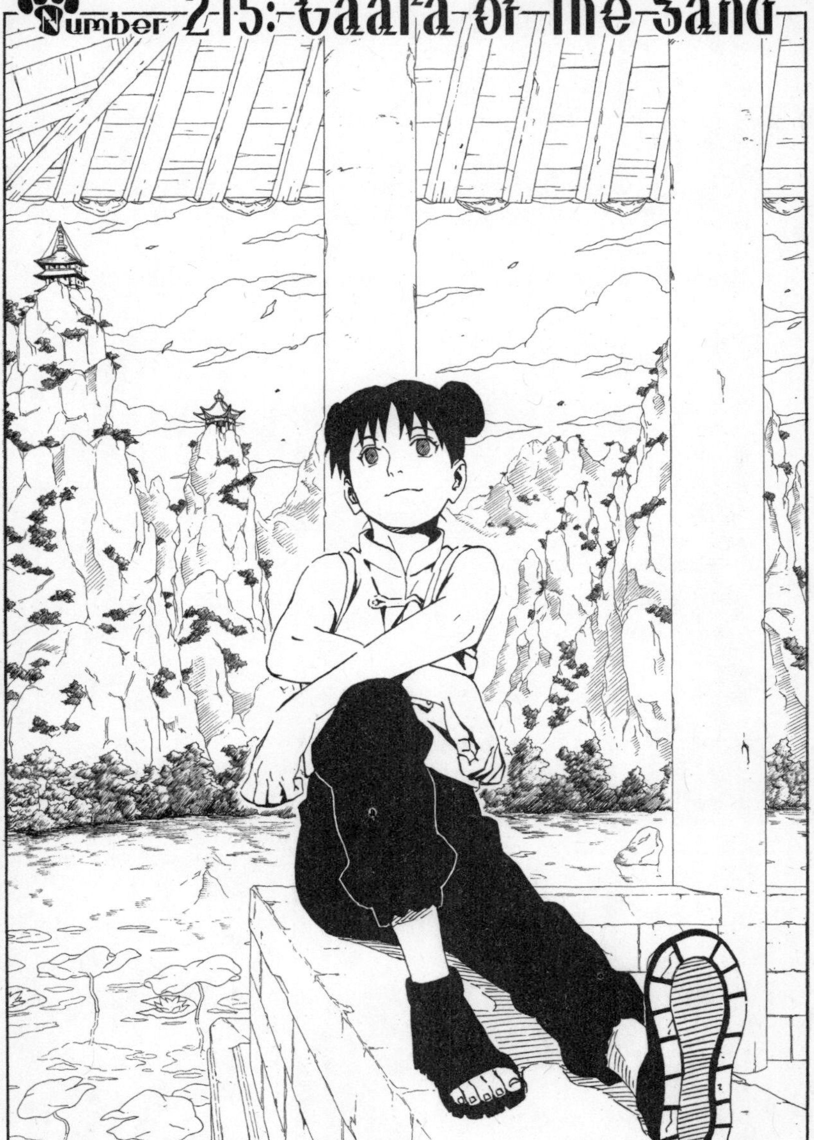

SHF

...

DRJP

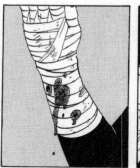

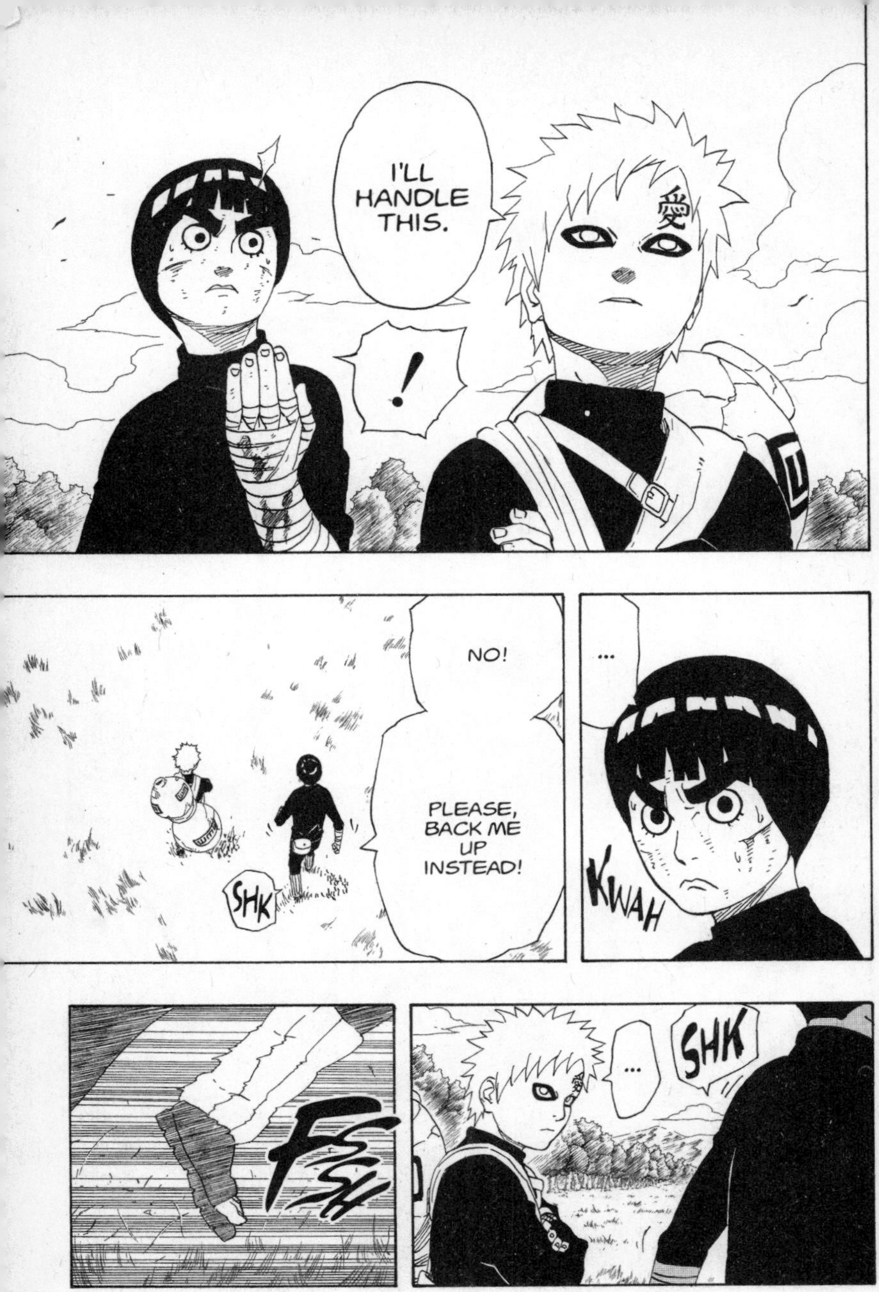
I'LL HANDLE THIS.
!
...
KWAH
NO!
PLEASE, BACK ME UP INSTEAD!
SHK
SHK
...
FSSH

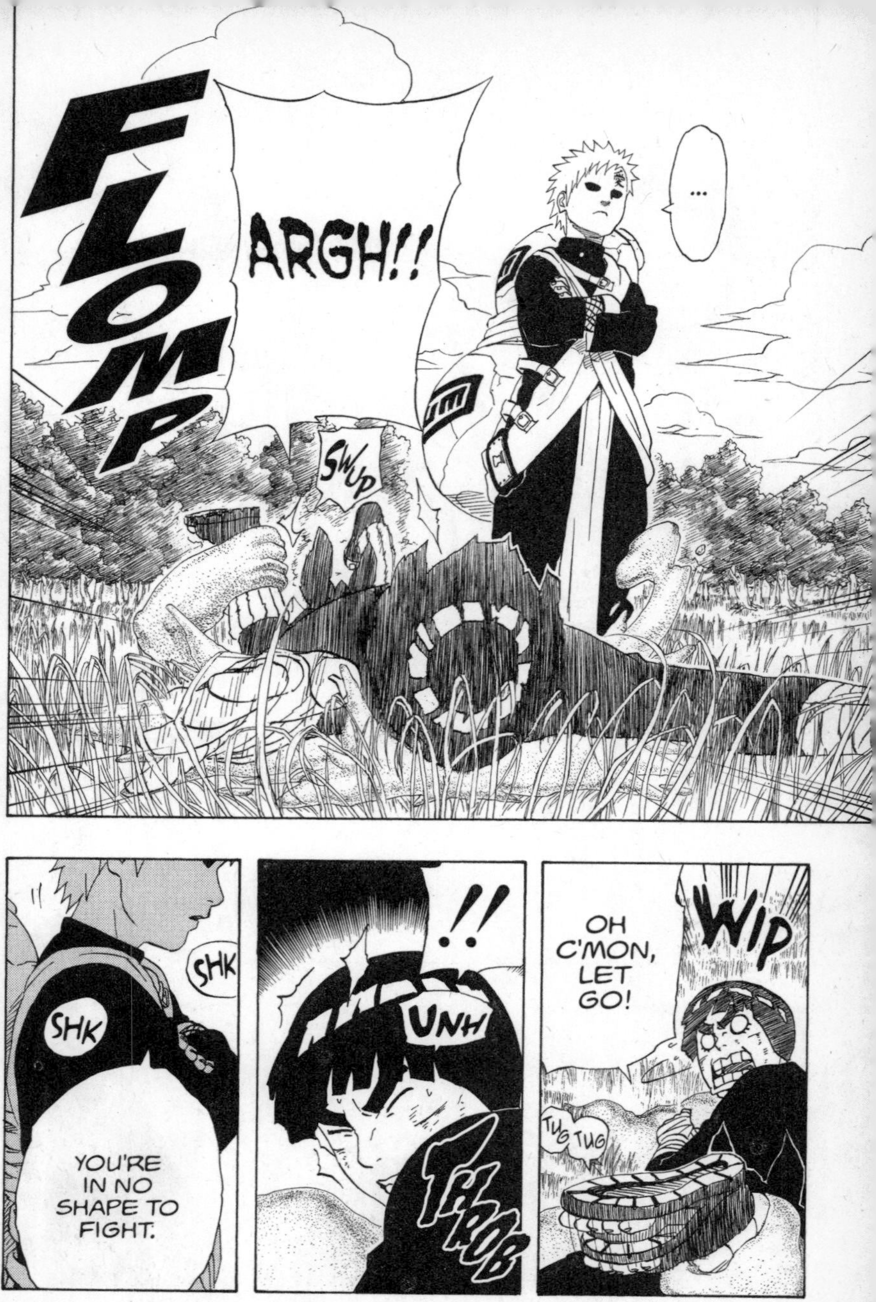
...
ARGH!!
FLOMP
SWUP
OH C'MON, LET GO!
WIP
TUG TUG
!!
UNH
THROB
SHK
SHK
YOU'RE IN NO SHAPE TO FIGHT.

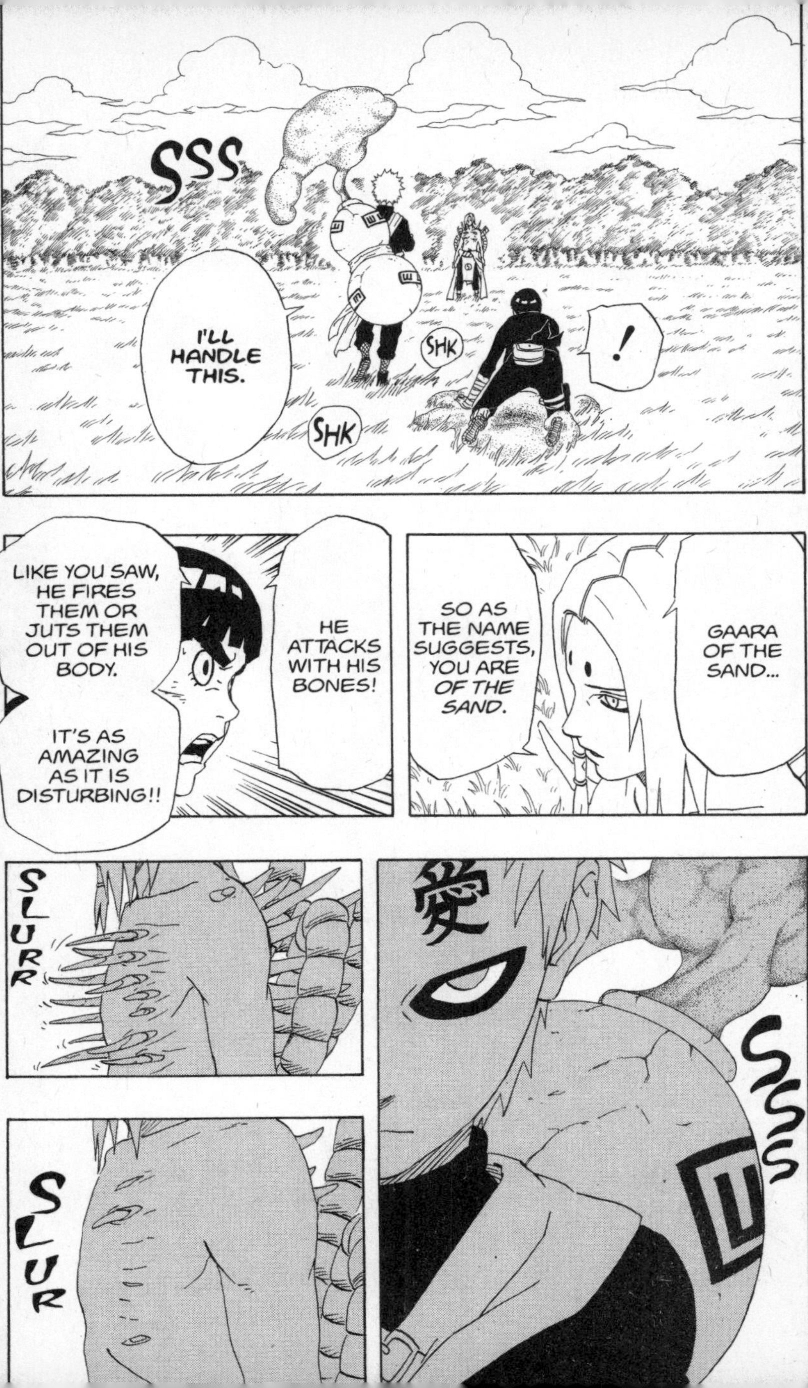
SSS
!
SHK
I'LL HANDLE THIS.
SHK
GAARA OF THE SAND...
SO AS THE NAME SUGGESTS, YOU ARE OF THE SAND.
HE ATTACKS WITH HIS BONES!
LIKE YOU SAW, HE FIRES THEM OR JUTS THEM OUT OF HIS BODY.
IT'S AS AMAZING AS IT IS DISTURBING!!
SSS
SLURR
SLUR

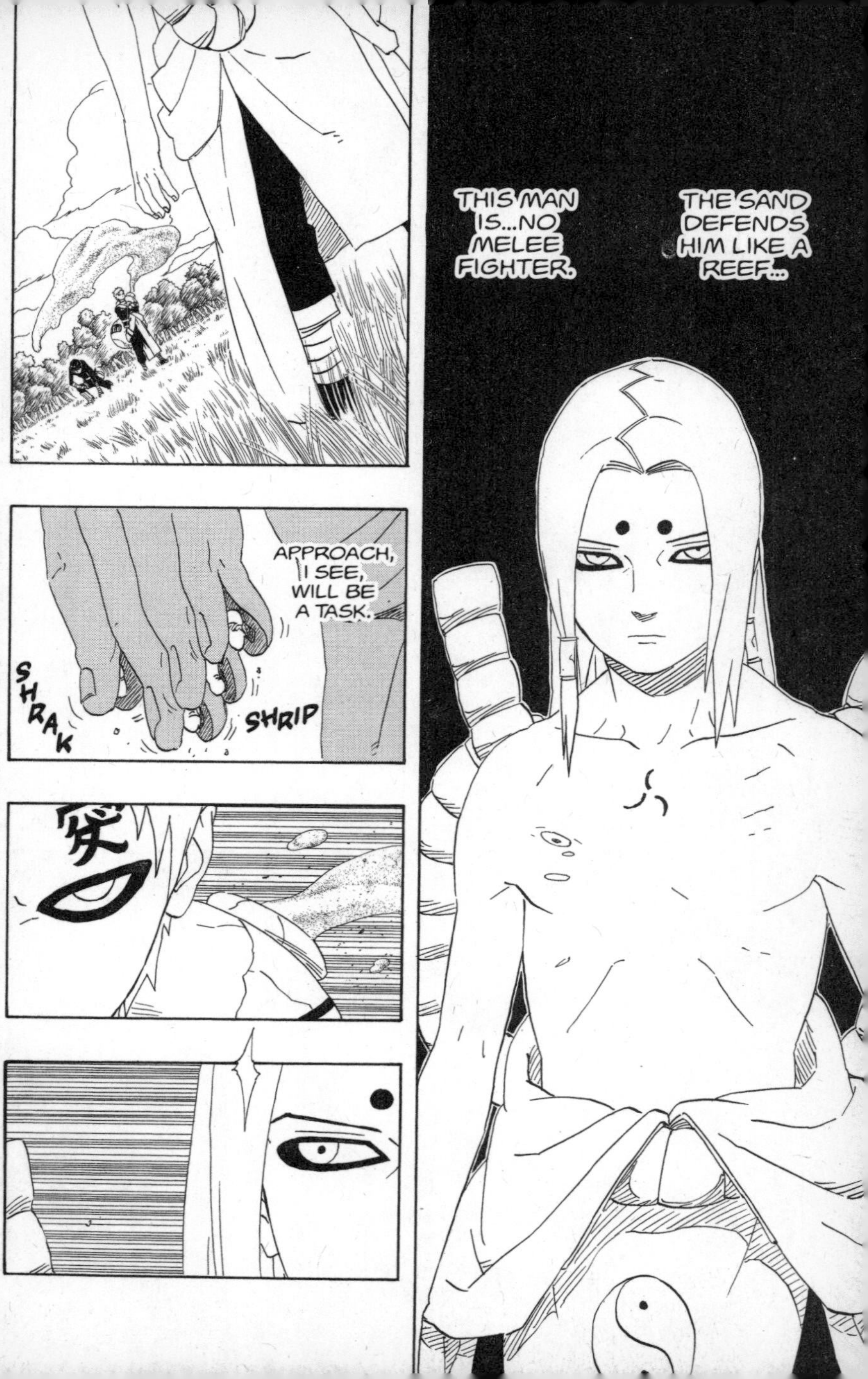
THE SAND DEFENDS HIM LIKE A REEF...
THIS MAN IS...NO MELEE FIGHTER.
APPROACH, I SEE, WILL BE A TASK.
SHRIP
SHRAK
突

READ THIS WAY

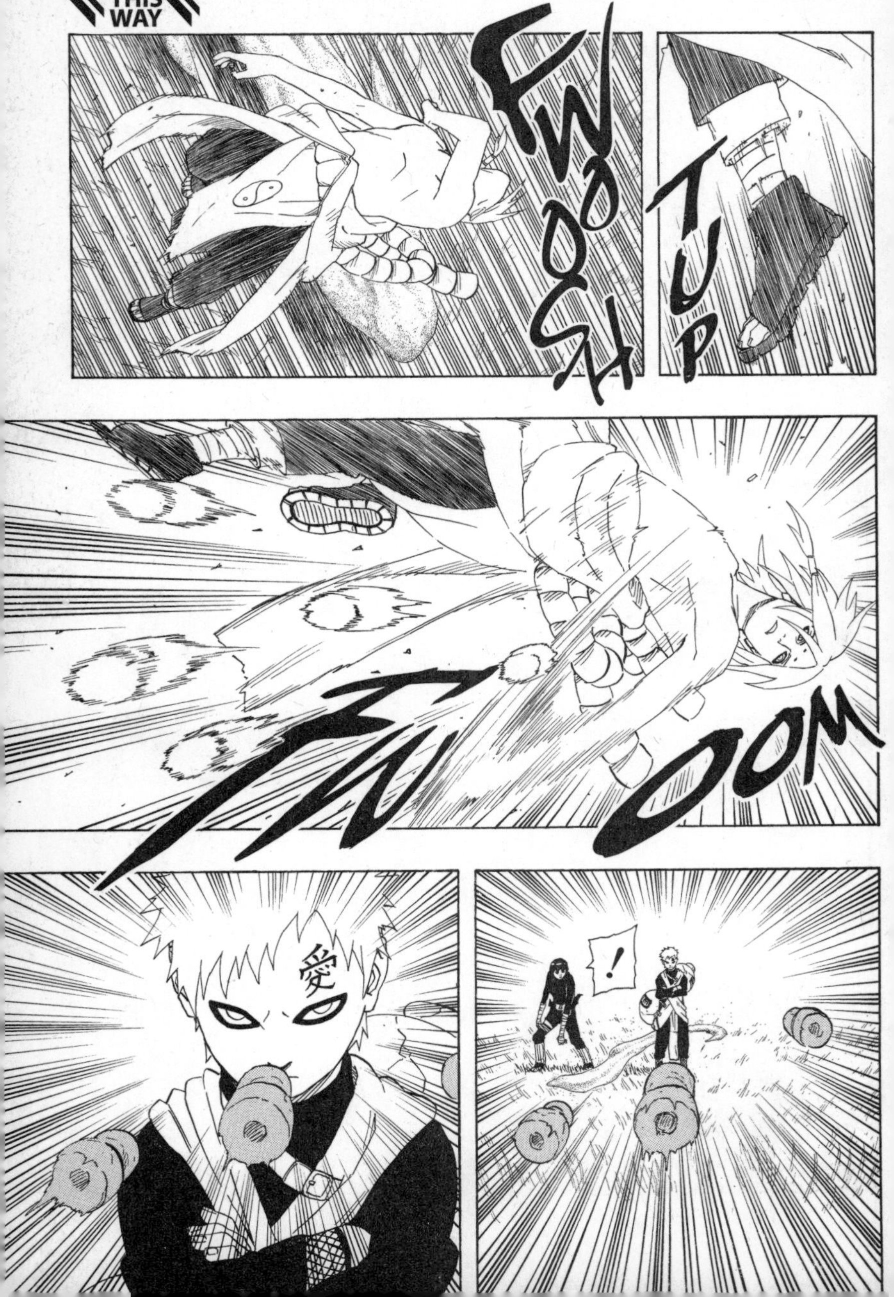
TUP
FWOOSH
FWOOM
!

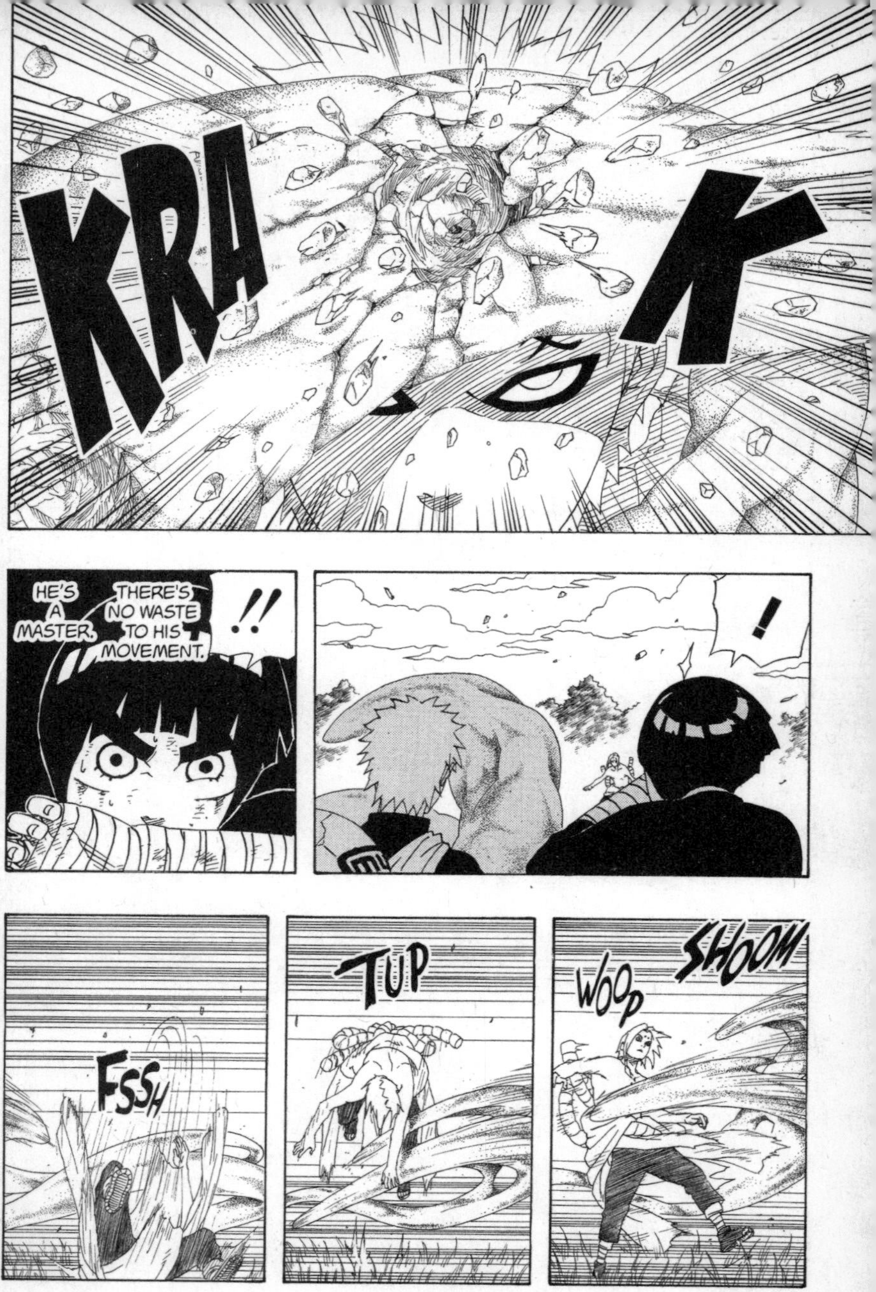
KRAAK
!
!!
THERE'S NO WASTE TO HIS MOVEMENT.
HE'S A MASTER.
SHOOM
WOOP
TUP
FSSH

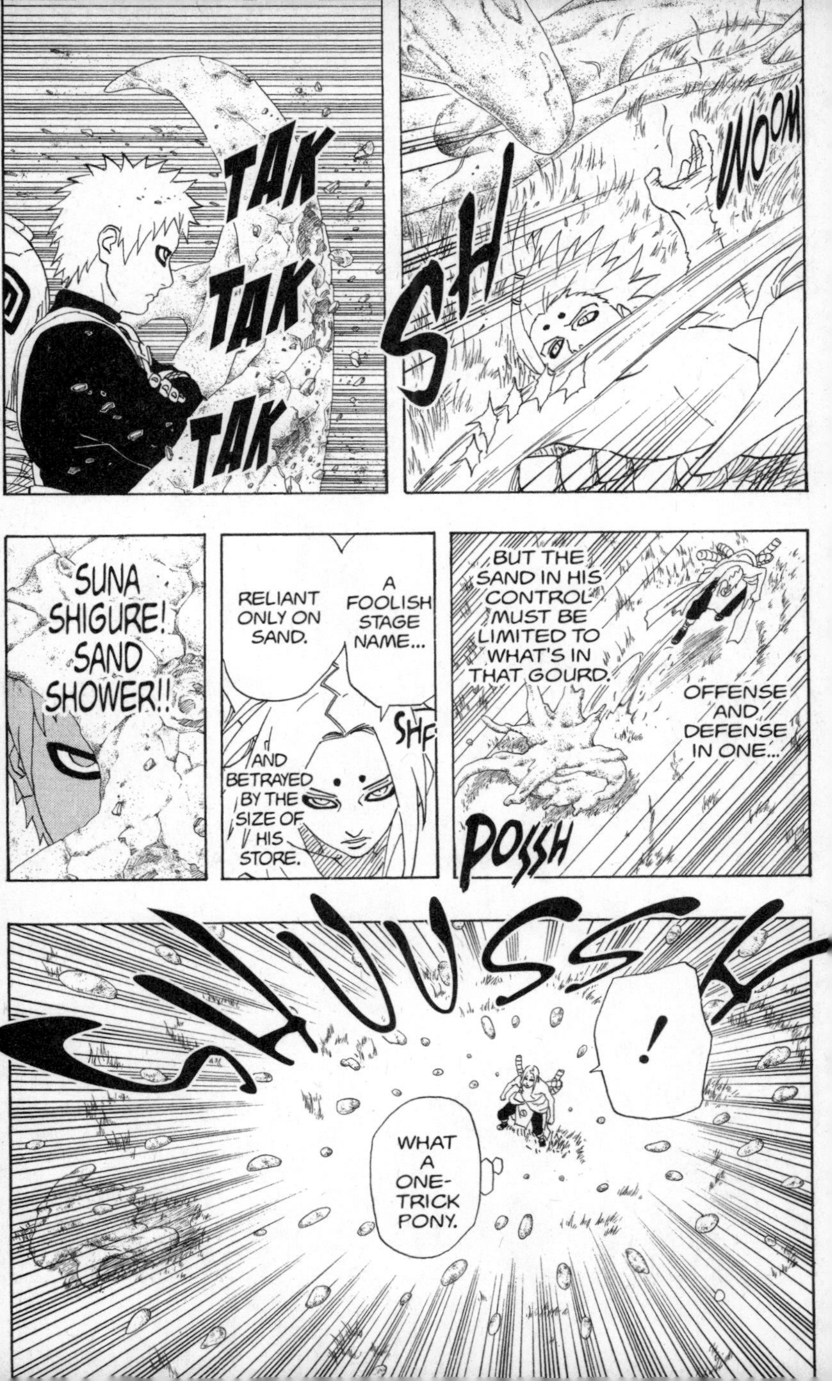
WOOM
SH
TAK
TAK
TAK
BUT THE SAND IN HIS CONTROL MUST BE LIMITED TO WHAT'S IN THAT GOURD.
OFFENSE AND DEFENSE IN ONE...
POSSH
A FOOLISH STAGE NAME...
RELIANT ONLY ON SAND.
SHF
AND BETRAYED BY THE SIZE OF HIS STORE.
SUNA SHIGURE! SAND SHOWER!!
SHUUSSH
!
WHAT A ONE-TRICK PONY.

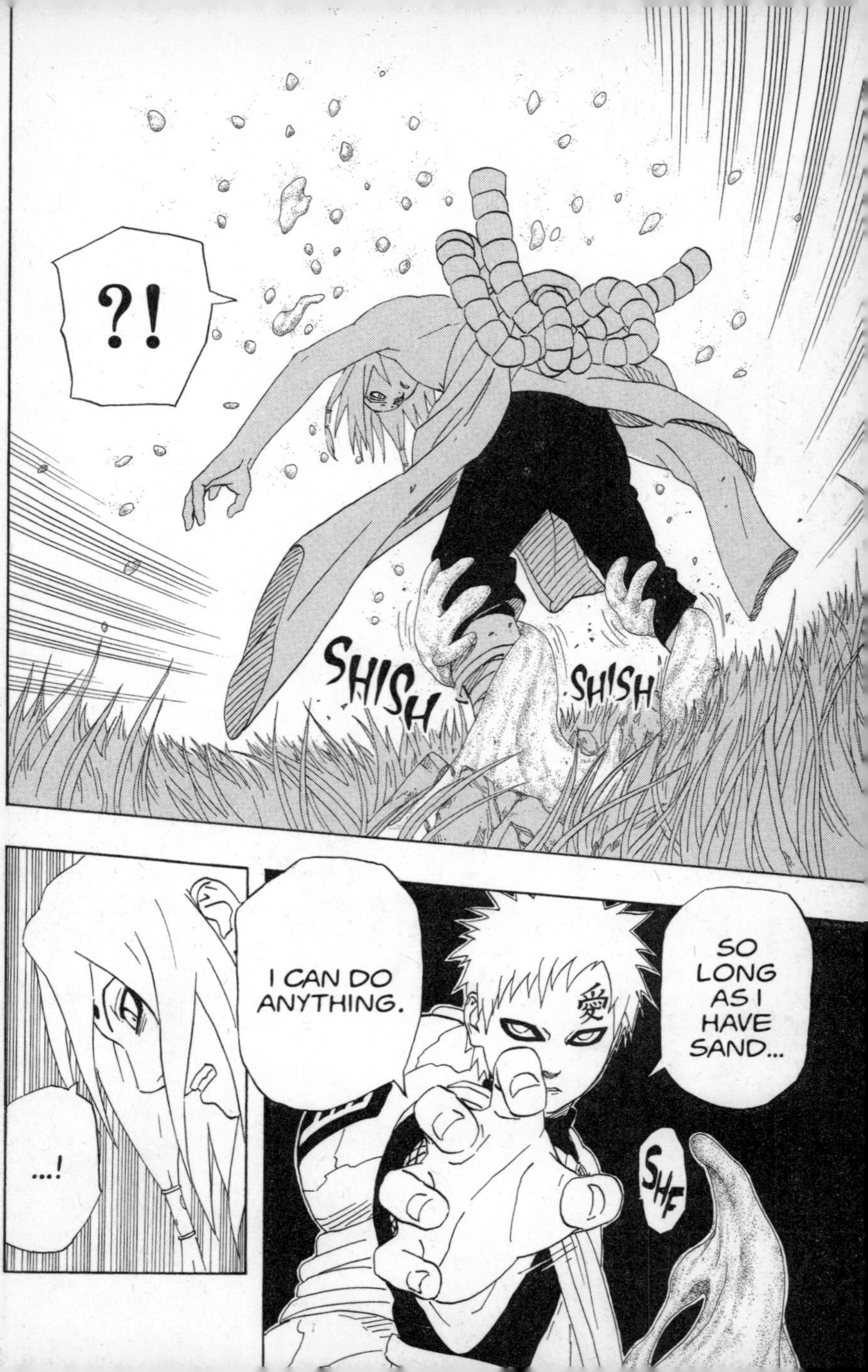
?!
SHISH
SHISH
SO LONG AS I HAVE SAND...
I CAN DO ANYTHING.
SHF
...!

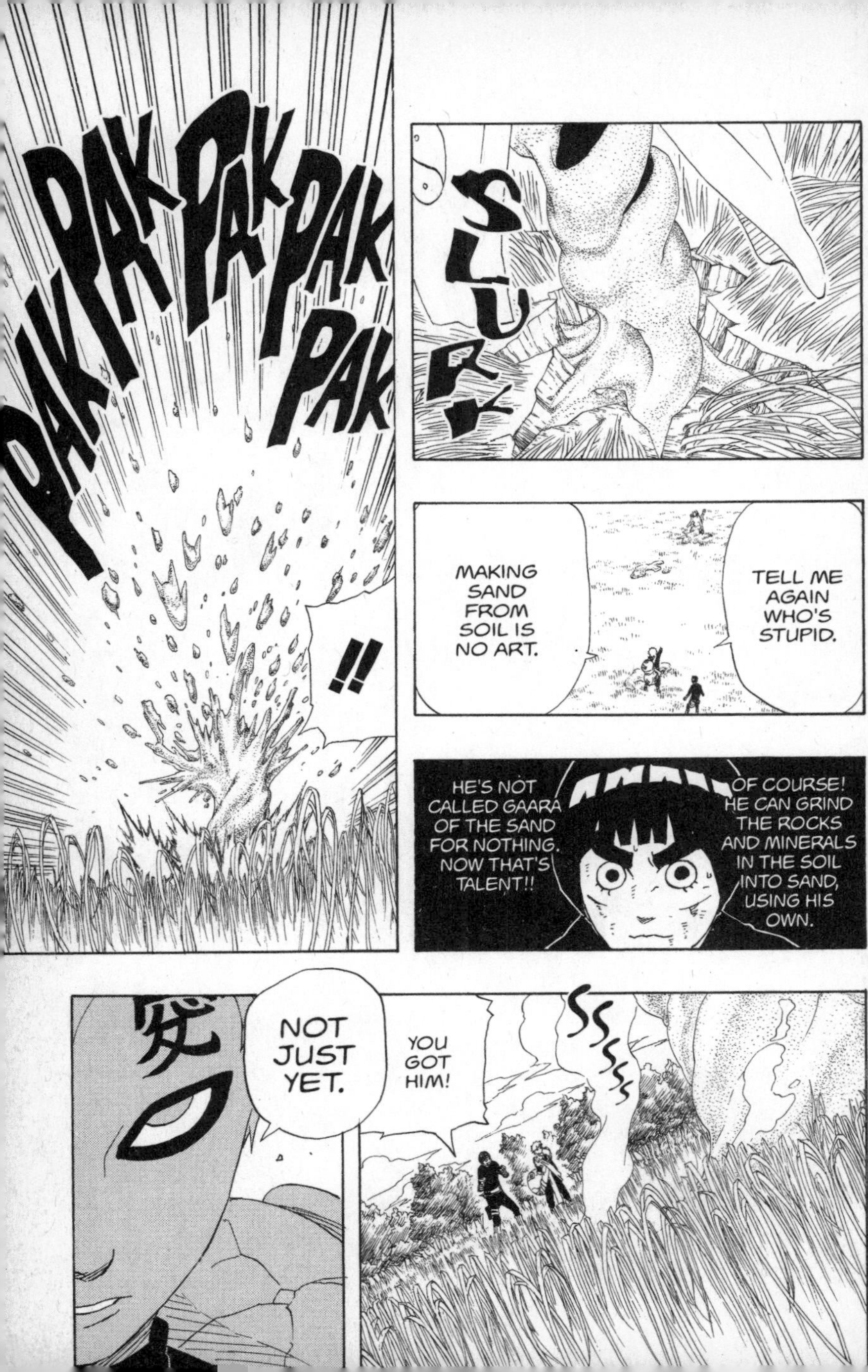
SLURP
TELL ME AGAIN WHO'S STUPID.
MAKING SAND FROM SOIL IS NO ART.
OF COURSE! HE CAN GRIND THE ROCKS AND MINERALS IN THE SOIL INTO SAND, USING HIS OWN.
HE'S NOT CALLED GAARA OF THE SAND FOR NOTHING. NOW THAT'S TALENT!!
PAK PAK PAK PAK PAK PAK
!!
SSSSS
YOU GOT HIM!
NOT JUST YET.

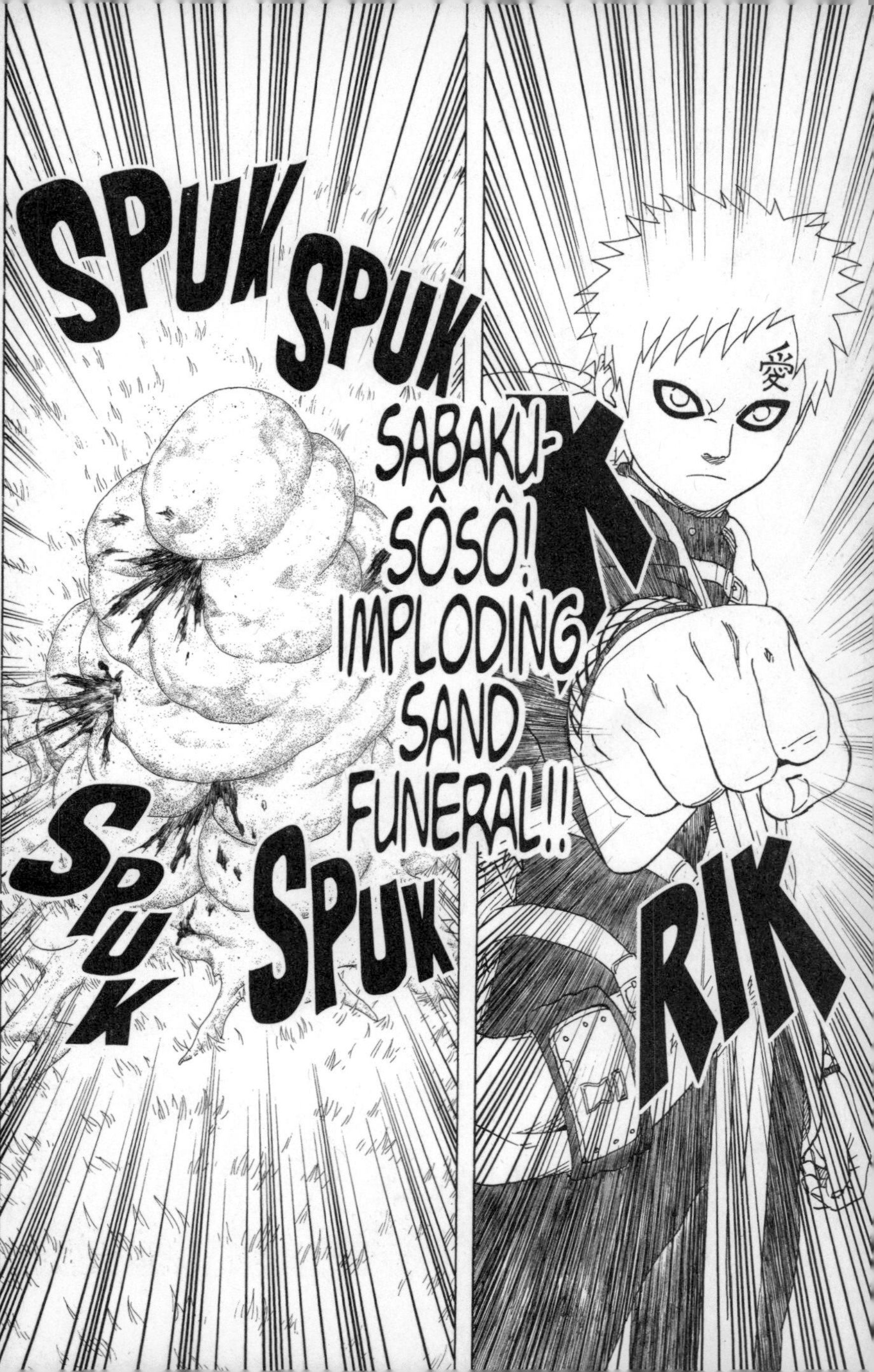
RIK
SPUK
SPUK
SABAKU-SÔSÔ! IMPLODING SAND FUNERAL!!
SPUK
SPUK

READ THIS WAY

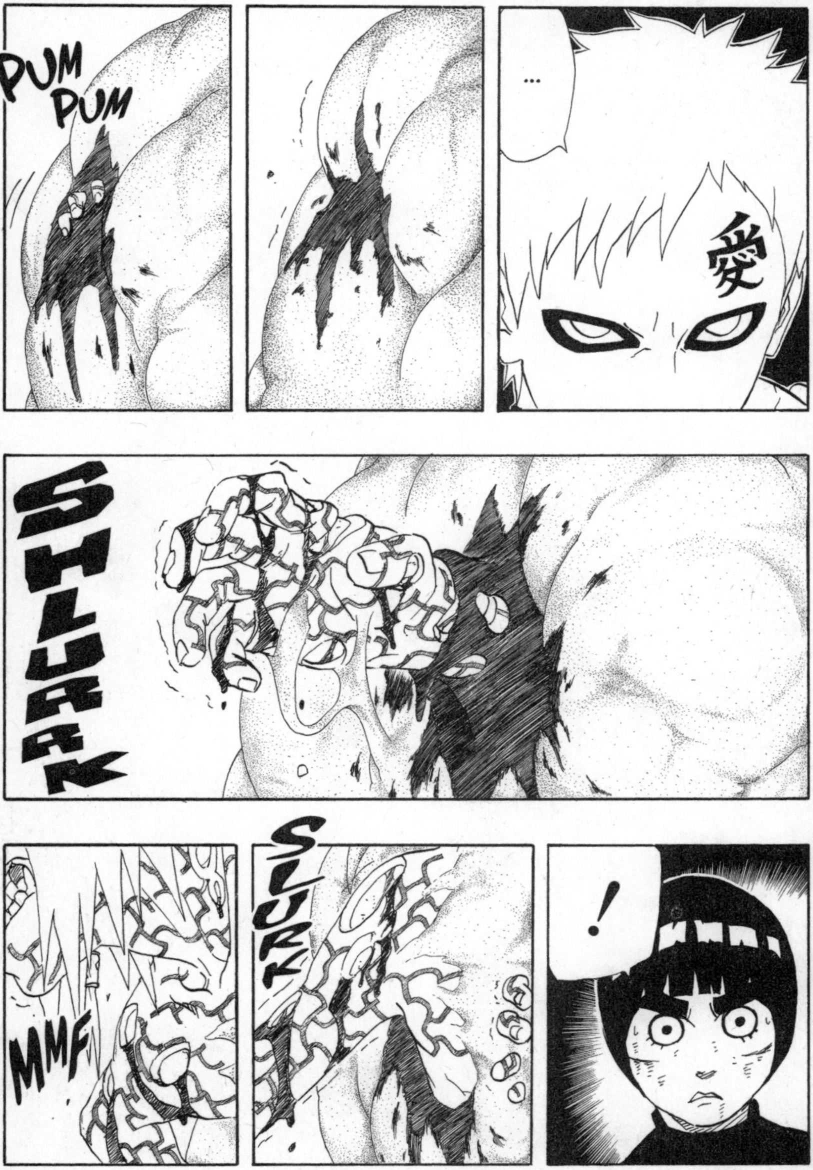
...
PUM PUM
SHLURRK
!
SLURK
MMF

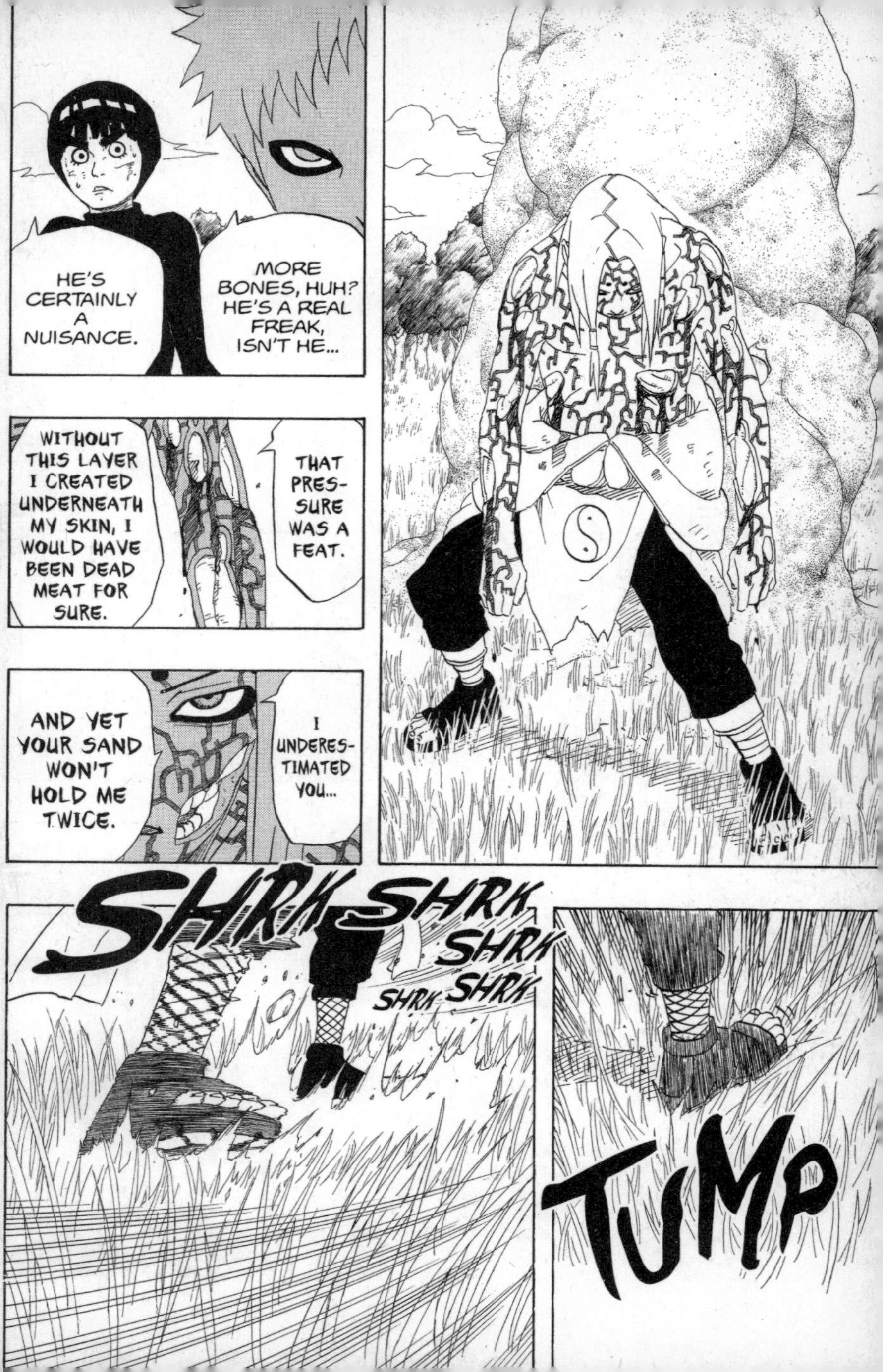
MORE BONES, HUH? HE'S A REAL FREAK, ISN'T HE...
HE'S CERTAINLY A NUISANCE.
THAT PRES-SURE WAS A FEAT.
WITHOUT THIS LAYER I CREATED UNDERNEATH MY SKIN, I WOULD HAVE BEEN DEAD MEAT FOR SURE.
I UNDERES-TIMATED YOU...
AND YET YOUR SAND WON'T HOLD ME TWICE.
TUMP
SHRK SHRK
SHRK
SHRK
SHRK SHRK

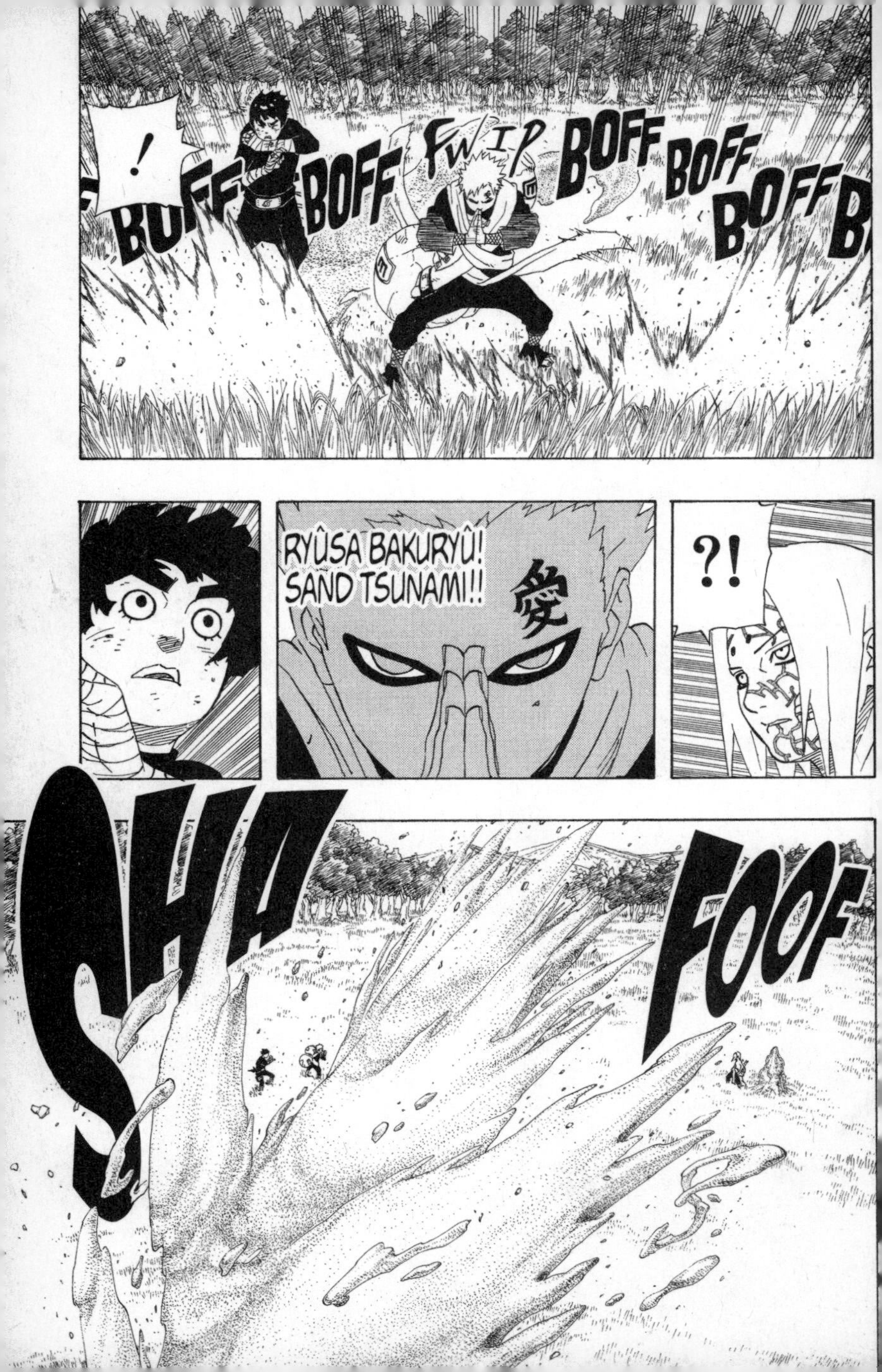
BOFF
BOFF
BOFF
FWIP
BOFF
!
?!
RYÛSA BAKURYÛ! SAND TSUNAMI!!
FOOF
SHA

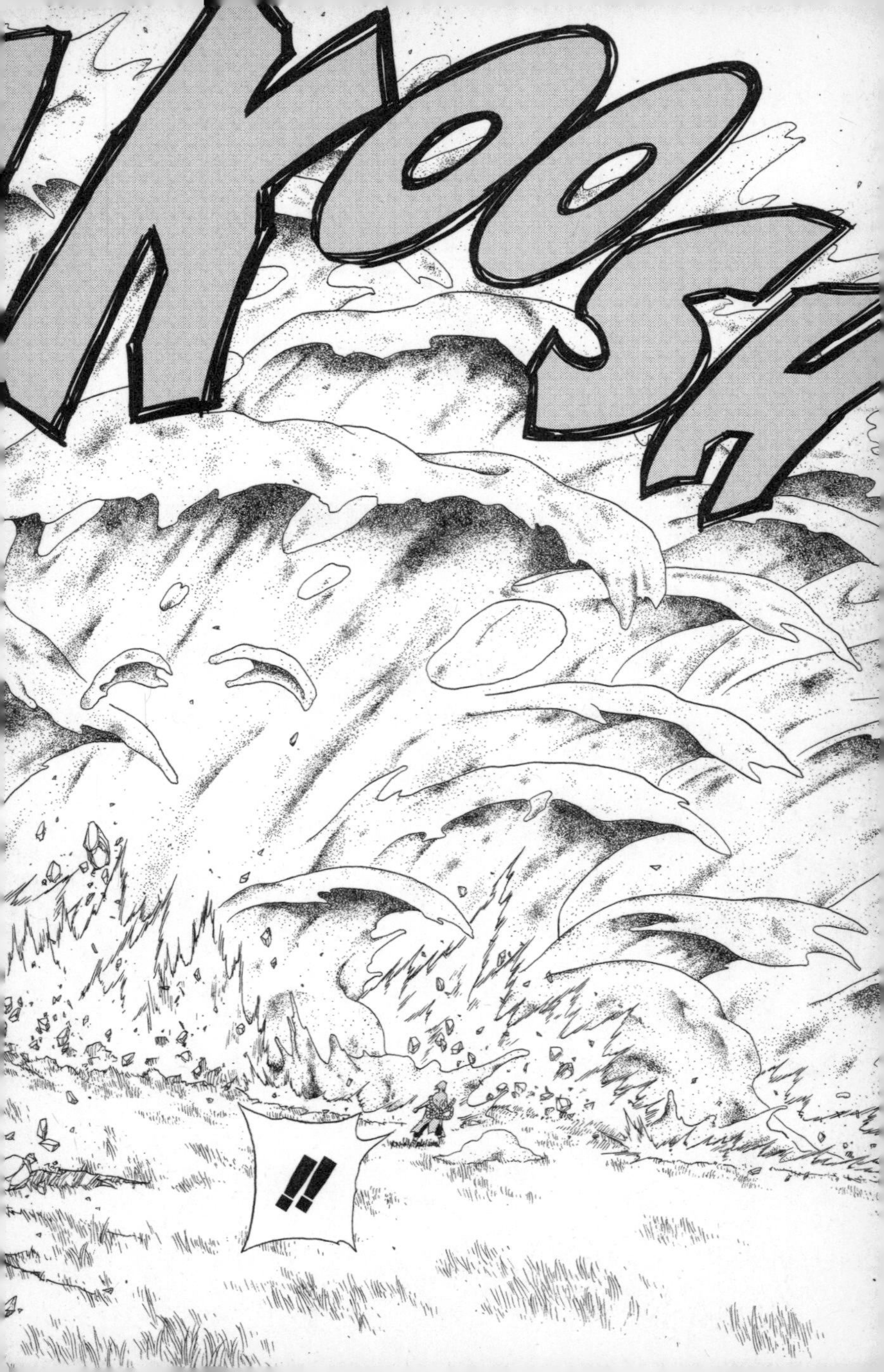
WOOSH
!!

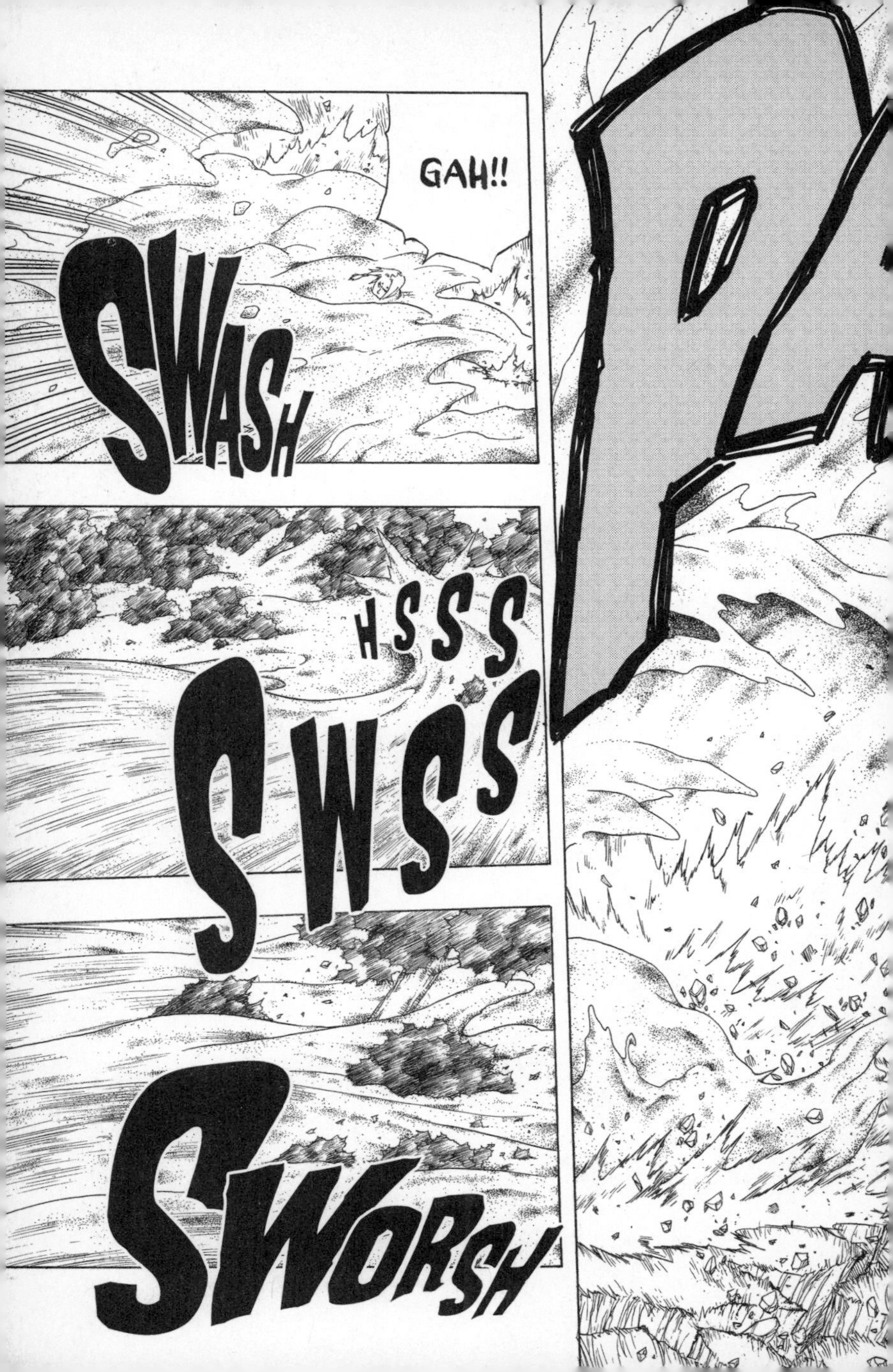
GAH!!
SWASH
HSSS
SWSS
SWORSH

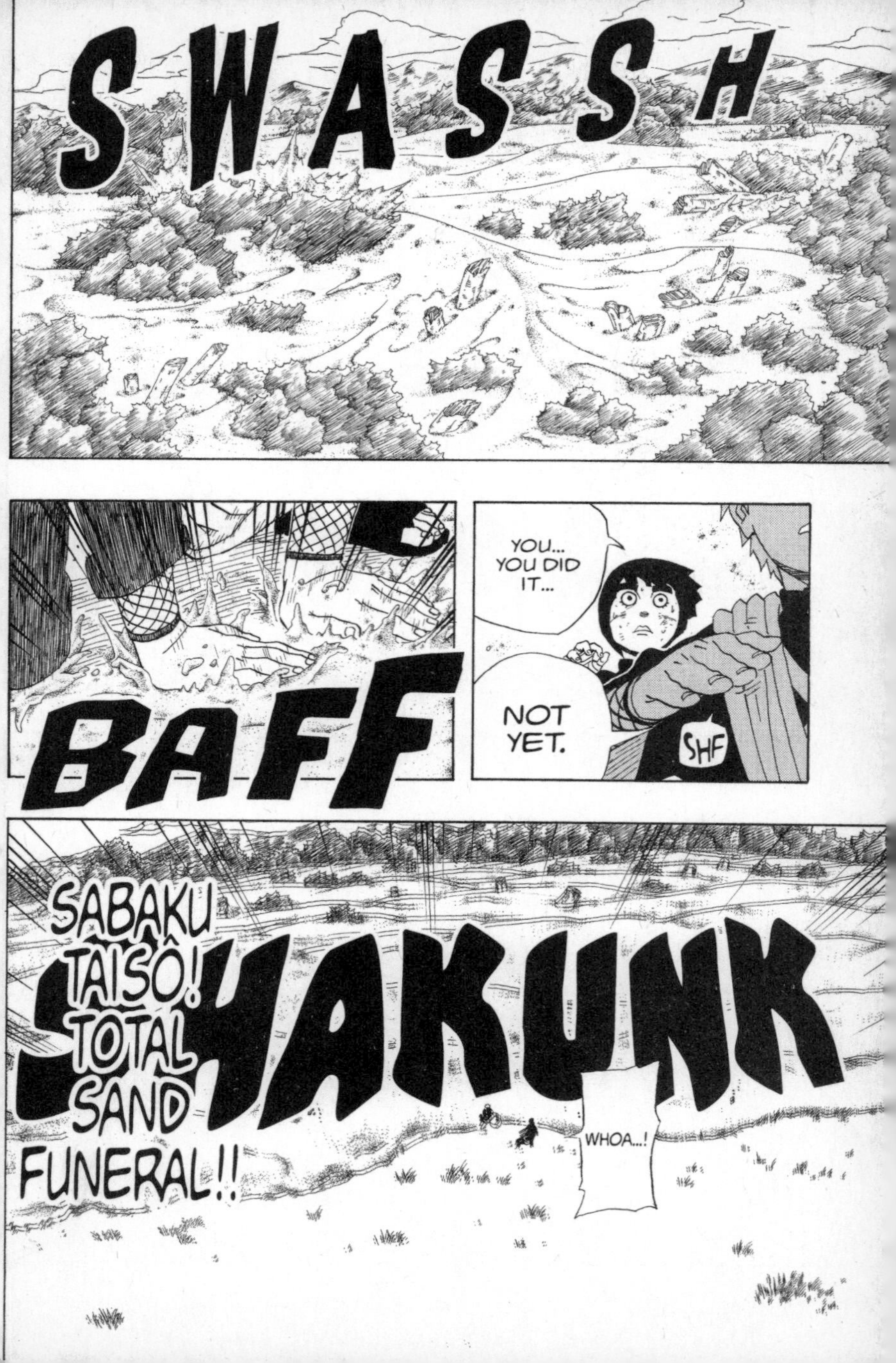
SWASSH
YOU... YOU DID IT...
NOT YET.
SHF
BAFF
SHAKUNK
WHOA...!
SABAKU TAISÔ! TOTAL SAND FUNERAL!!

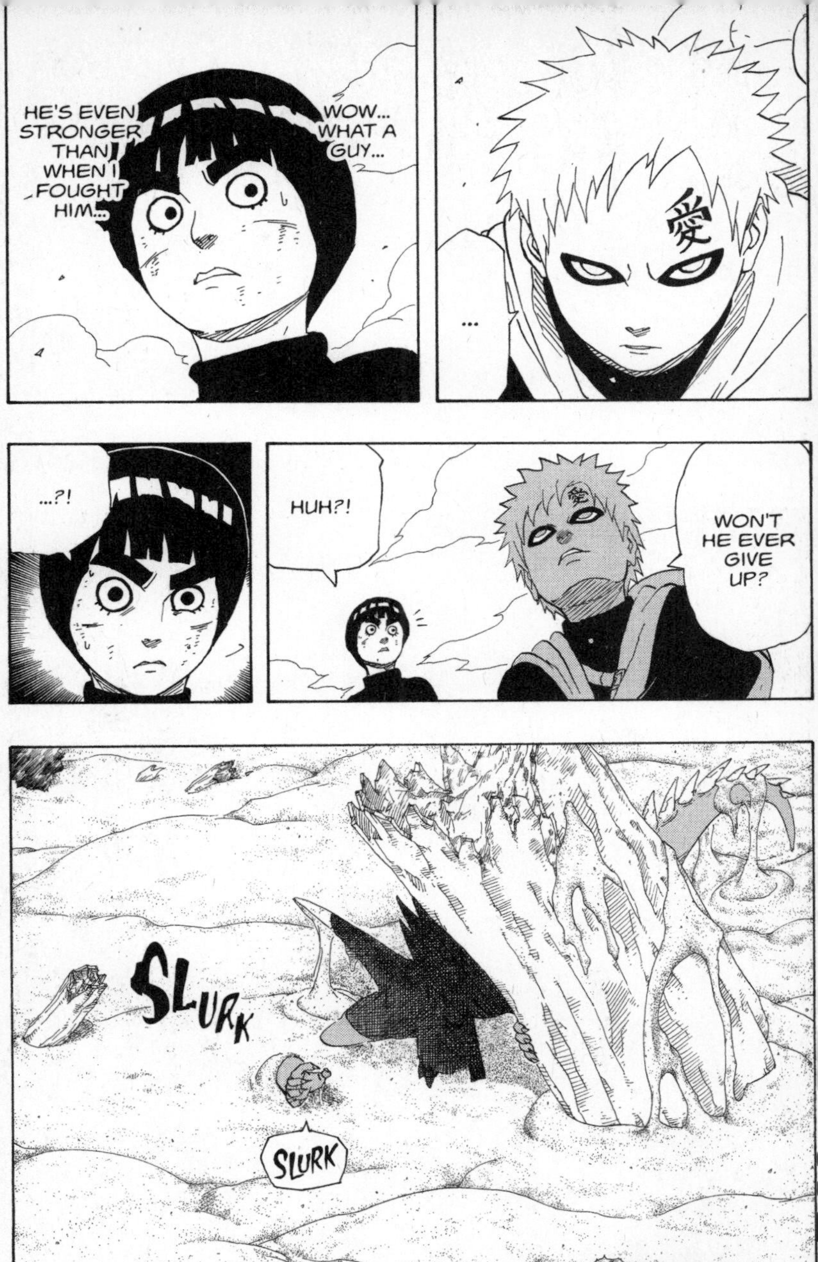
...
WOW... WHAT A GUY...
HE'S EVEN STRONGER THAN WHEN I FOUGHT HIM...
WON'T HE EVER GIVE UP?
HUH?!
...?!
SLURK
SLURK

Number 216: Halberd and Shield...!!

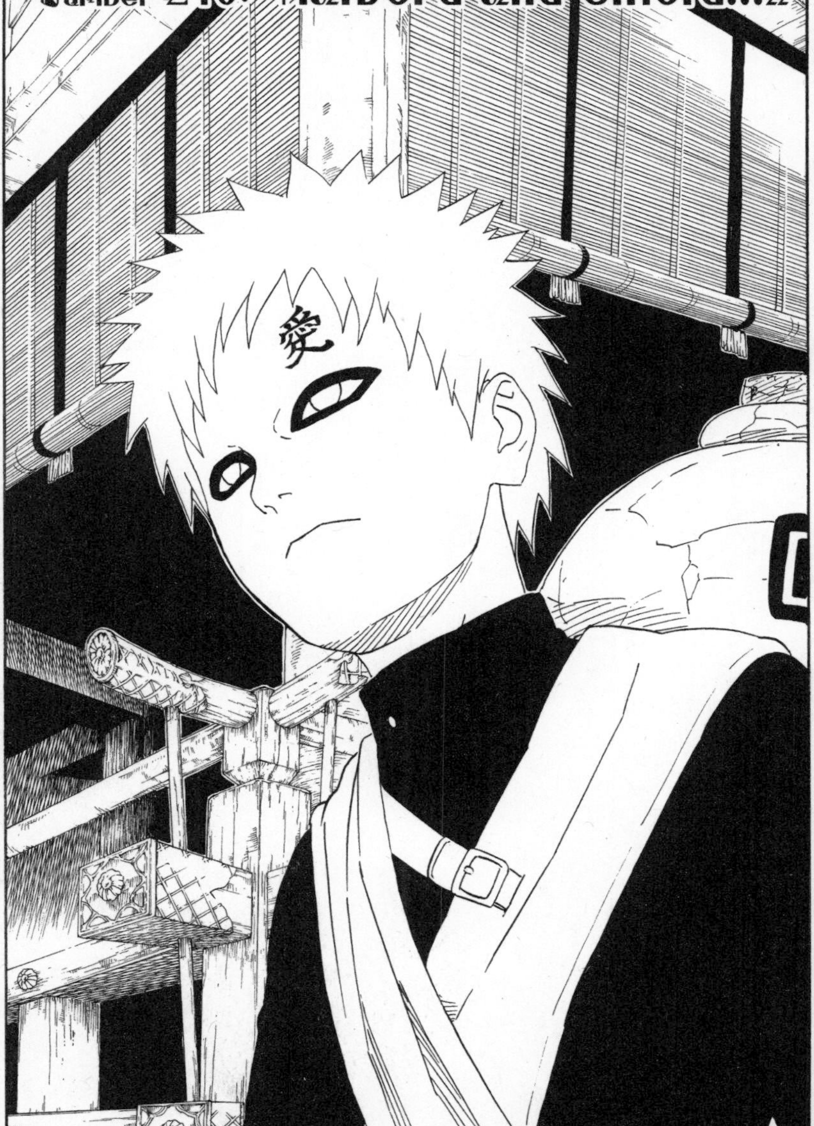
愛

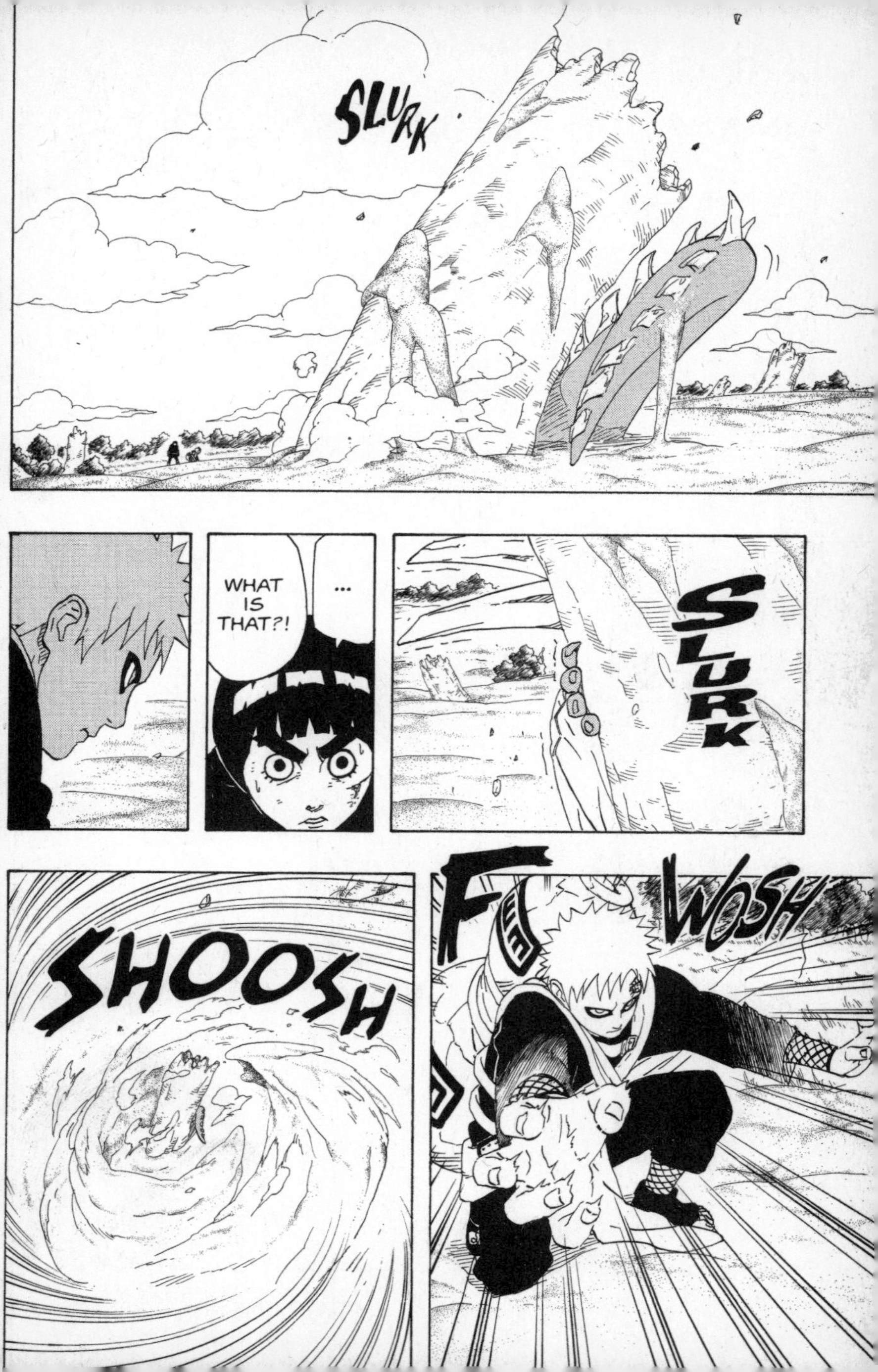
SLURK
SLURK
...
WHAT IS THAT?!
FWOSH
SHOOSH

READ THIS WAY

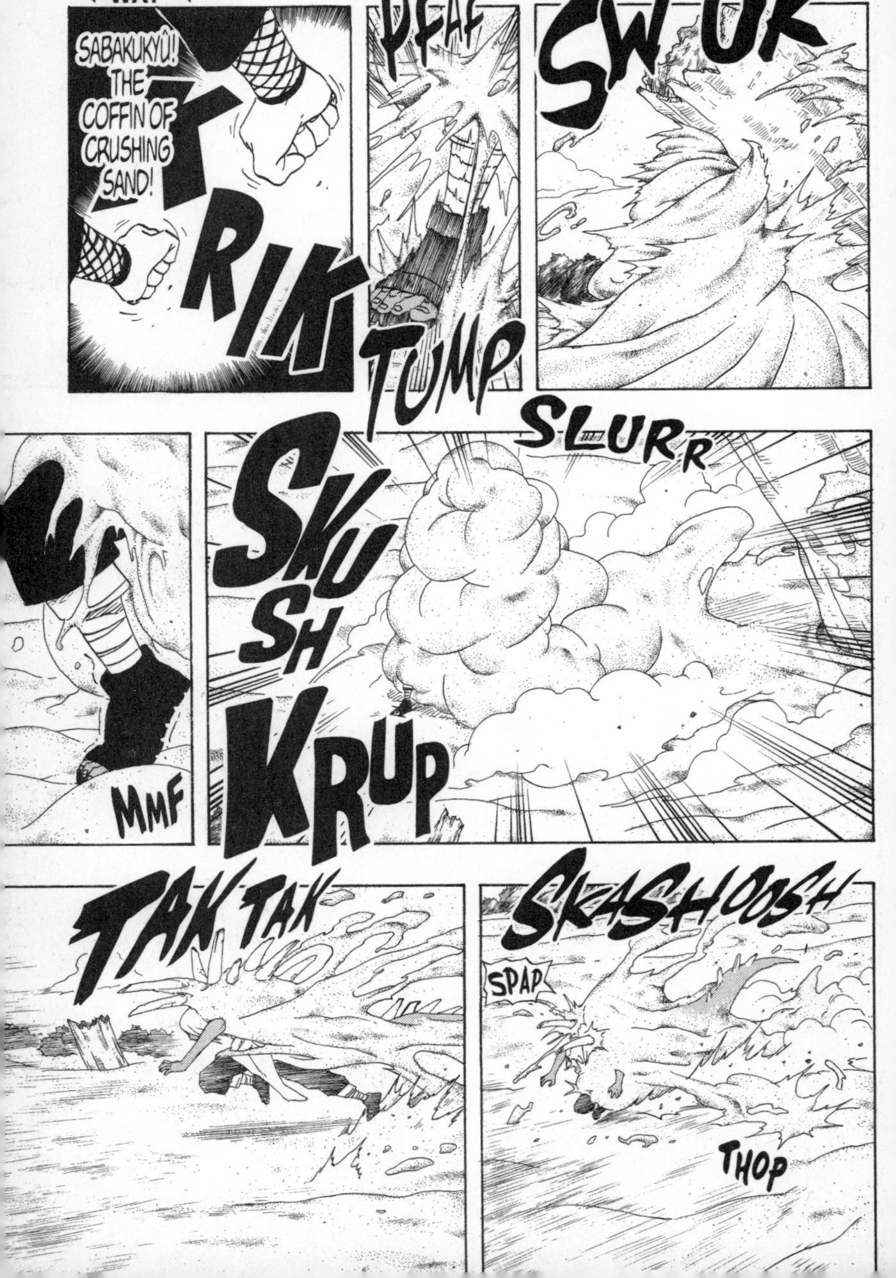
SWUK
PFAF
SABAKUKYÛ! THE COFFIN OF CRUSHING SAND!
TRIK
TUMP
SLURR
SKUSH
KRUP
MMF
SKASHOOSH
SPAP
THOP
TAK TAK

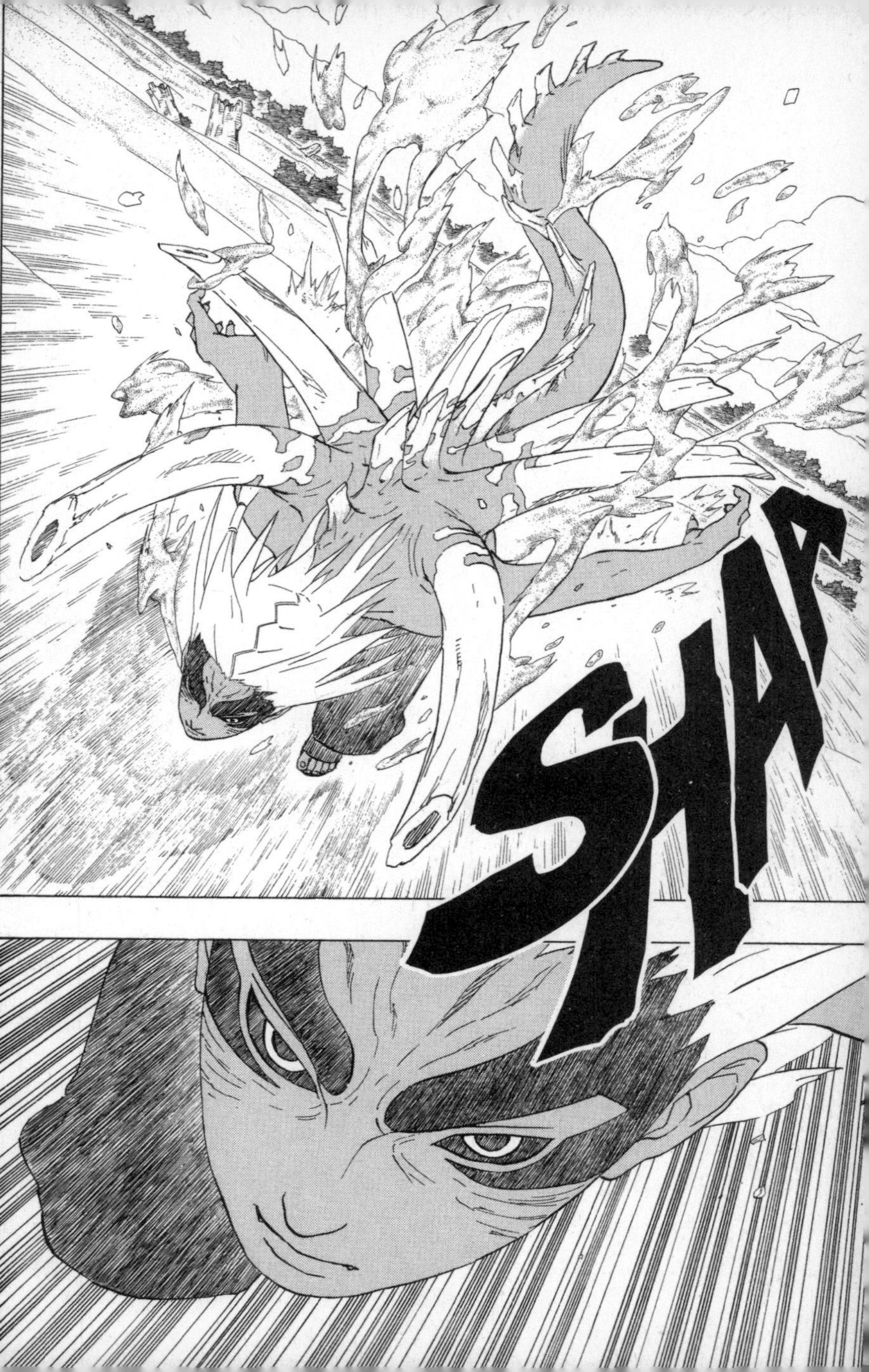
SHA

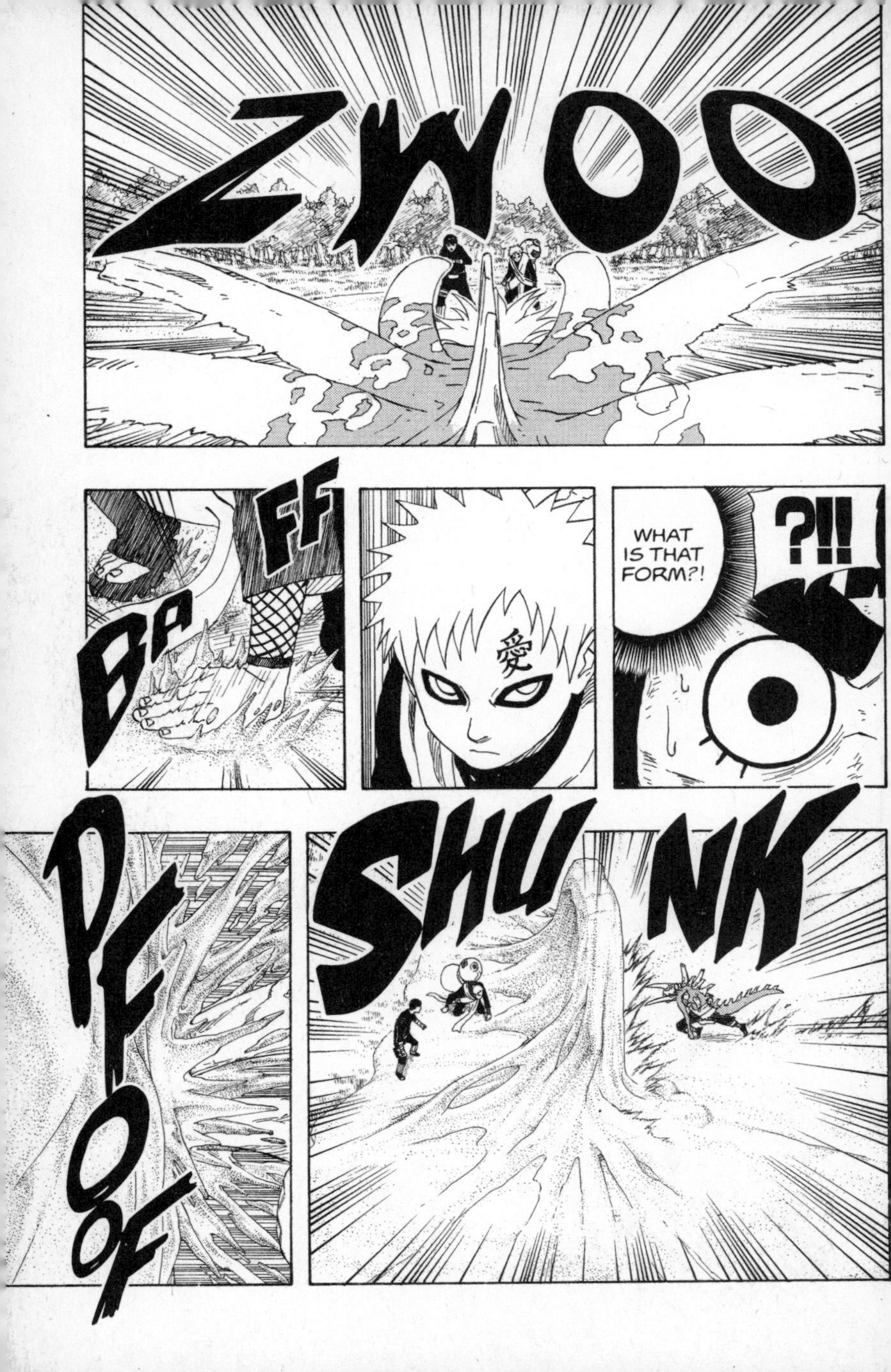
ZWOO
WHAT IS THAT FORM?!
?!!
BAFF
SHUNK
PFOOF

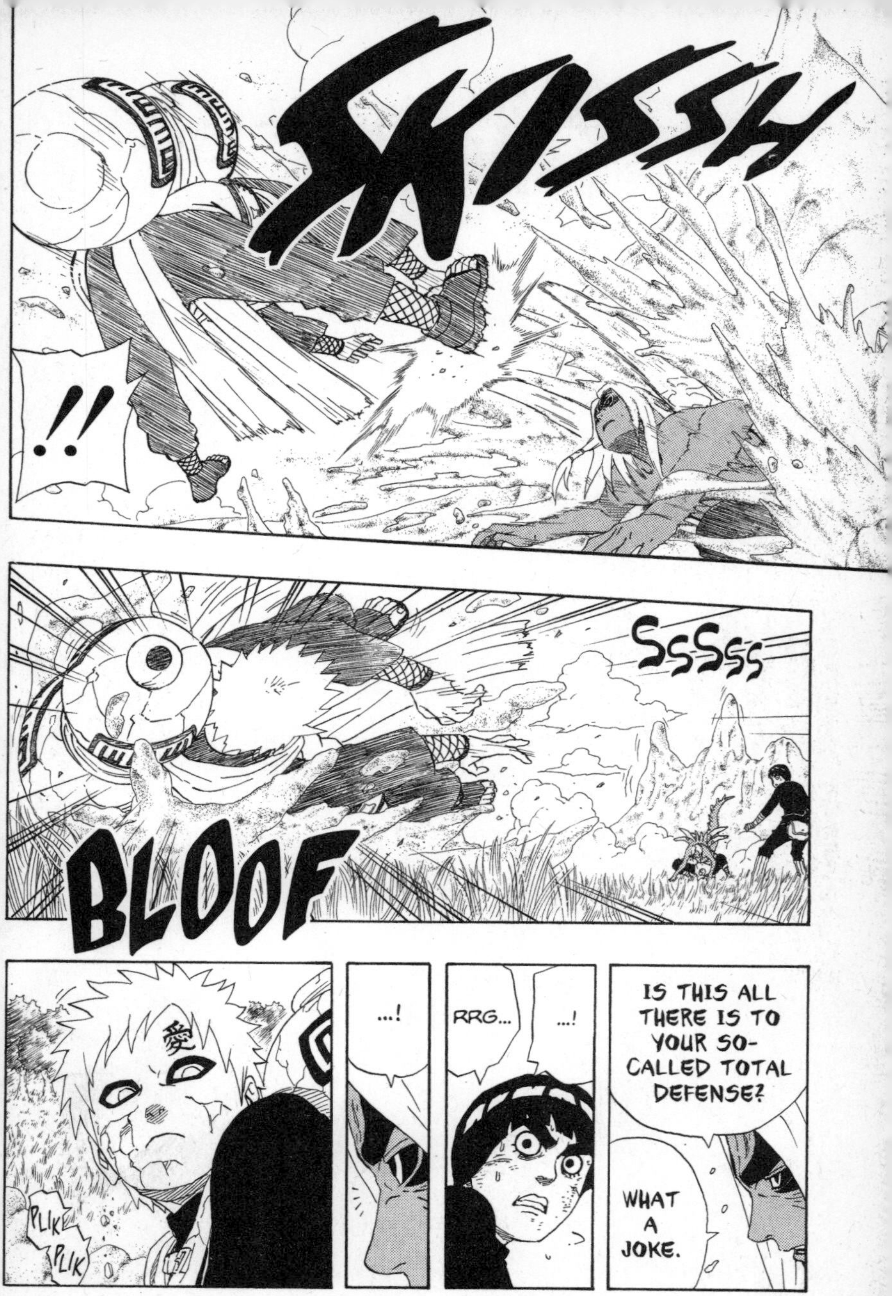
SWISSH
!!
SsSss
BLOOF
IS THIS ALL THERE IS TO YOUR SO-CALLED TOTAL DEFENSE?
WHAT A JOKE.
RRG...
...!
...!
PLIK
PLIK

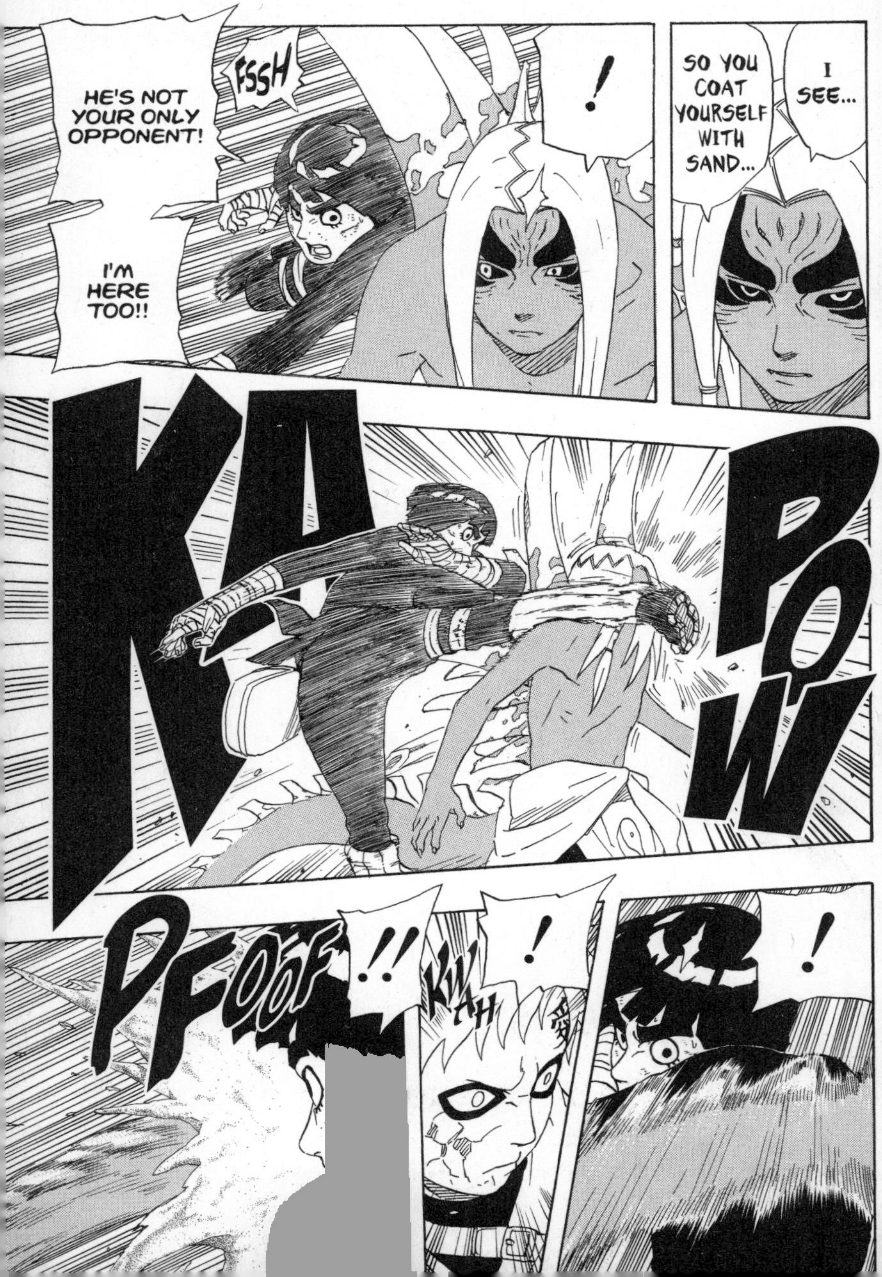
I SEE...
SO YOU COAT YOURSELF WITH SAND...
!
FSSH
HE'S NOT YOUR ONLY OPPONENT!
I'M HERE TOO!!
KA
POW
!
!
KWAH
PFOOF
!!

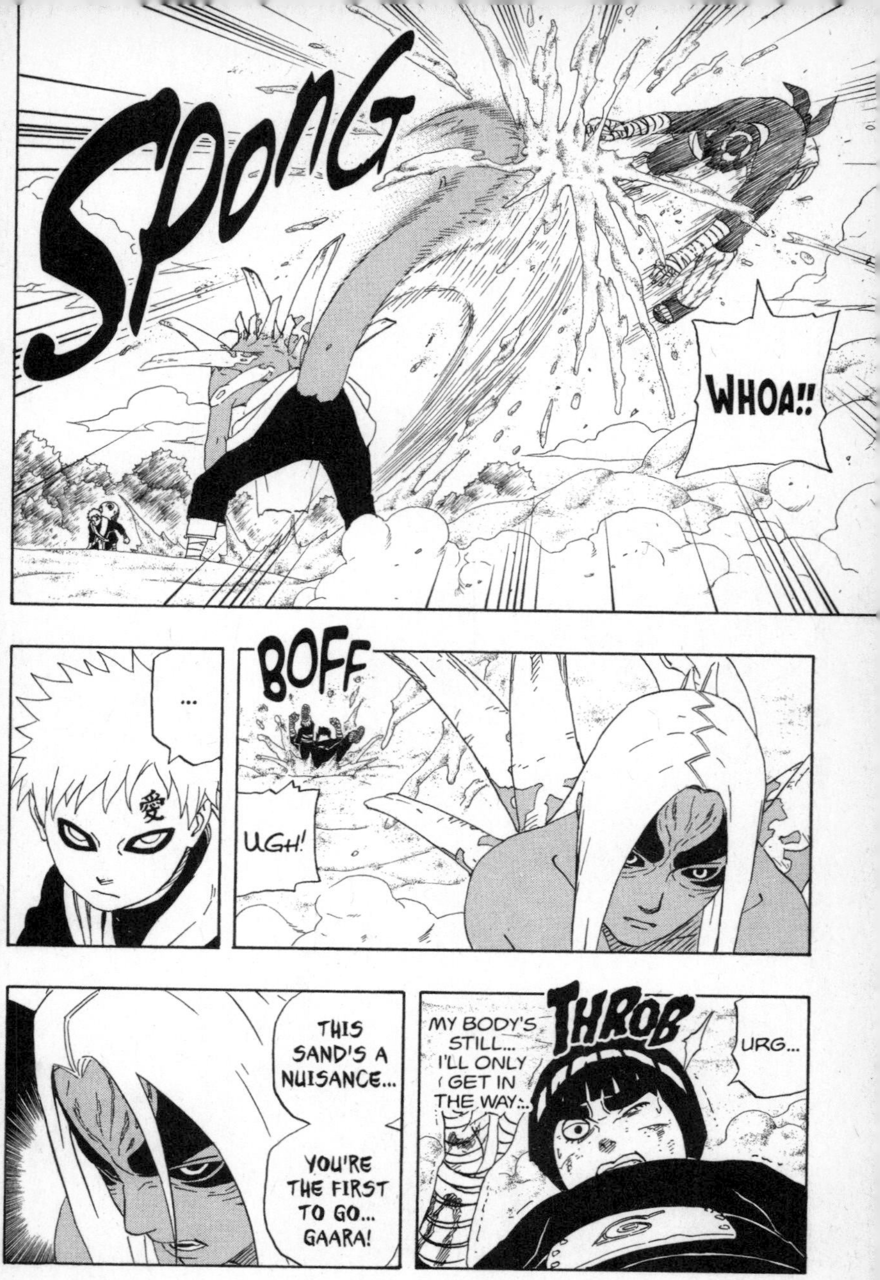
SPONG
WHOA!!
BOFF
UGH!
...
URG...
THROB
MY BODY'S STILL... I'LL ONLY GET IN THE WAY...
THIS SAND'S A NUISANCE...
YOU'RE THE FIRST TO GO... GAARA!

READ THIS WAY

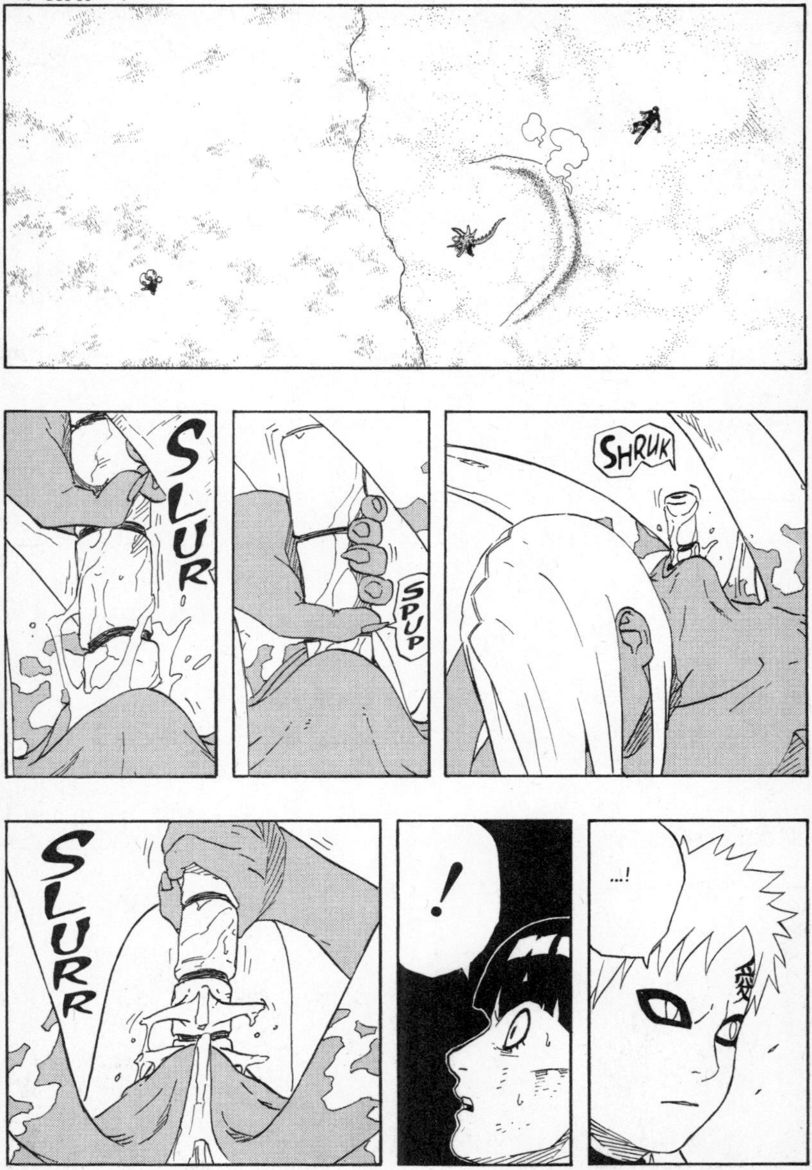
SHRUK
SPUP
SLUR
...!
!
SLURR

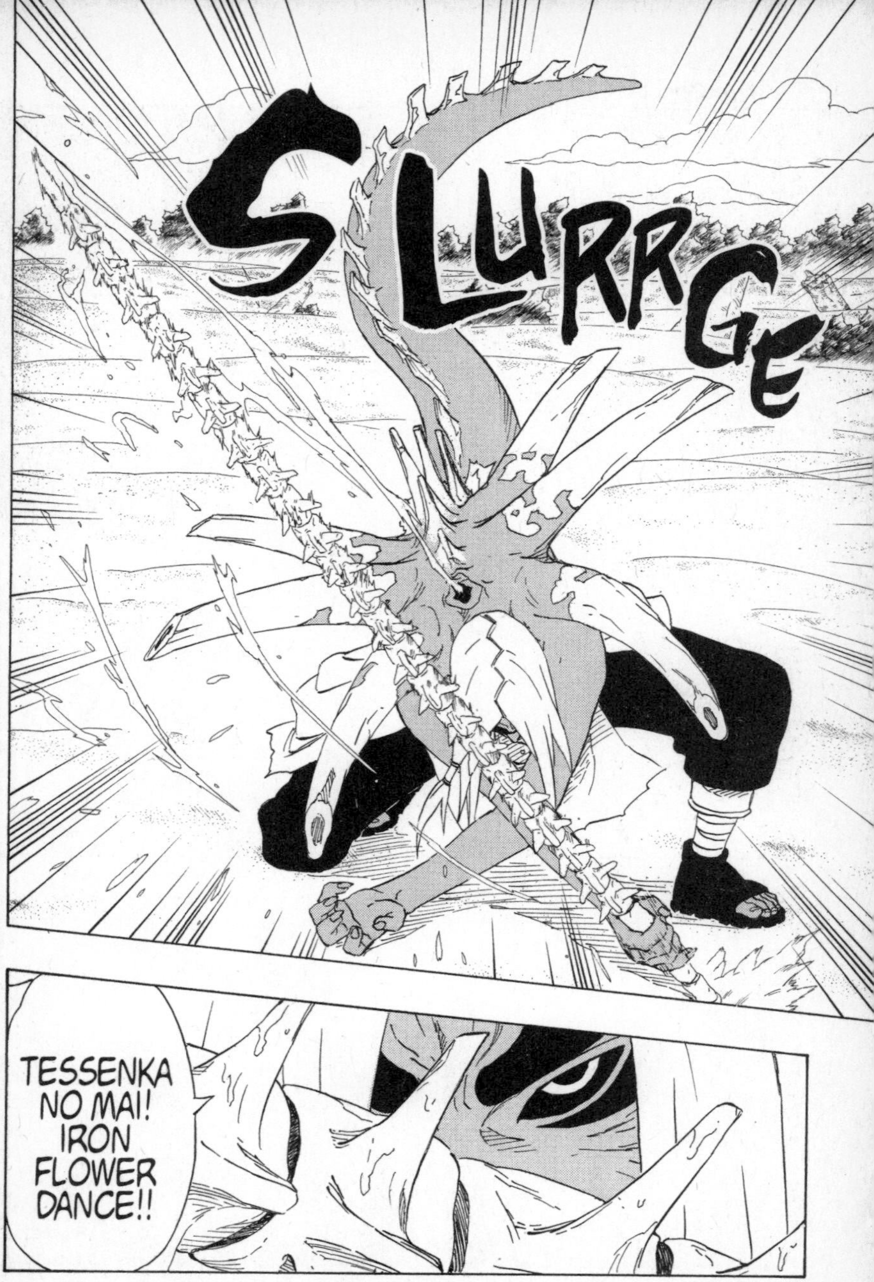
SLURRGE
TESSENKA NO MAI! IRON FLOWER DANCE!!

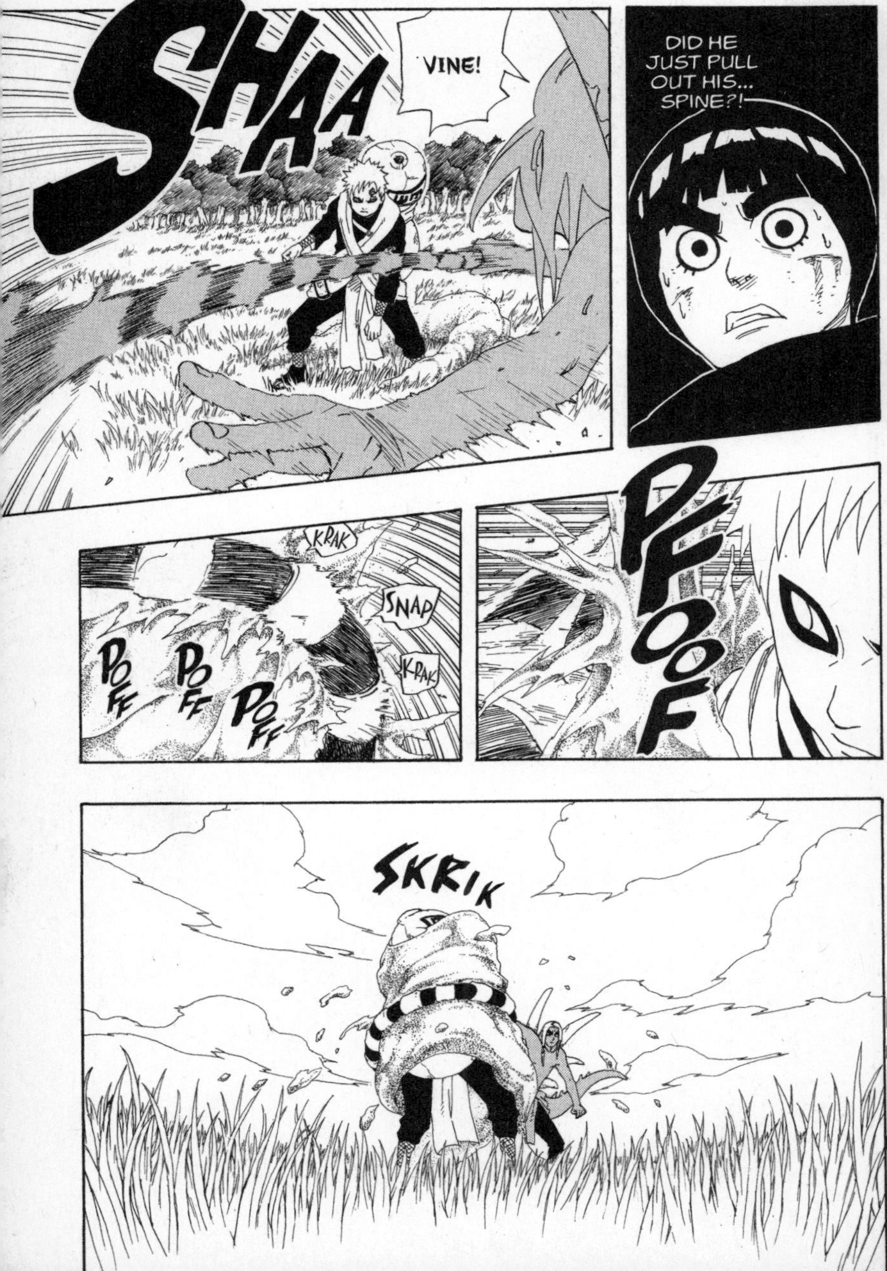
DID HE JUST PULL OUT HIS... SPINE?!
SHAA
VINE!
PFOOF
KRAK
SNAP
KRAK
POFF
POFF
POFF
SKRIK

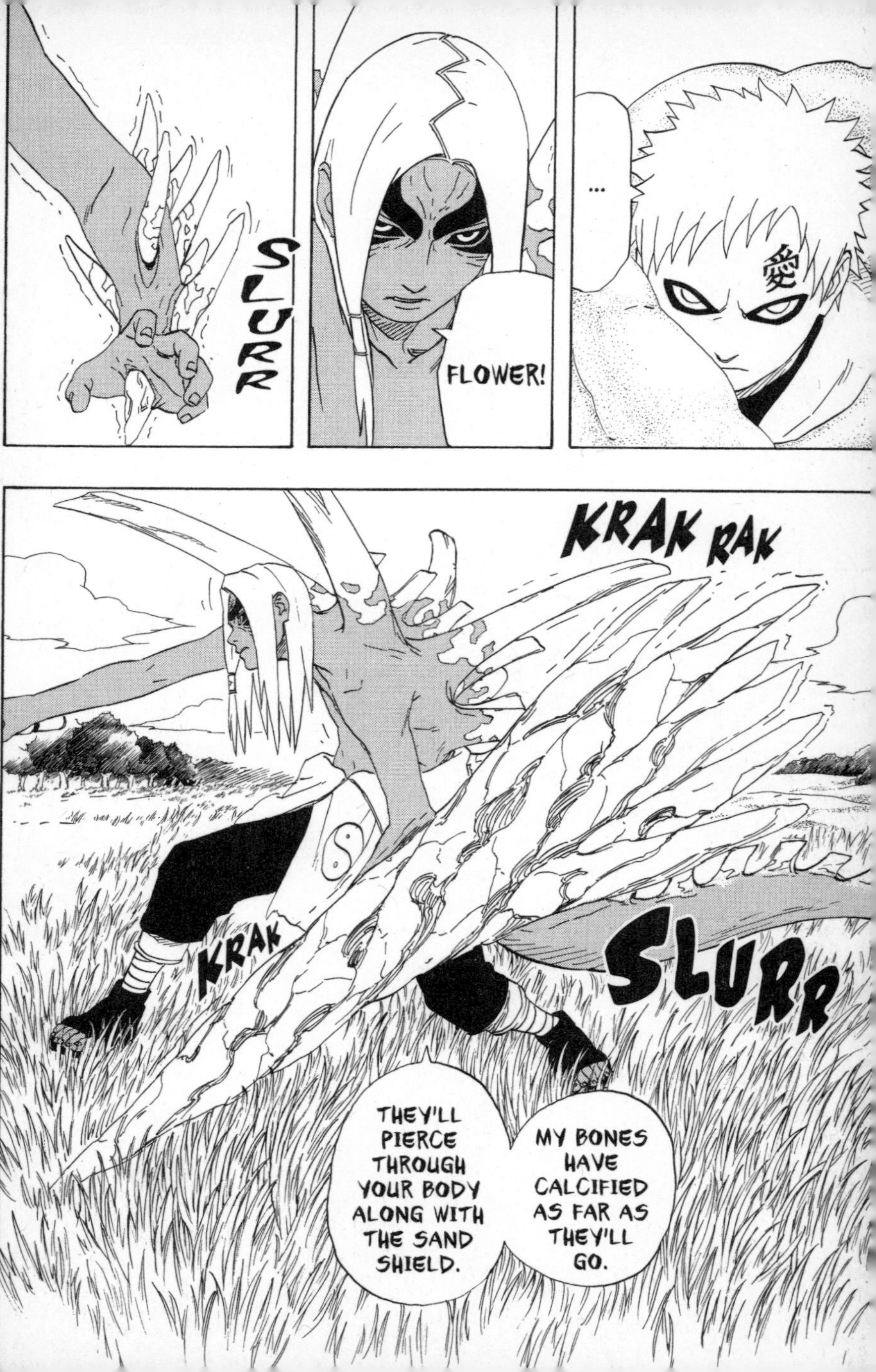
...
FLOWER!
SLURR
KRAK RAK
SLURR
KRAK
MY BONES HAVE CALCIFIED AS FAR AS THEY'LL GO.
THEY'LL PIERCE THROUGH YOUR BODY ALONG WITH THE SAND SHIELD.

READ THIS WAY

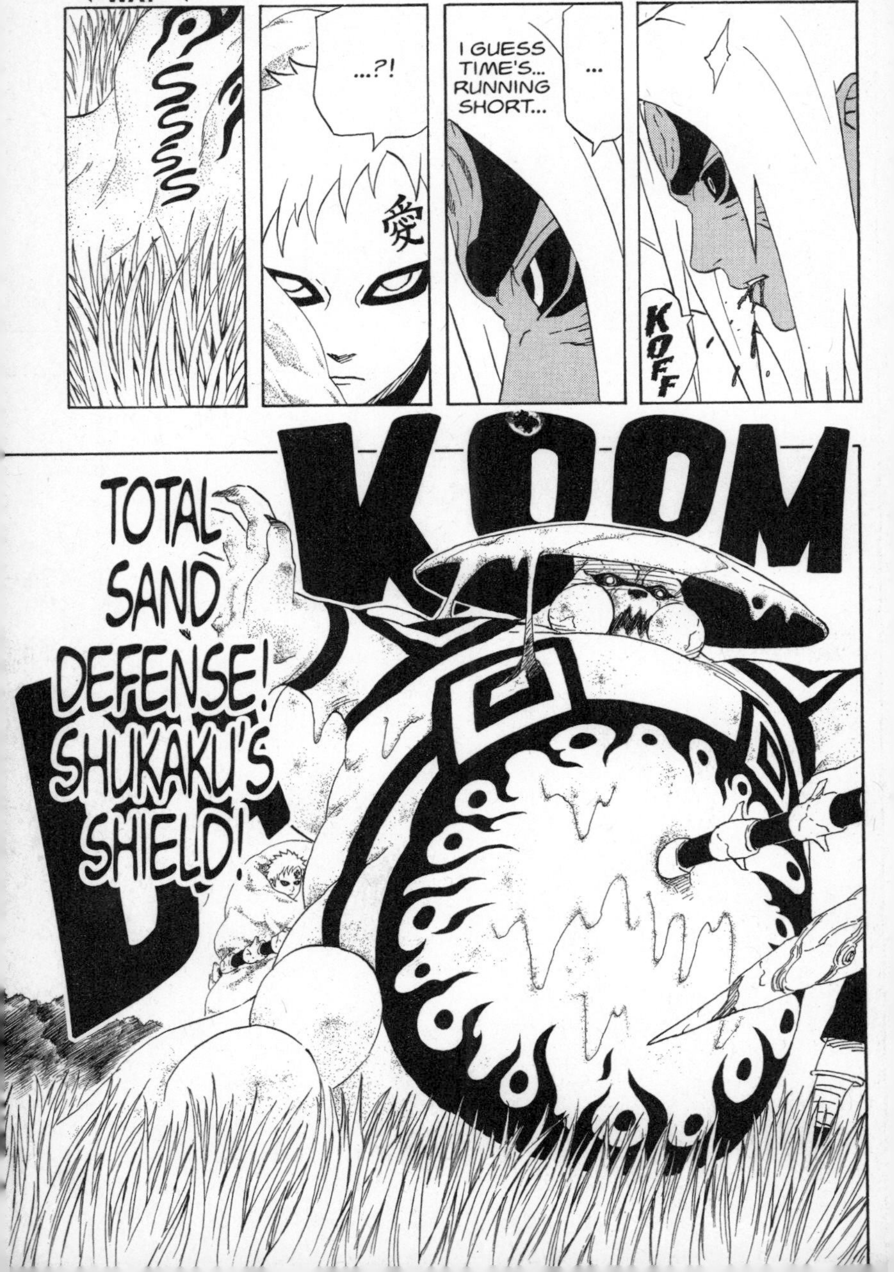
KOFF
...
I GUESS TIME'S... RUNNING SHORT...
...?!
SSSSS
KOOM
TOTAL SAND DEFENSE! SHUKAKU'S SHIELD!
D

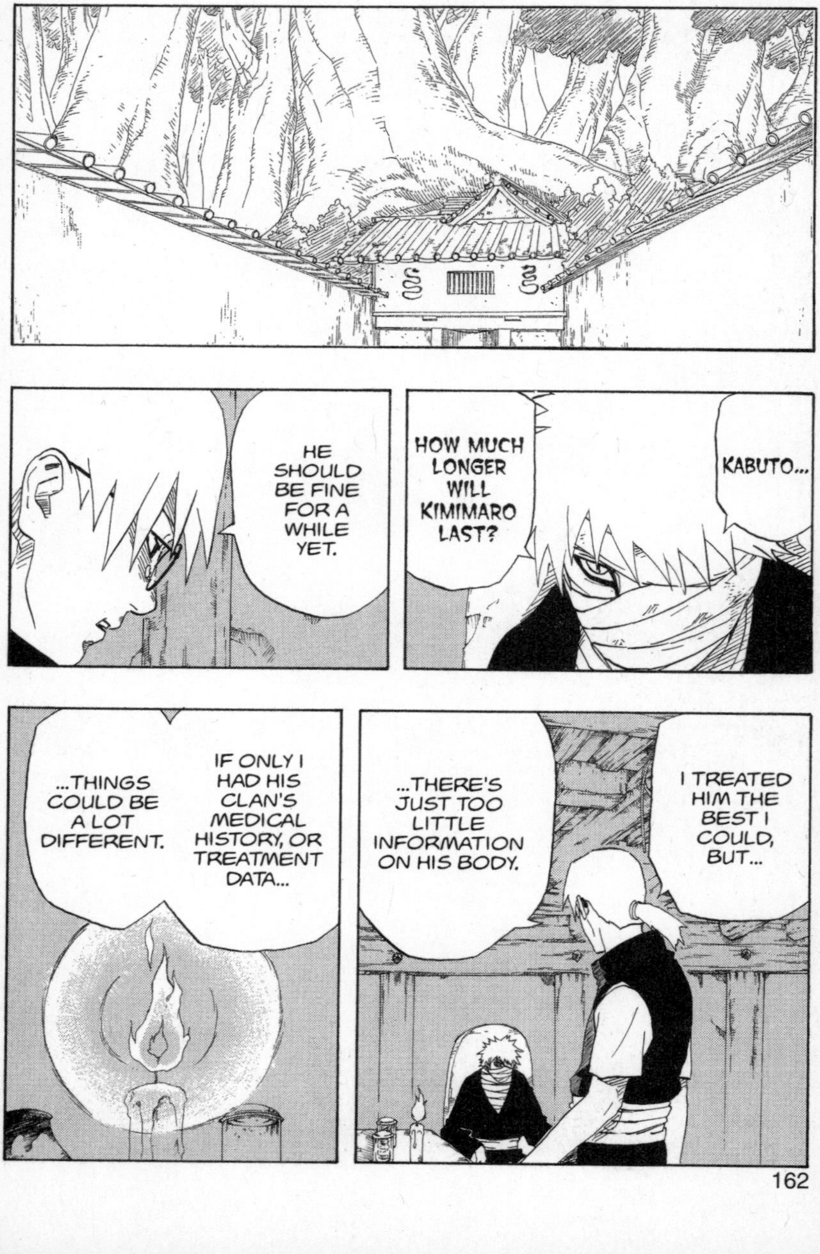
KABUTO...
HOW MUCH LONGER WILL KIMIMARO LAST?
HE SHOULD BE FINE FOR A WHILE YET.
I TREATED HIM THE BEST I COULD, BUT...
...THERE'S JUST TOO LITTLE INFORMATION ON HIS BODY.
IF ONLY I HAD HIS CLAN'S MEDICAL HISTORY, OR TREATMENT DATA...
...THINGS COULD BE A LOT DIFFERENT.

READ THIS WAY

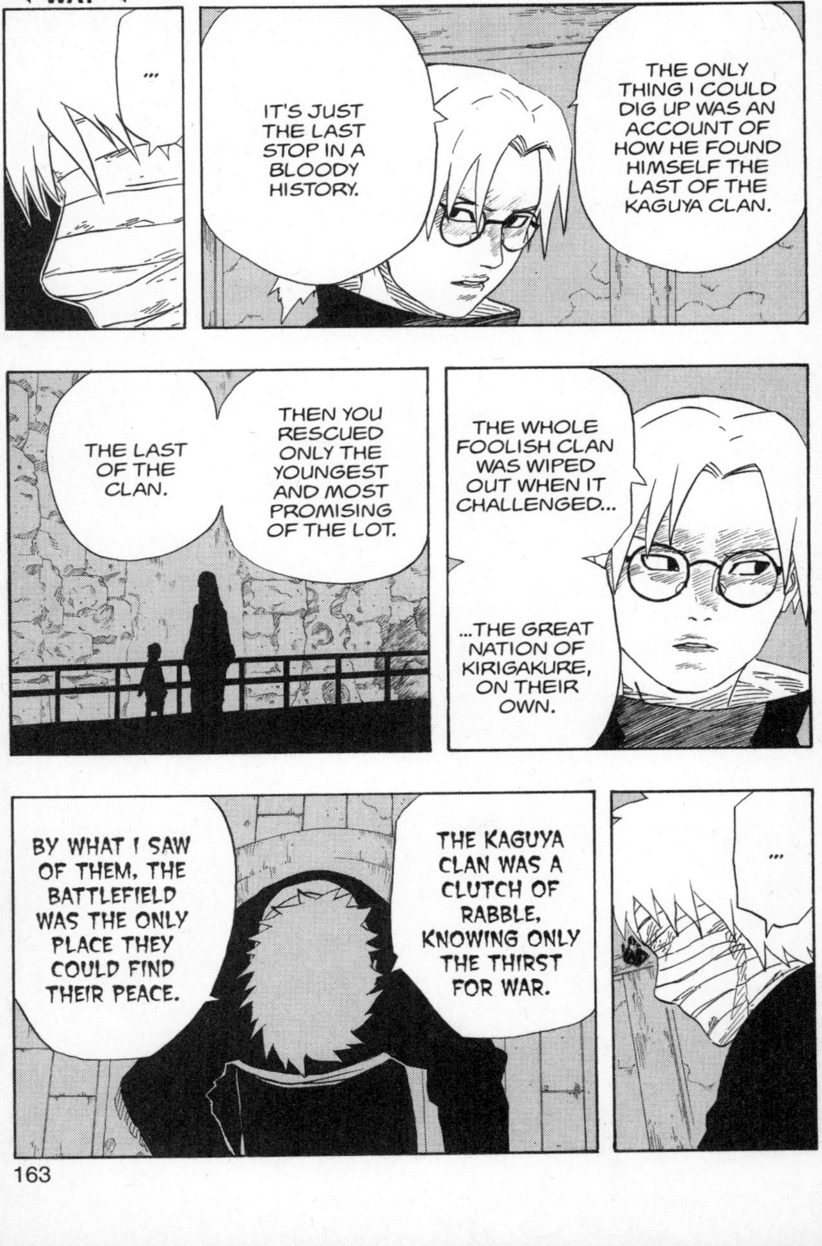
THE ONLY THING I COULD DIG UP WAS AN ACCOUNT OF HOW HE FOUND HIMSELF THE LAST OF THE KAGUYA CLAN.
IT'S JUST THE LAST STOP IN A BLOODY HISTORY.
...
THE WHOLE FOOLISH CLAN WAS WIPED OUT WHEN IT CHALLENGED...
...THE GREAT NATION OF KIRIGAKURE, ON THEIR OWN.
THEN YOU RESCUED ONLY THE YOUNGEST AND MOST PROMISING OF THE LOT.
THE LAST OF THE CLAN.
...
THE KAGUYA CLAN WAS A CLUTCH OF RABBLE, KNOWING ONLY THE THIRST FOR WAR.
BY WHAT I SAW OF THEM, THE BATTLEFIELD WAS THE ONLY PLACE THEY COULD FIND THEIR PEACE.

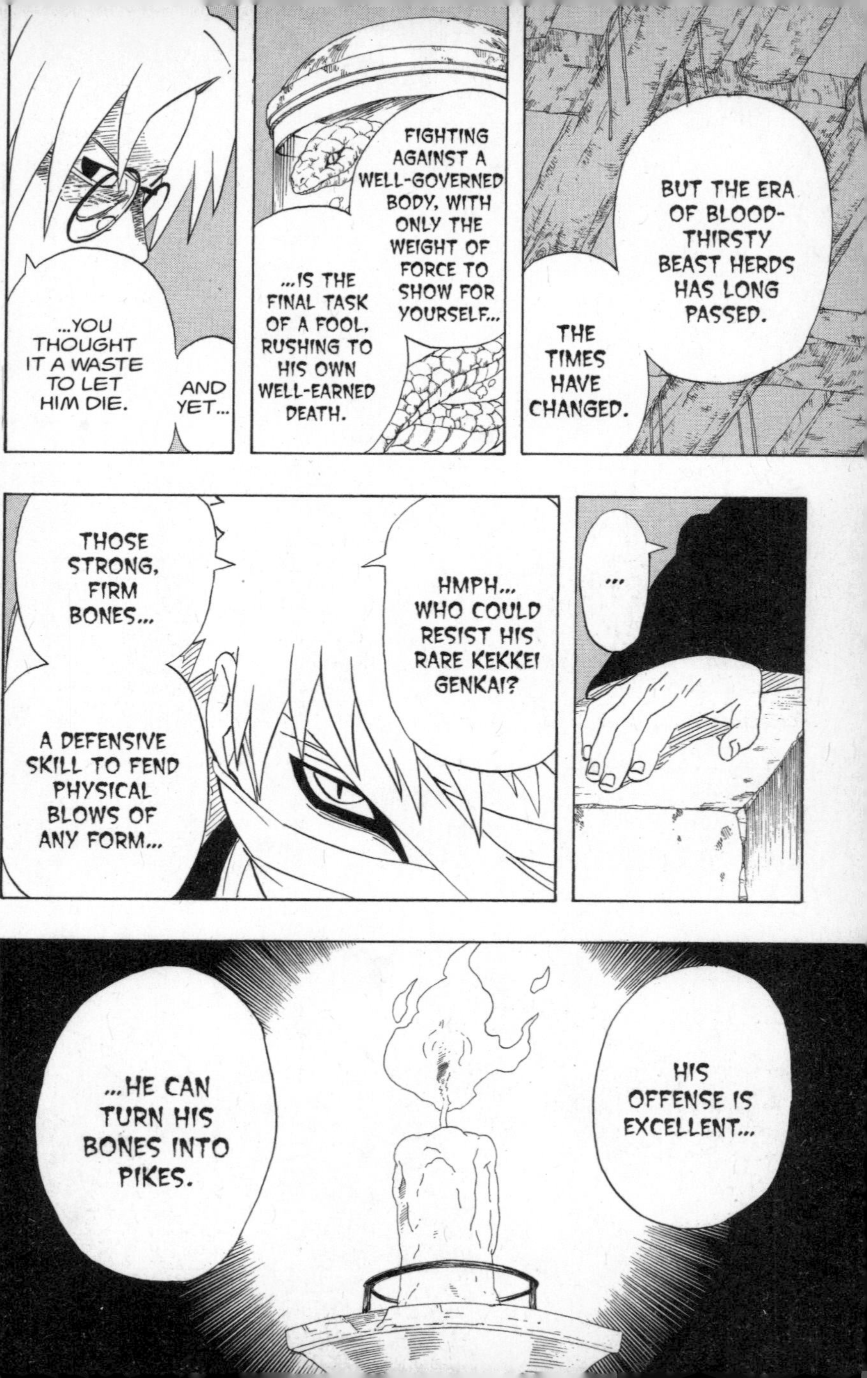
BUT THE ERA OF BLOOD-THIRSTY BEAST HERDS HAS LONG PASSED.
THE TIMES HAVE CHANGED.
FIGHTING AGAINST A WELL-GOVERNED BODY, WITH ONLY THE WEIGHT OF FORCE TO SHOW FOR YOURSELF...
...IS THE FINAL TASK OF A FOOL, RUSHING TO HIS OWN WELL-EARNED DEATH.
AND YET...
...YOU THOUGHT IT A WASTE TO LET HIM DIE.
...
HMPH... WHO COULD RESIST HIS RARE KEKKEI GENKAI?
THOSE STRONG, FIRM BONES...
A DEFENSIVE SKILL TO FEND PHYSICAL BLOWS OF ANY FORM...
HIS OFFENSE IS EXCELLENT...
...HE CAN TURN HIS BONES INTO PIKES.

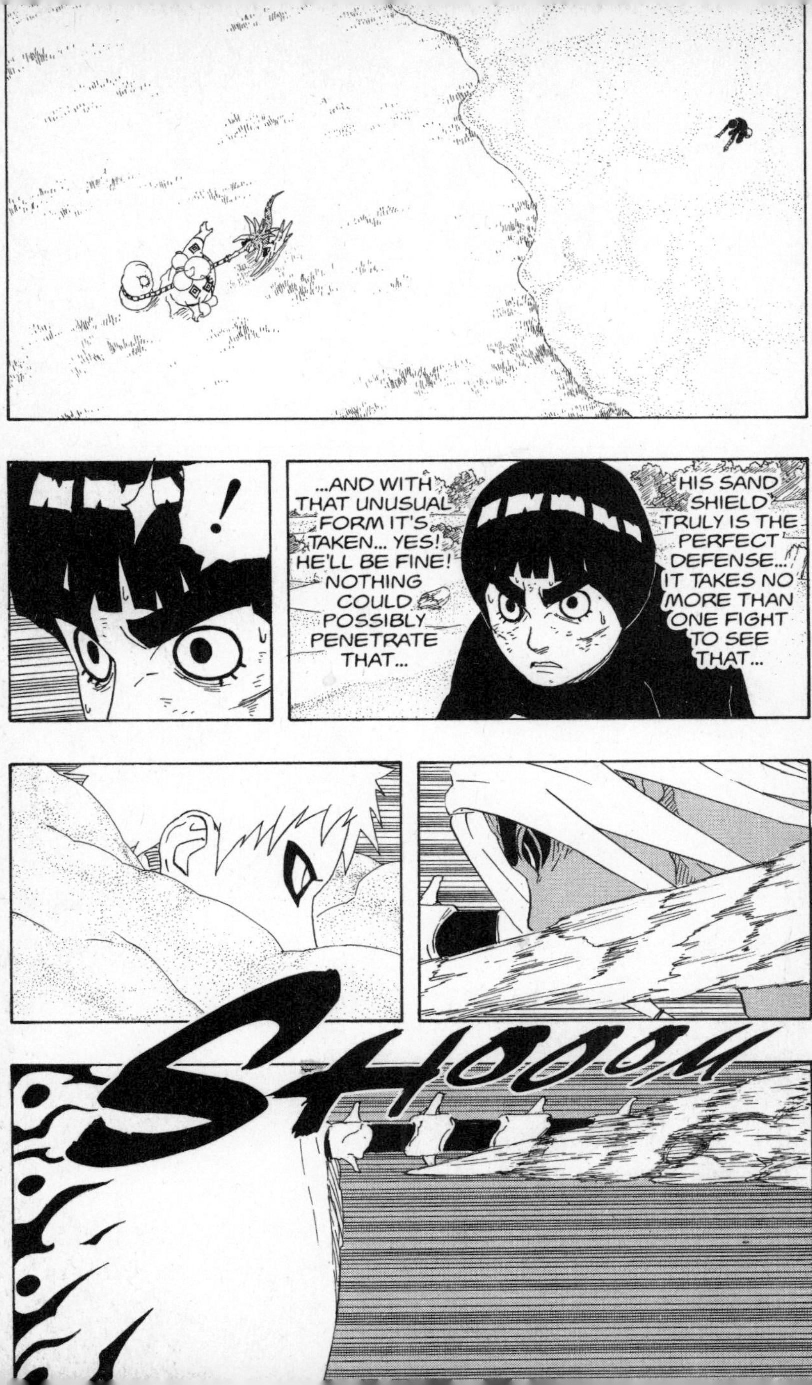
HIS SAND SHIELD TRULY IS THE PERFECT DEFENSE... IT TAKES NO MORE THAN ONE FIGHT TO SEE THAT...
...AND WITH THAT UNUSUAL FORM IT'S TAKEN... YES! HE'LL BE FINE! NOTHING COULD POSSIBLY PENETRATE THAT...
!
SHOOOM

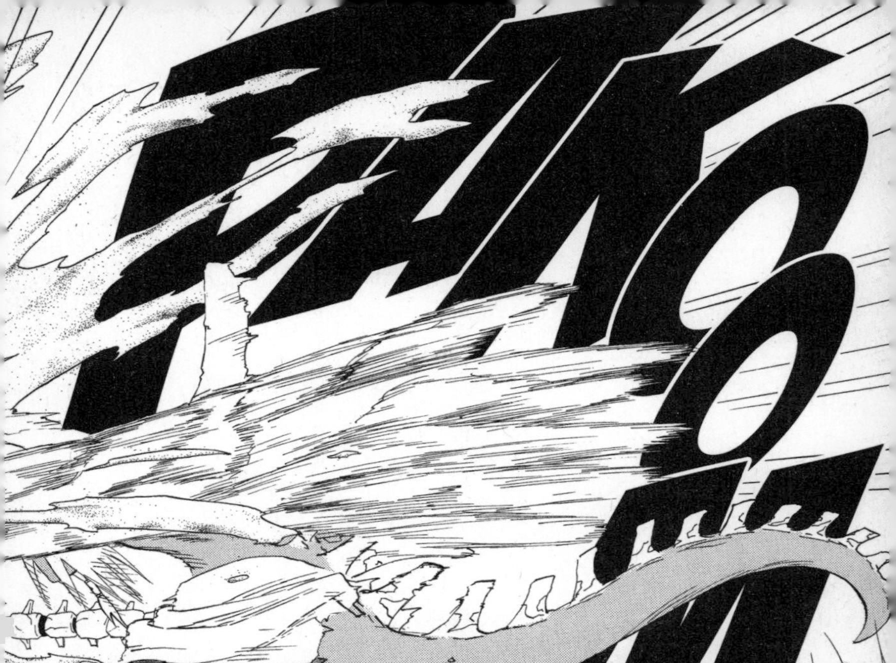

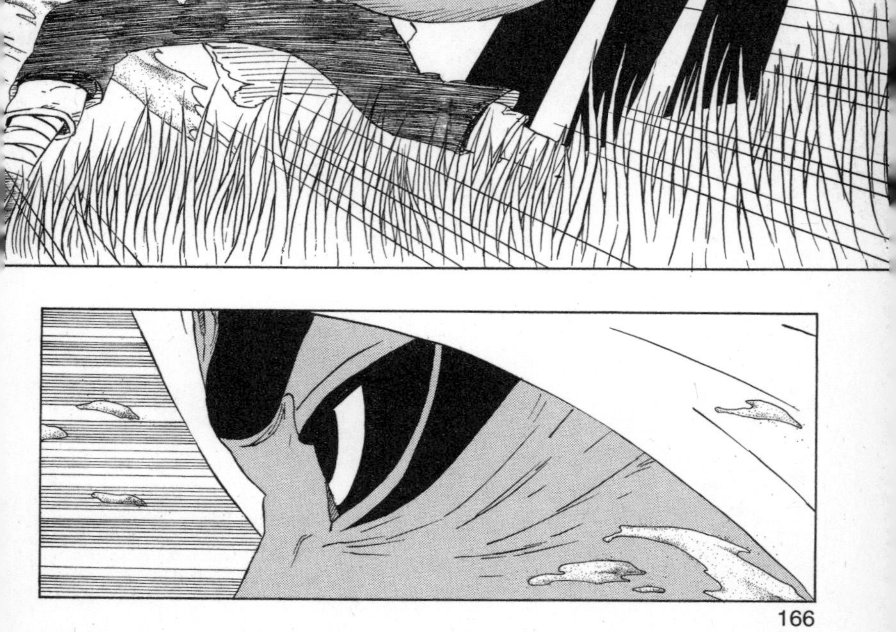

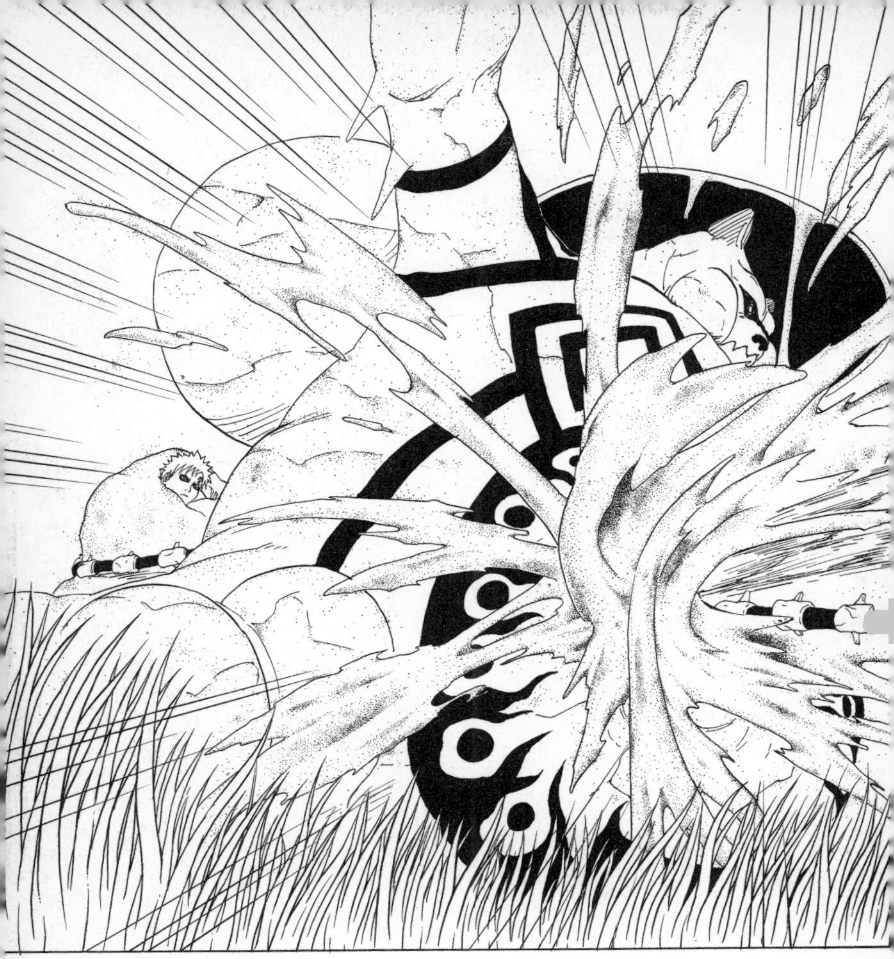

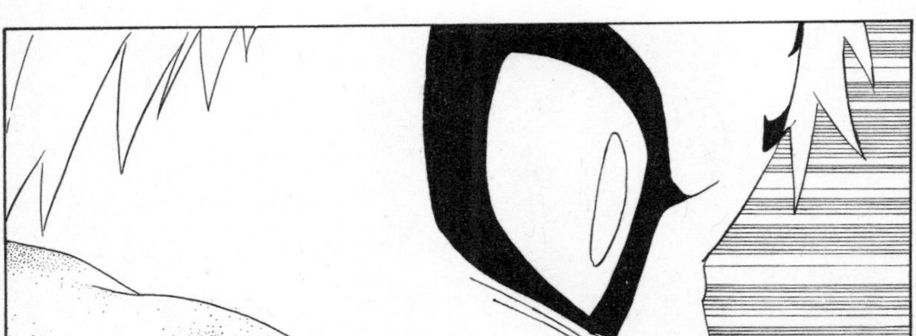

MEET KISHIMOTO MASASHI'S ASSISTANTS PART 8

ANOTHER YOUNG ASSISTANT HAS JOINED THE NARUTO STAFF. LATELY I'M BEGINNING TO FEEL THE AGE DIFFERENCE WITH MY ASSISTANTS. I GUESS I'M AN OLD MAN NOW.

ASSISTANT NO. 8: ITAKURA YÛICHI

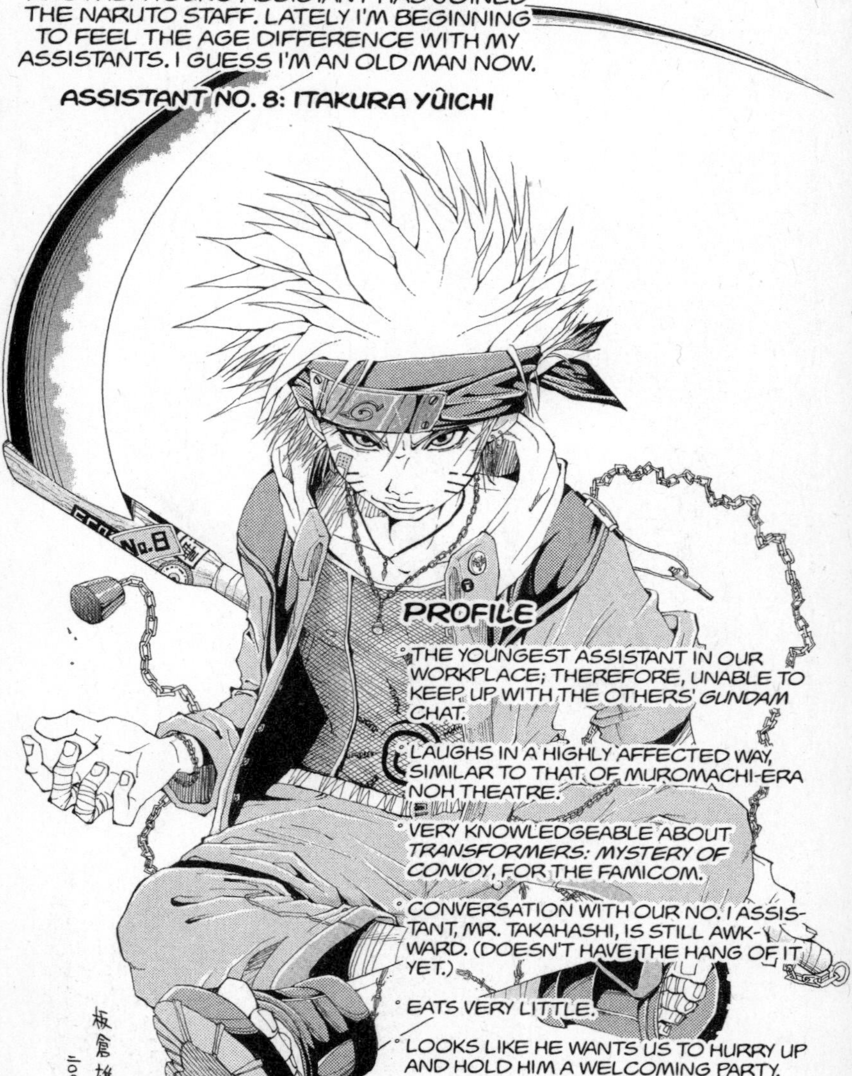
No.8
板倉雄一
二〇〇四

YÛICHI ITAKURA, 2004

PROFILE

- THE YOUNGEST ASSISTANT IN OUR WORKPLACE; THEREFORE, UNABLE TO KEEP UP WITH THE OTHERS' *GUNDAM* CHAT.
- LAUGHS IN A HIGHLY AFFECTED WAY, SIMILAR TO THAT OF MUROMACHI-ERA NOH THEATRE.
- VERY KNOWLEDGEABLE ABOUT *TRANSFORMERS: MYSTERY OF CONVOY*, FOR THE FAMICOM.
- CONVERSATION WITH OUR NO. 1 ASSISTANT, MR. TAKAHASHI, IS STILL AWKWARD. (DOESN'T HAVE THE HANG OF IT YET.)
- EATS VERY LITTLE.
- LOOKS LIKE HE WANTS US TO HURRY UP AND HOLD HIM A WELCOMING PARTY.
- IS A SWEET AND KINDHEARTED BOY.

Number 217: For The Most Precious

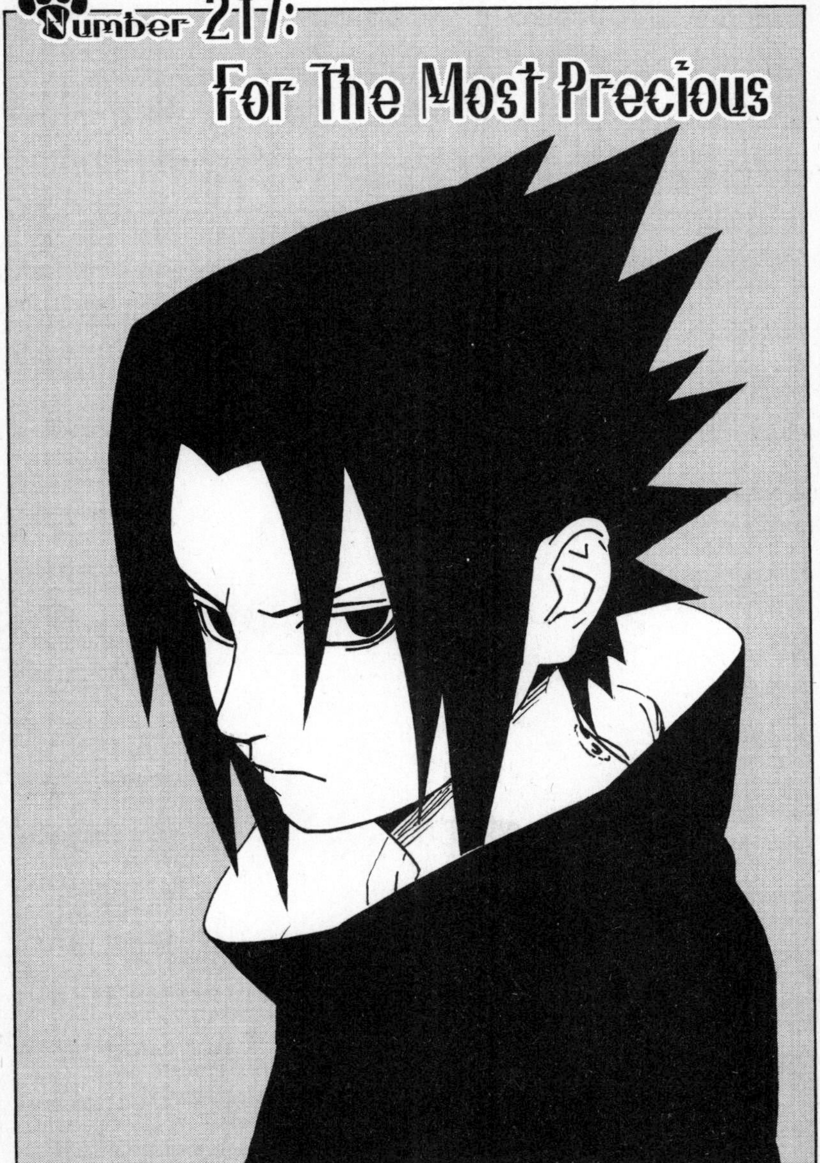

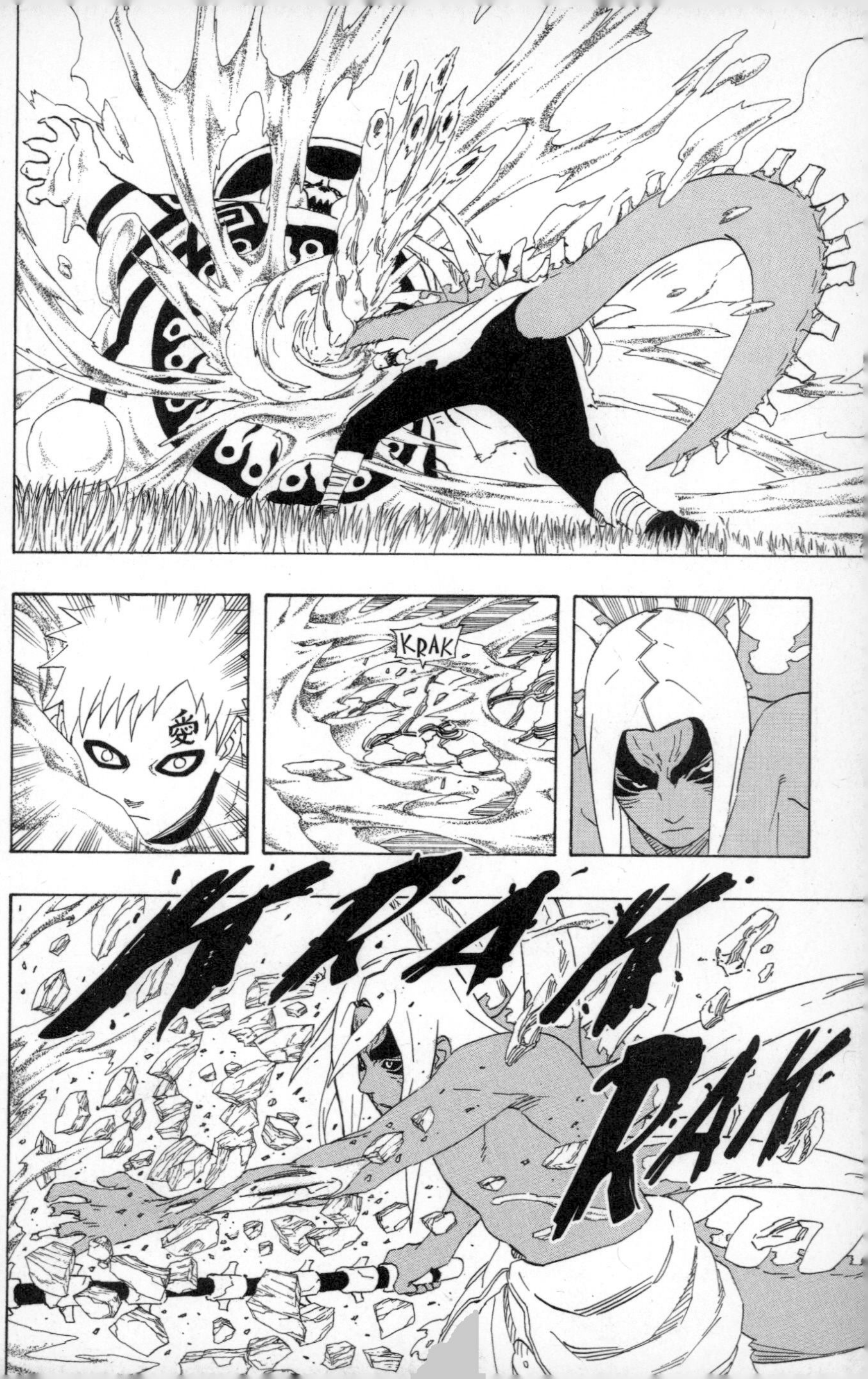
KRAK
KRAK
RAK

READ THIS WAY

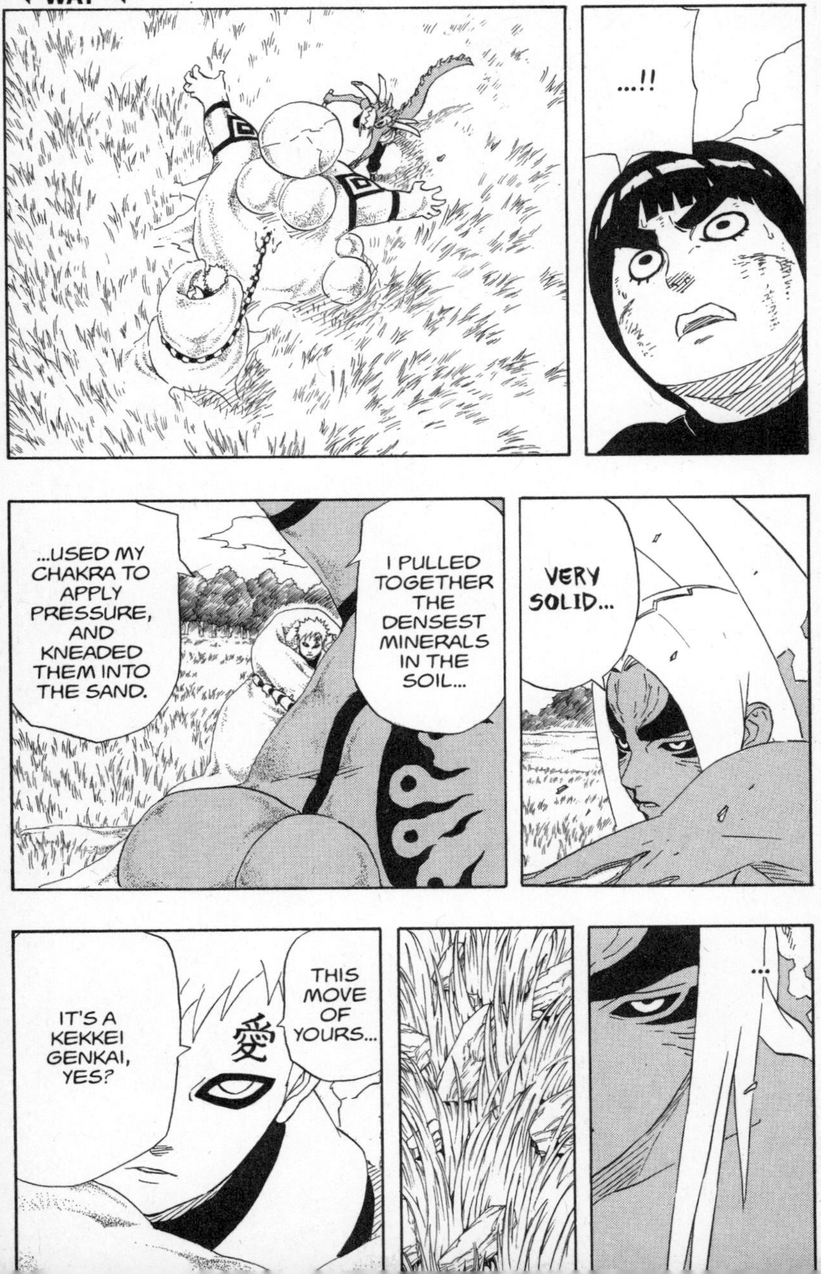
...!!
VERY SOLID...
I PULLED TOGETHER THE DENSEST MINERALS IN THE SOIL...
...USED MY CHAKRA TO APPLY PRESSURE, AND KNEADED THEM INTO THE SAND.
...
THIS MOVE OF YOURS...
IT'S A KEKKEI GENKAI, YES?

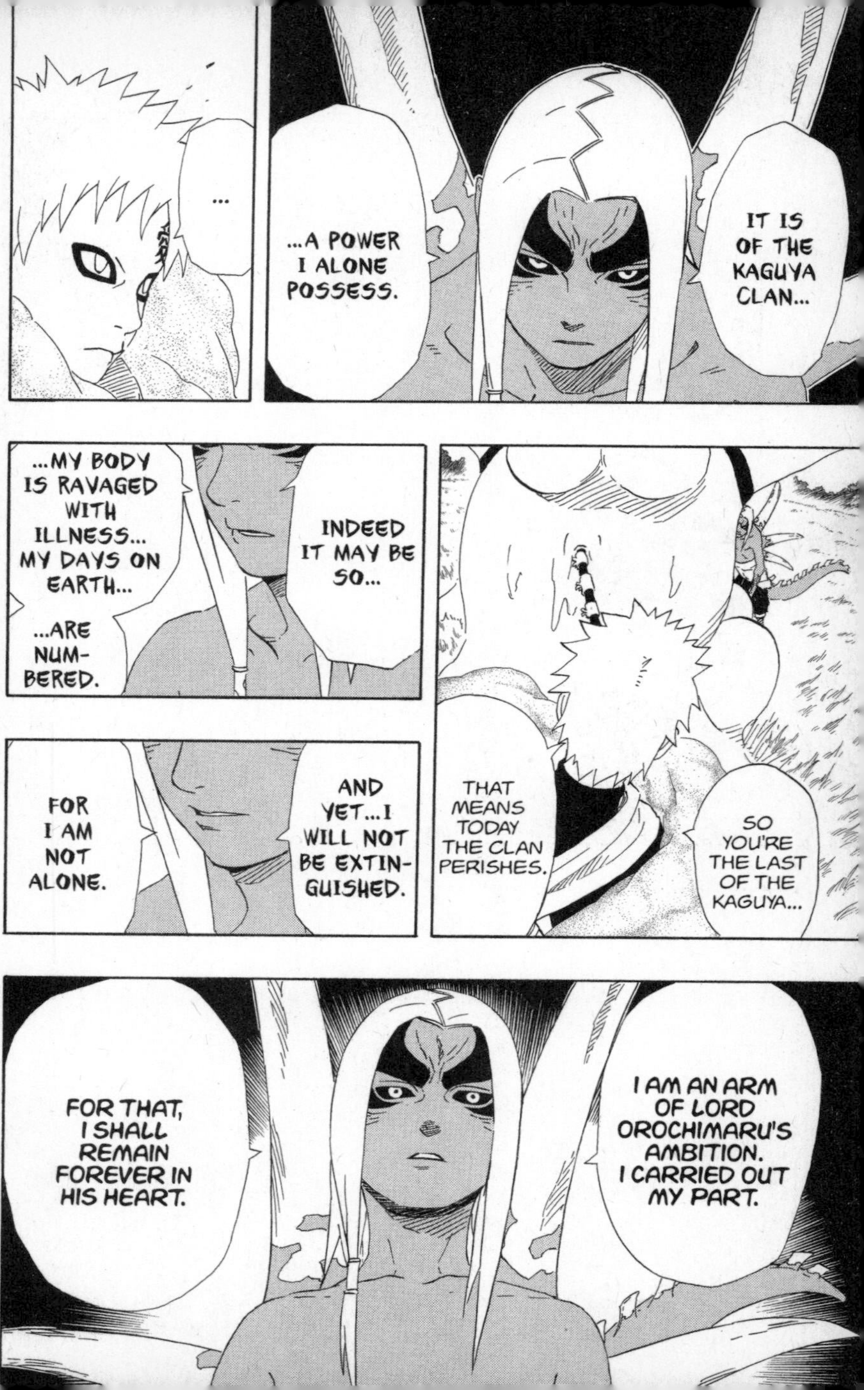

IT IS OF THE KAGUYA CLAN...
...A POWER I ALONE POSSESS.
...
SO YOU'RE THE LAST OF THE KAGUYA...
THAT MEANS TODAY THE CLAN PERISHES.
INDEED IT MAY BE SO...
...MY BODY IS RAVAGED WITH ILLNESS... MY DAYS ON EARTH...
...ARE NUM-BERED.
AND YET...I WILL NOT BE EXTIN-GUISHED.
FOR I AM NOT ALONE.
I AM AN ARM OF LORD OROCHIMARU'S AMBITION. I CARRIED OUT MY PART.
FOR THAT, I SHALL REMAIN FOREVER IN HIS HEART.

READ THIS WAY

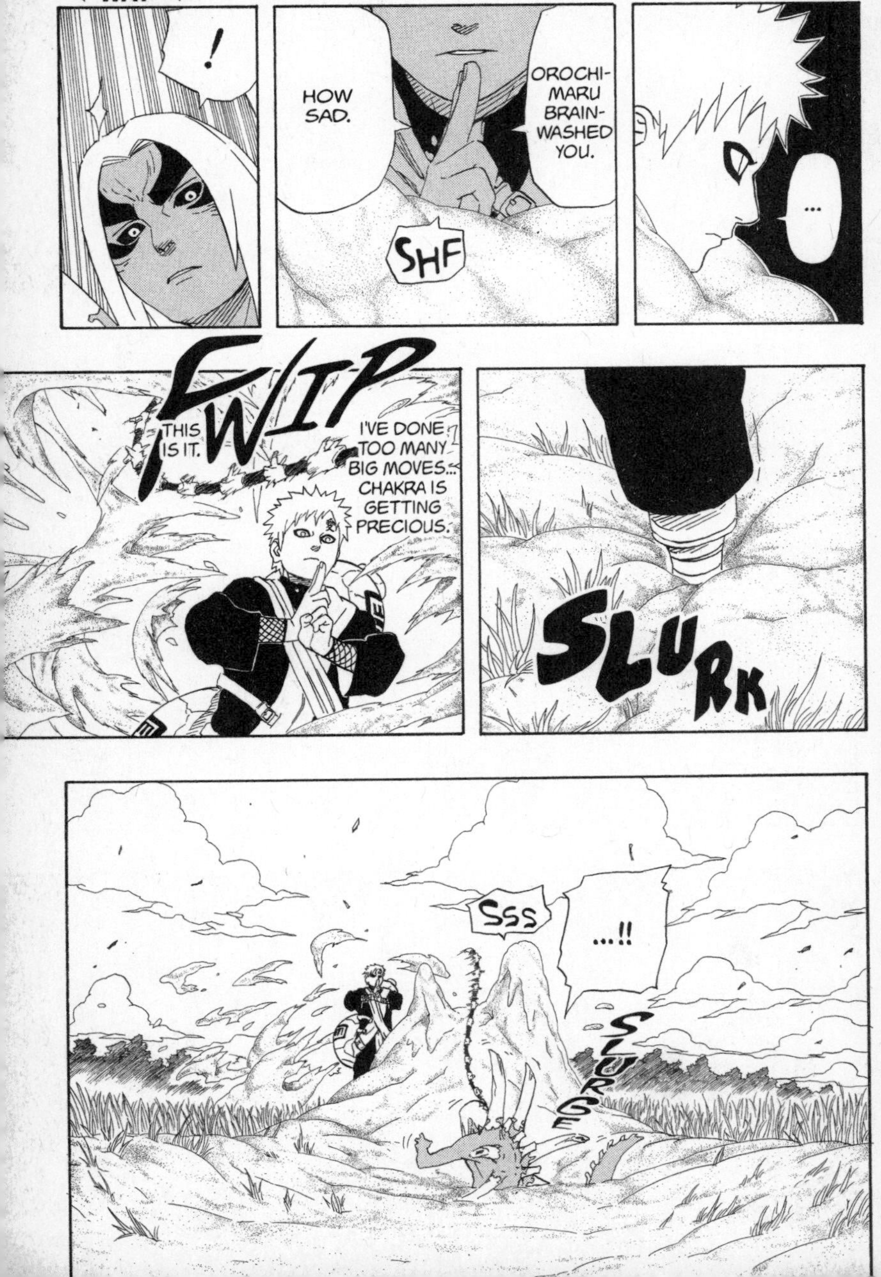
...
OROCHI-MARU BRAIN-WASHED YOU.
HOW SAD.
SHF
!
SLURK
FWIP
I'VE DONE TOO MANY BIG MOVES... CHAKRA IS GETTING PRECIOUS.
THIS IS IT.
...!!
SSS
SLURGE

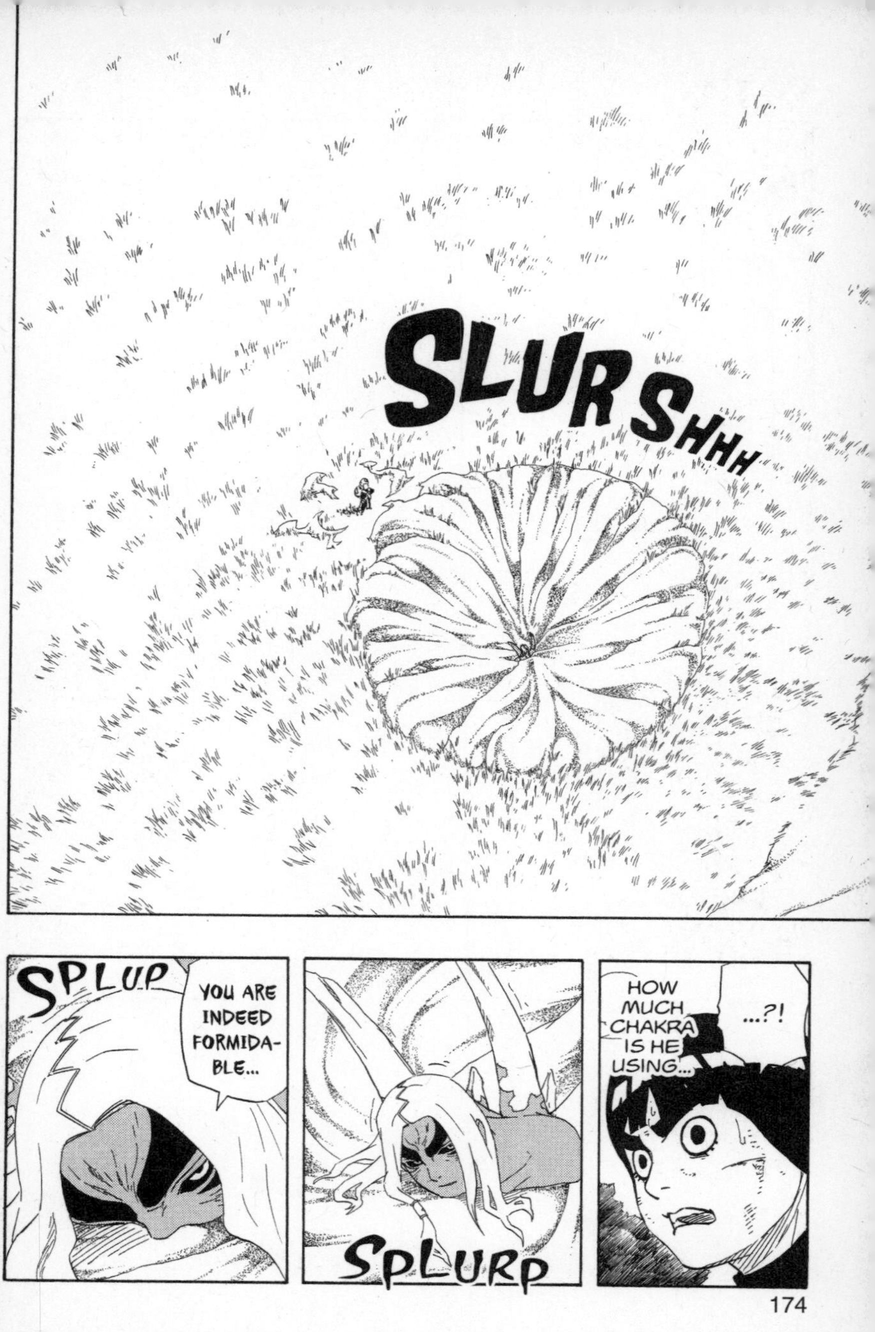
SLURSHHH
HOW MUCH CHAKRA IS HE USING...
...?!
SPLURP
SPLUP
YOU ARE INDEED FORMIDABLE...

READ THIS WAY

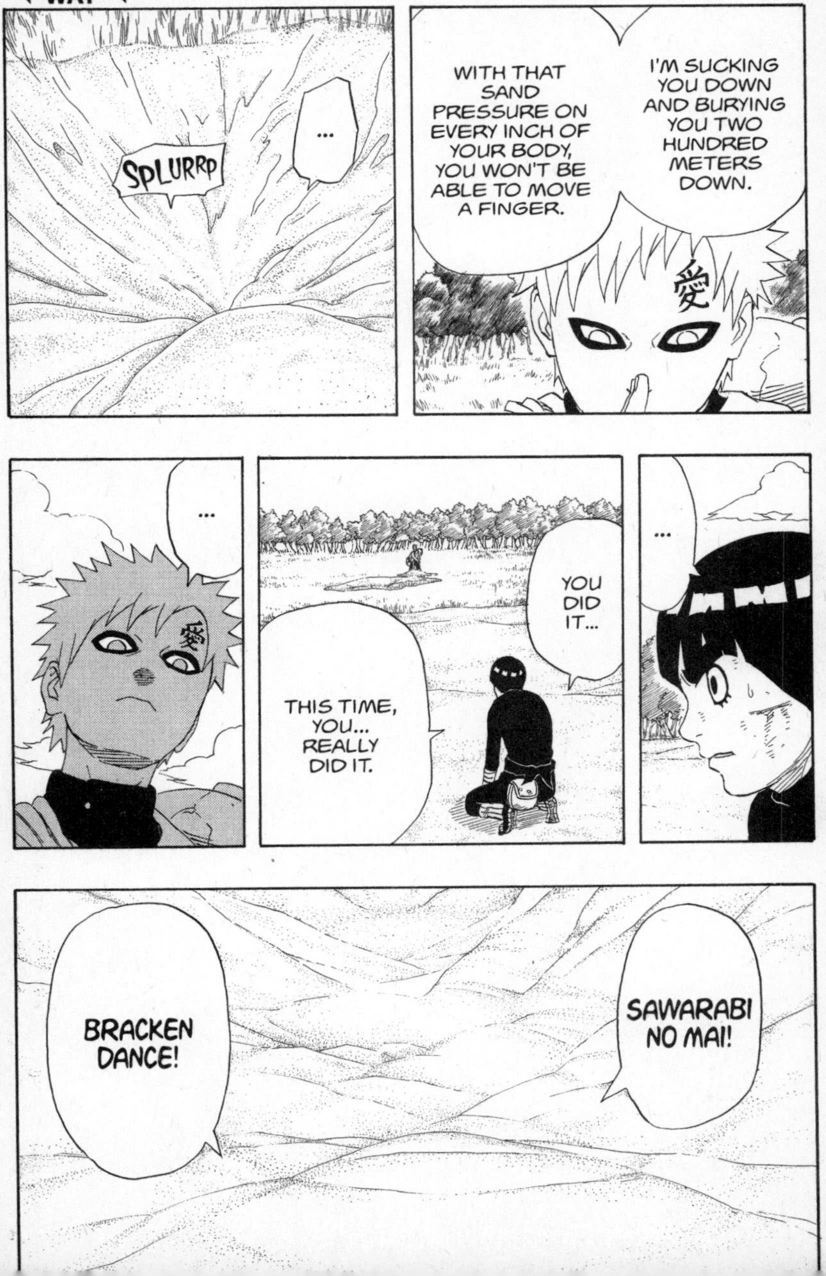

I'M SUCKING YOU DOWN AND BURYING YOU TWO HUNDRED METERS DOWN.
WITH THAT SAND PRESSURE ON EVERY INCH OF YOUR BODY, YOU WON'T BE ABLE TO MOVE A FINGER.
...
SPLURRP
...
YOU DID IT...
THIS TIME, YOU... REALLY DID IT.
...
SAWARABI NO MAI!
BRACKEN DANCE!

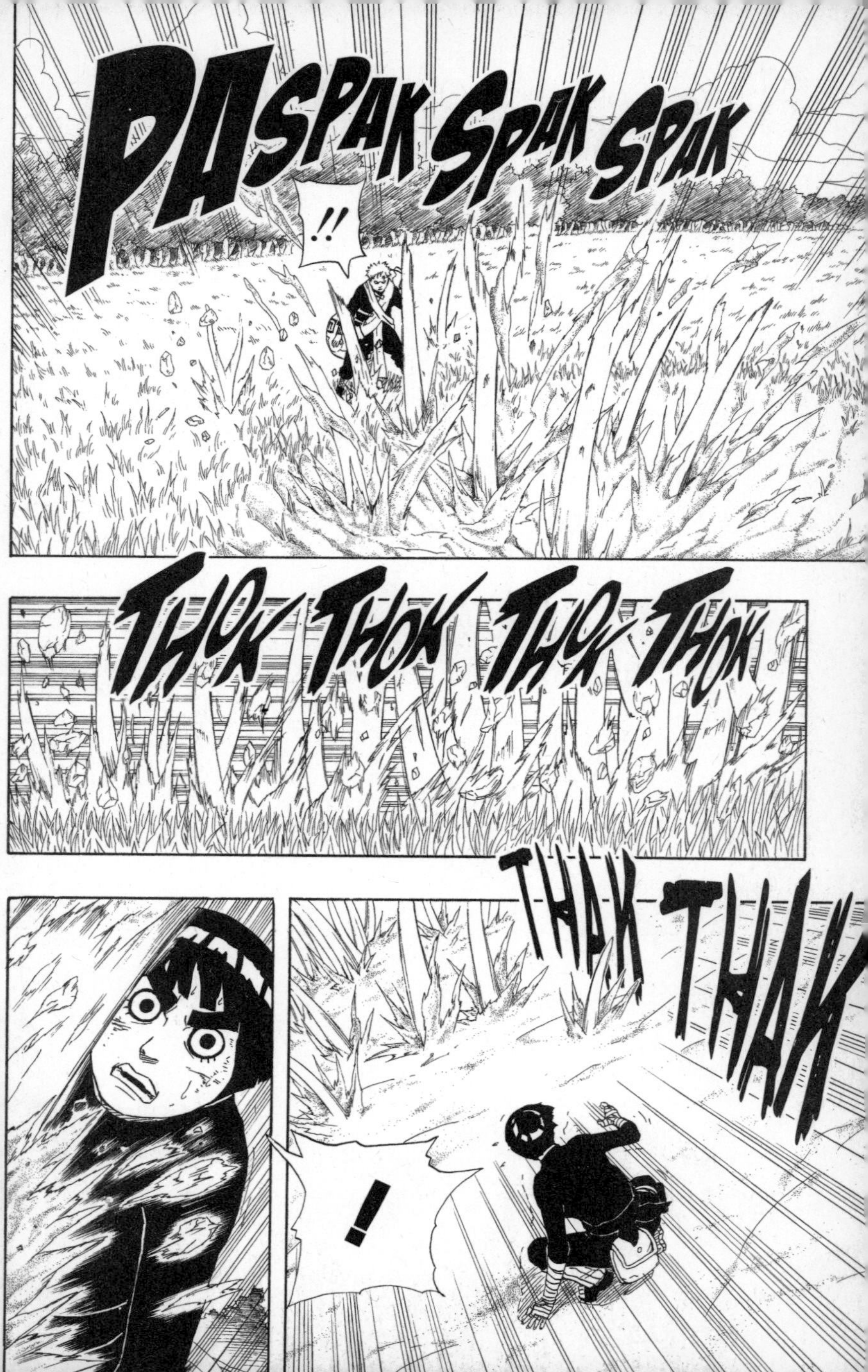
PASPAK SPAK SPAK
!!
THOK THOK THOK THOK
THAK THAK
!

READ THIS WAY

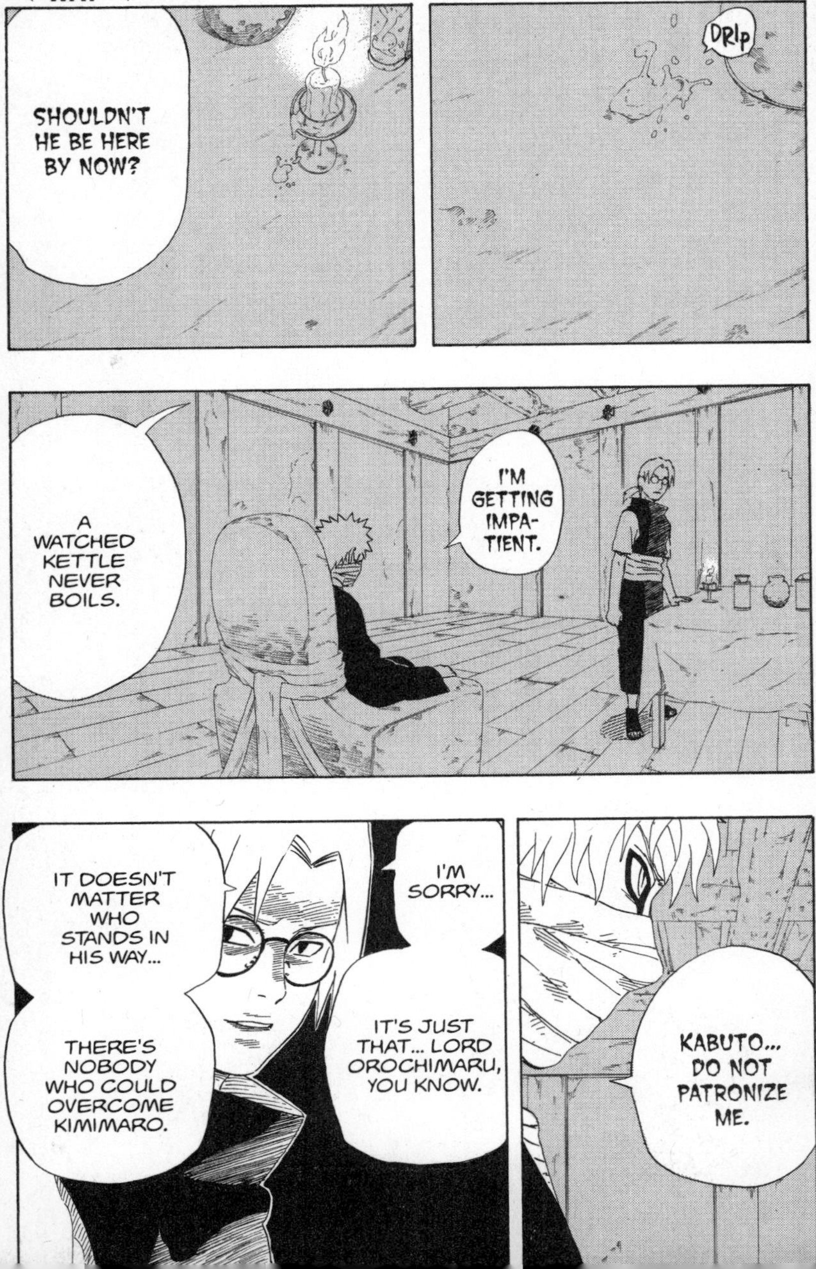
DRIP
SHOULDN'T HE BE HERE BY NOW?
I'M GETTING IMPATIENT.
A WATCHED KETTLE NEVER BOILS.
KABUTO... DO NOT PATRONIZE ME.
I'M SORRY...
IT'S JUST THAT... LORD OROCHIMARU, YOU KNOW.
IT DOESN'T MATTER WHO STANDS IN HIS WAY...
THERE'S NOBODY WHO COULD OVERCOME KIMIMARO.

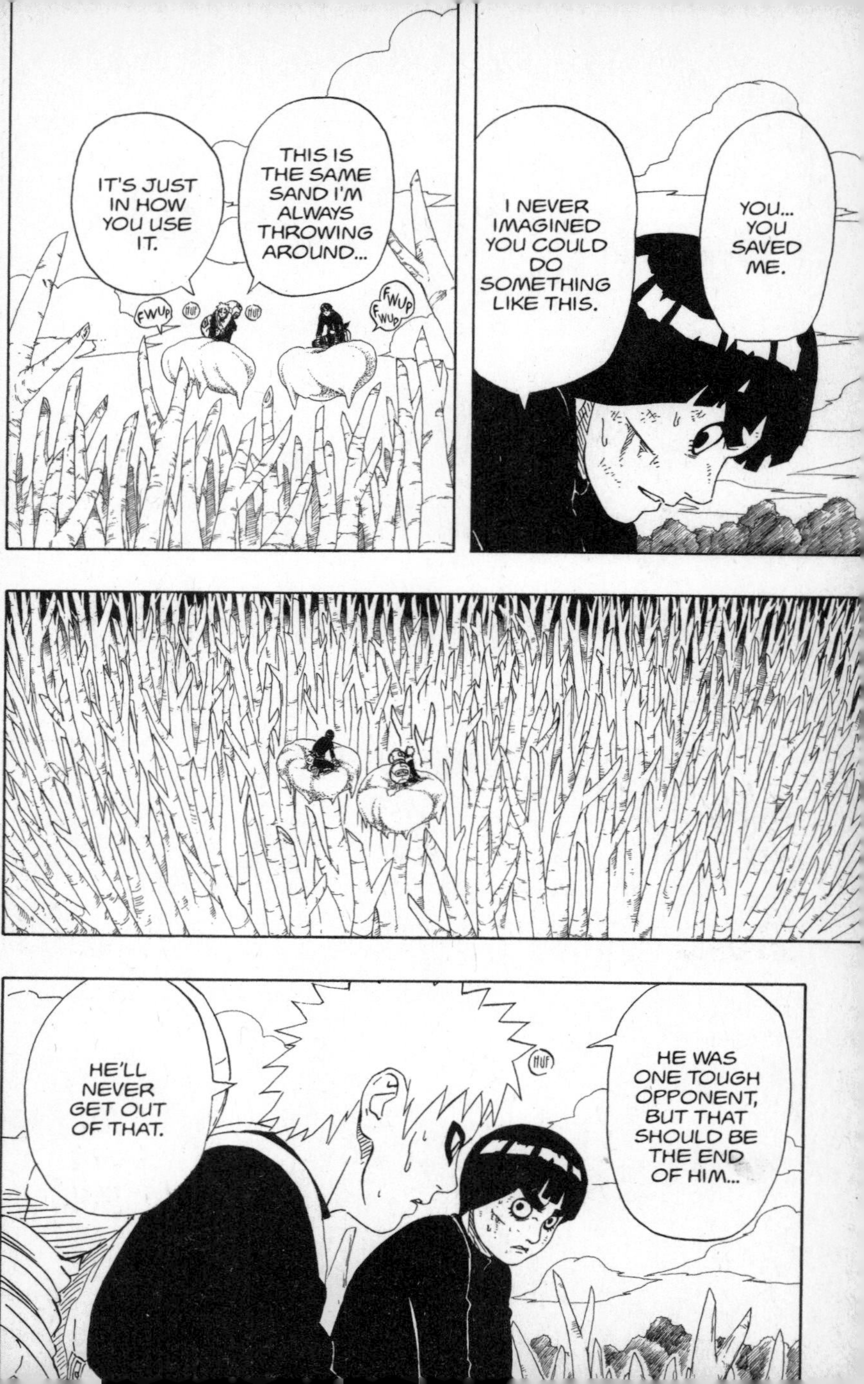
YOU... YOU SAVED ME.
I NEVER IMAGINED YOU COULD DO SOMETHING LIKE THIS.
THIS IS THE SAME SAND I'M ALWAYS THROWING AROUND...
IT'S JUST IN HOW YOU USE IT.
FWUP FWUP
HUF
HUF
FWUP
HE WAS ONE TOUGH OPPONENT, BUT THAT SHOULD BE THE END OF HIM...
HUF
HE'LL NEVER GET OUT OF THAT.

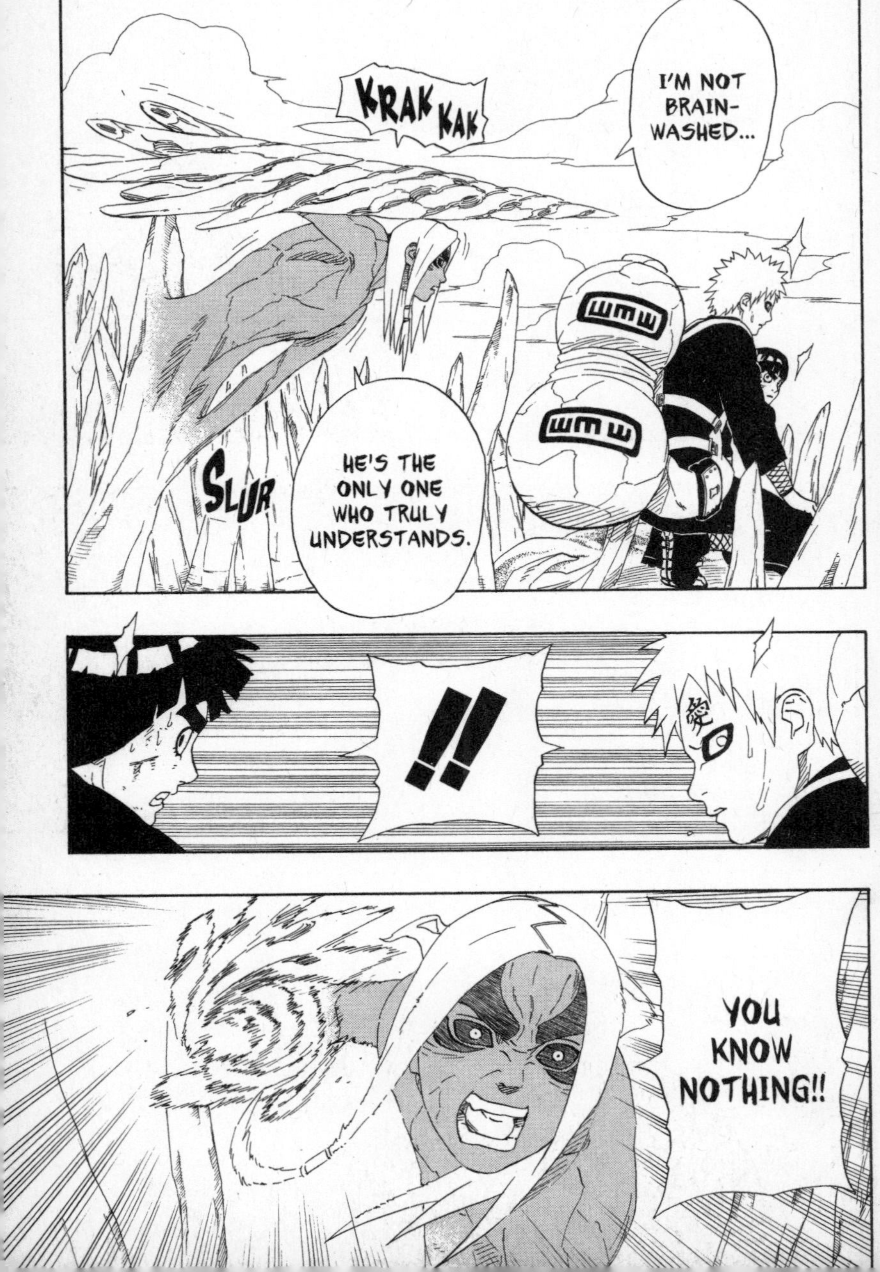
I'M NOT BRAIN-WASHED...
KRAK KAK
HE'S THE ONLY ONE WHO TRULY UNDERSTANDS.
SLUR
!!
YOU KNOW NOTHING!!

....!

WHA...

....?!

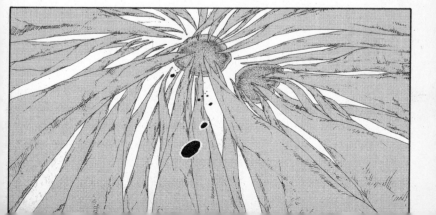

READ THIS WAY

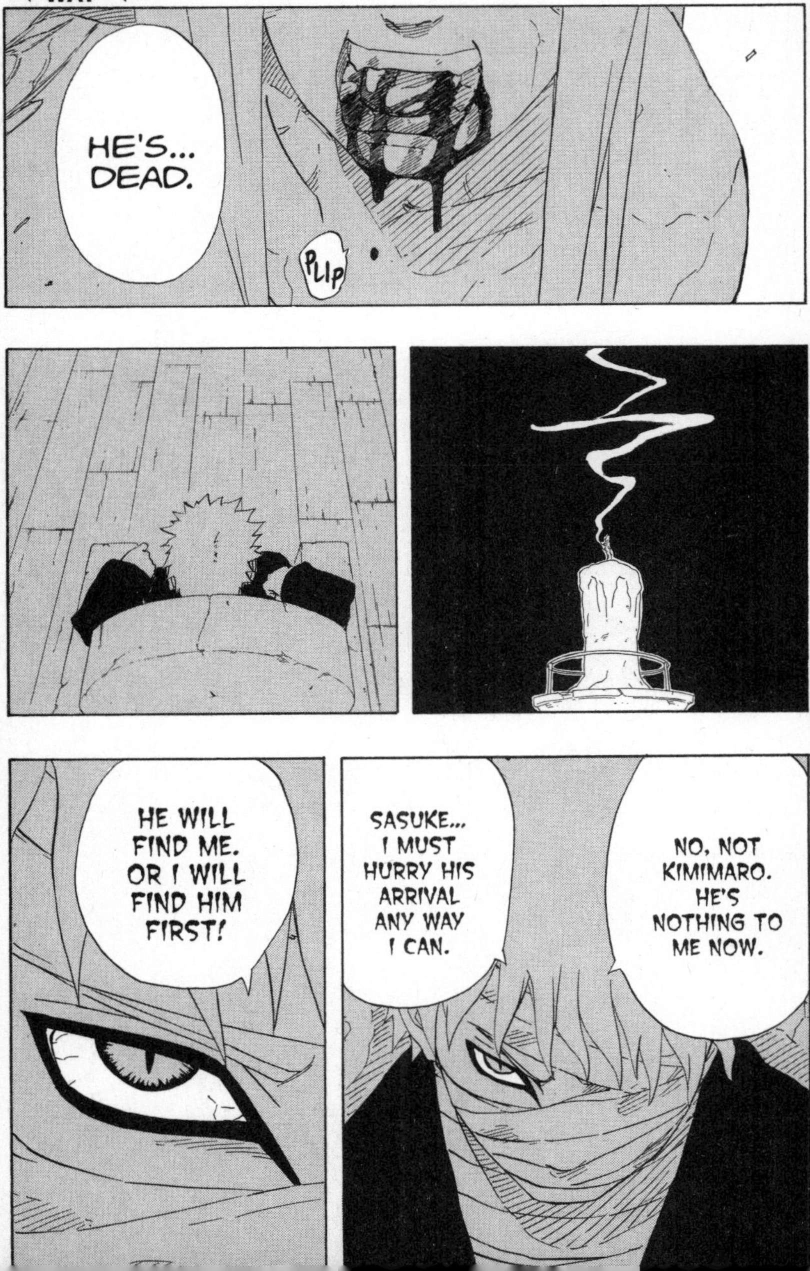
HE'S... DEAD.
PLIP
NO, NOT KIMIMARO. HE'S NOTHING TO ME NOW.
SASUKE... I MUST HURRY HIS ARRIVAL ANY WAY I CAN.
HE WILL FIND ME. OR I WILL FIND HIM FIRST!

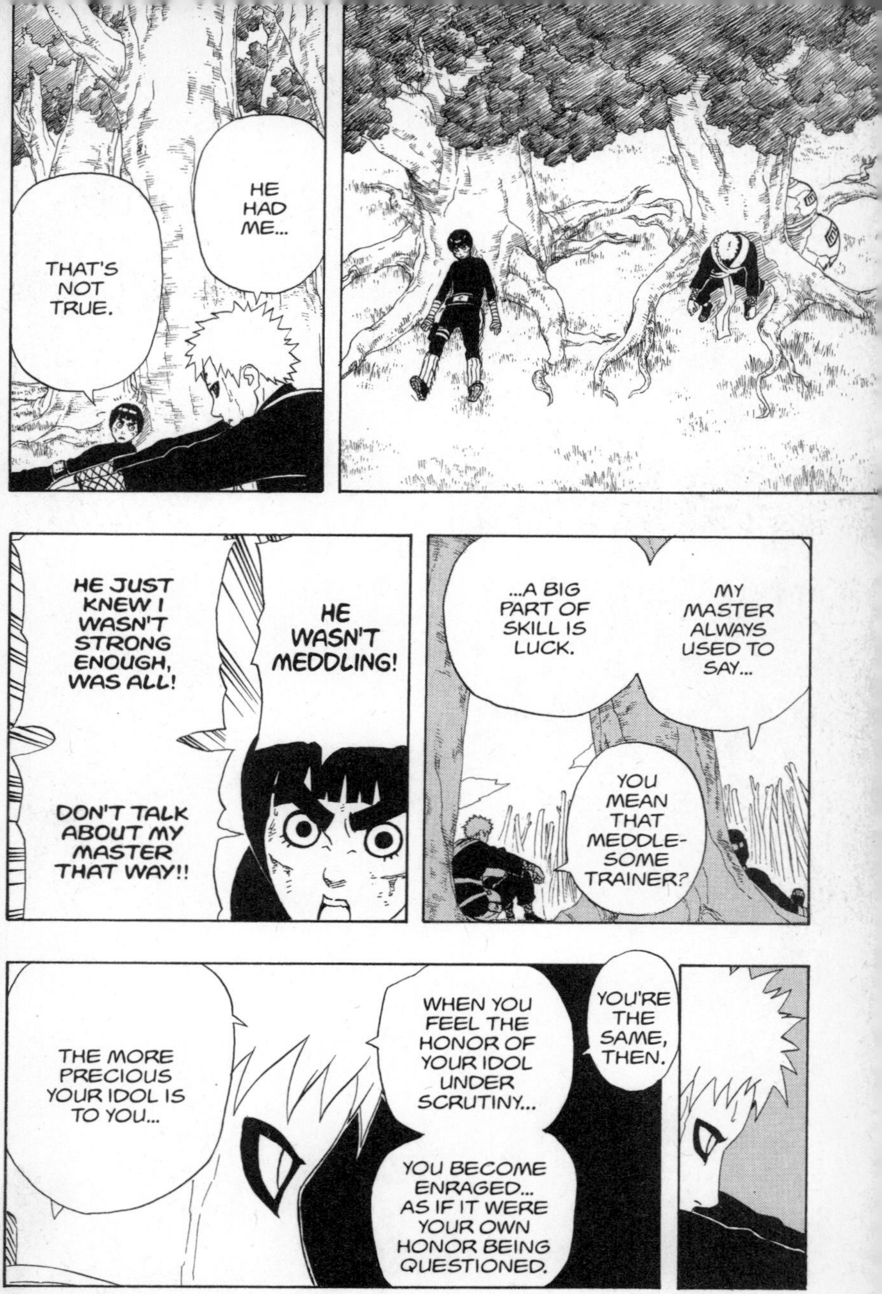
HE HAD ME...
THAT'S NOT TRUE.
MY MASTER ALWAYS USED TO SAY...
...A BIG PART OF SKILL IS LUCK.
YOU MEAN THAT MEDDLE-SOME TRAINER?
HE WASN'T MEDDLING!
HE JUST KNEW I WASN'T STRONG ENOUGH, WAS ALL!
DON'T TALK ABOUT MY MASTER THAT WAY!!
YOU'RE THE SAME, THEN.
WHEN YOU FEEL THE HONOR OF YOUR IDOL UNDER SCRUTINY...
THE MORE PRECIOUS YOUR IDOL IS TO YOU...
YOU BECOME ENRAGED... AS IF IT WERE YOUR OWN HONOR BEING QUESTIONED.

READ THIS WAY

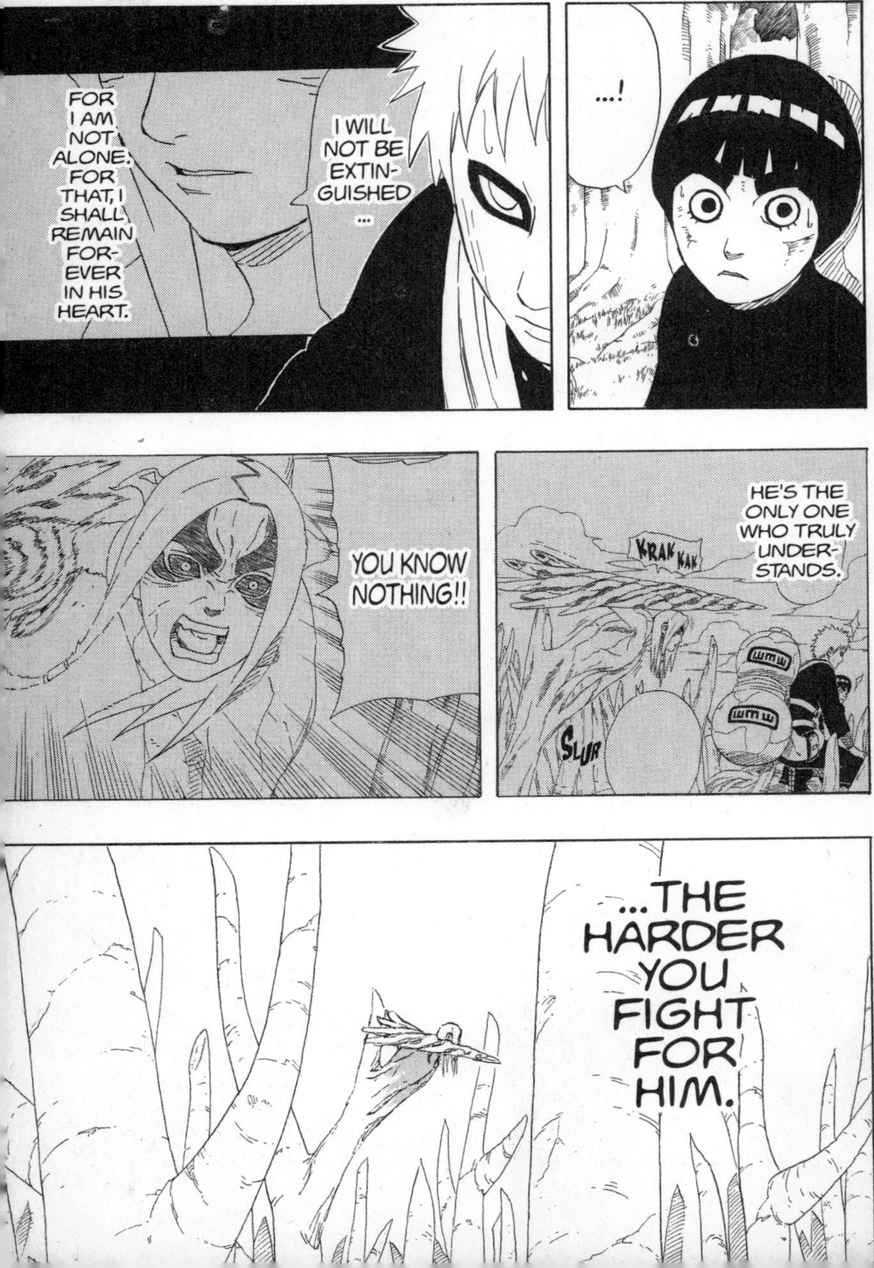
...!
I WILL NOT BE EXTINGUISHED...
FOR I AM NOT ALONE. FOR THAT, I SHALL REMAIN FOREVER IN HIS HEART.
HE'S THE ONLY ONE WHO TRULY UNDERSTANDS.
KRAK KAK
SLUR
YOU KNOW NOTHING!!
...THE HARDER YOU FIGHT FOR HIM.

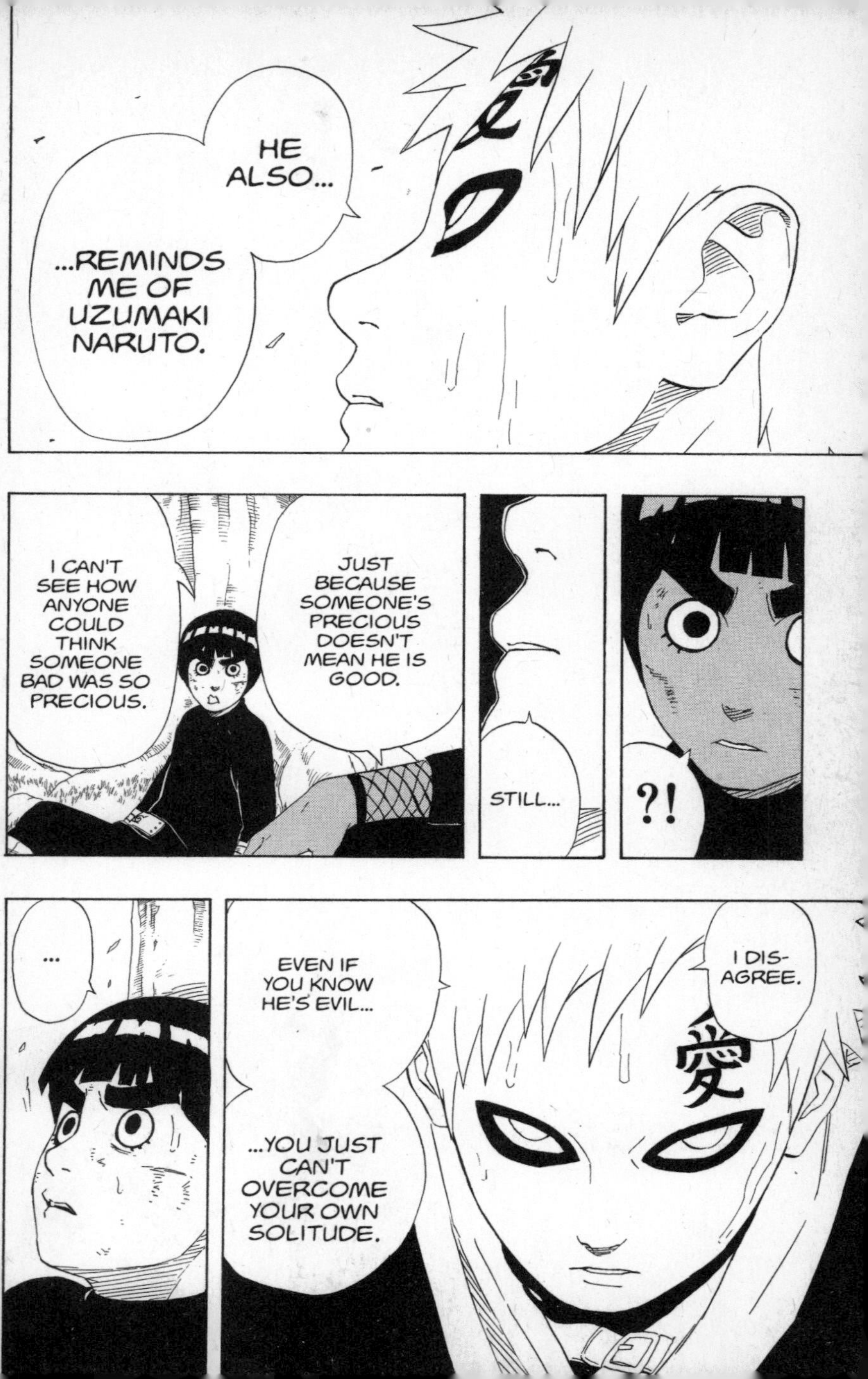
HE ALSO...
...REMINDS ME OF UZUMAKI NARUTO.
?!
STILL...
JUST BECAUSE SOMEONE'S PRECIOUS DOESN'T MEAN HE IS GOOD.
I CAN'T SEE HOW ANYONE COULD THINK SOMEONE BAD WAS SO PRECIOUS.
I DIS-AGREE.
EVEN IF YOU KNOW HE'S EVIL...
...YOU JUST CAN'T OVERCOME YOUR OWN SOLITUDE.
...

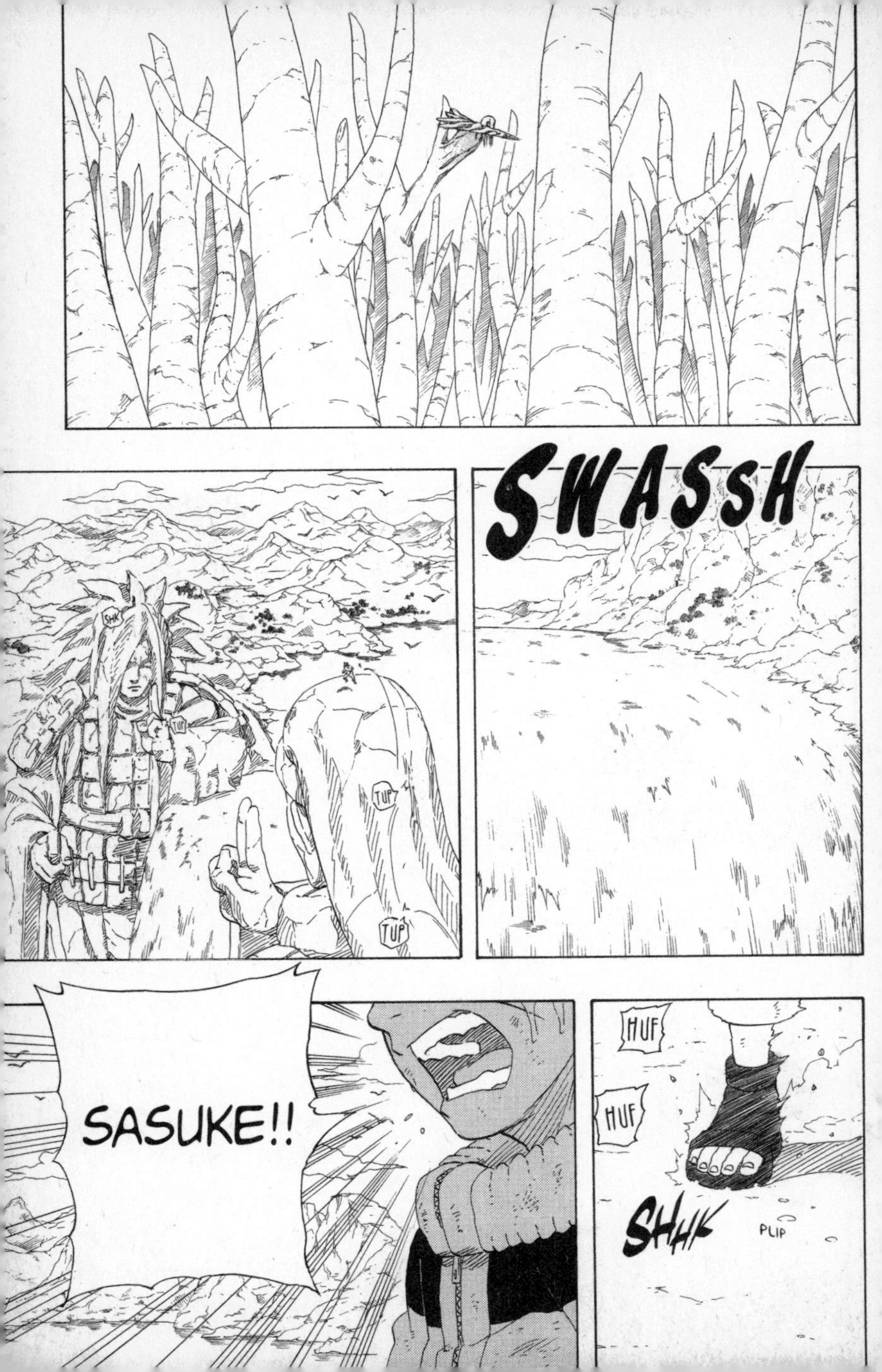
SWASSH
SHK
TUP
TUP
TUP
HUF
HUF
SHHK
PLIP
SASUKE!!

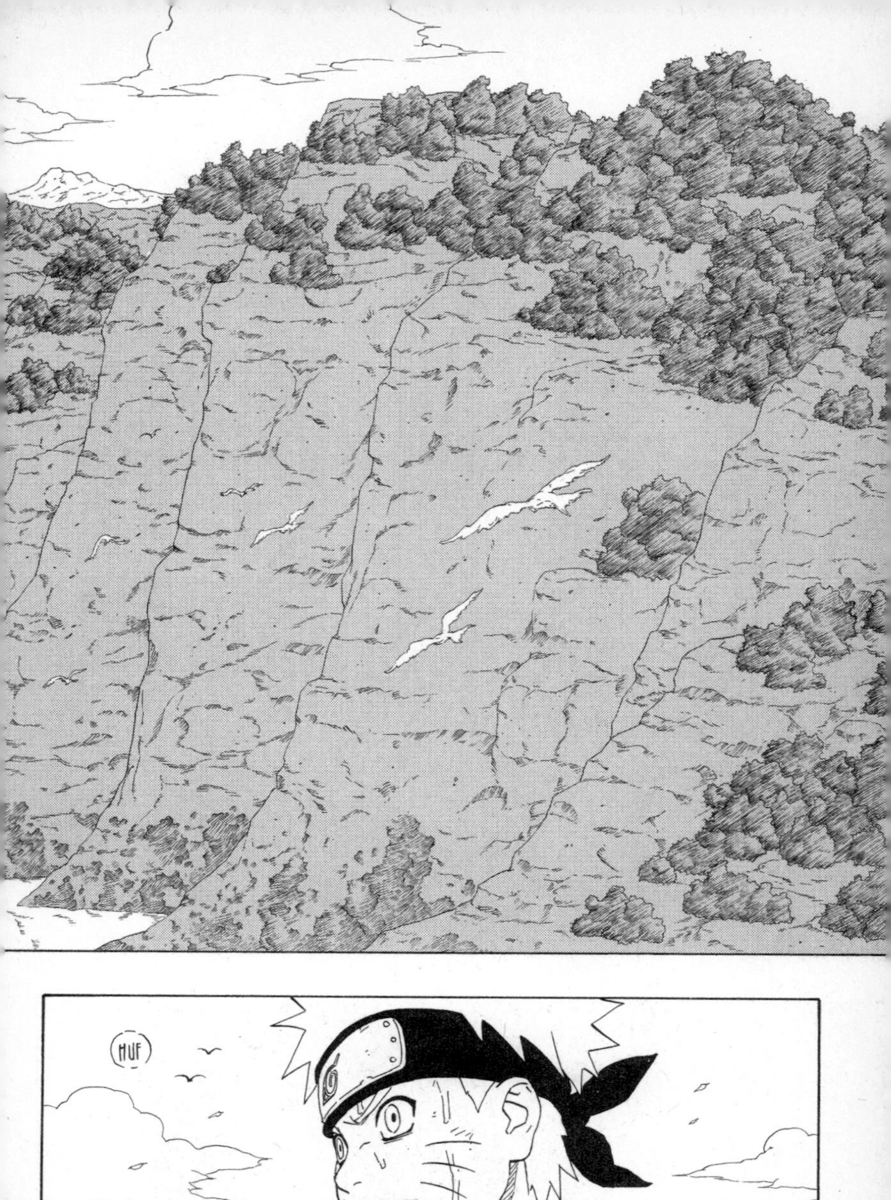
HUF
HUF

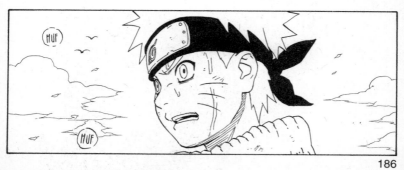

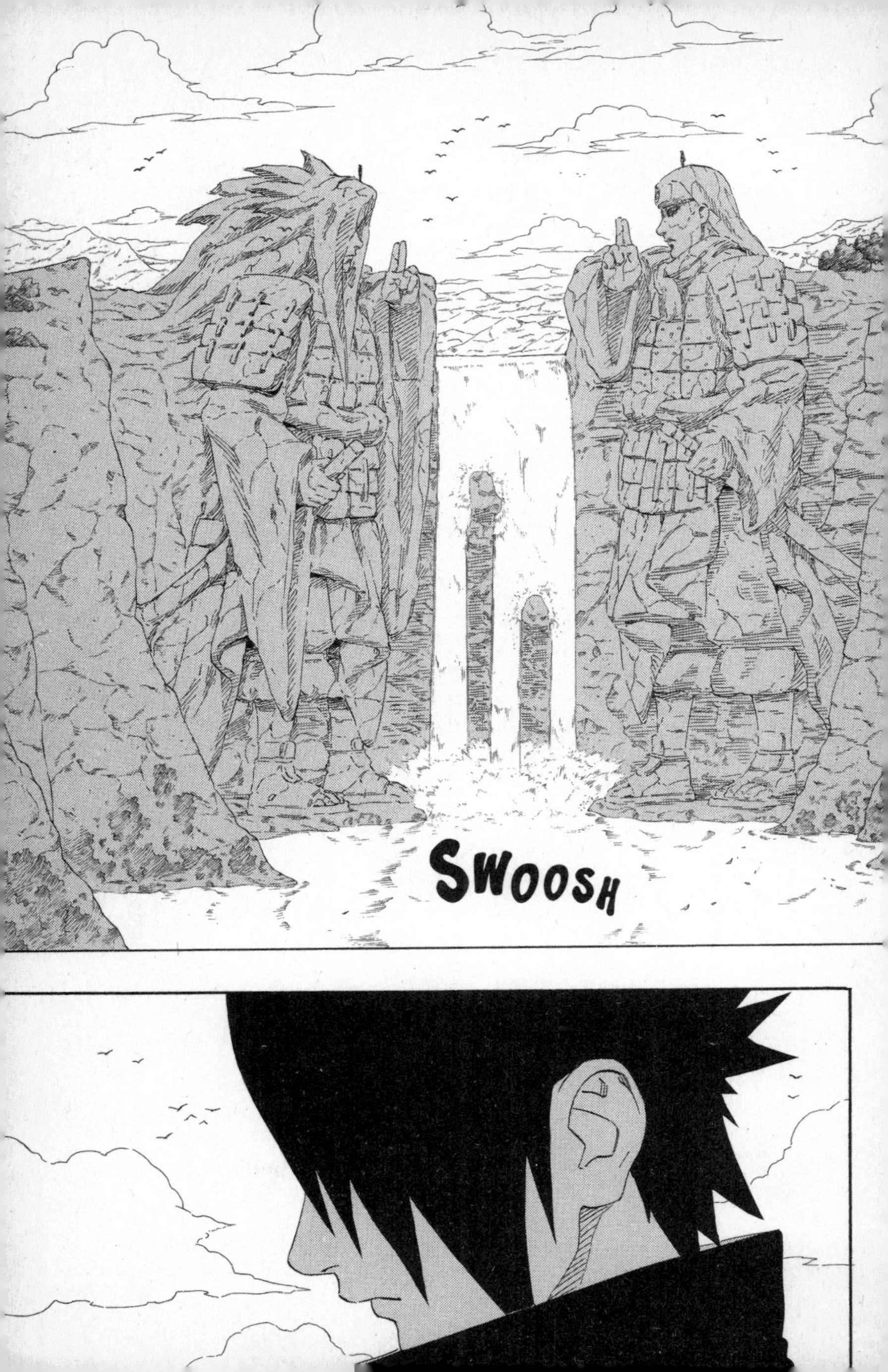
SWOOSH

IN THE NEXT VOLUME...

BROTHERS

Sasuke delves deep and remembers how his big brother, Itachi, became the feared ninja he is today – and how he may be able to achieve the same level of power. Will being friends with Sasuke mean Naruto's downfall?

AVAILABLE DECEMBER 2007!

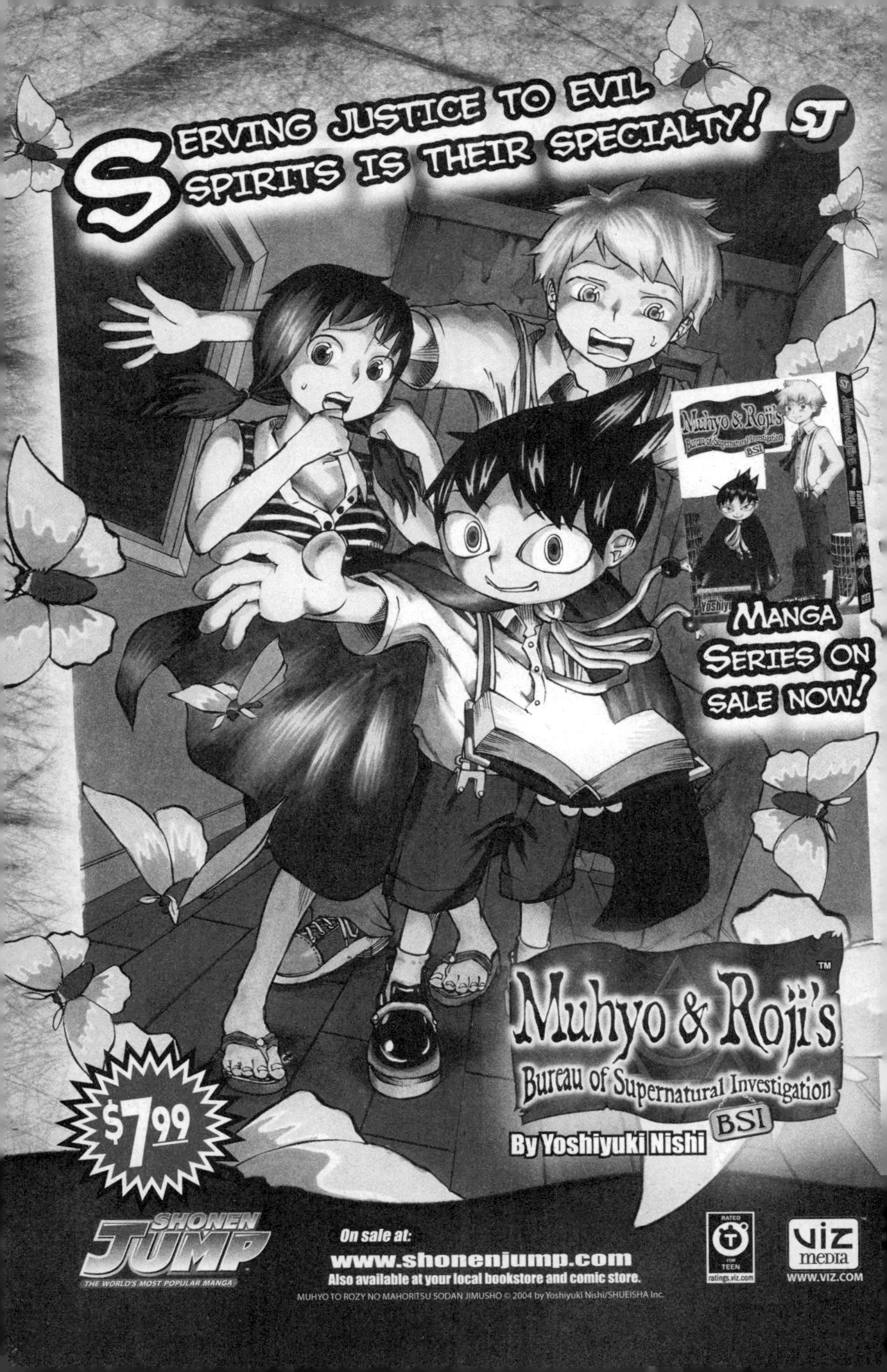
SERVING JUSTICE TO EVIL SPIRITS IS THEIR SPECIALTY!
SJ
MANGA SERIES ON SALE NOW!
Muhyo & Roji's
Bureau of Supernatural Investigation
BSI
By Yoshiyuki Nishi
$7.99
SHONEN JUMP
THE WORLD'S MOST POPULAR MANGA
On sale at:
www.shonenjump.com
Also available at your local bookstore and comic store.
MUHYO TO ROZY NO MAHORITSU SODAN JIMUSHO © 2004 by Yoshiyuki Nishi/SHUEISHA Inc.
RATED T FOR TEEN
ratings.viz.com
VIZ media
WWW.VIZ.COM

SHONEN JUMP™
NARUTO™

VIZ Media presents three new volumes of *NARUTO* manga per month from September through December 2007! Get more *NARUTO* than ever before! Big changes are coming for your favorite ninja in 2008. To get prepared, you'll want to read all the *NARUTO* you can!

September 4, 2007: *NARUTO* Volumes 16, 17, 18

October 2, 2007: *NARUTO* Volumes 19, 20, 21

November 6, 2007: *NARUTO* Volumes 22, 23, 24

December 4, 2007: *NARUTO* Volumes 25, 26, 27

Coming in March 2008: *NARUTO* Volume 28 Two and a half years pass, and we find Naruto taller, older, and wiser. A new look and new story arc! *NARUTO* manga volumes start releasing every other month.

Keep this schedule with you so you won't miss out on new releases of NARUTO!

SHONEN JUMP

THE WORLD'S MOST POPULAR MANGA

As a proud member of NARUTO NATION, VIZ Media's *SHONEN JUMP* magazine will continue to serialize the *NARUTO* series, provide in-depth background information for fans about the developments in the accelerated manga, and be the first place you can read the new adventures of Naruto beginning in the January 2008 issue!

October Issue:
On sale September 4, 2007
4 chapters of *NARUTO*

November Issue:
On sale October 2, 2007
Special *NARUTO* issue: Everything you ever wanted to know about the manga and more.

December Issue:
On sale November 6, 2007
The very first *NARUTO* chapter, drawn before the series even started!

January 2008 Issue:
On sale December 4, 2007
A new saga begins, with a new Naruto!

300+ Pages Every Month